Pro InfoPath 2007

Philo Janus

Apress®

Pro InfoPath 2007

Copyright © 2007 by Philo Janus

ISBN-13 (pbk): 978-1-59059-730-9

ISBN-10 (pbk): 1-59059-730-3

Printed and bound in the United States of America 9 8 7 6 5 4 3 2

Lead Editor: Jim Sumser
Technical Reviewer: Judith Myerson
Editorial Board: Steve Anglin, Ewan Buckingham, Gary Cornell, Jason Gilmore, Jonathan Gennick, Jonathan Hassell, James Huddleston, Chris Mills, Matthew Moodie, Dominic Shakeshaft, Jim Sumser, Keir Thomas, Matt Wade
Project Manager: Beth Christmas
Copy Edit Manager: Nicole Flores
Copy Editor: Damon Larson
Assistant Production Director: Kari Brooks-Copony
Production Editor: Ellie Fountain
Compositor: Kinetic Publishing Services, LLC
Proofreader: Elizabeth Berry
Indexer: Brenda Miller
Artist: Kinetic Publishing Services, LLC
Cover Designer: Kurt Krames
Manufacturing Director: Tom Debolski

Distributed to the book trade worldwide by Springer-Verlag New York, Inc., 233 Spring Street, 6th Floor, New York, NY 10013. Phone 1-800-SPRINGER, fax 201-348-4505, e-mail orders-ny@springer-sbm.com, or visit http://www.springeronline.com.

For information on translations, please contact Apress directly at 2855 Telegraph Avenue, Suite 600, Berkeley, CA 94705. Phone 510-549-5930, fax 510-549-5939, e-mail info@apress.com, or visit http://www.apress.com.

The source code for this book is available to readers at http://www.apress.com in the Source Code/Download section. You will need to answer questions pertaining to this book in order to successfully download the code.

For my father,
Lt. Col. Victor F. Janus (1922–2006).
I miss you, Dad.

Contents at a Glance

Contents

About the Author

PHILO JANUS graduated from the US Naval Academy with a BSEE in 1989 to face a challenging career in the US Navy. After driving an aircraft carrier around the Pacific Ocean and a guided missile frigate through both the Suez and Panama Canals, and serving in the US Embassy in Cairo, a small altercation between his bicycle and an auto indicated a change of career (some would say that landing on his head in that accident would explain many things).

Philo's software development career started with building a training and budgeting application in Access 2.0 in 1995. Since then, he's worked with Oracle, Visual Basic, SQL Server, and .NET, building applications for federal agencies, commercial firms, and conglomerates. In 2003, he joined Microsoft as a technology specialist evangelizing Office as a development platform.

About the Technical Reviewer

■**JUDITH M. MYERSON** is a systems architect and engineer. Her areas of interest include middleware technologies, enterprise-wide systems, database technologies, application development, web development, web services, object-oriented engineering, software engineering, network management, servers, security management, information assurance, standards, RFID technologies, and project management. Judith holds an MS in engineering, and several certificates. She is also a member of the IEEE organization. She has reviewed and edited a number of books, including *Hardening Linux, Creating Client Extranets with SharePoint 2003, Microsoft SharePoint: Building Office 2003 Solutions, Pro SQL Server Replication, Microsoft Content Management Server Field Guide, Microsoft Operations Manager 2005 Field Guide,* and *Pro SMS 2003.*

Acknowledgments

It's often said that books don't write themselves. I'll tell you what—they don't get written by authors, either, without a good project manager managing the process. My deepest thanks to Beth Christmas, whose supportive words and guidance kept me going even when I was horribly behind schedule. Many times I'd have an e-mail from her and dread opening it, only to read it and find nothing but encouragement. Thanks, Beth!

Also to Jim Sumser, the guy who got me into this and helped me take my first steps as an author.

A great big thank you to the technical reviewer, Judith Myerson, with whom I've fenced in comments for almost a year.

Thanks also to Damon Larson, my copy editor, who kept me honest on all the nitpicky stuff I always found a way to screw up.

A huge thank you to the InfoPath team, who have been incredibly supportive through some insanely stupid questions over the years; most notably Tudor Toma, Kamaljit Bath, Ned Friend, Kalpita Deobhakta, and Silviu Ifrim.

Thanks to my managers for encouraging me on tilting at this windmill: Rob Spanswick, Ryan Buma, and Jeff Rutherford.

Of course, my deepest, warmest thanks go to my family, who understood that "Daddy is working on his book" was just one more thing to put up with. That they seemed more excited than I was that I was writing a book really kept me going on some late nights. Big hugs to my wife, Christine, and my daughters, Antoinette and Samantha.

Finally I'd like to thank the crowd at Design of Software for keeping me sane through this writing process:

Allan Lane	Mark Theodore Anthony Wieczorek
Aaron F. Stanton, PhD	Geert-Jan Thomas
John Haren	Ian Boys
Tapiwa Sibanda	Dana L. Hoffman
Erik Springelkamp	Tim Becker
Luis A. Zaldivar	Wayne Venables
Kaushik Janardhanan	Rui Pacheco
Andrei Tuch	Colm O'Connor

Introduction

Electronic forms are the bane of developers everywhere. Laying out a form is generally designing a business process, so while it may seem like a fairly straightforward thing to do (I need this data, so I'll put these controls on the form), you start running into issues of validation, presentation, showing and hiding optional fields, and so on. InfoPath is a great tool exactly because the designer is so straightforward that the developer can have the business stakeholders design their own forms (or design the forms in conjunction with them in a joint-analysis design session).

InfoPath 2007 has evolved far beyond that initial vision. With the addition of browser-compatible forms, developers can design a form once and reuse it as a rich desktop form or a browser-based form, and even embed the form in their own solutions. And since InfoPath is completely XML-based, they're not locking into some proprietary stack—an InfoPath form could be the front end for a Java process, for example.

A problem with the growth of features and capabilities is that there are a lot more aspects of InfoPath to understand. With InfoPath 2003, you had to understand the InfoPath client and some basic SharePoint integration. InfoPath 2007 brings in not only browser capabilities, but also deeper integration with SharePoint, integration with Windows Workflow Foundation (WF) as both a tool and a client, and a host of additional programmatic interfaces.

This book is intended to introduce a power user or developer to InfoPath as a platform for developing form templates. While InfoPath is easy to use once you're used to it, there are sharp edges and dark nooks and crannies that can be a bit frustrating. Having gone through these travails myself, I felt the need to share the lessons I've learned with other "newbies." Hopefully, you'll be able to read through it in a weekend to understand what you can do with InfoPath, but also use it as a reference to work from as you implement a solution.

The first parts of the book are oriented toward any InfoPath power user—they show you how to use the controls, views, validation, and other user interface features without writing any code. Later chapters start delving into code and the Visual Studio environment, and are intended for experienced developers with a background in C#.

You do not need to have worked with InfoPath, SharePoint, or WF previously—I introduce and explain the concepts you need to understand how they interact. (Hopefully, after reading this book, you'll be hungry to learn more about SharePoint and WF development!)

To start off, you can get by with just the InfoPath client. As you dig into SharePoint integration, you will need access to a SharePoint server (either Windows SharePoint Services or Microsoft Office SharePoint Server). And of course, to work through the sections covering code, you'll need Visual Studio 2005.

I hope you enjoy reading this book as much as I've enjoyed writing it. If you have questions or feedback, please feel free to contact me at philo89@msn.com.

■■■

CHAPTER 1

Introducing InfoPath

Microsoft introduced InfoPath in 2003 as part of the Office System. While it may appear to be a simple form designer, its apparent simplicity masks an incredibly powerful tool for building the user interface for any number of applications. InfoPath can cover a multitude of situations, from basic workgroup forms that produce XML to enterprise applications that submit data, via web services, to an enterprise application integration (EAI) engine such as BizTalk Server.

This book will examine how InfoPath 2007 along with Microsoft Office SharePoint Server can address each of these scenarios. In addition, since InfoPath is a common thread among them, it eases migration from one scenario to another.

InfoPath

The design interface of InfoPath is very straightforward (see Figure 1-1). A user who wishes to design a form from scratch simply needs to start with a layout table, and then use table structures within the form to establish the look and feel of their form. From there, it's simply a matter of dragging and dropping the various control structures (repeating or optional sections, repeating tables, master/detail sections, etc.), and then the controls needed to establish the data characteristics of the form itself. These simple actions alone can produce a form that can create arbitrary XML or publish to a number of XML-based servers.

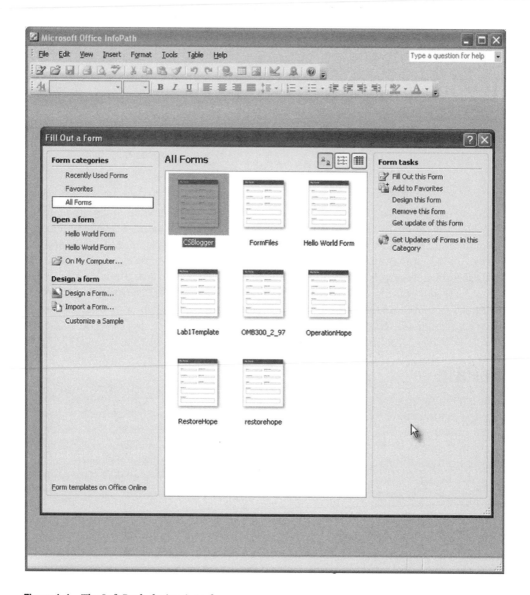

Figure 1-1. *The InfoPath design interface*

One of the major benefits of InfoPath is that it is wholly XML-centric. The form design is based on XML schemas (XSD). Form designers have a choice of either designing a form from scratch (which will result in a schema being built automatically by InfoPath), or building a form based on a preexisting schema. A blank InfoPath form with an attached schema is shown in Figure 1-2.

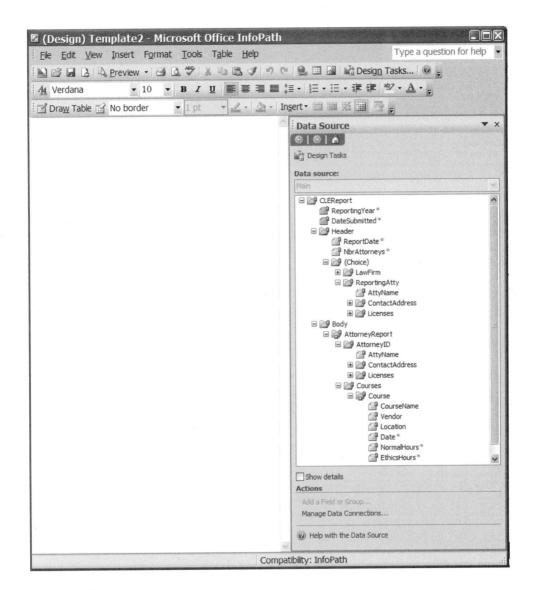

Figure 1-2. *XML schema in an InfoPath form*

InfoPath views are based on XSL transforms (XSLT). Form developers can build various views of their data, and those views are rendered by XSLT automatically generated by InfoPath. Some examples of the uses for views include the following:

- A personnel review in which the manager's comments aren't visible to the employee being reviewed.

- A routed approval form in which previous approvals are read-only for subsequent approvers.

- A multipurpose form (like those at DMV offices) where certain fields are shown to the user based on the form's purpose.

- A user-friendly data entry interface as well as a formal printed view.

Figure 1-3 shows two views of an asset tracking form: one summary view and one that shows the details of the asset.

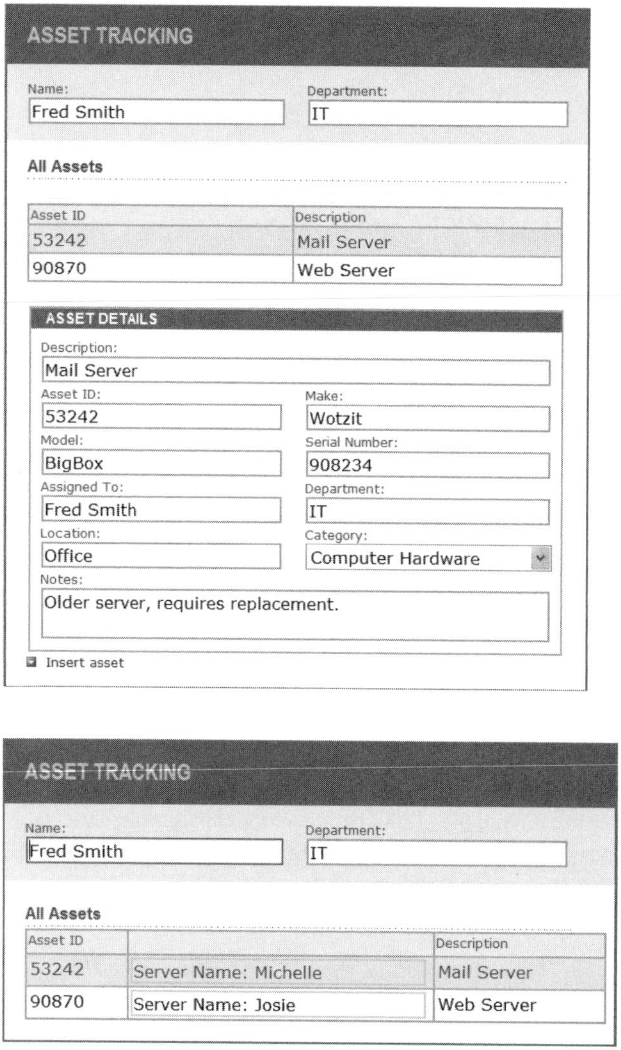

Figure 1-3. *Two views within an InfoPath form*

Finally, all InfoPath data is saved as XML. This enables InfoPath to coexist with other industry standard tools and processes in an XML-oriented solution. The ubiquity and power of XML tools also means that InfoPath can serve as a form UI (user interface) in an environment that isn't XML-based.

For example, consider a document-centric environment for processing invoices. Invoices are all processed as XML documents (as shown in Figure 1-4), and there is an established schema for the invoices within the organization. However, working with the invoices is painful—there are some XML-editing tools, but most people simply work in a text editor to deal with the invoices.

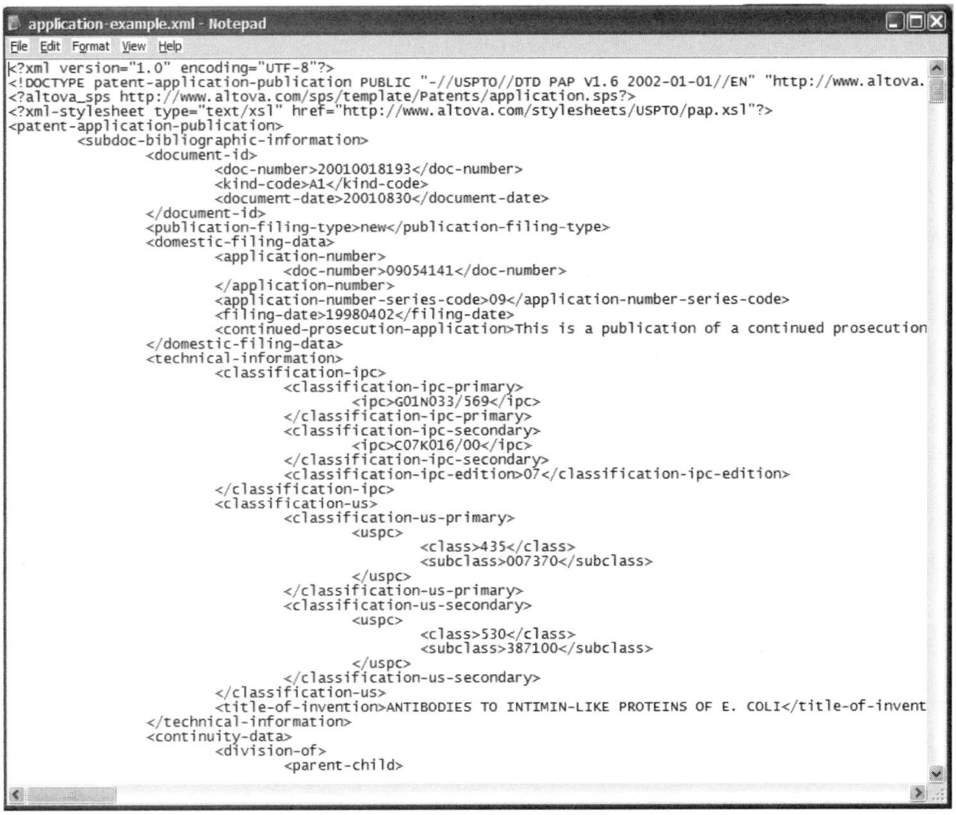


```
<?xml version="1.0" encoding="UTF-8"?>
<!DOCTYPE patent-application-publication PUBLIC "-//USPTO//DTD PAP V1.6 2002-01-01//EN" "http://www.altova.
<?altova_sps http://www.altova.com/sps/template/Patents/application.sps?>
<?xml-stylesheet type="text/xsl" href="http://www.altova.com/stylesheets/USPTO/pap.xsl"?>
<patent-application-publication>
	<subdoc-bibliographic-information>
		<document-id>
			<doc-number>20010018193</doc-number>
			<kind-code>A1</kind-code>
			<document-date>20010830</document-date>
		</document-id>
		<publication-filing-type>new</publication-filing-type>
		<domestic-filing-data>
			<application-number>
				<doc-number>09054141</doc-number>
			</application-number>
			<application-number-series-code>09</application-number-series-code>
			<filing-date>19980402</filing-date>
			<continued-prosecution-application>This is a publication of a continued prosecution
		</domestic-filing-data>
		<technical-information>
			<classification-ipc>
				<classification-ipc-primary>
					<ipc>G01N033/569</ipc>
				</classification-ipc-primary>
				<classification-ipc-secondary>
					<ipc>C07K016/00</ipc>
				</classification-ipc-secondary>
				<classification-ipc-edition>07</classification-ipc-edition>
			</classification-ipc>
			<classification-us>
				<classification-us-primary>
					<uspc>
						<class>435</class>
						<subclass>007370</subclass>
					</uspc>
				</classification-us-primary>
				<classification-us-secondary>
					<uspc>
						<class>530</class>
						<subclass>387100</subclass>
					</uspc>
				</classification-us-secondary>
			</classification-us>
			<title-of-invention>ANTIBODIES TO INTIMIN-LIKE PROTEINS OF E. COLI</title-of-invent
		</technical-information>
		<continuity-data>
			<division-of>
				<parent-child>
```

Figure 1-4. *XML data for an invoice*

With the XML schema at your disposal, it would be short work to point InfoPath at the schema and create a user-friendly form, with validation, that hides the complexity of the XML documents and allows users to interact with something that looks properly like an invoice, such as the one shown in Figure 1-5.

Patent Application			

Version:		Distribution:	
[Electronic Version 1.6]		1/1/2002	

St 32 Name	B100, DOC	St 32 Name	B200
Doc Number	20010018193	Application Number Series Code	09
Document Date		Filing Date	19980402
Kind Code	A1	Continued Prosecution Application	This is a pul
Country Code			
St 32 Name	B100, DOC		
Doc Number	09054141		
Document Date			
Kind Code	A1		
Country Code			

Italic:	E. coli
Subscript:	
Bold:	

Italic:	E. coli
Subscript:	
Bold:	

Italic:	E. coli
Subscript:	
Bold:	

Figure 1-5. *Invoice form in InfoPath*

InfoPath As a Smart Client

An additional benefit with InfoPath is that since it has a rich client for filling out forms, a user that has InfoPath installed doesn't need to be online to fill out a form. For example, let's say a government official needs to fill out a project justification and financials package, which is about 12 pages of detailed data. He may fill it out in one sitting, but it's more likely that he will have to stop in the middle and put it aside for various reasons: interference of other work, the need to research some aspect of the project to properly fill in the form, or simply the lack of enough time in one day.

With a web-based or desktop custom form, the ability to save a user's progress and return to it requires additional coding. If the official wants to travel with the form (on a laptop, for example), that may require even more code (and with a web form, it's simply not possible).

InfoPath, on the other hand, has built-in capability for a user to save form data locally to be opened later. In addition, even if the form template were hosted on a server when the user opened the form, InfoPath caches the form template locally so that the user can continue working on the form even if the original template location (web server or file share) is no longer available.

InfoPath also has a rich collection of controls: a date picker, repeating sections, check boxes, radio buttons, drop-down lists—all the client controls forms designers have come to expect. In addition, InfoPath provides spell checking out of the box.

Finally, for organizations that have a public key infrastructure (PKI) in place, InfoPath provides the ability to digitally sign forms. Enabling this capability simply requires selecting a single option in the form options when designing a form. Once the digital signature option is enabled, users can digitally sign their forms, providing authentication and nonrepudiation of the data in the form. Additional options provide the capability of signing independent sections of the data, as well as co-signing (parallel signatures) and counter-signing (signing a previous signature).

A major limitation with InfoPath 2003 was that users were required to have InfoPath installed on their desktops to fill in InfoPath forms. This limited usage to internal/intranet scenarios— forms for users outside the organization (e.g., the general public, customers, or users from other companies) still had to be implemented by other means. A further limitation was that in the area in which it was best suited—intranet applications—a forms solution generally required a workflow solution. Unfortunately, there was no readily available workflow solution that could interact with InfoPath with the same ease at which users could create forms.

InfoPath 2007 addresses these shortcomings very nicely. In the first case, the new Microsoft Office InfoPath Forms Services (part of Microsoft Office SharePoint Server) provides a capability to publish InfoPath 2007 forms to browser-based forms. As a result, a developer (or power user) can design a form in InfoPath, leverage the InfoPath rich UI capabilities inside the firewall, and publish the same form to an Office SharePoint server for consumption by users outside the firewall.

With respect to workflow, Microsoft Office SharePoint Server is built on Windows SharePoint Services, and provides all the collaboration capabilities inherent in that platform. In addition, the newest version of Windows SharePoint Services provides powerful new workflow capabilities based on the Windows Workflow Foundation (WF). Windows SharePoint Services version 3 provides out-of-the-box workflow capabilities that can be configured by power users and administrators. In addition, the WF development model means that .NET developers can expand and extend the workflow capabilities to provide for any possible circumstance.

■**Note** Lest you think that there is a glaring typo in the preceding paragraph, the proper abbreviation for Windows Workflow Foundation is indeed "WF." It seems that after the Worldwide Wrestling Federation lost a legal battle with the World Wildlife Fund over the initials WWF, Microsoft decided discretion was the better part of valor.

These are just two of the exciting new capabilities in InfoPath 2007. Other new benefits include the following:

- Control templates, with which power users or developers can create templates of controls in frequently used layouts or combinations

- Integration with Outlook for offline folder capabilities

- The design checker, which is used to validate your form designs

- The multi-select list box, which is now a standard control in the toolbox

- Ability to publish a form directly to an installable MSI file

- Data connection libraries in Microsoft Office 2007 Server

- Built-in ability to publish to PDF or Microsoft's new XPS format

- The Trust Center, for managing trusted forms

- Additional form events

- Offline caching of lookup data

- InfoPath forms hosted in the designer when working in Visual Studio

We'll look deeper into these capabilities in the next chapter.

E-forms

Every company or agency has a problem with forms. They have paper forms in filing cabinets, submitted by customers or constituents, in folders routing around the office, and so on. The problems these forms cause are well known—routing takes time and frequently requires rekeying of data (potentially introducing mistakes). Data is difficult to find once the process is complete, and metrics are nearly impossible to generate.

Hosting the forms electronically has long been recognized as a solution to these problems, but that simple concept opens a whole new Pandora's box: how to design the forms; how to design workflow; how to ensure that forms are available internally, externally, online, offline, and in print; how to process forms or publish data into other business systems; and so on.

Part of the problem is the desire to find a "one size fits all" solution—something that can solve the problem for

- Enterprise intranet applications (time cards, purchase requests, etc.)

- Workgroup applications (configuration management, status reports, etc.)

- Ad hoc applications (shift scheduling, equipment tracking, etc.)

- Internet applications (customer requests, constituent form submission, etc.)

Traditionally, these have been solved by myriad solutions—heavyweight code development, web development, Access databases, Excel spreadsheets, and so on. Each serves its purpose, but each has varying degrees of supportability. In addition, the use of different platforms for each style of application makes migrating an application from one "slot" to another difficult (e.g., taking a grassroots workgroup application and creating an enterprise application from it).

InfoPath for Forms Solutions

Workgroups everywhere have a horde of data-handling requirements that aren't being met. They have a need to collect structured and semi-structured data, aggregate it, and search and report on the results. These requirements often find a home in Excel, Access databases, or other small custom applications. Consider a hypothetical office that is required to track certain types of training for regulatory requirements (continuing legal education for lawyers, accountants, auditors, etc.). Those records probably started on ledger paper (see Figure 1-6).

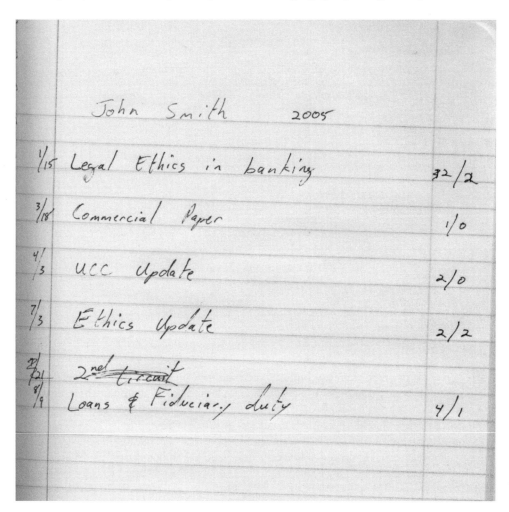

Figure 1-6. *Twentieth-century record keeping*

The problems here are obvious—reporting has to be completed by hand, correcting mistakes requires good old basic "line out and rewrite," and the potential for both data entry and compilation errors is immense. Data entry is tedious, and if someone wants to verify their status, they have to either look at the paper records themselves (lack of security) or get the auditor responsible for tracking coursework to look it up for them (wasting personnel resources).

Basically, this process gets reduced to "publish one warning report four weeks before the end of the year, spend a week reconciling updates, and then publish again at year's end." There *might* be quarterly updates if management (and the bookkeeper) has the time to collate and publish them.

The quickest and most obvious fix would be to address the constant retotaling by hand, and that could be done in Excel (Figure 1-7).

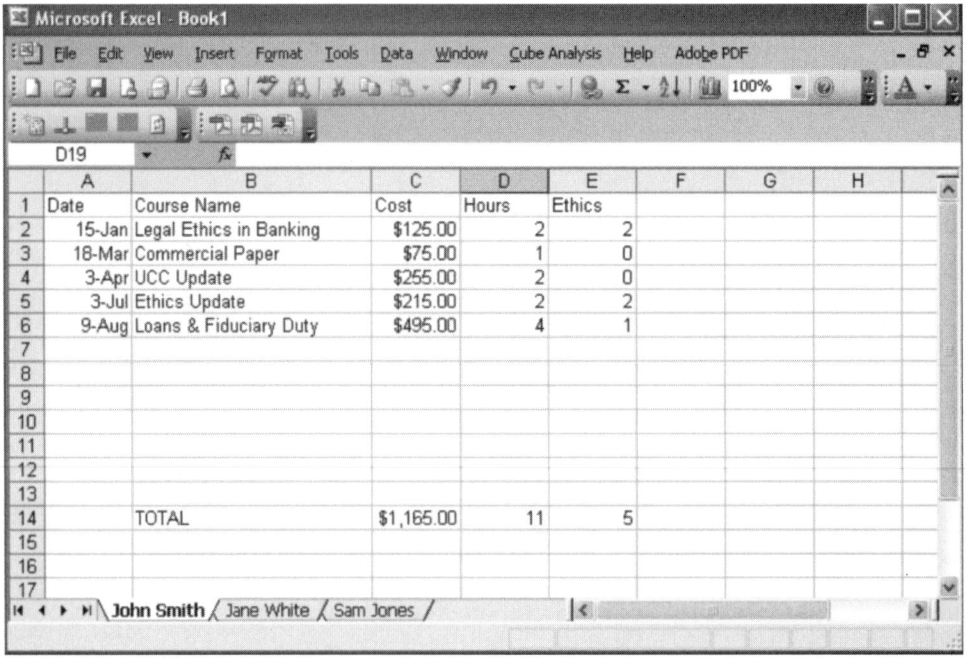

	A	B	C	D	E
1	Date	Course Name	Cost	Hours	Ethics
2	15-Jan	Legal Ethics in Banking	$125.00	2	2
3	18-Mar	Commercial Paper	$75.00	1	0
4	3-Apr	UCC Update	$255.00	2	0
5	3-Jul	Ethics Update	$215.00	2	2
6	9-Aug	Loans & Fiduciary Duty	$495.00	4	1
14		TOTAL	$1,165.00	11	5

Figure 1-7. *Using Excel for record keeping*

Of course, the problems here are similar—you have very little control in terms of security, so most likely someone would have to be disturbed for an individual to update their file or get their status. Compiling reports is also still problematic—someone has to go through and compile the data by hand. The math is already done, but generating the report isn't.

At some point, an enterprising individual in the office would have started adding macros to the spreadsheet to implement some business rules, and the truly industrious would have started building a training tracking application. Over time, this application would evolve, and the bible of business rules and validations would grow along the lines of the following:

- Any course more than $500 must be approved by a senior partner.
- Ethics hours cannot be more than total course hours.
- Course dates cannot be after today's date (coursework can't be pre-entered).
- Courses cannot be more than $75 per hour of training.
- Due to the load in tax filing work, no training may be entered for April.

Then there are reporting requirements—year end reports, delinquency reports, quarterly updates, accounting reports, spending per attorney, and so on.

What happens after this generally varies, but the worst case is that the application grows in popularity and is adopted by another department. Once the application becomes a serious dependency for the organization, it will need to be migrated to a more robust architecture. This may (probably will) require a relational database back end, forms with the same validations, a reporting solution, and other improvements.

One major task in such a migration is ensuring that the new UI (the forms) meets all the user requirements of the old solution while keeping the same program logic and validations. The existing forms must be picked apart, and every rule or criterion documented to be reimplemented in the new solution.

InfoPath can ease these types of migrations because while it can act as a front-end tool for power users, it can also act as the front end of a server-based enterprise solution. Since InfoPath is XML-based and can hook natively to web services, InfoPath forms cover the full spectrum, from ad hoc workgroup "micro-applications" to enterprise solutions.

Summary

This book will cover InfoPath 2007 from the ground up, using a solution-based approach. It will cover the basics of the forms package, and how you can use InfoPath to build a pretty powerful form just by dragging controls to a design surface, publishing to Windows SharePoint Services, and using the native forms libraries in Windows SharePoint Services for aggregating data and providing a basic reporting capability.

You'll then move on to more advanced concepts: using data connections, workflow, publishing to browser-based forms, and custom code for those things that simply can't be done through the InfoPath UI.

By the end, you'll see how InfoPath can ease a lot of application development pain.

■ ■ ■

CHAPTER 2

Tour of the InfoPath Client

The InfoPath client is very straightforward—opening it presents you with a wizard that allows you to select from a number of forms in a gallery of samples, from a list of recently used forms, and from an online library of forms. In addition, you can design and publish forms, guided by wizards in the client. This chapter will cover the fundamentals of the InfoPath interface, design concepts, and some of the underlying architecture concepts.

Form Templates vs. Form Data

One basic concept to understand with InfoPath (indeed, with electronic forms in general) is that the "form template" is separate from the "form data." In InfoPath, the form template is a new format with an .xsn extension. Traditionally, the word "form" has been generic for a paper with formatting and data on it. Forms were differentiated as to whether they were "blank " or "filled in." The important difference is that with paper forms, when a form was filled in, you got both the questions and the answers, as shown in Figure 2-1.

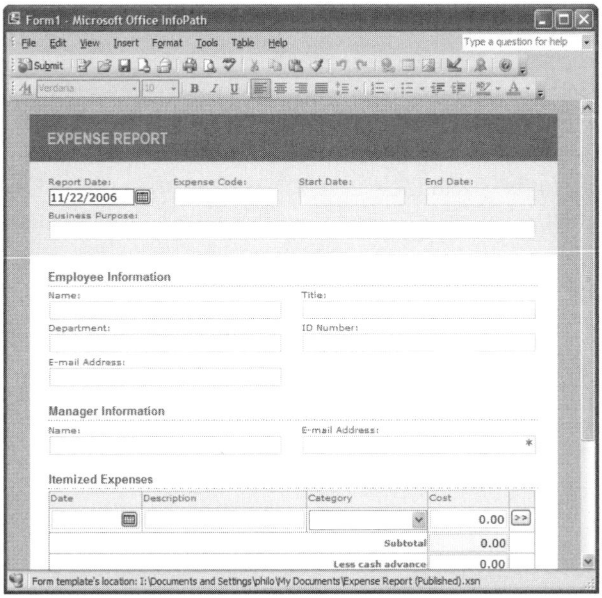

Figure 2-1. *A standard form*

With electronic forms, the form data is generally stored separately from the form template. While this eases storage requirements, it introduces new concerns—namely that the meaning of the answer can depend on the question asked. Consider the following answers to the form in Figure 2-1, if they were stored on their own, without the questions attached:

- CO1239078

- 1/27/2006

- Zeus Conversion

- 394-23488

- 05-11-235899

- R0248349

Without the questions, the answers are meaningless. Thus, when designing an electronic forms solution, it is critically important to put as much thought into storage and maintenance of the form templates as the form data. InfoPath makes this somewhat easier by using a schema to define the form as well as automatically understanding and maintaining form template versioning.

InfoPath and Form Maintenance

Not only can InfoPath open form templates from network locations, it is designed to. Forms can be opened from network shares (URN publishing), web servers, or SharePoint (either Office SharePoint Server or Windows SharePoint Services). When the developer publishes a form template, the form template is tagged with the location it is being published to. When InfoPath opens a form template, it caches a copy of the template locally so that the form can be opened again later if the computer is offline, or so that data files referring to the form template can be opened even if the template is unavailable.

When the form is filled out, the form data (an XML file) is also tagged with the parent location of the form template—this enables the data file to find the template file when it is opened again. (This is important, since the template information is not part of the form data file!)

When the form is reopened, it checks to see if the parent location is available. If it is, then InfoPath checks the version of the current form and the parent form. If the parent form is newer, InfoPath asks the user if they want to download the newer version of the form template. If the parent form file is not available, then InfoPath will open the form from the cache (assuming the form template has been opened at least once previously and is therefore cached).

Tour of the InfoPath Client

When you first open InfoPath, you're presented with the Getting Started dialog (Figure 2-2). This offers options such as selecting a form (template) to open from various categories (including a package of sample forms included with the product), opening an existing form (data), and designing a form (template). Down the center of the dialog is the form gallery. You can maintain this gallery with the options on the right-hand side.

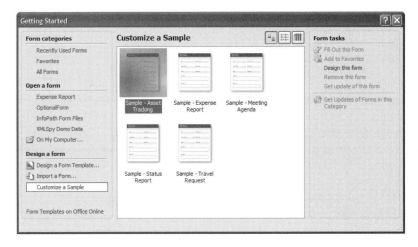

Figure 2-2. *The Getting Started dialog*

As an example, select the Expense Report sample form and open it (Figure 2-3). You will see a fairly standard InfoPath form—text boxes, a date picker with a default of today's date, tables with radio buttons, optional sections, and rich text sections. In addition, the ribbon icon in the toolbar (Figure 2-4) indicates that the form can be digitally signed.

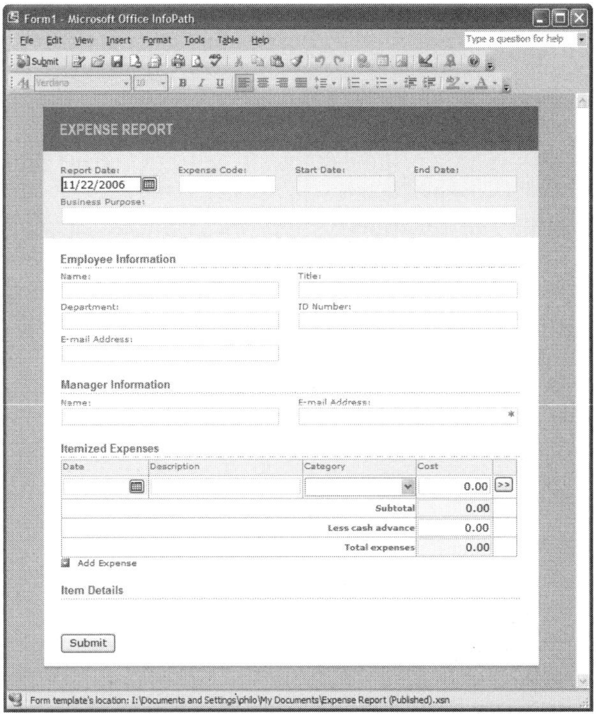

Figure 2-3. *Expense Report sample form*

Figure 2-4. *Ribbon icon indicating digital signature capability*

The text boxes are fairly standard text box controls—the user types to fill them out, and can tab from field to field. The Employee Information text boxes have spell checking disabled, but if you type in the Business Purpose field and misspell a word, you'll see that InfoPath presents spell checking capabilities with a similar interface to the rest of the Office suite (Figure 2-5). (InfoPath also uses the Office dictionaries, so any customizations the user makes or special dictionaries they add will also apply here.)

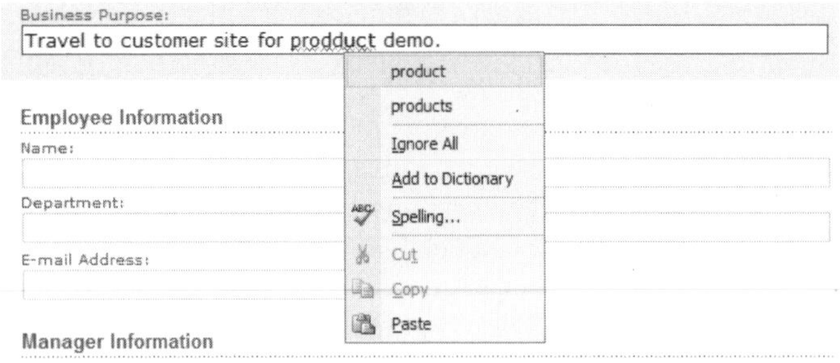

Figure 2-5. *Spell checking in InfoPath*

The Date field in the Itemized Expenses section is of interest as well. Type **123** into the field and hit the Tab key. Note that the field is highlighted in red. If you right-click in the field, you'll see why this warning is shown ("Only Date Allowed"). Change the entry to **1/1** and tab out, and the error will go away.

Look at the Itemized Expenses table. At the top left of the table is a small arrow icon (hidden behind the dialog in Figure 2-6). If you click this icon, you'll be presented with the option to add another row or remove the existing row. This indicates that this table is in a repeating group— you can have one or more rows in the table.

Figure 2-6. *Repeating group indicator icon*

Add a few rows in the Itemized Expense table and enter some costs—note that the subtotal is computed automatically. This can be done either with code or with custom rules in the InfoPath designer.

Rich Text Fields

Multi-line fields can be rich text fields, which means you can apply Word-style formatting to the text in the fields. Apart from using the standard font control (which includes bold, italic, etc.), you can also insert tables, numbered lists, highlighting, and so on.

Rich text fields offer the option to use limited rich text capability (basic fonts, sizing, text formatting), or full rich text capability, which also allows tables and embedded images. Images embedded in the rich text control can be either embedded (in which case they will be base64 encoded inline into the XML) or linked.

One feature to note is the table designer (Figure 2-7). By clicking and dragging from this button, you can easily create a basic table of any dimension. The inserted table can then be formatted by right-clicking and selecting the formatting option desired.

Figure 2-7. *The table designer*

Repeating and Optional Sections

InfoPath provides capabilities for optional sections and repeating sections—areas of controls that can be added by the user, by rules depending on data in the form, or by code. The various types of sections include the following:

- *Optional section*: Put simply, this is a section that isn't required. It can be configured to be inserted by the user (either with a shortcut or via a menu option), or can be added via rules or code. If the form is configured to automatically insert the section, there is also an option to either allow or prevent the user from inserting it. Optional sections only insert a single instance of the section—to add more than one copy, use a repeating section.

- *Repeating section*: This section allows multiple "copies" of a section of a form to be added or removed. Again, this can be done by the user or through automatic action of the form (e.g., a matching section can be added for each member of a comma-separated list). If the user is given the option to add or remove copies of the section, they can add via a link on the form, add or remove with the shortcut link on the top-left of the section, or add through the Insert menu (see Figure 2-8).

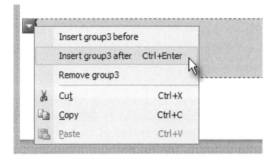

Figure 2-8. *Managing repeating sections*

- *Repeating table*: The repeating table (Figure 2-9) is similar to the repeating section, with the additional capability of adding an optional header and footer. The header can contain titles, and the footer can contain summary information (easily configured by the designer). Again, rows can be inserted by the user or by the form.

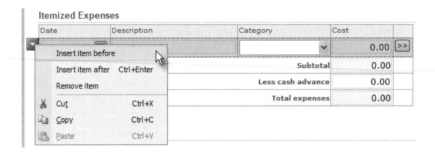

Figure 2-9. *Repeating tables*

- *Horizontal repeating table*: Similar to the repeating table, this table allows the user to dynamically add columns to a defined table (see Figure 2-10). (Columns can also be added by form action or code.)

Item Details		
Student	Jack Smith	Jane Monroe
Date	2/14/2006	3/15/2006
Score	23.4	75

Insert item

Figure 2-10. *Horizontal repeating table*

- *Master/detail*: The master/detail controls provide a way of managing and navigating large quantities of data. A master control (repeating table) is linked to the child control (another repeating table) and filters the data presented in it based on the record selected in the master. Figure 2-11 shows a master/detail control with the first record selected and the data in the child table filtered appropriately. Figure 2-12 shows the result of selecting the last row/record.

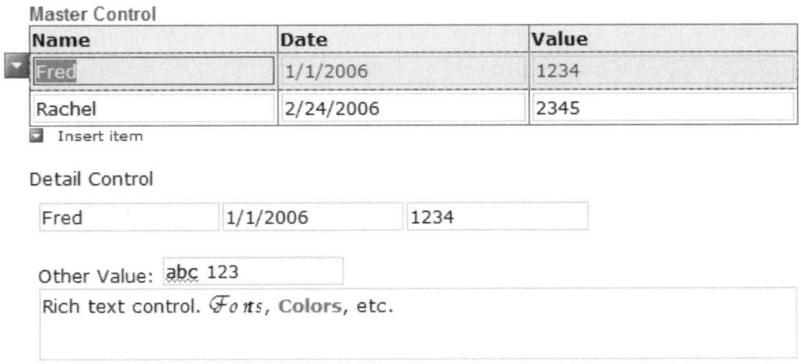

Master Control

Name	Date	Value
Fred	1/1/2006	1234
Rachel	2/24/2006	2345

Insert item

Detail Control

Fred	1/1/2006	1234

Other Value: abc 123

Rich text control. *Fonts*, **Colors**, etc.

Figure 2-11. *Master/detail controls*

Master Control

Name	Date	Value
Fred	1/1/2006	1234
Rachel	2/24/2006	2345

Insert item

Detail Control

Rachel	2/24/2006	2345

Other Value: q987098

Table in rich text

Insert item

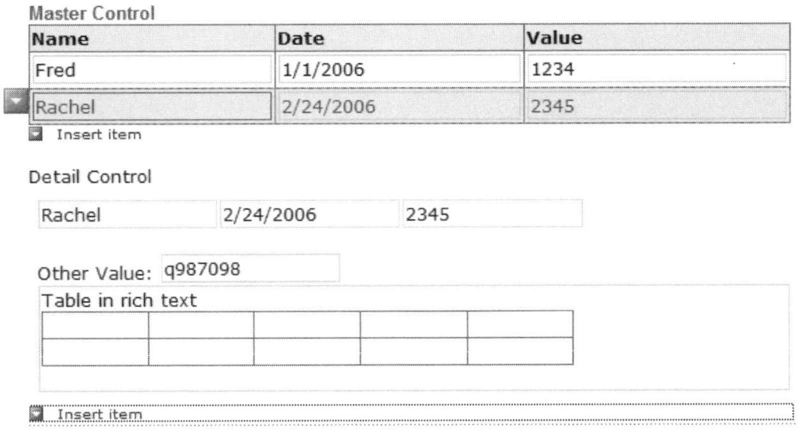

Figure 2-12. *Master/detail controls with different record selected in the master*

- *Bulleted list, numbered list, and plain list*: These offer various ways of simply listing data bound to repeating nodes (see Figure 2-13). With any of the repeating lists, the user simply has to type information, and then press the Enter key to add another item. Tabbing takes the user out of the list to the next control.

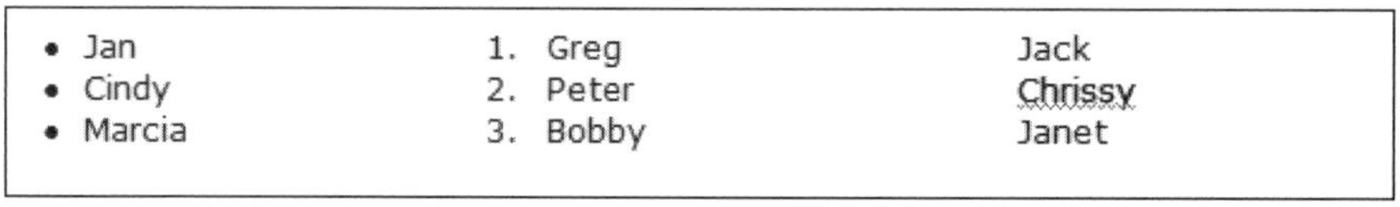

• Jan	1. Greg	Jack
• Cindy	2. Peter	Chrissy
• Marcia	3. Bobby	Janet

Figure 2-13. *Bulleted list, numbered list, and plain list controls*

- *Multi-select list box*: This simple variation on the list box allows the user to select multiple choices from the preconfigured list (see Figure 2-14). (There's no option to allow the user to enter their own choices.)

☑ First Choice
☐ Second Choice
☑ Third Choice
☐ Fourth Choice

Figure 2-14. *Multi-select list box*

File and Picture Controls (and Ink)

InfoPath 2003 Service Pack 1 added some very powerful file and ink controls to InfoPath, and they remain in InfoPath 2007. When used on a tablet PC, InfoPath will perform text recognition on handwriting inked into text boxes and other text fields (see Figure 2-15).

Figure 2-15. *Ink-enabled form in InfoPath*

The ink drawing control enables you to draw using a tablet stylus and save the image into the form. This allows you to capture sketches, handwritten notes, annotations on predefined templates, and so on (see Figure 2-16).

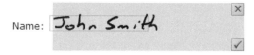

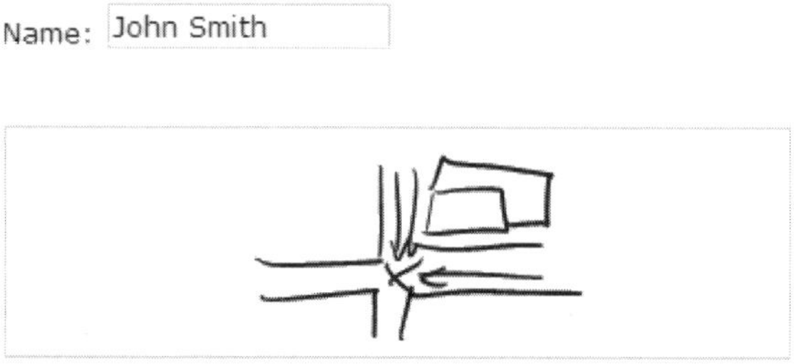

Figure 2-16. *Ink drawing control*

InfoPath also provides the ability to embed or attach images, and attach files to a form. The image control can be configured to either embed the image in the form data or simply embed a link to the image. The file attachment control embeds the file as base64 encoding in the XML. It also allows the form designer to limit what file types can be attached to the form.

Views

InfoPath offers the ability to show multiple views of a form. By showing different views of the data, a designer can make the form easier for a user to understand and fill in.

Various uses of multiple views include the following:

- *Multiple-purpose forms*: Imagine a standard DMV form, which is quite long—but for any given use (new license, replacement license, car registration, etc.), the user only has to fill in a few fields. An InfoPath form can have a different view for each use—one view for new licenses, which shows the fields for the new license; another view for car registration, which uses the same personal information but shows different fields for the automobile information; and so on.

- *Forms with multiple pages*: Some forms require a lot of fields, and can run many pages. InfoPath allows the form designer to break the fields up into views that can represent pages. Microsoft's OMB Form 300 solution uses this method of paging.

- *Forms in which different users get different representations of data*: A performance review form will have information that may be editable, read-only, or hidden, depending on who is viewing the form. For example, the summary info can be viewed by anyone looking at the form; the employee's remarks can be read by the employee's manager, but not edited; and the manager's remarks can't be viewed by the employee. InfoPath allows views to be designed to fulfill each of these uses, and the views can be locked down by user role.

InfoPath also has provisions for print views, as well as the use of custom XSLT for generating a print view for Microsoft Word. Form designers can set views by user role, through form logic, or via form code. Forms can also be designed to allow users to switch views via the View menu.

Errors

InfoPath has a number of validation capabilities. The form designer has everything from basic options (e.g., preventing a field from being blank, or excluding certain values) to some very complex validation formulas. In addition, any requirements from underlying schemas will also be enforced.

Errors are indicated by a dashed red highlight around the control. You can view details by mousing over the errored control. Full details can either be shown to the user through a dialog box or by selecting Show Error Message from the Tools menu (Figure 2-17).

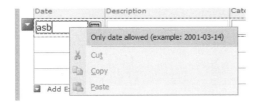

Figure 2-17. *Error display in an InfoPath form*

Digitally Signing a Form

Digital signatures are a way of guaranteeing that digital content has not changed since it was submitted by the person who signed it, and that it was signed by the person who indicated that they authored the form.

WHAT IS A DIGITAL SIGNATURE?

Digital signatures are a way for a user to apply the legal equivalent of a signature to data. To understand digital signatures, it is necessary to first understand public/private key encryption.

Public/Private Key Encryption

Public/private key encryption is a special type of encryption in which a user has two keys: a public key and a private key. This allows messages to be encrypted by anyone using the public key; only the user can decode the message using his/her private key.

More importantly for the subject of digital signatures, a message encrypted with a user's private key can only be decoded with that user's public key. In other words, if you know that a given public key belongs to John Doe, then decrypting a message using his public key guarantees that John is the person who encrypted it.

To digitally sign a document, the user creates a special summary of the document, called a *hash*. The hash is much, much smaller than the original document, but uniquely represents it—a given document will always produce the same hash.

After creating the hash for the document, the user then encrypts it using their private key. After sending the form, future users can decrypt the hash with the original user's public key (guaranteeing who encrypted the hash in the first place). They can then run the hash function on the form data as submitted, and compare the hashes. If the hashes match, then the user has a guarantee that the form has not been changed since it was originally signed.

Luckily, InfoPath takes care of all this behind the scenes.

To digitally sign a form, the user must have a *digital certificate*. A digital certificate is a small encrypted file that acts as the private key in a public/private key pair. Certificates can be obtained from commercial signing companies, such as VeriSign or thawte. These certificates are useful when form data is going to be sent outside the company or organization—when another group needs to verify the signatory of a form.

For purely internal use, it's a fairly straightforward effort to generate your own certificates, either with Windows Server 2003 or another package. For more information on configuring Windows Server 2003 as a certificate generator, or public key infrastructures in general, see `http://www.microsoft.com/PKI/`.

Finally, InfoPath offers an option to create an ad hoc digital signature, using either the user's typed name or an image of an actual signature (see Figure 2-18).

Figures 2-18. *Creating an ad hoc digital signature*

If you have a certificate installed and a form is enabled for digital signing, then you can sign the form by clicking the small ribbon icon.

Clicking this button brings up the digital signature wizard (Figure 2-19). This allows the end user to either sign the whole form or sections of the form, depending on how the form is designed. Forms can be designed either way: they can be signed in their entirety (in which case the user applies their digital signature to the entire form data such that no part of the form can be changed without invalidating the signature); or you can select specific sections of the form data to be signed (in which case each section you designate can be signed independently).

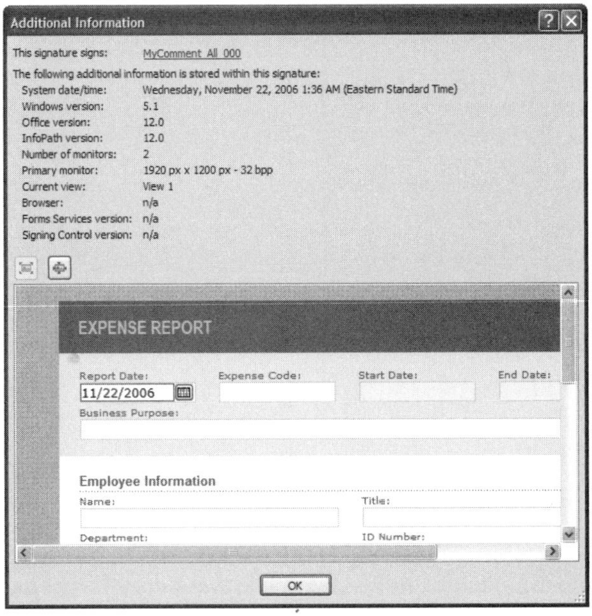

Figure 2-19. *Signing a form*

In addition, sections of a form can be co-signed or counter-signed. *Co-signing* means that multiple people can sign a form or section. However, the signatures exist in parallel—prior signatures can be removed without affecting later signatures. This could be used to indicate multiple witnesses, for example—one witness could remove their signature without changing the fact the other people signed the document.

Counter-signing means that later signatures are, in effect, signed over the prior signatures. The classic example of this would be a performance report—once an employee signs their report, their manager then signs, indicating that they are signing the employee's signature as well. In this case, the employee cannot remove their signature without corrupting the manager's signature.

Form Settings

You can change InfoPath form settings using the Options dialog under the Tools menu. The following bullets give descriptions of the InfoPath options, which are pretty rudimentary in form-filling mode:

- *General*: You can change the most recently used file list, print background colors and pictures, show the Fill Out a Form dialog on startup, and enable or disable auto-advance (Figure 2-20).

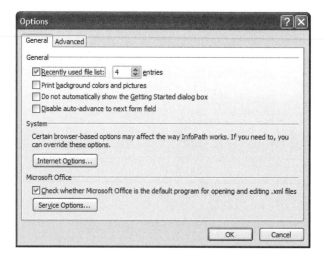

Figure 2-20. *The Options dialog*

- *System*: You can change the Internet security settings for InfoPath. This leverages the security dialog from Internet Explorer.

- *Office*: You can set Office as the default program for opening XML files.

- *Advanced*: You can set autorecover options. InfoPath will automatically store form data while you are filling out forms. You can set the duration between saves here (the default is 10 minutes), and you can also control notifications for managed code errors and digitally signed forms (Figure 2-21).

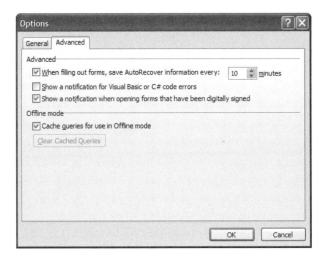

Figure 2-21. *The advanced form options*

- *Offline mode*: InfoPath can cache the results of data connection queries so that the form operates correctly when used offline. The end user can also clear cached data from this dialog.

Submitting Forms

InfoPath offers many ways of handling form data once the form is complete—the user can save the data, submit it to a data source, e-mail it, print it, export it, or merge it with other forms. When the user saves a form, the XML form data is saved as an XML file to the location the user selects: the local file system, a network location, or a SharePoint document library (shown in Figure 2-22).

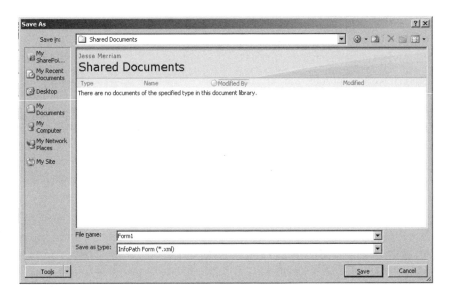

Figure 2-22. *Saving form data to a SharePoint document library*

If the form is built to enable submitting a form, then the user will have a Submit button (Figure 2-23) that performs whatever the submit action may be (e-mailing the form, posting it to a database or web service, saving it to a file location, etc.). It is possible to disable the file save functionality if submitting is enabled (to discourage users from saving forms instead of submitting them).

Figure 2-23. *Submit button on an InfoPath form*

Exporting Forms

InfoPath normally saves or submits forms in XML format—it saves the form data only to an XML document. However, there may be reasons to save a copy of what is traditionally thought of as the "filled-in form." With the Export command, InfoPath offers the ability to save off the "actual view" of the form.

Go to File ➤ Export To to find the options for exporting an InfoPath form. The options available are as follows:

- *Web*: Exports the form to a single-file web archive in the .mht format.

- *PDF or XPS*: Exports the form to Adobe's PDF Acrobat format or Microsoft's new XML Paper Specification (XPS) full-fidelity print format.

- *Excel*: Exports the data to an Excel spreadsheet. This gives you the option of exporting all the data in the form or just the data that's visible in the current view. You can also bring in data from other forms.

Digital Rights Management

Windows Server 2003 introduced Rights Management Services (RMS), a server technology that enables Office clients to produce documents protected with strong encryption, enabling sharing of sensitive business information while maintaining control over it. A central server grants access rights for protected documents to users designated by the document author.

In Office 2003, RMS protection was available natively in Word, Excel, and Outlook. InfoPath 2007 gains the ability to protect forms with RMS encryption. Under File ➤ Permission, you will find the settings to apply RMS protection to the form data such that only designated users can open and read it.

Browser Forms

While InfoPath 2003 required users to have InfoPath installed on their desktops to fill out forms, InfoPath 2007, in conjunction with Office Forms Services, provides a browser-based capability for forms submission (see Figure 2-24). There are some restrictions on the form as it's being designed, but once the form is submitted to a SharePoint forms library, the experience to the user is transparent.

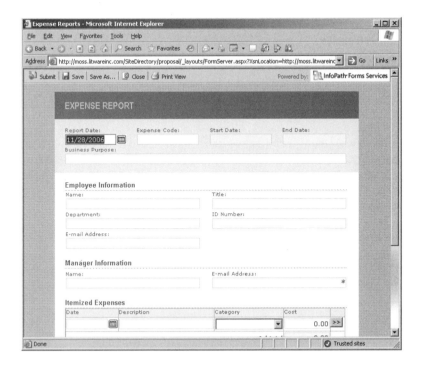

Figure 2-24. *InfoPath form in a browser*

As you can see, the browser-based experience is remarkably similar to the InfoPath experience, including drop-down calendars (see Figure 2-25), complex form validation rules, optional groups, repeating tables, and so on. Browser-based InfoPath forms will run in Internet Explorer (IE) 6+, Safari, Mozilla, Netscape 6+, and Firefox.

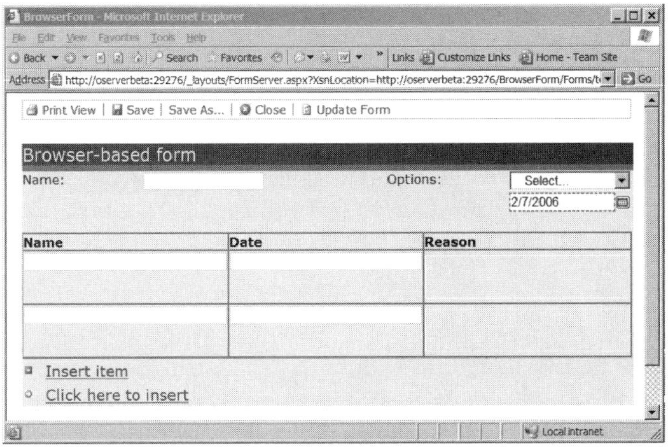

Figure 2-25. *Date picker in an InfoPath browser form*

Browser-based forms even offer rich text editing. When editing a rich text field in a browser-based form, a small toolbar pops up, giving a rich text editor with which the user can add tables, hyperlinks, and richly formatted text.

Note Browser-based forms do not allow images to be embedded.

E-mailing Forms

InfoPath 2007, in conjunction with Outlook 2007, gives users the ability to e-mail fully editable forms to other users (see Figure 2-26). Instead of e-mailing an attachment that someone needs to open, edit, save, and then attach to a new e-mail, users can e-mail out a full-fidelity form embedded within the e-mail itself. The recipient can then fill out the form and simply return it to the original sender (or forward it on to another user).

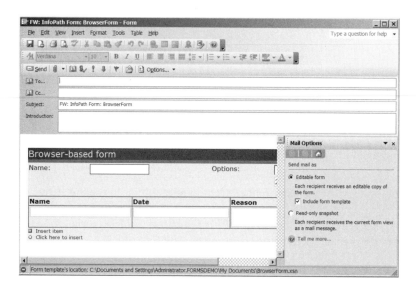

Figure 2-26. *InfoPath form in an Outlook e-mail*

You'll see from the options in the task pane that this form can be sent as a fully editable form or a simple read-only image of the form data (useful for users that don't have InfoPath installed). You can also use this capability in workflows—forms can be e-mailed out as part of a workflow, and the workflow can take an action based on the responses in the returned form.

Forms for Metadata

There's one more interesting new use for InfoPath forms in the new Office SharePoint Server. In SharePoint 2003 (Portal Server or Windows SharePoint Services), users could add metadata to documents in a document library. If the metadata were made mandatory, then a user submitting a document to the library would be prompted for the data before being allowed to save.

But other than that, there was no way to access the document's metadata from within the Office application the user was editing the document in.

In Office 12, document metadata is pulled down to the Office application so that the document author can edit the metadata while still editing the document. That metadata is presented in a header bar under the ribbon. That header bar is actually an embedded InfoPath form (see Figure 2-27).

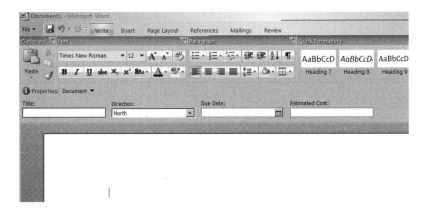

Figure 2-27. *Word document with SharePoint metadata*

The forms can actually be edited in InfoPath, so a designer can add images, change the design, add validation rules, pull lookup data in, leverage other code, and so on—basically anything InfoPath can do, these form headers can do.

Summary

That's the whirlwind tour. Hopefully it's helped you understand the InfoPath client from the user's view. From here, we'll dive into the designer and the forms capabilities for the power user and developer.

CHAPTER 3

■ ■ ■

Tour of the InfoPath Designer

This chapter will tour the InfoPath designer, cover some of the basics, and generally try to fully cover all the design features of InfoPath. It will cover some basic design concepts and tour the InfoPath form designer features. This is the entry point for building everything from basic data entry forms to powerful enterprise e-forms.

Introduction to InfoPath Form Design

InfoPath forms are all XML-based. Understanding this is critical in designing forms, as it will help explain some of the form behaviors that you should take into consideration while you are laying out a form. The form definition is a schema, whether the form is designed against an arbitrary schema or a blank form is laid out (in which case InfoPath implicitly creates the schema underneath the form).

A power user can be happily oblivious to the XML/XSD magic that is going on behind the scenes while creating a form, and still produce a working, scalable front end for their business process. But a developer who is laying out a form (or troubleshooting a form they didn't design) will be much happier with the results if they're aware of InfoPath's XML underpinnings.

Form Design Philosophy

There are a number of ways to start designing a new form—there may already be a schema defined (including the schema for a web service), and the form must be designed against that schema. Alternatively, the form may be the first part of a new solution, so the form will, in effect, define what the remainder of the solution looks like (or the form may be designed with the intent that it be "stand-alone"—rendering user data into XML is the entire intent of the current solution). Of course, the form you're designing may be an intersection of the two—a business process may exist with a currently defined schema, and you might be designing an electronic version of a paper form to integrate with the process.

Whenever possible, I strongly recommend designing a schema first. The main reason is that from a schema, all things can flow. There are tools that can take an XML schema and render a database schema (such as Altova's XMLSpy). Microsoft's BizTalk Server uses the schema as its common denominator for XML document translation. Obviously, InfoPath works with XML schemas natively, making it easy to design a form against an XML schema. Finally, Visual Studio includes a tool (XSD.exe) that can generate an entire class tree from a schema. So if you have an XML schema as your starting point, you can auto-generate major portions of your solution. Starting from any other point means adding the step of creating the XSD from where you started.

There's one notable exception here, and that's that if you design a form in InfoPath, InfoPath generates a W3C-compliant schema with the form. If you use groupings, repeating sections, optional sections, and the like, you can judiciously generate a fairly solid XSD simply by laying out a form. The interesting thing about this approach is that it seems that people are better at laying out requirements by looking at a form than they are from being interviewed by an analyst. Project an InfoPath form up during a design session with the users, and you may find ideas and business rules flowing faster than ever.

Creating a New Form

Open the Design a Form dialog (Figure 3-1)—either by clicking the Design a Form Template link on the Getting Started wizard or in the File menu.

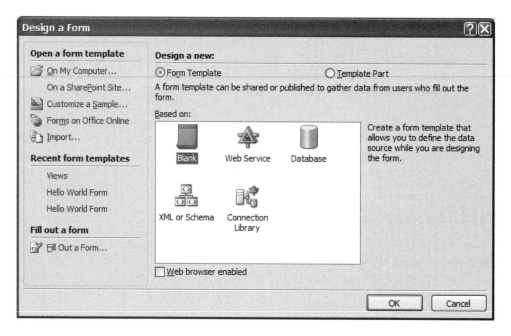

Figure 3-1. *The Design a Form dialog*

You are presented with the options to open a form template for editing, choose from a list of recent form templates, switch back to the Fill Out a Form wizard, or design a new form template or template part. A check box provides the option to create a form template or template part that can be viewed via browser from Office Server.

BROWSER FORMS

InfoPath 2007, in combination with Office SharePoint Server 2007, allows you to author forms that can be served to a web browser (see Figure 3-2). The forms have full fidelity with the rich client forms—including drop-down lists, optional and repeating sections, rich text, and validation—with a minimum of round trips to the server. Browser-based forms are compatible with Internet Explorer (IE) 5+, Netscape 6+, Firefox, Safari, and Mozilla, providing a cross-platform capability not previously available with InfoPath forms.

There are a number of features that are *not* available in browser forms. Obviously, inking controls are not, nor are image controls, combo boxes, master/detail controls, or lists. The best way to approach this is to create a form as a browser form from scratch; by indicating the form is browser-based, only those options permitted in browser forms will be available. Should you decide to change once a form is designed, then you can use the design checker in the Design Tasks pane to validate the suitability of a form for browser use.

One other option to note with respect to the limitations of browser forms is that it is possible to designate a view as "client-only." If you do so, the view will not be available to browser form users, and the full InfoPath client capabilities will be available in that view.

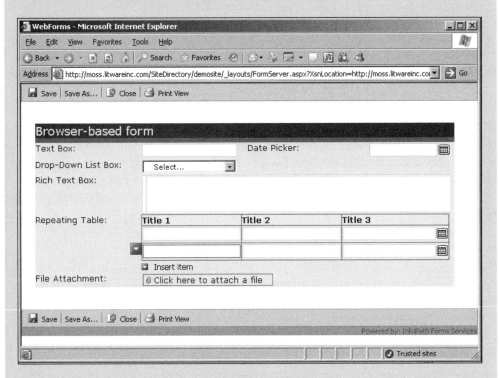

Figure 3-2. *An InfoPath form in a browser*

Types of InfoPath Forms

Let's look at the various ways to create a new InfoPath form.

Blank

This option starts you with a completely blank canvas. The form is not bound to any data sources and has no layout or controls. You then build the form by dragging and dropping controls onto the design surface to lay out the form. InfoPath builds a schema behind the scenes to represent the controls placed on the form.

Web Service

With this option, the wizard will prompt you to enter the URL of a web service that has implemented a SOAP 2.0–compliant WSDL. From the web service, InfoPath will list the methods available. When you select a method, the schema for the WSDL will become the schema for the form—input parameters will become query fields and return parameters, and structures will be presented as the data fields.

Database

This option lets you create a form bound to an Access or SQL Server database.

■**Note** InfoPath uses the operating system's data connection builder to create a new data connection. As a result, when the wizard provides data provider options, you may see other databases listed (Oracle, Sybase, etc.) if you have installed the drivers for them. This is an artifact of reusing the wizard—rest assured that InfoPath cannot natively connect to any database except MS Access or MS SQL Server. It is for this reason that I advocate building *all* your InfoPath forms against web services, to make maintenance easier across all platforms.

The wizard will walk you through building a data connection, and then the form will have a data source reflecting both query and data fields representing the database tables or views you have hooked. This will allow you to design the form to retrieve data from the database and post it back if you choose.

XML or Schema

InfoPath lets you design a form against an existing XML document or schema. If you design the form against a schema, the form data source is locked down to that schema, and the form UI must be designed against that data source.

On the other hand, designing a form against an XML document allows InfoPath to infer the schema from the XML. It also leaves the data source unlocked so that the designer can add nodes or alter the data source on which the form is then designed.

Connection Library

InfoPath allows you to store and reuse data connections in Windows SharePoint Services. You can store the connection to a data connection library, and then reuse the connection in other forms.

Control Template Part

Another new option in InfoPath 2007 is the ability to build a custom control template from other InfoPath controls. If there is a collection of controls you regularly use (an example would be an HR department that has a standard personnel information section), then you can lay out the controls in a control template and save that off for reuse in other forms.

The Design Tasks Pane

Once you're in design mode for a form, you'll see the list of design tasks in the right-hand task pane. These tasks are your options for managing and designing your form. Let's walk through each of the tasks in detail.

Form Layout

This task pane (Figure 3-3) provides the basic structure for laying out your form. You have a number of predefined table layouts you can insert, as well as a complement of table actions that you can perform. I've found it most useful to start with Table with Title, and then nest tables within the main table to provide structure to the form.

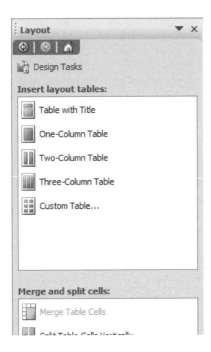

Figure 3-3. *The Layout task pane*

■**Note** Design tables only affect the display of the form—they have no effect on the underlying schema or XML data.

You can also access a table designer from the Layout Table button in the button bar at the top of the designer.

InfoPath uses a "flow layout" paradigm, so without layout tables, all the controls simply fall together (Figure 3-4). There is no way to explicitly place items on the form canvas—it takes tables to manage layout of a form (Figure 3-5).

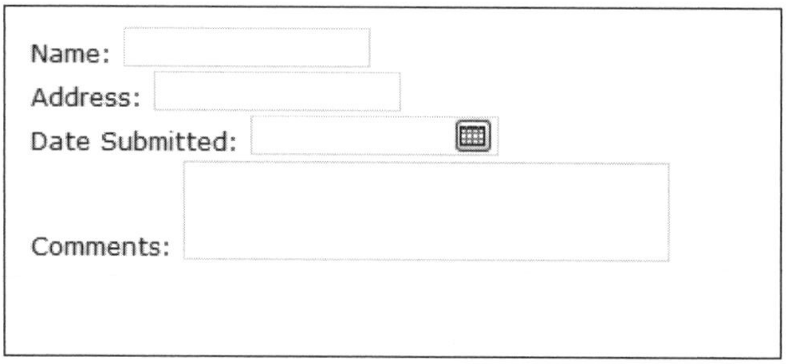

Figure 3-4. *A form with no layout tables*

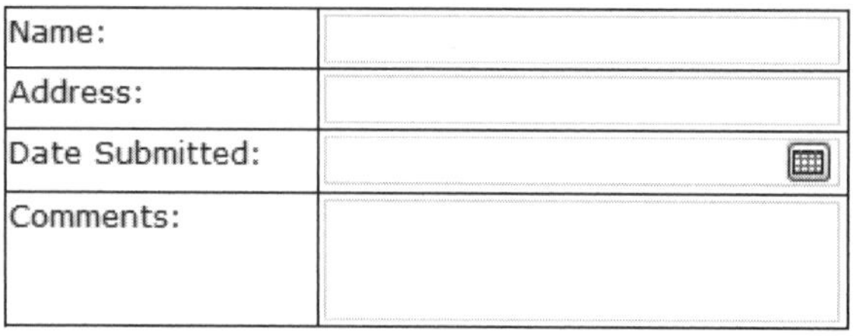

Figure 3-5. *Using layout tables to lay out an InfoPath form*

Laying out forms with tables takes some practice—you generally want to provide separate cells for labels and controls, as well as a blank cell between adjacent controls for some separation. Get used to the cell formatting buttons on the toolbar—merge cells, split cells, and cell formatting get heavy use when you're laying out an InfoPath form!

Let's try laying out a basic form just to get an idea of how it works.

Exercise 3-1. Laying Out an InfoPath Form

1. Create a new blank form. (Go to File ➤ Design a Form, and then select New Blank Form from the task pane.)

2. From Design Tasks, select Layout.

3. Select Table with Title.

4. In the area where it says "Click to add a title," click and type **Hello World Form**.

5. Click in the area where it says "Click to add form content."

6. Click the Design Tasks link in the task bar, and then click Controls.

7. Add a section control—this will allow you to group the header info of your form.

8. Click inside the section control.

9. Under Insert Layout Tables in the layout task pane, click Custom Table.

10. Select 5 columns and 3 rows, and then click OK.

11. You'll see that you've added a table within the main layout table.

12. Click and drag the sides of the center column to make it narrower—this will be a buffer between two columns of controls and labels (see Figure 3-6).

Figure 3-6. *Initial form layout*

13. Type **Name** in the first cell, and then click in the second cell. In the task pane, click Controls, and then click the text box control. Note that InfoPath inserts a text box into the cell, sized to the width of the cell (see Figure 3-7).

Figure 3-7. *Inserting a text box into the form*

14. Type **Date** in the fourth cell (after the buffer), and then put a date picker control in the fifth cell. You can either click in the cell and then click the control, or click and drag the control from the task pane.

15. In the first cell in the second row, type **Description**.

16. Click in any empty space in the second cell in the second row, and drag to the right to select the remaining four cells (see Figure 3-8).

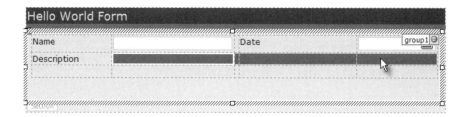

Figure 3-8. *Selecting and merging cells in an InfoPath table*

17. Right-click and select Merge Cells, and then add a rich text box to the newly merged cell.

18. Now you're going to add a repeating table to the form for some detail data. Right-click in the empty table space below the section control, to the right of the Section tab, and select Insert ➤ Rows Below. Do this again to get two new rows in your layout table.

19. Select the upper empty row and add a color fill (either through Format ➤ Background Color, by selecting Borders and Shading from the context menu, or by using the Fill tool from the formatting toolbar) to split the form visually.

20. Click in the lower row, and then click the repeating table control. Change the number of columns to 5, as shown in Figure 3-9.

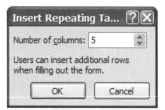

Figure 3-9. *The column picker dialog for a new repeating table*

21. Add the following labels to the header of your form: **Description**, **Item Nbr**, **Unit Cost**, **Qty**, and **Subtotal**. Your form should now look like the one in Figure 3-10.

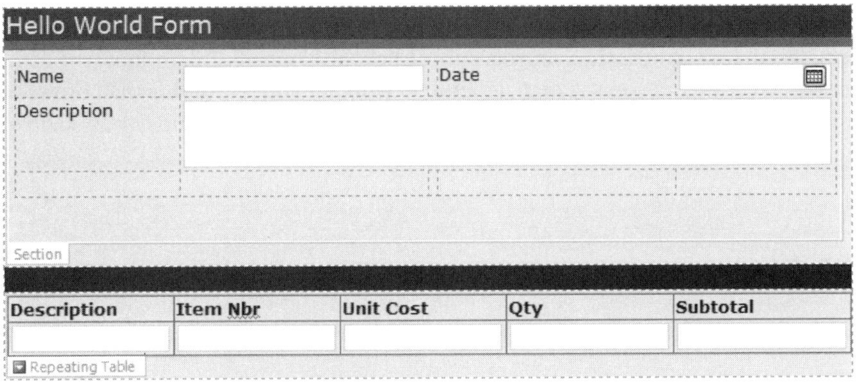

Figure 3-10. *The completed Hello World form*

22. You can click the Preview Form button to see how the form will look.

23. Save the form (File ➤ Save; you will get a note about needing to publish it later).

INFOPATH DESIGNER QUIRKS

I want to point out a few "features" of InfoPath that may drive you crazy:

- It is possible to resize objects to be larger than the cell they are in. For example, select the text box you laid down in step 10 of Exercise 3-1, and then drag the right side of it to the right—you can make it larger than the cell. When you select the control, its handles are visible, so you can grab them even if they're beyond the edge of the cell.

- Sizing tables is not as easy—if a nested table becomes larger than the cell that contains it, you'll have to drag the edge of the outer table out to expose the wayward inner table, and then resize it down.

- When you nest tables, there will be a gap between the bottom of the child table and the bottom of the parent (see Figure 3-11). This is there by design to give you room to add other content. It will not appear when the form is published.

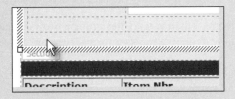

Figure 3-11. *Design gap below a design table*

Controls

The next design task pane is the controls pane. Click the Controls link to show the Controls pane (Figure 3-12). What you see may depend on whether you're working on a browser form. The controls are broken down into five groups: Standard, Repeating and Optional, File and Picture, Advanced, and Custom.

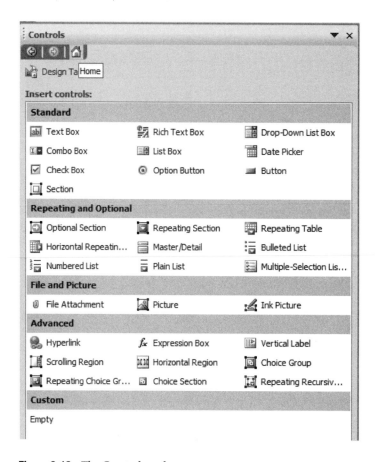

Figure 3-12. *The Controls task pane*

Not all controls are available in browser forms. When you are designing a browser-based form, InfoPath will only show the controls that will run in a browser form. These are as follows:

- Text box

- Rich text box

- Drop-down list box

- List box

- Date picker

- Check box

- Option button

- Button

- Section

- Optional section

- Repeating section

- Repeating table

- Hyperlink

- Expression box

Text Box

Let's start with the basic text box and use that to examine some of the common features of all controls. From the text box on the form you designed in Exercise 3-1, open the Text Box Properties dialog (either double-click the text box or right-click and select Text Box Properties). The Text Box Properties dialog is shown in Figure 3-13.

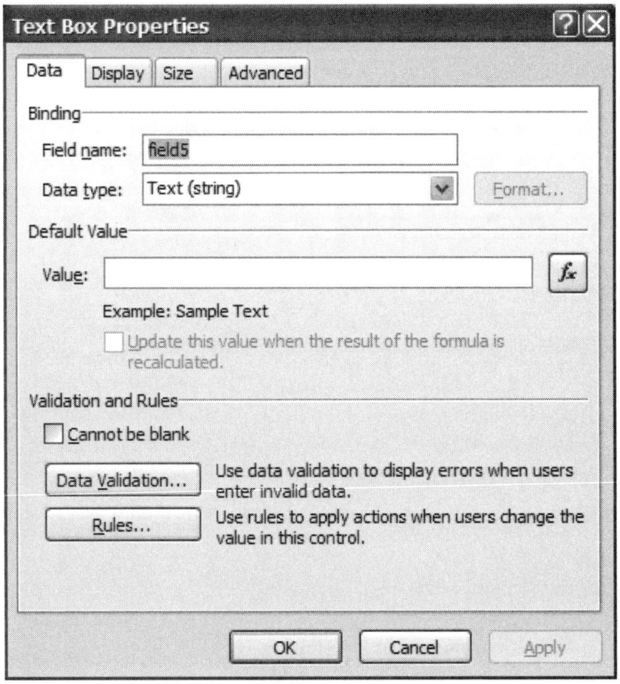

Figure 3-13. *The Text Box Properties dialog*

Field Name

The field name refers to the name of the underlying element. If you are designing a blank form, you can change this and it will rename the underlying schema element (a good idea if you don't want a schema with elements named "field1," "field2," etc.) There are naming restrictions on this field:

- No spaces or special characters are allowed.

- The name must start with a letter or underscore.

- It can only contain letters, numbers, hyphens, underscores, and periods.

■**Note** If you are designing a form against a predefined schema or web service, this field will be read-only (you can't rename an element in a predefined schema).

Exercise 3-2. Field Names and Form Data Structure

1. Open the Hello World form you created in Exercise 3-1.

2. In the Controls task pane, click the Design Tasks link, and then click Data Source.

3. You'll see that your data source is an unreadable stack of sequentially numbered nodes (group1, group2, field1, field2, etc.).

4. The section you put in for the header data is group1. Right-click the section, and then select Section Properties.

5. Rename the section **Header**, and then click OK. The name "group1" will change to "Header."

6. Change the names of the field1, field2, and field3 controls to **Name**, **Date**, and **Details**.

7. Right-click the repeating table and select Repeating Table Properties. Note that you can't change the name in this dialog box. Close the dialog.

8. In the Data Source task pane, right-click the group2 node and select Properties. Change the name to **OrderDetails**. This is the name of the parent container for the repeating nodes representing order items.

9. Change group3 to **OrderItem**.

10. For the text boxes in the table, you can change the name either from the control or the data source. The data source looks more intelligent and self-describing (see Figure 3-14).

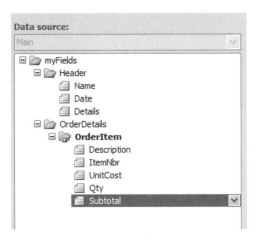

Figure 3-14. *A well-defined data source*

11. Save the form again.

Data Type

The data type indicates what kind of data will be allowed in this field. This governs validation of the field during data entry (and if you are designing a new, blank form, setting the data type on the control will establish the data type of the element in the underlying schema). A list of data types and descriptions is shown in Table 3-1.

Table 3-1. *Data Types Available in InfoPath Text Boxes*

Data Type	Example	Comments	Allows Formatting?
Text	Mr. Jones	Any text string; can be restricted with pattern validation	No
Whole Number	3245	Any string of digits	Yes
Decimal	34.546	A decimal value	Yes
True/False	True	Can be either True/False or 1/0	No
Hyperlink	//ftpserver/path	Corresponds to the any URI data type in XML schemas	No
Date	1/13/2005	Accepts various date formats	Yes
Time	12:23:45 PM	Accepts various time formats	Yes

When you select a data type, the text box will restrict user input accordingly—the user can enter data, but if the data doesn't conform to a format for the given data type, then InfoPath will indicate an error by highlighting the text box with a red dashed border and will give the user an error prompt, along with an example of proper data formatting (see Figure 3-15).

Figure 3-15. *Data type error in an InfoPath form*

Format

The contents of a text box can be formatted in a variety of ways depending on the data type of the text box. The formats are applied in the display, but do not affect the saved value. For example, an integer with currency formatting applied may display "($23,325)," but the value stored in the underlying XML data document will be "23325."

The formats that can be applied come from a fixed list based on the data type of the text box. For example, whole numbers can be formatted either as a raw display, as a number with optional grouping symbols and negative value display, or as currency (again with optional grouping symbols and negative value display).

To format a text box, open the Text Box Properties dialog and select a data type that provides formatting (see Table 3-1), which should enable the Format button next to the data type selector (Figure 3-16).

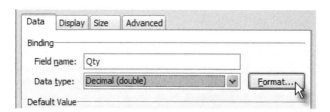

Figure 3-16. *Selecting the format for a text box*

This opens the formatting dialog box. Figure 3-17 shows the formatting dialog for a text box with a date data type. You'll see that you have the option to either leave the raw data or provide a friendlier format. Since this is a regionalized value, many of the options will be formatted in accordance with the end user's regional setting in Windows.

Figure 3-17. *The Date Format dialog box*

Default Value

The Default Value property can set the value for a text box (or other control) until it's edited. One example would be to insert today's date into a date picker when a form is opened. Another would be to perform some calculations on other values (e.g., a subtotal box showing the product of quantity and cost). InfoPath makes it easy to show a running total as well—if you have a repeating group or repeating table, you can simply sum the values of an element in each of the groups.

Exercise 3-3. Using Default Values

1. Open the form you designed in Exercise 3-2.

2. Double-click the date field, which will open the Text Box Properties dialog.

3. Click the "fx" button next to the Value text box in the Default Value section (see Figure 3-18).

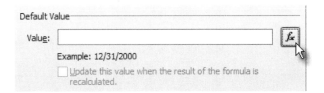

Figure 3-18. *The function button on the Text Box Properties dialog*

4. Click the Insert Function button.

5. Select each of the categories, and note the options available.

6. Select "Date and Time" from the Categories list, and then select "today" from the Functions list. Click OK. The formula text area should now show the formula `today()`.

7. Click OK.

8. Click the Preview Form button in the toolbar. The date picker will default to today's date.

9. Click Close Preview.

10. In the repeating table, double-click the text box in the last column (Subtotal).

11. Click the "fx" button next to the Value text box in the Default Value section.

12. Click Insert Field or Group, and the Select a Field or Group dialog will open (see Figure 3-19).

Figure 3-19. *Selecting a field or group in the Text Box Properties dialog*

13. Select the Qty element, and then click OK.

14. Type a * (for multiplication).

15. Open the Select a Field or Group dialog again, and select the UnitCost element.

16. Click OK, and then click OK again.

17. Right-click the repeating table, and select Repeating Table Properties.

18. Select the Display tab, and make sure Include Footer is checked.

19. Click OK.

20. Add a text box in the footer in the rightmost column (see Figure 3-20).

Description	Item Nbr	Unit Cost	Qty	Subtotal
☑ Repeating Table				

Figure 3-20. *A repeating table footer*

21. Right-click the text box you just added. Name it Total. To the right of the Default Value section, you will see a small button labeled "fx"—this opens the Function Designer dialog. Click it now to open the dialog.

22. Click Insert Function, select Sum, and then click OK.

23. Double-click where it says "double click to insert field."

24. Open the Items group, and then the Item group. Select the Subtotal element.

25. Click OK, another OK, and then another OK.

26. Preview the form. Enter some values for Qty (quantity) and UnitCost. Click the Insert Item link to add additional rows. Note that the subtotals and grand total are calculated automatically.

27. Save the form.

Validation and Rules

InfoPath provides a number of methods for validating data and automatically taking actions based on the value in a field.

The "Cannot be blank" check box obviously makes a field mandatory. This option can be tricky—again, it may be unavailable if the underlying schema is designed in such a way that the field is already mandatory (e.g., a date that is not nillable).

Data validation allows you to set one or more rules on what data a user can enter in a control. Data entry can be restricted by absolute value (e.g., "Total price cannot be greater than 10,000"), a relative value (e.g., "Date submitted must be after today"), or even based on values in other fields (e.g., "Number of days requested must be less than number of days available").

■**Tip** Recognize that the rule you are entering in the wizard is the *error condition*, which is the inverse of the desired result. Therefore, if the date submitted must be after today, the actual condition you want to enter is "If the date submitted is today or before, raise an error."

You can indicate an alert by highlighting the control with the error condition and showing a tool tip, or by popping up a dialog box.

■**Note** Browser-based forms cannot show a dialog box on error.

Notice the section at the bottom of the Validation dialog labeled "Script"—this is where you can add script or code to the controls on your form. You can add JScript or .NET code when control data is changed—either before the update is posted to the underlying XML file, after it's posted, or when the code is validated. You'll learn more about adding code to InfoPath forms in Chapter 4.

In the next exercise, you'll set date validation and error conditions on the fields on your form. They should display error messages when you enter invalid data on the fields on your form.

Exercise 3-4. Validation and Error Conditions

1. Open the Hello World form.

2. Double-click the Date field to open the Properties dialog.

3. Set the data type to "Date (date)."

4. Click the Data Validation button.

5. Click the Add button to open the Data Validation dialog.

6. Under "If this condition is true," the Date field should already be selected. Change the second drop-down box (which should say "is equal to") to "is less than" (see Figure 3-21).

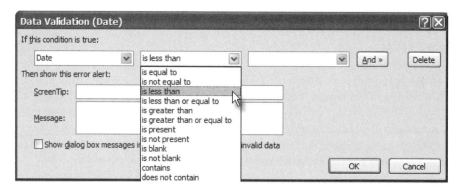

Figure 3-21. *The Data Validation dialog*

7. In the final drop-down box, select Use a Formula. The Insert Formula dialog will open.

8. Click the Insert Function button to open the Insert Function dialog (see Figure 3-22).

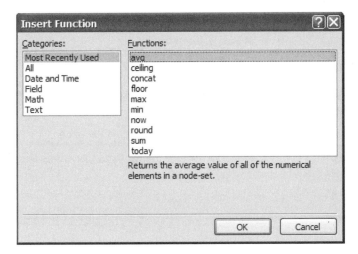

Figure 3-22. *The Insert Function dialog*

9. The Category will default to Most Recently Used—in the Functions selector, you should have "today" selected (if you don't, then select Date and Time on the left).

10. Select "today," click OK, and then click OK again.

11. In the Data Validation dialog, add a screen tip and message for the error (Figure 3-23).

Figure 3-23. *The Data Validation dialog when complete*

12. Click OK, click OK, and then click OK again.

13. Open the Text Box Properties dialog for the Qty text box in the repeating table.

14. Set the data type to Whole Number (integer).

15. Click the Data Validation button, and then the Add button.

16. In this case, you want the quantity to be greater than zero. So your error condition is "Quantity" "is less than."

17. In the final drop-down box, select "Type a number," and then type **1**.

18. Click OK, then OK, and then OK again to close the Properties dialog.

19. Preview the form.

20. Type some letters in the Date field, and then tab out of the control. Note that the control is outlined in red because the text violates the data type condition.

21. Delete the text and type in yesterday's date. Note that you now get the error you added.

22. Try the same with the Qty box in the repeating table. Add extra rows and violate the various conditions, noting that the errors are called out appropriately.

23. Save the form.

Rules are similar to data validation, except rules perform specific actions when certain conditions are met within a control. The conditions wizard is similar to the wizard from the validation option, but the actions are different (see Figure 3-24).

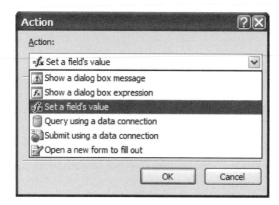

Figure 3-24. *The Actions dialog*

You can have multiple rules on a control (and stop processing additional rules if a given rule fires), and each rule can have multiple actions. The options available in the Actions dialog are shown in Table 3-2.

Table 3-2. *Options in the Actions Dialog*

Action	Description
Show a dialog box message	Pops up a dialog with a specific text message.
Show a dialog box expression	Shows a dialog box with a calculated message (using the expression builder).
Set a field's value	Allows you to select a field and set it to a calculated value.
Query using a data connection	Pulls additional data from a defined data connection (perhaps updating a data connection or bringing in new data on a separate connection).
Submit using a data connection	Provides a way of submitting data before the Submit button is clicked, and a way of submitting to multiple data connections.
Open a new form to fill out	Opens a new form. An example would be that if the country code on a shipping form was in another nation, a customs form would be automatically opened for the user to fill out.

Display

On the Display tab are, amazingly, a number of options affecting how the control and its contents are displayed.

The Placeholder option puts placeholder text in a control, which can give some quick contextual guidance to a user.

Read-only, as indicated, prevents a user from editing a control. You may often use this on calculated controls (e.g., your subtotal and grand total fields in Exercise 3-2) so that the user doesn't change the calculated totals.

Enable Spelling Checker and Enable AutoComplete give you control over when these fields may not make sense (e.g., disable spell checking on proper name fields, and disable auto-complete on fields that may have sensitive or often-changing data).

Checking the Multi-line option gives you the option to make a multi-line text box. Simply check "multi-line" and "wrap text," and then size the text box larger vertically to get multi-line capability. Checking "Paragraph breaks" also gives a paragraph formatting style to the text box.

The "Limit text box to [x] characters" option gives you a way to put a maximum length on a field. As indicated by the tab name, this only affects the display of the data, not the underlying schema. If you set this option, you also have the option to automatically skip to the next control when the control is full.

Alignment lets you set the alignment of the text within the text box (left, center, right, or justified).

Conditional Formatting

Conditional formatting applies conditions to the control itself based on the contents. If you click the Conditional Formatting button, you will get the Conditional Formatting dialog, which is simply a container for your formatting rules. Click the Add button to bring up the Conditional Format rule dialog (Figure 3-25).

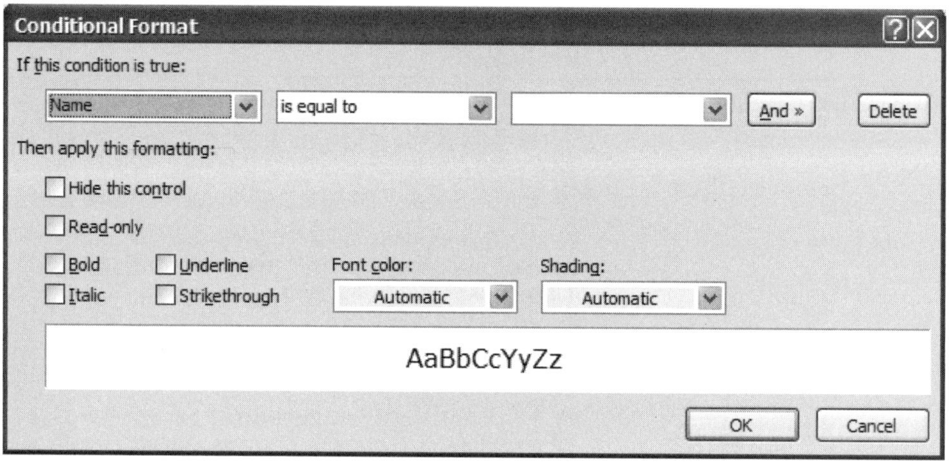

Figure 3-25. *The Conditional Format rule dialog*

The conditions editor should be getting fairly familiar—it's exactly like the validation conditions editor. You can add multiple conditions and AND or OR them as necessary. When a rule is satisfied, the formatting indicated in the lower part of the dialog is applied. You have a variety of options here—a number of text formatting options to apply (with a preview section to show what you're doing), as well as the ability to make a control read-only or hide it.

The conditions don't restrict you to the current control—you can change the formatting of a control based on conditions in a completely different control. For example, you can have a justification text box that only shows if the total is greater than a certain value.

Tip Again, you need to consider carefully how you state your conditions to achieve the desired result. For example, assume that the business rule is "If the total is greater than 1,000, then show the justification block." In InfoPath, the way you have to define this is to add the conditional formatting to the *justification block* and set it to be hidden if the total is less than or equal to 1,000.

Size

The Size tab simply has options for the size, location, and padding of the controls. You can select various units, including percentage, ems, pixels, or inches. The Align button sets the alignment of the control to the nearest label.

Advanced

The Advanced tab provides a collection of sections that give the user control over accessibility features, how controls are merged when forms are merged, and so on.

Accessibility: This option provides access to the various accessibility aspects of the controls. Screen Tip, Tab Index, and Access Key are all fairly self-explanatory.

Merging Forms: This button brings up a wizard that allows you to assign what happens to the control data if this form is merged with another form. If the control holds data that cannot be easily merged (e.g., numerical data), then InfoPath will raise an error. Data of all types can be merged into a repeating control, since InfoPath will simply add additional nodes to the repeating control.

When merging, you have the option to either keep the underlying data in the target form (the form that other form data is merged into) or combine the values. Of course, you get various options for combining data—ignoring blank fields, separating data with a defined character or value, prefixing each value with a character or dynamically defined value (using the ubiquitous "fx" button), and so on.

Code: This section provides the control's ID for use in code (see Chapter 4).

Input Recognition: When an InfoPath form is being filled in using a tablet PC, InfoPath offers handwriting recognition capabilities. The result is that the form user can hand-write data, and the form will be filled in with typed data. This option allows the form designer to "hint" to the recognizer what type of data the field should hold, improving accuracy on handwriting recognition.

Rich Text Box

While the standard text box control allows only POA (plain ol' ASCII), the rich text box control allows end users to format their text using either basic formatting (bold, italic, font formatting, etc.) or full rich text (including tables, images, etc.). The formatted text is stored using markup tags in the underlying XML. Images that are placed in a rich text box control can be embedded or linked. Embedded images are stored as base64-encoded text within the XML.

The underlying properties for the rich text box control are generally similar to those of the text box control.

Drop-Down List Box

The drop-down list box control has a unique issue in that it can be data driven; as a result, there are options available to establish the list that InfoPath presents to the user to choose from.

InfoPath offers the user options to type in a list or get a list dynamically. The following bullet points describe the options:

- *Enter list box entries manually*: This option simply allows you to enter the form items. This is good for items that won't change very often, such as sex, days of the week, months of the year, and so on.

- *Look up values in the form's data source*: You would use this option to draw the list items from any repeating section of the form. For example, in your Hello World form, you may want to provide a list of items in the order to choose from (see Figure 3-26).

Figure 3-26. *Using a drop-down list box to choose from existing data*

- *Look up values from an external data source*: Finally, you can use external data sources to populate a drop-down list. You can add an XML file to the form as a data source, pull data from a web service or database, or use data from a SharePoint list.

Combo Box

The combo box operates exactly like a drop-down list box, except that it has the added feature of allowing the user to enter values that aren't in the list. This is both a blessing and a curse: it is convenient in that the developer can allow users to enter free-form data or select formal data from a list; but on the other hand, this makes binding a list to a lookup table problematic. You may also run into problems if you try to have a schema in which the value is an integer foreign key, since any user-typed value is going to be passed as a string.

Date Picker

The date picker is fairly straightforward—you have a control that is bound to a datetime data type and offers users a calendar control to choose a date. You can indicate whether the value should be saved as a string, a date, or a datetime data type. You can set the time display format (defaulted to "do not display") in the formatting for the control if the data format is set to text or datetime. In the following sample, I have taken an InfoPath form and put three date picker controls on it, each set to a different data type. I entered **3/17/2006 9:00** into each and saved the form (which produces an XML document). Opening the XML document shows how each data format affected the date saved:

```
<my:myFields xmlns:my="http://schemas.microsoft.com/office/infopath/2003/myXSD/➥
2006-03-17T23:43:09" xml:lang="en-us">
    <my:DateString>2006-03-17T09:00:00</my:DateString>
    <my:DateDate xmlns:xsi="http://www.w3.org/2001/XMLSchema-instance">➥
2006-03-17</my:DateDate>
     <my:DateTime xmlns:xsi="http://www.w3.org/2001/XMLSchema-instance">➥
2006-03-17T09:00:00
</my:DateTime>
</my:myFields>
```

Note the varying data types of the XML elements—the first is a simple text value; the following two are set with namespace pointers. Also note that the second element only has the date, while the third has the date and time.

Finally, note the formatting of the datetime strings in the elements with time included. The "T" is used to separate the date and time elements, and the time is reported using 24-hour clock standards. This is the standard datetime format for XML elements, and is worth knowing if you're going to generate your own XML.

Check Box

The check box is fairly straightforward, but it has one interesting twist. Placing a check box on a form gives you a simple yes/no-style control, and will add a label with the element's name.

Looking at the properties, you can see that the default data type is True/False (Boolean). You can indicate the default state of the control (checked or unchecked), you can select the value of the control for the cleared and checked states (True/False or 1/0), and you can invert the results.

It gets more interesting if you change the data type. If you change it to Text, instead of being limited to True/False or 1/0, you have free-form text boxes to put values for checked and cleared. Switching to decimal lets you put in decimal values. The same applies for Date, Time, Hyperlink, and so on. This means that you can use the check box to truly switch between two values without having to manipulate them with code.

For example, let's say you were figuring out a discount that varied based on veteran status— the normal discount is 10 percent, but veterans get an extra 5 percent off, so their discount is 15 percent. You could have a check box captioned "Veteran" for the user to check. If the box is cleared, the value is .90, and if it's checked, it's .85. Then you simply show the value in the Discount text box.

Option Button

Option buttons are similar to check boxes, except that you can have multiple values instead of a single yes/no. When you add an Option button to a form, you will be prompted for how many to insert (see Figure 3-27). The buttons are added with text labels for the element to which they're assigned (you can change these labels without affecting the operation of the buttons). All the buttons added are bound to the same element in the data source, and InfoPath manages the code to ensure that only one button is selected at a time.

Figure 3-27. *Prompt for option buttons*

If you look at the properties, you will see that, as with the check box, you can change the data type of the option button and indicate what value the individual button will represent. If you change the data type of one button, you will change it for all buttons bound to the same element (and possibly lose the values you had entered for them).

You also have a check box to indicate which button is selected by default (or you can deselect all to not have a default).

Button

The button control is a little different from the controls covered so far. It is not related to a data source element—the button does what buttons do best: it fires off some kind of action.

If you look at the properties for the button, you'll see that you have some different options from what you've seen so far (see Figure 3-28). The Action option offers two selections: Rules and Custom Code, and Submit. Selecting either action changes the options in the Properties dialog to reflect your choice.

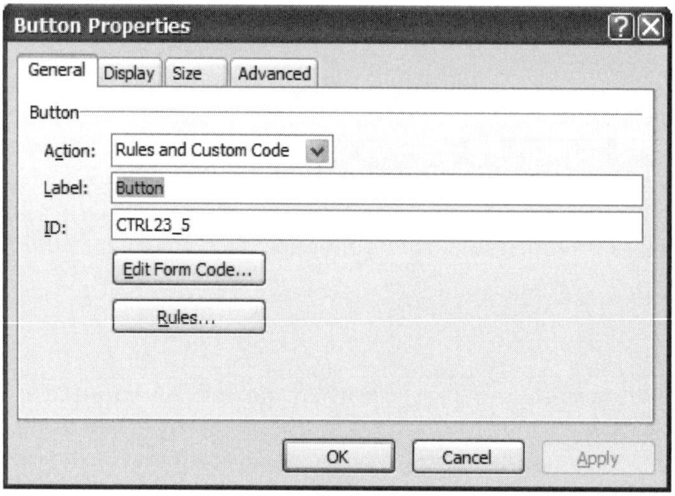

Figure 3-28. *The Properties dialog for a button control*

The Submit action gives you a place to set the label for the button and a button for the submit options for the form (for more details, see Chapter 4).

The Rules and Custom Code action allows you to set the label and the button ID. You also get a button to edit the code associated with the button (see Chapter 4) and/or rules associated with the button. The Rules dialog is the common one used throughout InfoPath.

Section

A section control doesn't directly affect the user. The form designer can use it for grouping controls. The first reason you may want to do this is to provide some structure to your data—by putting in a section to group, say, all your "header" elements, you can then add some additional structure to your data in the resulting XML.

Another reason you may want to use a section is to hide data—by putting conditional display rules on a section, you can hide or show a section based on values in other fields.

Optional Section

An optional section is similar to a section control—used for grouping and for allowing the insertion of groups of controls. However, there is a unique difference—when controls are *hidden* using conditional formatting rules, the elements remain in the data source, with their default values.

Caution Hiding a date control that doesn't have a default value may cause problems if the element is not marked as nillable in the underlying schema—the date control will fail validation as InfoPath tries to post it with a null value.

On the other hand, when an optional section is removed using the section controls, the elements are not actually posted as part of the XML. (An obvious side note here is that the underlying schema must provide for the group to be absent from the XML document—marked as minoccurs=0).

Looking at the properties for an optional section, you can see that the section can be included in the form by default or not. If you include the section by default, you can also allow users to delete it. If it is not included, then you can optionally allow users to insert it, and customize the text shown to indicate that the option exists (see Figure 3-29).

Figure 3-29. *Customizing the text for inserting an optional section*

■Note The only way to programmatically insert or delete an optional or repeating section is with code. (This is covered in Chapter 9.)

If the section is not included by default, then you also have options to add rules to the section (most notably, if the section is not already present, to take effect if the user adds the section). You can also edit the default values of the section as it is added to the form (setting dates to today's date, setting totals based on calculations from the form, etc.).

You can also customize the commands you use to insert the optional section in the form. In this dialog, you can indicate which menus and toolbars will show the options for adding or removing the section. You can also customize the label shown to the user for each location you choose to show the command. (Note again that you may choose not to allow the user to insert or delete the section at all, instead opting to do so using program logic.)

The remainder of the settings in the dialog are similar to those already covered.

Repeating Section

The repeating section is similar to the optional section—adding or removing copies of the section also adds or removes groups of elements to or from the underlying XML. You can allow users to insert and delete sections, or not (and do so programmatically).

■Note Again, adding or removing sections automatically requires code.

■Note If you want to have a repeating section but don't want any instances inserted by default, go to Tools ➤ Default Values. This will open the Default Values dialog, where you can set the default values for any data-carrying element in your form. From here, find your repeating section—it will automatically be checked. If you uncheck the section, it will not be inserted by default.

Another interesting capability is that you can set up multiple types of repeating sections to be inserted. They must all have the same data construction (to match the underlying schema), but you can customize the default data of the section. So, for example, you can offer the user the option to insert a new widget section for various types of widgets. Using nested advanced controls, this can become a very powerful feature.

On the Display tab, you can indicate whether additional sections should be added vertically or horizontally.

The Filter Data button allows you to add a filter to the repeating section so that only sections with data matching the filter are displayed. You can map the filter to another control so that you can use a control to dynamically filter the displayed data. Or you can use a fixed filter for a particular view to provide a less cluttered display.

■**Caution** Filters such as these should not be considered a security feature. There is nothing stopping a user from simply saving the XML data and examining it with an XML editor. Context, data, and role-based filtering of data that is in the underlying data source are for UI design use only.

Repeating Table/Horizontal Repeating Table

The repeating tables are stylized repeating controls—they provide a tabular view of repeating section data. When you add a section to these tables, you will get additional rows or columns as appropriate.

The new options in the options dialog are dwindling. Now the only new options you have are the Show Header and Show Footer check boxes, which are fairly self-descriptive. Show Footer is unchecked by default, but adding it will give you a good section for total-style controls to summarize the table contents.

You also have the Master/Detail tab—see the accompanying sidebar for a discussion of master/detail controls in InfoPath 2007.

MASTER/DETAIL CONTROLS

InfoPath can easily link controls, allowing one control (the master) to filter the data in the other (the detail). A repeating table can be either a master or a detail control, while a repeating section can only be a detail control.

There is also a master/detail control that will insert a repeating table and repeating section already configured and linked together. The master control applies a filter to the detail section, effectively linking each row in the repeating table to a section of the repeating section.

The default behavior is to link the text boxes in the repeating table to the text boxes in the repeating section, but of course you can add additional controls and formatting to the repeating section—the sections will be displayed (with their unique data) as the corresponding row is selected in the master control.

Bulleted List/Numbered List/Plain List

The list controls are fairly straightforward—they are essentially repeating elements in a group. The types of list only affect the display in the form—they are each saved as similar XML (i.e., the numbered list does not encode the numbering in any way in the underlying XML).

Multi-Select List Box

The multi-select list box is new to InfoPath 2007. This provides a check box–tagged list similar to the other list boxes covered so far. The list can be populated manually, or it can pull data from elsewhere in the form or from a data source. In addition, a check box at the bottom of the Options dialog indicates whether the user will be able to add additional values to the list.

File Attachment

The file attachment control allows the user to attach a file to the form for submission. The attached file is encoded into the actual form data using base64 encoding, so it is transmitted with the form data without your having to worry about accessibility or relative links. (On the other hand, you *do* have to worry about excessive file sizes!)

Looking at the properties for the file attachment control shows some new options—whether to show the file placeholder (Figure 3-30) or insert a default file (perhaps a file related to the form that the user has to fill out/file/submit in association with the form).

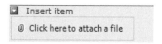

Figure 3-30. *The file attachment control*

There is an option for allowing the user to browse, delete, and replace files. You will most often use it when the attached file is a read-only instruction or information for the user filling out the form.

You also have an option for restricting which types of forms can be attached to the form (governed by file extension). Adding extensions here will put a filter on the file browser that the user uses to attach their file; it will also check when the file is attached (in case the user copies and pastes a file path directly into the file browser).

The Display and Advanced tabs are similar to others shown before. Nothing new here, so let's move on.

Picture

The picture control allows a user to either paste an image or load an image from a file into the control. One unique option you have with the picture control, presented when you add the control to a form template, is whether the picture will be saved inline (encoded into the XML as base64 text) or included as a link.

■**Note** The potential problem you face when you allow inserting pictures as links is that if the user browses to an image on their local hard drive, you will end up with a link to the image on their hard drive, which isn't accessible by anyone else.

Ink Picture

The ink picture control is similar to the picture control, except that it enables a tablet user to ink directly into a picture control, drawing an image that will be encoded with the form. The only unique property is that you can actually embed a background image. For example, if you were designing a hospital triage form, you could add an ink picture control and then embed a background image of a body where triage workers could mark injury locations (Figure 3-31).

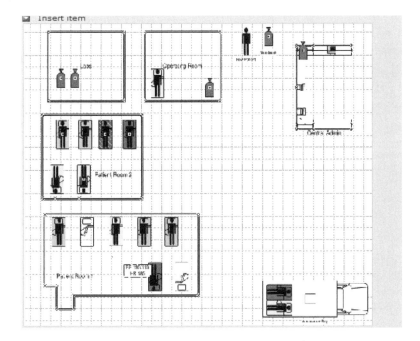

Figure 3-31. *An ink picture control with embedded background image*

Hyperlink

The hyperlink control does exactly as the name implies—it allows you to add a clickable hyperlink to a form. If you add a hyperlink control to a form, you'll be prompted for the text to display and the link address. By default, the form designer can enter any text they like—but both link and text can also be bound to fields in the data source.

■**Note** To "build" a hyperlink, you need to go into the properties for the element and set a default value concatenating the string for the hyperlink and the data value you want added.

Expression Box

The expression box is a control that doesn't bind to the data source. You can use this to display data or dynamic messages on the form without having the control bound to an underlying element. This is useful for displaying the results of operations on other controls or other data that is useful to the user, without saving the data to the XML data file.

Tip The expression box has one other interesting use—it's a great "xpath cheat sheet." When you're working in code in an InfoPath form, you often need to reference InfoPath data elements. Trying to sort out the references and namespaces can be tricky, so it's often easier to drag an expression box to the form and select the element you're trying to refer to. The expression box will then give you the full xpath to the element.

Custom Controls

InfoPath can also host custom controls, built in C++, C#, or VB.Net. Building custom controls won't be covered in this book, but to learn more about them, see the InfoPath team blog (http://blogs.msdn.com/infopath/) article in December 2006.

Template Parts

Template parts provide a way to reuse collections of controls you may find yourself using repeatedly. For example, an HR department may have a "Personnel Information" group of controls (including name, address, employee ID, etc.) that they use on almost all their forms (see Figure 3-32). They could create a control template for the controls and simply reuse that template in forms moving forward.

Figure 3-32. *An example of a template part in the toolbox*

Of course, one drawback is that the schema for the template isn't mappable—the section of schema representing the controls will always be the same. This pretty much limits their use to forms designed from scratch or possibly public schemas that have sub-schemas or defined complex groups.

Data Source

The Data Source task pane is the view into the underlying data structure of your form. I mentioned earlier that InfoPath forms are directly bound to the schema—this is where you can look at the schema itself. I cannot reiterate this often enough—in InfoPath, the form template *is the schema*. Realizing this will help you understand how controls should be laid out, what design decisions you should make, and why certain things may not work the way you expect (the most notable example being trying to place an element from a group outside the control governing that group—it won't go well).

At the top of the treeview displaying the data source, there is a drop-down list box that you can use to select from the various data connections in the form. If you only have the main data source (i.e., you haven't added any connections), then this will be disabled.

From the Data Source task pane, you can drag elements to the design surface to create controls. By default, InfoPath creates a label for the control when you drag it over. You can switch this behavior on or off by going to Tools ➤ Options, and then on the Design tab checking or unchecking "Create labels for controls automatically when adding from data source." (The subordinate option, "Convert field or group names into friendly names," when checked, will try to parse a label into intelligent words and capitalize appropriately.)

If you are designing the form against a schema, the schema in the Data Source pane will be read-only (you can still drag elements, groups, or whole chunks of the data source to the design surface to automatically create bound controls). On the other hand, if you are working on a new, blank form (and thus designing the schema as you go along), you can edit the schema in the Data Source pane.

Tip Keep an eye on your data source when you are working on a new, blank form. If you add a control, then the underlying data node is automatically created as well. However, if you then delete the control, the associated element is *not* deleted. If you add and delete a lot of sections and controls, you can find yourself with a data source that has a lot of leftover debris. You can right-click unwanted elements and groups to delete them in the Data Source pane.

Design Checker

The design checker is a new feature in InfoPath 2007. It is most helpful when designing (or converting) forms for browser-based use. The design checker will review the form design for the targeted platform and list errors and/or warnings regarding the form design.

You can also change the targeted platform for InfoPath forms here—click the "Change compatibility settings" link, and you will see the Form Options dialog opened to the Compatibility tab, where you can change the browser compatibility settings.

Publishing the Form Template

The final design task is publishing the form template. As this is a large subject in itself, it will be covered in more detail in Chapter 5.

Summary

This chapter has covered the technical details of who's who and what's where in the InfoPath form designer. However, even though we've put a name to every tool in the toolbox, we're still not quite ready to build a chair. In the next chapter, we'll cover views—essential tools for really powering up an e-form solution, since they provide a way of slicing and presenting data within the InfoPath client depending on user need, role, or form design.

CHAPTER 4

InfoPath Views

Remembering that InfoPath form data is all about the underlying XML, one has to ask the question, "If the form is just a view on the data, can I have different views?"

The answer is "Yes! How perceptive of you!"

InfoPath offers forms designers to build different views on the same data using the same easy designer covered in Chapter 3. You can use views to provide a number of features to your form:

- Various views on data for various purposes (e.g., a header view for one group and a detail view for another)

- Functionality for paging through longer forms

- Multipurpose forms with the same underlying schema

- The option of alternate functionality on a form (e.g., a search form)

- Views on forms by user role

- Print views for printing forms

This chapter will cover some scenarios in which you would use multiple views, how a user would experience the views, and how to design the various types of views.

InfoPath Views in Detail

InfoPath views are generally underappreciated. While many people understand their usefulness in paging or role-based views, they are often locked into the paper form–centric way of things. Instead, consider that an InfoPath form template can actually function as a small application, with search, summary, and detail views on the data. Each of these features can be embedded in a view of the form, and the user can dynamically move around to perform the functions.

InfoPath 2007 adds a few new twists. With browser-capable forms, you may want to have two views on the same schema—for example, a browser-based view for the users who will be filling out the form via the Web; and a richer, client-based view for the internal users who will be using InfoPath to edit the forms after submission.

Another aspect of multiple views is InfoPath's forms workflow. You will probably want to present a different view of the form depending on what stage of the workflow the form is at. For example, the form might start with the submitter, who may need to fill in a long page of detail before submitting. Once submitted, the form might go to an initial screener, who only needs to see a read-only view of some summary data, and perhaps edit a few fields or use forward/reject buttons. Then, the form might go to a final reviewer, who needs a read-only view of the full form in order to read the screener's comments and add his or her own.

Let's look at how a user may experience views.

Form Paging

As I mentioned, a common and obvious use of views is paging through longer and more complex forms. Figures 4-1, 4-2, and 4-3 show three pages of Microsoft's OMB Form 300 solution. This is an InfoPath version of a very long, complex government project submission form.

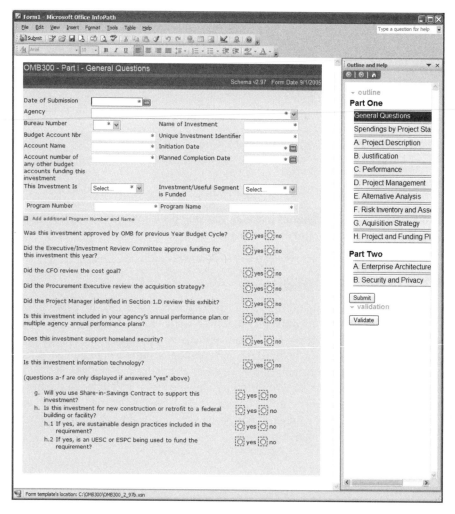

Figure 4-1. *The initial page of the OMB Form 300 solution*

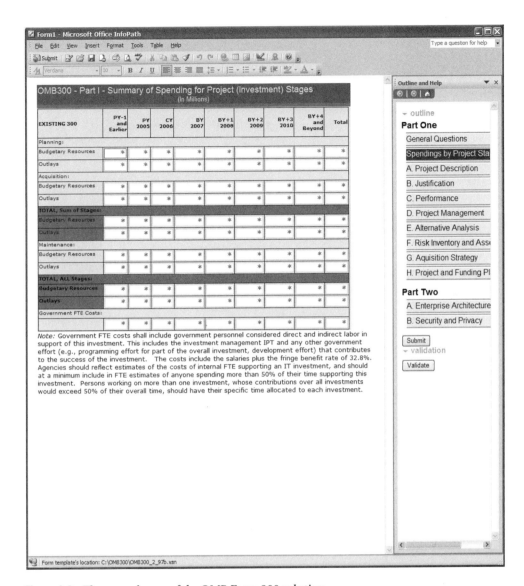

Figure 4-2. *The second page of the OMB Form 300 solution*

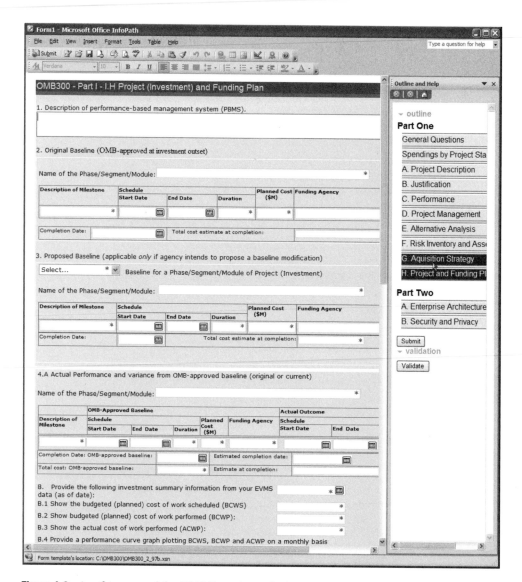

Figure 4-3. *Another page of the OMB Form 300 solution*

These are just 3 of 12 total pages in the InfoPath form (I said it was complex).

■Note Right now, I have to make a pitch for one of InfoPath's truly winning features—this form should help make it obvious why InfoPath is a very powerful offline tool. It's doubtful anyone would complete filling out a form this long in one workday. With InfoPath, users can save the XML data file to their local desktop and exit InfoPath (or take the file on their laptop to work on elsewhere). They only need to submit the form when they are completely finished with it. Storing and restoring user data in a web form is generally a complex development effort—InfoPath does it out of the box!

The user interface for changing pages in this case is the View menu (see Figure 4-4). By default, every view in a form is added to the View menu, so a user can get to the view by simply selecting View ➤ [view name]. You can, of course, configure a view so that it doesn't show up in the View menu, if you choose.

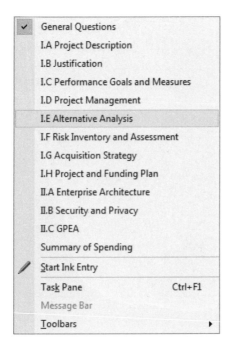

Figure 4-4. *The View menu*

Alternative Views

Another use for views is to show different perspectives on the same data. Let's consider a travel request form—the person initiating the request has to fill in a large number of fields to cover all their needs and desires for a particular trip. However, a lot of that information is of no interest to someone reviewing the request—they want to know "where and why?" So they may get a summary view that also pulls in amplifying information about past trips (see Figures 4-5 and 4-6).

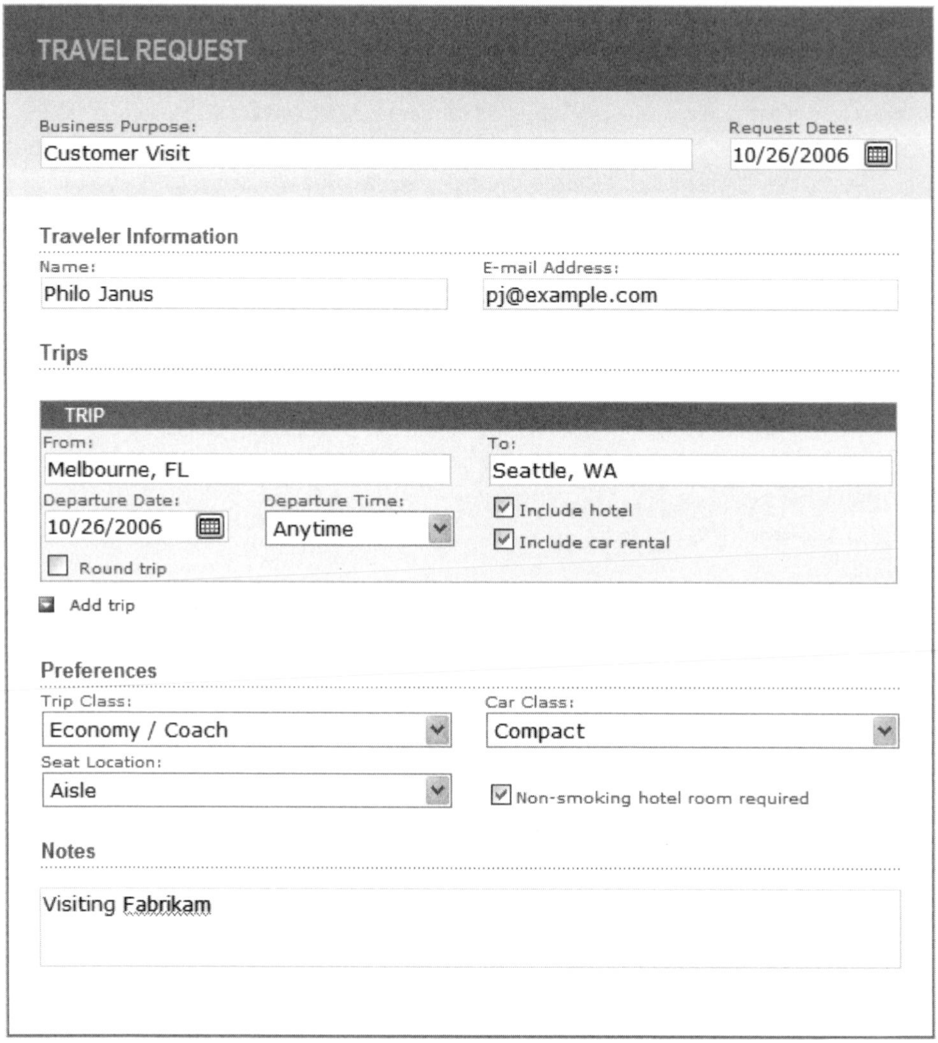

TRAVEL REQUEST

Business Purpose:

Customer Visit

Request Date:

10/26/2006 📅

Traveler Information

Name:

Philo Janus

E-mail Address:

pj@example.com

Trips

TRIP

From:

Melbourne, FL

To:

Seattle, WA

Departure Date:

10/26/2006 📅

Departure Time:

Anytime

☑ Include hotel
☑ Include car rental

☐ Round trip

📩 Add trip

Preferences

Trip Class:

Economy / Coach

Car Class:

Compact

Seat Location:

Aisle

☑ Non-smoking hotel room required

Notes

Visiting Fabrikam

Figure 4-5. *Submitter's view of a travel request form*

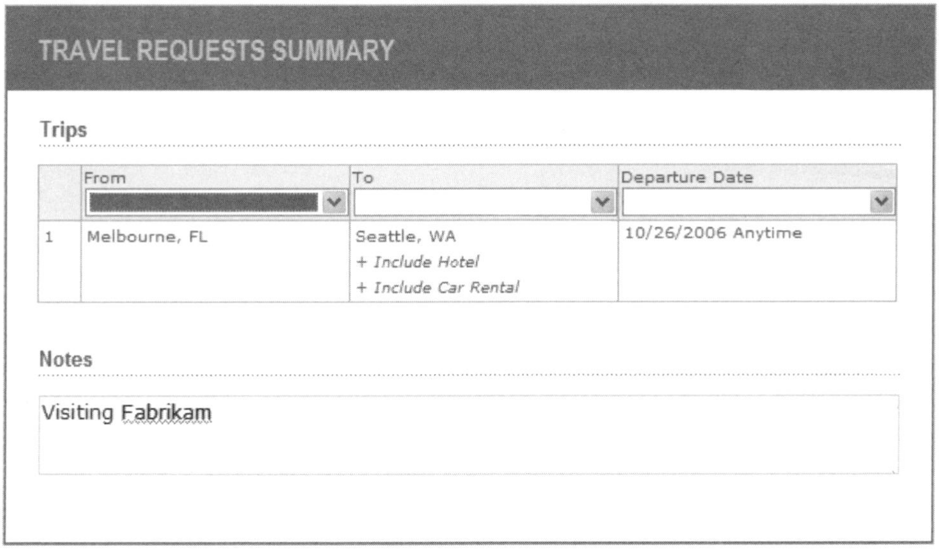

Figure 4-6. *Reviewer's view of the same travel request form*

Also note that in the submitter's view, all the fields in the form are editable, while in the reviewer's view, the submitted data is read-only; the reviewer can only type in a comments field and indicate whether the form should be approved or rejected.

Exercise 4-1. Creating Multiple Views for a Form

1. Open the Hello World form in design view.

2. Click the link for "Design tasks" in the task pane on the right. (If you don't see the task pane, press Ctrl+F1.)

3. Click the Views link.

4. In the View task pane, under "Select a view," you should see "View1 (default)" in the list.

5. First, you'll add a new view to present an alternate view of your form. Under Actions, click Add a New View.

6. Give the view a new name, and then click OK. You'll be presented with a blank canvas.

7. Click Design Tasks from the drop-down list, and then click Layout.

8. Click Table with Title in the task pane, and type **Hello World Summary** in the title area of the inserted table.

9. Select Design Tasks from the task pane header menu, and then click Data Source.

10. Click the folder icon labeled "Header" in the Data Source pane, and drag it to the data area of the layout table. When you stop dragging and let go, you will get a context menu offering format options. Select Controls in Layout Table (as shown in Figure 4-7).

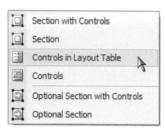

Figure 4-7. *Data node context menu*

You'll see that InfoPath has parsed the controls into a layout table and added labels based on the control names. (You can enable and disable auto-labels under Tools ➤ Options on the Design tab.)

11. Preview the form. Use the View menu to switch back and forth between views (see Figure 4-8). Enter some data and see how it's presented in the controls in each view. When you're finished, click the Close Preview button.

Figure 4-8. *The View menu*

■**Note** The Preview button has a drop-down menu, which is new in InfoPath 2007. You can click the button to preview the form or use the drop-down menu to access the Preview Settings dialog. In the Preview Settings dialog, you can select to preview the form as a specific user role, designate sample data for the form, and assign a domain for the form's security.

View Options

Let's look at the various options you have available to set up views in InfoPath.

If you click the View Properties button in the Views task pane, you are presented with the View Properties dialog (see Figure 4-9). Let's review some of the options presented in this dialog.

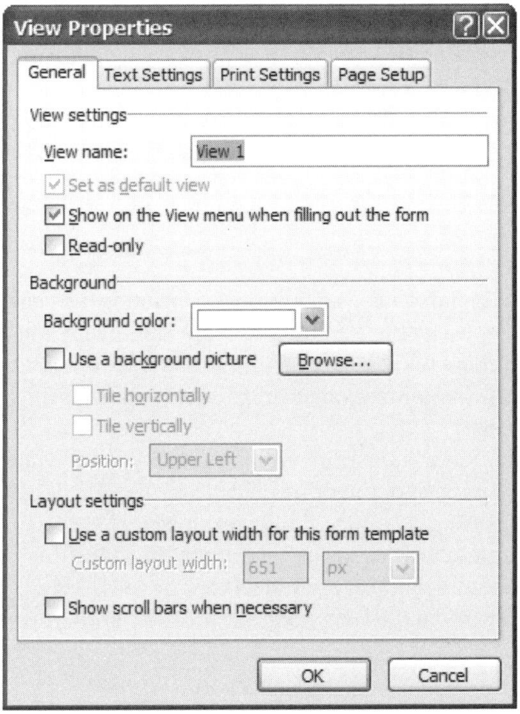

Figure 4-9. *The View Properties dialog*

View Settings (General Tab)

Here you can set the name of the view—an intuitive name to indicate to the form user what the view is used for. If you have multiple data entry views in the form, you can also select which one to use as the default view when the form is opened. You can also hide the view from the user filling in the form by unchecking "Show on the View menu when filling out the form." Finally, you have the option to make the view read-only by simply checking the Read-only check box.

If you are designing a browser-capable form, you'll have one additional option here: "Allow InfoPath-only features." This allows you to designate a view as rich client–only; it won't be available in browser-based forms. The benefit here is that you can have a "hybrid" form in one package: browser-based forms for use in web scenarios, and client-based (and more powerful) forms for users that have InfoPath installed.

Background (General Tab)

The background settings allow you to set the background for the view, behind any elements you put on the page. You have a color picker to set the background color and a browser to select a background image. If you choose a background image, you can tile it horizontally or vertically, and also set the position of the image.

Text Settings Tab

This tab allows you to effectively set a "style sheet" for the whole view at once. Using this, you can set the font for similar controls throughout the view with one setting. Select a control in the list, and then select a font, size, color, and style from the selectors on the right. This will apply that style to all the controls on the form. (You can still apply styles to individual controls if you choose.)

Print Settings Tab

The Print Settings tab offers a number of options related to—you guessed it—printing the view. This allows you to offer views as reports (each view can be formatted with specific layout and print options). For example, in addition to the views necessary for filling in and reviewing the form, you can offer a final approval view that shows summary data and is configured to print three copies.

The first option allows you to designate one view as the print view for another view. When this is set up, if the user chooses to print a particular view, the printout will look like the designated print view. (This gives the form designer the opportunity to hide text boxes, clean up layout, substitute text boxes for radio buttons, etc.). You will probably want to then hide the designated print view from the user to reduce confusion. You can hide a view by unchecking "Show on the View menu when filling out the form" on the General tab of the View Properties dialog.

■**Note** If you add a print view for Word (see Exercise 4-2), that view *will not show up in the Views task pane.* Imported print views for Word will only appear in the "Designate print view" drop-down list (in addition to the other views designed for the form).

The Orientation, Copies, and Print Range options set the default values for a print job (e.g., a given form can always be set to print in triplicate—this option allows setting the copies to "3" so that users don't have to do this every time they print the form).

■**Note** The print-specific settings are disabled for Word print views.

The Headers and Footers options allow you to designate dynamic content to be printed on every page of a form. Using autotext tokens (like &p for the current page number) gives you significant control over what's printed in the headers and footers.

InfoPath solves this problem by offering two types of print views: Print View and Print View for Word.

Creating a new view using Print View basically creates a new blank view, but sets it as the print view for the view you selected when you created it. You can then design the view to suit your dead tree needs.

Print View for Word is entirely different—this option allows you to designate an XSLT that will take the form data and apply the transform to render out WordProcessingML, which can be opened by Word 2003 and later. You can find guidance on creating this XSLT in the InfoPath SDK—but as an introduction, I'll walk you through the creation of a Word print view for your Hello World form.

Exercise 4-2. Creating a View Using Print View for Word

1. You'll need the form you designed in Exercise 4-1, but don't open it.

2. Install the InfoPath SDK (available online—search for "InfoPath SDK" on www.microsoft.com).

3. You should find the Word print wizard in %Program Files%\Microsoft Office 2003 Developer Resources\Microsoft Office InfoPath 2003 SDK\Tools\WordPrint—the file is wizard. hta (a single-file web page).

4. Run the Word print wizard by double-clicking wizard.hta. Figure 4-10 shows the wizard's welcome page.

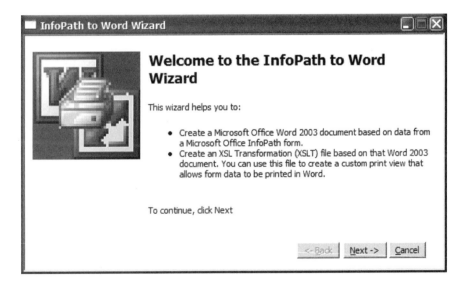

Figure 4-10. *The welcome dialog for the Word print wizard*

5. Click Next.

6. On the next screen, browse to your form and select it. Note that you could just use a schema, but the wizard provides some additional functionality if you point to the InfoPath form template (*.xsn).

7. Click Next.

8. The next screen offers the option of opening Word 2003 to edit your print view. What this does is create a blank Word document, with the schema from the InfoPath form attached, so that you can design the Word print view. Click the Open Word 2003 button to proceed.

■**Note** If you get an error regarding missing or unregistered DLL files, you must register the DLL files yourself (in particular, `wordprint.dll` and `imageDecode.dll` from the `Tools/WordPrint` folder, and `html2xhtml.dll` from the tools folder of the SDK). To do so, use `regsvr32` from the `Windows\System32` directory to register the DLLs. If you get a security warning about the action, accept the warning.

■**Note** For more information about XML documents in Microsoft Word, start at `http://msdn.microsoft.com/office`.

9. You'll be presented with a blank document in Word 2003, with the XML Structure pane open. The form's XML structure is already attached in the list at the bottom of the pane, as shown in Figure 4-11.

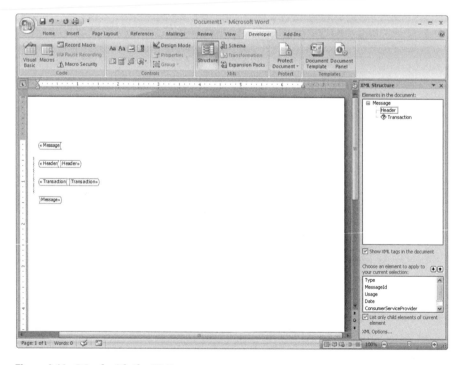

Figure 4-11. *Word with the XML pane open*

10. You must start with the myFields node, which is usually at the bottom of the list. Scroll down and click it—this will insert a myFields node in the document, filter the element list to just show the children of myFields, and show the document structure with the myFields node (see Figure 4-12).

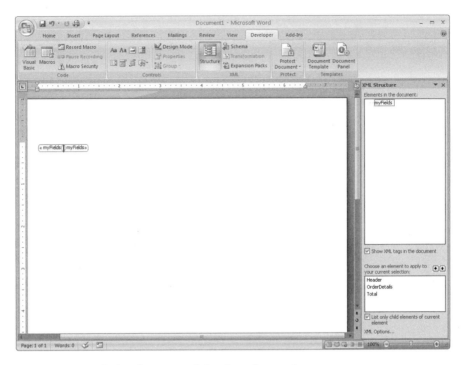

Figure 4-12. *Word after the root node has been inserted*

11. Click the Header node to insert it between the myFields nodes, and then insert a two-column-by-three-row table inside the Header nodes.

12. Add labels and each of the Name, Date, and Details nodes into the table, as shown in Figure 4-13.

Name:	«Name( )Name»
Date:	«Date( )Date»
Details:	«Details( )Details»

Figure 4-13. *The Word form after the table and Header nodes have been added*

13. Click after the closing Header node, and add the OrderDetails node. Then add the OrderItem node inside that.

14. Finally, insert a five-column table and place the child nodes of OrderItem (Description, ItemNbr, UnitCost, Qty, and Subtotal) in the columns. Your document should now look like Figure 4-14.

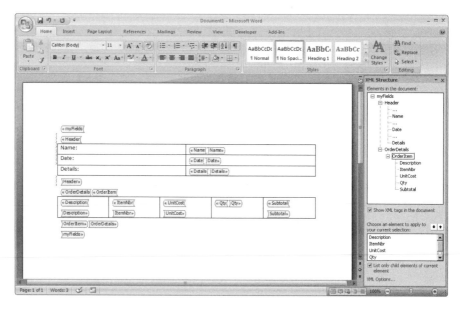

Figure 4-14. *The finished Word form*

Obviously, this is very simplistic, but you can see how you could leverage this with a complex schema to provide rich form formatting, including headers and footers, page numbering, watermarking, and so on.

15. Save the Word document in a convenient location and close Word.

16. Back in the wizard, click the Next button.

17. The page that displays will ask for the Word document you've just created. Browse to it and select it. Check the box to store a copy of the document inside the form (keeping everything in one package).

18. Click Next.

19. Click Finish. This will generate an XSLT file in the same location as the Word document. Click Congratulations on the final screen.

20. Now reopen your InfoPath form in InfoPath 2007 design mode.

21. In the task pane (press Ctrl+F1 if it isn't visible), click Views.

22. Select the link at the bottom of the Views task pane that reads "Add Print View for Word."

23. This wizard will install the XSL file into your InfoPath form template. Click the Next button on the first page.

24. On the next page, browse to the location where the Word print wizard stored your XSL file, and select it. Click Next.

25. Give your Word print view a memorable name.

26. Click Next, and then click Finish.

Note Your print view will not show up in the views listing; you will have to select it as a print view for an existing view, as shown in the following steps.

---

27. Select a view, and then click the View Properties button at the bottom of the task pane.

28. Select the Print Settings tab—you will want to select your print view from the drop-down list (see Figure 4-15).

Figure 4-15. *Selecting the print view for an existing view*

29. You're done—you can test it by previewing the form, filling in some data, and printing.

Exporting Views

Previously, InfoPath had the capability to export form data to either a single-page web view (MHT) or Excel. InfoPath 2007 adds the capability to export to Adobe PDF format or Microsoft's new XPS (XML-based full-fidelity print) format.

WHAT IS XPS?

In 2005, Microsoft announced the XML Paper Specification (XPS), an XML-based full-fidelity printing standard. A document represented in XPS format has a reliable, repeatable appearance. Microsoft refers to it as "electronic paper."

Why not use PDF? For one thing, the XPS specification is XML-based, so it's far easier to generate. XPS also provides authentication and digital rights management packaging, enabling users to secure documents from editing, viewing, and printing; and even to expire documents based on a calendar date.

XPS technologies will be native in both Windows Vista and the WinFX platform, which will enable developers to truly leverage trustworthy, fixed-format document packaging with just a few lines of code or built-in libraries.

A practical application of XPS will be described later in the book. For more information, go to www.microsoft.com/xps.

■Note You can enable or disable view exporting in the Open and Save section of the Form Options dialog.

Changing Views

I've gone over some of the basic methods for changing views, but to make sure you've learned them all, here's the list:

- The user can change views using the View menu. Views can also be hidden from the View menu or made read-only in the View Properties dialog.

- You can design the form template to select a view automatically based on user role.

- You can select which view to display when the form is opened (by going to Tools ➤ Form Options ➤ Open and Save ➤ Rules).

- You can program a button to display a specific view when the user clicks it.

- You can assign a specific view to use when printing a form.

Summary

I've reviewed the various aspects of views—how they can provide added richness for your forms as well as allow you to present information dynamically. In closing, I'd like to give you a strong reminder that views are not meant to be a security mechanism—the user can always open the underlying XML file and read any data contained therein! The only proper way to truly protect data from a user is to simply not provide it to their client in the first place.

CHAPTER 5

■ ■ ■

Publishing InfoPath Forms

Once you've designed a form template, what are you going to do with it? If you want other people to be able to fill it out, you need to publish it to an accessible location. With InfoPath, there are a number of ways to publish form templates—you can publish to a shared file location on a server, to a web server, or to a SharePoint form library. You can also "publish" by creating an installation package that you can send to users to install and fill out.

Publishing Overview

Form templates aren't much use sitting on the designer's desk—you have to get the template out to the people who are going to use it. InfoPath provides publishing capabilities built into the client, and makes getting your new form out to your users very easy. At the same time, InfoPath's publishing capabilities, especially in conjunction with Microsoft Office SharePoint Server, provide powerful enterprise-level management of forms templates.

InfoPath has a number of options to provide access to end users. The publishing wizard can publish the form template to SharePoint (2003 or 2007), via e-mail, to a network shared folder, or to an MSI file that can be distributed to end users to install.

Note InfoPath has a complex security and reference architecture between the client, form template, and form data. You generally cannot just take an XSN file (form template) and "hand it around" for people to fill out—it must be published to an authoritative location for the system to work properly. Trying to open an XSN file from any random location will likely give you an error like that in Figure 5-1.

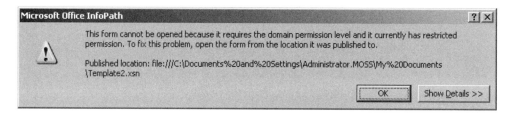

Figure 5-1. *InfoPath error due to opening from the wrong location*

When you publish an InfoPath form template to a specific location, the form template is encoded with that location. Form data (XML files) saved from that template are also stamped with the published location of the form template. This is so that when a user opens a data file, InfoPath understands where to find the form template to properly render the form.

Note Remember that in InfoPath (and indeed in most electronic form solutions), the form *template* and the form *data* are stored separately. In InfoPath, form data files (the XML files) have a processing instruction (also known as a PI) that (1) indicates that InfoPath is the application associated with this data, and (2) tells InfoPath where to find the form template associated with this form data.

Should you have a need to maintain true renderings of the form for archival purposes, InfoPath Forms Services (running on Microsoft Office SharePoint Server) has an API to render out a TIFF image of a form. The InfoPath client also has the capability to render a form in MHT format (a single-file web archive), Adobe PDF format, or Microsoft's new full-fidelity print format, XPS.

Form Security

What you can do with an InfoPath form depends on what you are doing inside the form. Forms that are only "dumb forms" (no program logic or data connections) can actually be deployed by simply e-mailing the XSN file—they will run in restricted mode and can be opened from anywhere. On the other end of the spectrum, a form that has managed code behind it or makes data connections across domains requires full trust and will have to be deployed by an administrator.

You set the security level for the form in the Form Options dialog (Figure 5-2). By default, the option for "Automatically determine security level" is selected. This option means that InfoPath will determine the required security level based on what features you are using in the form. Alternatively, you can uncheck that option and select the security level you desire for the form. You cannot select a security level lower than InfoPath would impose—this is only for selecting a *higher* security level.

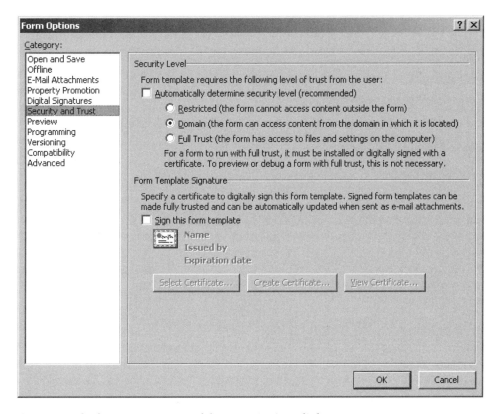

Figure 5-2. *The form security page of the Form Options dialog*

The security options allow you to choose between the following types:

- *Restricted*: Restricted forms are your basic "collect some information" type forms. They can be deployed via e-mail or by simply sharing the XSN file. Restricted forms cannot have any data connections or managed code. Restricted forms cannot be deployed as browser forms. Finally, since they are "divorced" from a server-based deployment point, there is no auto-update capability in restricted mode forms.

- *Domain*: Domain security forms are the middle ground between restricted forms and full trust forms. They must be deployed to a fixed location that is consistent to every user (e.g., a shared network drive or a web server). Your best option for deploying domain security forms is Windows SharePoint Services or Microsoft Office SharePoint Server. With domain security, a form can only connect to the server it's hosted on (unless it uses a trusted data connection library). Browser forms in this security mode cannot have any code.

- *Full trust*: Full trust forms are as the name implies—fully trusted. They can run any managed code, cross domain boundaries with data connections, and so on. However, since this is a significant security risk, fully trusted forms must either be digitally signed by the designer, installed with an MSI installer, or be part of the .NET code group indicating full trust on the assembly. Full trust forms published to a SharePoint location must be activated by an administrator at the local console before they can be used.

Xcopy Publishing

This is the simplest approach to publishing a form—simply copying it to a specific location or e-mailing the XSN file to an end user. However, it is also the most restrictive. To enable a form template to be used this way, its security must be set to Restricted (see the preceding section), meaning that it cannot contain any code or reference any data sources. In addition, since the form template is not published to a fixed location, this method doesn't provide any versioning capabilities.

Another more significant problem with this approach is the danger that the user will move, misplace, or delete the form template. I hate to sound like a broken record on this, but one more time: to render a form, you must have both the form *data* (XML file) and the form *template* (XSN file). If the user fills in a form template with InfoPath, saves their data as an XML file, and then later wants to view the form but has deleted the XSN file, they are out of luck (more likely you are out of luck, since you will have to answer the angry phone call . . .).

Network Location

You may ask, "If xcopy publishing is fraught with such danger, how do we get our form template to our end users?" (You may also ask, "Who uses the word 'fraught' these days?")

I'm glad you asked that question! A better way to provide access to a form template for your end users is to make it available from a network resource. The best alternative for publishing an InfoPath form template for internal consumption is actually to publish it to a SharePoint form library—I'll cover that in detail later in this chapter. However, if you don't have access to SharePoint, you can publish to a network file share or a web server. (These options are interesting in that, since they are solely acting as a file repository, they do not have to be Windows-based. The file server can be any Samba or WebDAV-style folder server; the web server need only be HTTP compliant).

Publishing to a file share is the most straightforward way to publish an InfoPath form—you are essentially copying the form template to a server-based location so that other users can access it. Note that this is essential for domain security form templates.

■**Caution** The trickiest part about publishing to a file share is the requirement that the path to the form template be the same for both the form designer and every form user. This may be especially problematic when considering development versus production domains—the mapped drives and locations may be completely different. Beware the situation in which the developer has a path mapped to the T drive but for the users it is mapped to the P drive—domain security forms published in this environment will fail when opened from the different drive letter. The InfoPath publishing wizard actually provides options for the location to have different paths for the administrator and the user, but it is still a critical issue to be aware of.

■**Note** To publish to a network file share, you will need full control permissions in the folder you will be publishing to. You need the ability to create a file when you first publish a form template, and then the ability to overwrite it when you update it.

Now let's take one of the sample form templates and publish it to a file share.

Exercise 5-1. Publishing to a Network File Share

1. For these exercises, you're going to use the Expense Report sample form. Open InfoPath, and select "Customize a sample" from the wizard. (If you already have InfoPath open, go to File ➤ Design a Form, and then select "Customize a sample.")

2. Double-click "Sample-Expense Report." You'll see the Expense Report sample InfoPath form open in design mode, with the familiar design tasks panel open to the right.

3. Click File ➤ Publish.

4. You'll be prompted to save the template—click OK.

5. Give the template a name, select a location to save it, and click Save.

6. On the first screen of the Publishing wizard, select "To a network location" (see Figure 5-3).

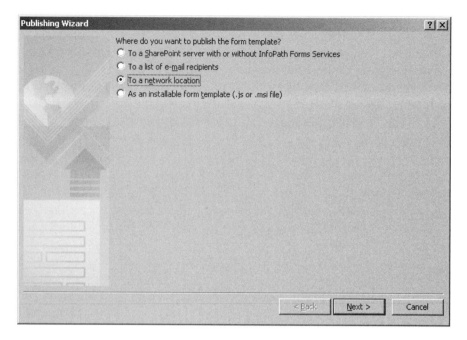

Figure 5-3. *The Publishing wizard*

7. Click Next.

8. On the next screen, you need to enter a network location and a name for the form template. For a network share, the format of the network location is of the style:

```
file://localhost/infopathforms/myform.xsn
```

9. Click Next.

10. The next screen gives you the opportunity to deal with the fact that the share the users see may not be the share you publish to. On this screen, you can enter the location the *users* will access the form from (see Figure 5-4).

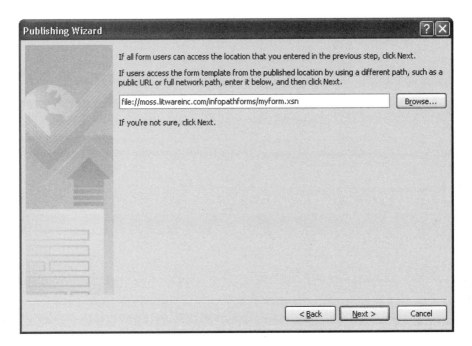

Figure 5-4. *Publishing wizard screen for user location*

11. Click Next.

12. The final screen verifies your publishing information. Click the Publish button.

13. Your form is now published and available from the URL you entered.

Via E-mail

InfoPath 2003 had the capability to enable submitting a form by automatically posting the form into Outlook for the user to send. However, this was accomplished by generating an e-mail with some preformatted text and attaching the XML file that comprised the form data. InfoPath 2007, combined with Outlook 2007, gives form designers the capability to embed a form inside the e-mail body dynamically, so the recipient can fill out the form without opening InfoPath. In this manner, a form may be published by e-mail out to the recipients; when the recipient gets the form, they can fill it in inside their e-mail client, as shown in Figure 5-5.

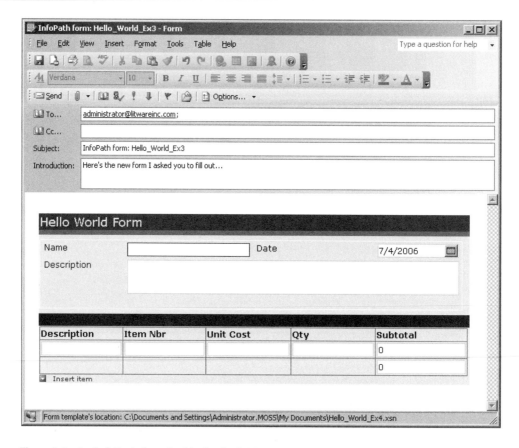

Figure 5-5. *An InfoPath form inside Outlook 2007*

■Note The embedded InfoPath forms capability only works when both the sender and recipient are using Outlook 2007. Users of other e-mail applications will receive the form template as an attached XSN file and send back the form data as an attached XML file.

Managing e-mailing of a form is handled through the publishing process. The person designing the form saves the template to a file folder and then chooses to publish the form to an e-mail recipient.

■Tip You can only publish self-contained forms to e-mail. Forms that reference external elements (such as Word print views, external schemas, or connections) will fail the InfoPath compatibility check.

Note You can't publish a form with Word print views to e-mail. To remove Word print views from an InfoPath form, go to View ➤ Word Print Views—this will give you the list of Word print views in the form template. You must remove all Word print views before publishing the form template via e-mail.

Exercise 5-2. E-mailing an InfoPath Form

1. In this exercise, you're going to take the Hello World form you built in Chapter 4 and e-mail it to an end user. Open the form in design mode.

2. Remove Word print views if necessary.

3. Select File ➤ Publish.

4. The wizard will prompt you to save the form—save the form in a convenient location.

5. From the location dialog (Figure 5-6), select "To a list of e-mail recipients," and then click Next.

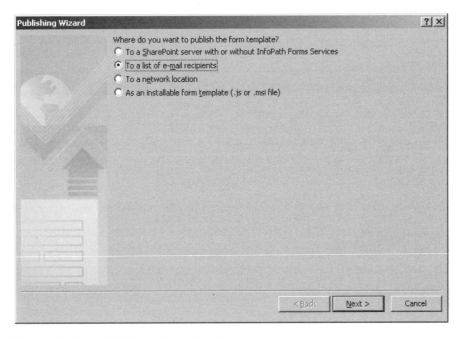

Figure 5-6. *The publish locations wizard*

6. Give the template a unique name, and then click Next.

7. The next screen allows you to select columns to be promoted to the container as metadata.

8. Click the Add button, and the field selector will open (see Figure 5-7).

Figure 5-7. *The Select a Field or Group dialog*

9. Open the Header group by clicking the + symbol next to it, and then select the Name node.

10. Click OK.

11. Add the Date and Total fields in the same way.

12. Click the Next button on the Publishing wizard.

13. You'll see a final screen. Click the Publish button. If you've done everything correctly, you'll be presented with an e-mail editor with the form embedded, as shown in Figure 5-8.

14. Address the e-mail to another Outlook 2007 user and send it.

15. Open Outlook 2007 on the recipient's computer. Note the new e-mail in their inbox.

16. Although the form is rendered in the preview pane, you must actually open the e-mail item to fill in the form (see Figure 5-8).

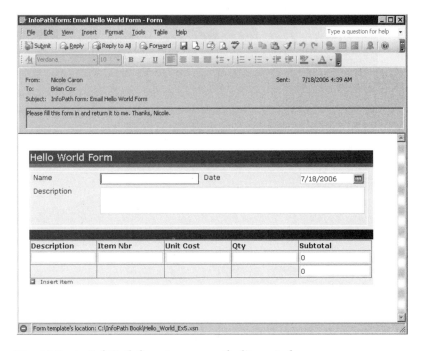

Figure 5-8. *An InfoPath form in an e-mail editor window*

17. Fill in the form and click the Submit button on the toolbar. Clicking the Submit button will open an e-mail header editing dialog to allow the submitter to fine-tune the e-mail headers (see Figure 5-9).

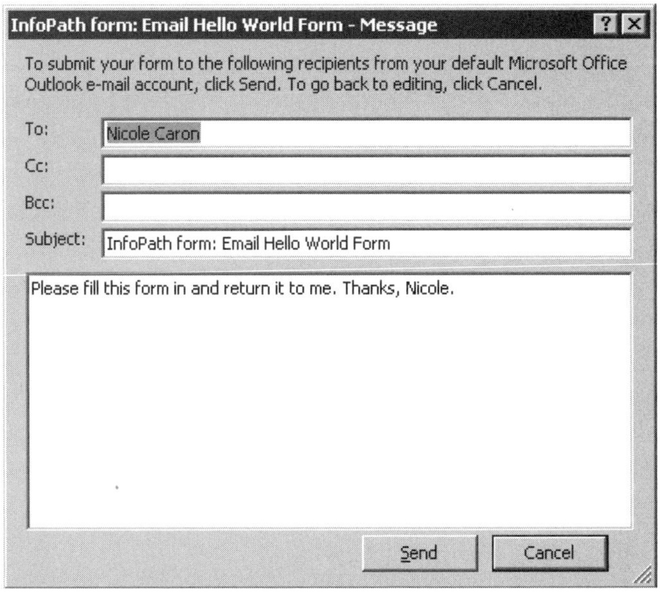

Figure 5-9. *InfoPath e-mail submission dialog*

You should get a dialog indicating the form was submitted successfully.

18. Note that the form header now has a line indicating when the form was submitted.

19. Close the form. Note that when you do, InfoPath asks if you want to create a form folder for the current form (see Figure 5-10). Click the Create Form Folder button.

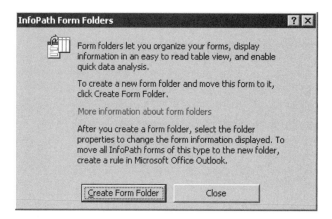

Figure 5-10. *The Form Folders dialog running InfoPath in an Outlook form*

This will create a form folder in Outlook (see Figure 5-11)—a new feature that provides a way of keeping and organizing InfoPath forms in Outlook. Since the folder syncs with Exchange, the user has the full features of Exchange available—offline caching, online storage, web-based access, and so on.

Looking at the list area for the folder, you should also note that the data fields you promoted in step 8 are viewable. This gives you an easy way to maintain your forms without having to open every one to determine the contents.

20. Also note that you have other Outlook and InfoPath functions available—tagging the form for follow-up, exporting or merging forms, indexing and searching, and so on.

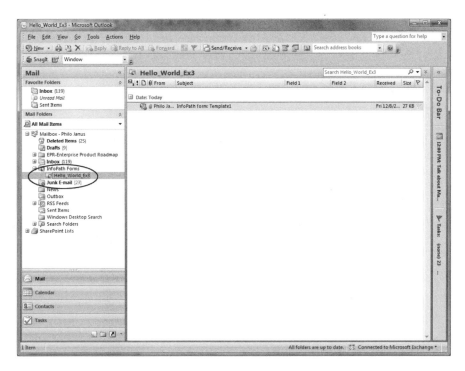

Figure 5-11. *An InfoPath form folder in Outlook 2007*

SharePoint

In the interest of completeness, I'm presenting this topic here, even though SharePoint itself is covered more fully in the next chapter.

SharePoint is a very natural complement to InfoPath. SharePoint form libraries offer a web-based repository for InfoPath form templates and data. In addition, through property promotion, key fields from an InfoPath form can be displayed in the form library interface, making it easier to find specific forms.

Don't worry too much about what SharePoint is or does—think of it first as a simple repository for InfoPath form data files with their associated template file. Publishing an InfoPath form template to a SharePoint site creates a form library (see Figure 5-12) and loads the form template as the default form for that library. SharePoint then provides an easy web-based way for users to fill out forms, store them, and edit them. (Microsoft Office SharePoint Server 2007 adds the capability to fill out forms through a browser interface.)

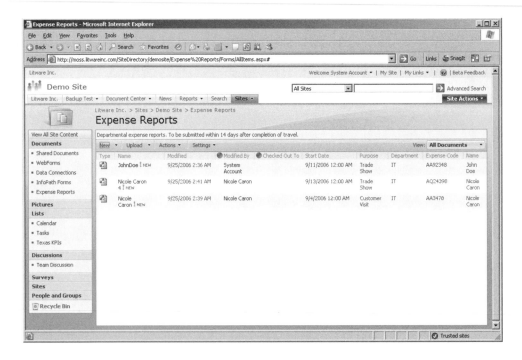

Figure 5-12. *A SharePoint form library*

With SharePoint 2007, there are two ways to publish an InfoPath form template to SharePoint—you can either publish to a form library or as a content type. Content types are new in SharePoint 2007—by publishing a form library to SharePoint as a content type, you make that form template available to SharePoint users to create new form libraries based on that form template.

Let's take a look at the two methods.

Publishing to a SharePoint Form Library

This publishes your form template (XSN file) to SharePoint and creates a form library within a SharePoint site to act as the main location for users to store InfoPath form data when they've filled out the form. You can also promote columns of data so that they are displayed in the form library web interface (see Figure 5-12). I will cover property promotion more fully in Chapter 6.

Publishing to a SharePoint form library also gives your form template a central network location to manage version control for the form template. (Form libraries also provide a native version control capability for the form data within the library.) The one main drawback of a form library is that it's "single-use"—when you create a form library, it only exists for that single form template and library of form data. If you want a reusable library, you'll want to publish the form template as a content type. (See the following section, "Publishing to a SharePoint Site As a Content Type," for more info.)

Exercise 5-3. Publishing to a SharePoint Form Library

1. You're going to use the Expense Report sample again. If you don't have it running, open InfoPath.

2. Select Customize a Sample, and then double-click Sample – Expense Report.

3. Select File ➤ Publish to open the Publishing wizard. Save the template if you are asked to.

4. Select "To a SharePoint server with or without InfoPath Forms Services" (see Figure 5-13).

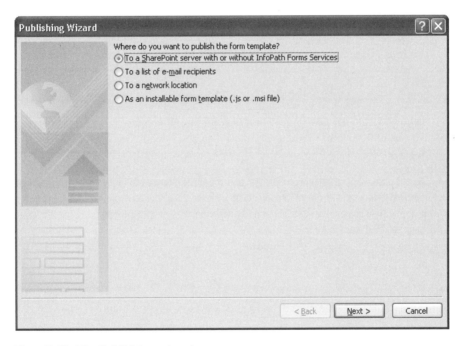

Figure 5-13. *The Publishing wizard*

5. On the next page, enter the URL for the SharePoint site you want to publish your form template to. The easiest way to do this is to open a browser to the site home page and copy the URL out of the address bar (see Figure 5-14).

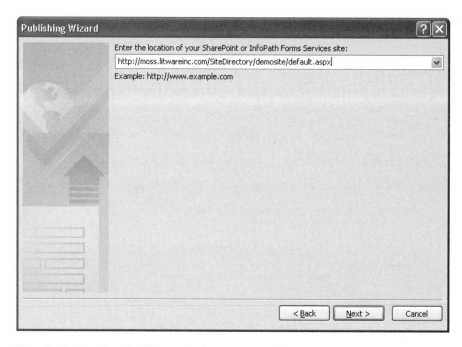

Figure 5-14. *Entering the SharePoint location to publish to*

6. Click Next.

7. The next page offers you the option to publish as a document library, a site content type, or an administrator-approved form template. Select Document Library. Note the check box option for "Enable this form to be filled out by using a browser." I'll cover browser-compatible forms in the next chapter; leave this option selected (see Figure 5-15).

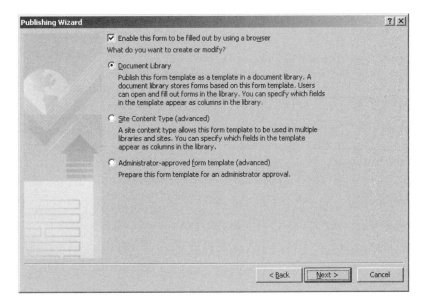

Figure 5-15. *Selecting how to publish to SharePoint*

8. Click Next.

9. The next page shows you the existing libraries in the current SharePoint site and offers you the option to create a new library or overwrite an existing library. Leave "Create a new document library" selected, and click Next (see Figure 5-16).

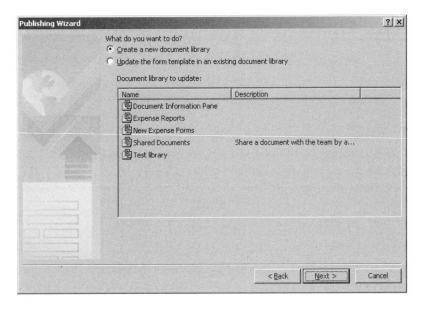

Figure 5-16. *Selecting whether to create a new library or replace an existing one*

10. On the next page, you simply need to give your new form library a title and description. Name it "Expense Reports" (how original!) and type a brief description of the form library. Click Next.

11. The next page is very important—this is the heart of how InfoPath and SharePoint interact. This page allows you to indicate which elements of data from the InfoPath form data will be promoted to SharePoint to be displayed in the form library. Click Add and add a few fields from the element list. Don't worry too much about the Site Column Group or other options in the dialog—I'll cover those in Chapter 6. Once you've selected a few elements, click Next (see Figure 5-17).

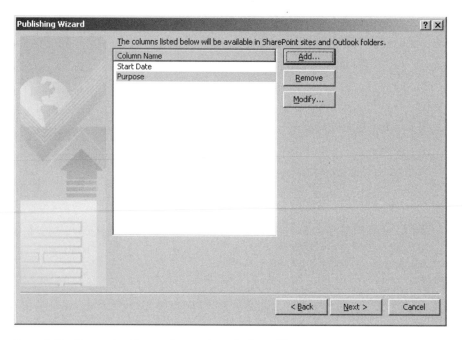

Figure 5-17. *Promoting form columns into the form library*

12. The next page simply summarizes the actions for the Publishing wizard. Click the Publish button at the bottom.

13. The final page offers you the option to e-mail the form template to e-mail recipients, or to open the form library. Selecting "Send the form to e-mail recipients" opens the form template in an e-mail, similar to publishing via e-mail, covered earlier. Click Done and you're finished.

Publishing to a SharePoint Site As a Content Type

As I mentioned in the previous section, the drawback to publishing a form template as a form library is that you can only use that template in that particular library—there's no reusability unless you open the XSN file and publish it again to a new form library. This is somewhat troublesome, as it requires the form developer to "be on call" to publish the template any time the form needs to be reused. As an example, consider the expense report template—if you have a large organization, it's likely that there will be a need for multiple libraries of the same expense report template (at the very least, a library per department).

Requiring the form author or a SharePoint administrator to dust off the XSN file and publish the template to a new form library every time a new one is required was a significant drawback in the 2003 product suite.

The content type allows an administrator to create a "blueprint" for a form (not just InfoPath forms—also documents). This way a library can be configured with specific information columns, lookup data, workflow settings, and so on. Then any user with the appropriate permissions can add a form of that type by simply choosing to create new content—the content type will be listed as an option.

Publishing a form template as a site content type is very similar to publishing a form template—the major difference is the requirement to store the form template (XSN file) in a document library in the site somewhere. (I recommend creating a Templates document library and using that.)

Installable Form Template

The installable form template allows you to share a form that requires full trust with users that may be outside the firewall, or won't otherwise have access to a common network location. With this option, you can create a JS or MSI installer file for your form template. The JS file is a JavaScript file that you can ship with your XSN file for the user to register their form—running the JS file will register the form template in the proper location on the end user's computer. (Remember that the XSN file needs to be registered with its location so that the XML files that users create with it are properly registered with the right template location.)

The MSI file creates a full installer package—a single MSI file that an end user can run to install the XSN file on their client system. The wizard options are very straightforward—simply indicate the company name for the MSI file, the language in which the file should be built, and the location InfoPath should place it in.

■**Note** You must have Visual Studio 2005 installed to select the MSI file publishing option.

Summary

You should now understand the basics of designing a form template, and know how to get the template to your users. The next chapter will look into expanding the capabilities of InfoPath with SharePoint and the Microsoft Office SharePoint Server system.

■ ■ ■

CHAPTER 6

SharePoint Integration

InfoPath 2007 and SharePoint are designed to work well together. SharePoint has built-in form libraries and content types, and the newest version has Forms Services to present forms in a browser for users who don't have InfoPath installed. In turn, InfoPath has a built-in capability to publish form templates to SharePoint, creating a form library in the process. It can also pull data from SharePoint lists for lookup lists, and leverage SharePoint workflow.

Finally, InfoPath has a unique niche in SharePoint—InfoPath forms can be embedded in Office 2007 documents to provide a rich user interface for managing SharePoint-based document metadata. We'll cover each of these aspects of SharePoint integration in this chapter.

WHAT IS SHAREPOINT?

Microsoft Office SharePoint Server 2007 is the third version of SharePoint. SharePoint 2001 was an Exchange-based application that offered the basic team services capability and a more advanced portal capability.

SharePoint 2003 consisted of two different server applications: One was Windows SharePoint Services 2.0 (commonly referred to as WSS), a collaborative web-based framework based on ASP.NET 1.1—the data repository of which became SQL Server. The other, SharePoint 2003 Portal Server, was for enterprise portals, and added personalization, enterprise search, single sign-on, and other features.

The 2007 version of SharePoint is truly a revolutionary upgrade. Windows SharePoint Services 3.0 is based on the ASP.NET 2.0 Web Parts framework, and has Windows Workflow Foundation (WF) built into its underpinnings. Microsoft Office SharePoint Server 2007, in addition to personalization and a hugely upgraded enterprise search capability, offers content management capabilities such as workflow and publishing approval templates, metadata management and enforcement, records expiration, and document policy management; InfoPath Forms Services; Excel Services; a business data catalog; and far more.

Obviously, SharePoint 2007 is too vast to be covered as a subsection of this book—it deserves a book of its own. Luckily there is one! For more information about SharePoint 2007, read Scot Hillier's *Microsoft SharePoint: Building Office 2007 Solutions in C# 2005*.

SharePoint Form Libraries

InfoPath integrates into SharePoint most notably through SharePoint's form libraries. These are web-based structures that host a form template and act as a repository for form data. Form libraries offer a powerful hybrid between a simple file share and a full e-forms application.

A SharePoint form library appears similar to a basic network file share viewed through a browser (Figure 6-1). However, there are a number of features that SharePoint adds that you would only get through an actual electronic forms application. The first, most obvious feature is the promotion of form metadata into the library, which makes it easier to identify the forms you may be looking for.

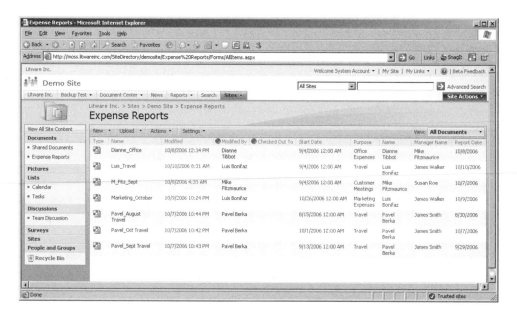

Figure 6-1. *A SharePoint form library*

This metadata is published to the form library when the form template is published. In SharePoint 2003, the metadata was one-way—it would be promoted from the form, but if edited in a form library view, the changes would not be reflected in the form data. In SharePoint/InfoPath 2007, any changes made to the metadata in the form library will be reflected in the form data itself.

Another feature of the SharePoint form library is the ability to have multiple views of the library, with sorting, grouping, and filtering capabilities (see Figure 6-2). These library views can be filtered on specific values, and SharePoint offers a number of variable values, such as the current user's login name and today's date.

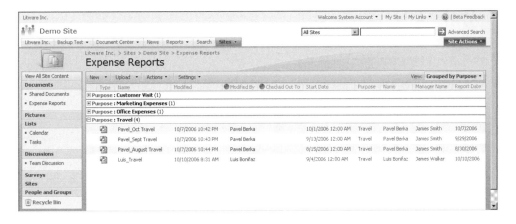

Figure 6-2. *A form library grouped by the Purpose field*

The ease of publishing InfoPath form templates to SharePoint form libraries makes InfoPath coupled with SharePoint a compelling replacement for the myriad other workgroup-level solutions that have exploded over the years to collect and store data (Excel spreadsheets, Access databases, homegrown scripted applications, etc.).

SharePoint form libraries offer a number of other features as well, including check-in and check-out, item-level security, e-mailing form data, versioning, and alerts.

Check-In/Check-Out

SharePoint form libraries provide a check-in/check-out function to streamline collaboration on documents stored in SharePoint. Checking out a form is as simple as selecting the option from the context menu (Figure 6-3). Note that check-in/check-out is not a security mechanism—it's simply a way of "enforcing politeness," or tagging documents that you may be working on. Anyone who has rights to edit the file can cancel the check-in and take the file to edit it. (This possibility is more palatable than needing an administrator to recover a document when the person editing it is on vacation, out sick, or otherwise unavailable.)

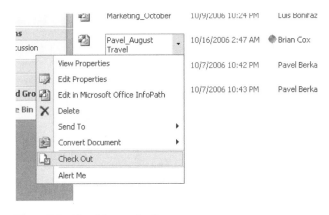

Figure 6-3. *Checking out a form*

When you check a form back in, you will be prompted for an optional comment that's saved to the comments field.

Item-Level Security

Users that have administrative permission over the form library have the ability to edit the permissions of individual items in the form library (this is new to SharePoint 2007). To edit item-level permissions, select Manage Permissions from the item's context menu. This will take you to a permissions page for the item.

By default, items inherit from the form library (which inherits from the site), so you will see a read-only list of the inherited permissions. From the Actions menu, you can then select to copy the parent permissions to the item. Once copied, you then have the ability to edit the permissions for that specific item (see Figure 6-4).

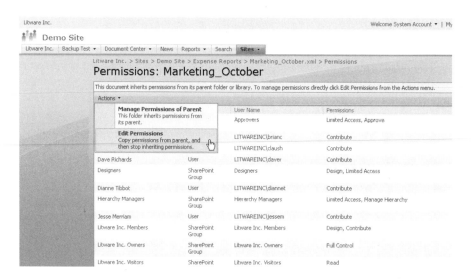

Figure 6-4. *Item-level permissions in SharePoint*

Once you've set item-level permissions, you can always revert to inheriting permissions from the parent—the item menu will have an Actions item, which has an option for "Inherit permissions"—of course, you will lose any custom permissions you have assigned.

■**Note** SharePoint was designed for collaboration—for people to work together. Excessive reliance on item-level or even folder-level permissions defeats the purpose (and can become a maintenance nightmare). For any given scenario, you should try to set permissions at the site level if at all possible.

Versioning

SharePoint also offers built-in versioning for form data files. To enable form versions, click the Versioning Settings link in the form library settings. In the versioning settings, you can set content approval, version history, and some security settings. The following list describes the settings and their details:

- *Content Approval*: "Content approval" refers to keeping submitted items in a draft state until someone with the appropriate permissions approves them. This, in conjunction with the Draft Item Security setting (described following), will hide draft items from other users until they are approved.

- *Document Version History*: This indicates whether a copy of the form data is retained every time a user edits the form. With this set to "No versioning," only the current copy is kept. "Create major versions" will give a major version number (1, 2, 3, etc.) to each version as it's saved. "Create minor versions" will assign major versions for approved edits and minor versions (2.1, 2.2, 2.3, etc.) to edits of drafts. You also have options to limit the number of versions retained.

- *Draft Item Security*: When Content Approval is enabled, this indicates who can see draft versions of submitted forms.

- *Require Check Out*: This option requires users to check out a document before editing it. Otherwise, checked-in documents can be edited freely.

When versioning is enabled, an option to view the version history of a form will show up on the form's context menu. The Version History page lists all saved versions (subject to the restrictions set for the library), as well as who modified it, the date of the change, and the comments when it was checked in. From the context menu, versions can be viewed, deleted, or restored to the library. Restoring a version replaces the current version in the form library.

Alerts

SharePoint has an alerting capability so that you can receive an alert by e-mail when a form is changed. On the context menu, you'll see an option called "Alert Me"—selecting this will open the New Alert page. From this page, you can view the alerts you have on the site (via a link near the top of the page). You can select when to send an alert (when anything in the form data changes, when it's changed by someone else, or when changes are made to a form created or last modified by you).

You can also set an option to receive an alert when a form that only appears in a specific view is changed. For example, if you have a view that only shows forms submitted in the last two weeks, you can set an alert on that view so that you only receive a notification when recent forms are edited.

Finally, you can indicate whether to receive an alert immediately, or as part of a daily or weekly summary.

Form Property Promotion/Demotion

As I pointed out in the previous chapter, when you publish an InfoPath form to a SharePoint form library, you can select data elements to be published up, or *promoted*, to the library. These data elements can be used in views on the library for sorting, filtering, and grouping. They can also be leveraged by workflows—a workflow can change a field value based on the status of the workflow (e.g., changing a status field on the form).

In SharePoint 2003, form property promotion was a one-way street. Once a value was promoted to the library, there was no way to post it back into the form (or *demote* the value). In SharePoint 2007, form library properties are bidirectional—if a field value is changed in the library, that change is reflected in the form data, provided that type of editing is allowed when the form is published (see Figure 6-5).

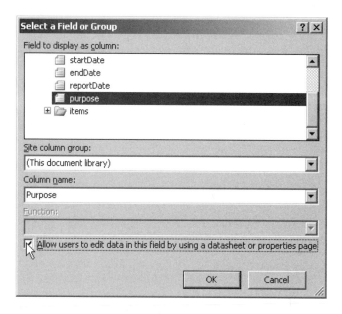

Figure 6-5. *Enabling property editing when selecting fields to promote*

If this setting is enabled for a promoted property, then a user who has the permissions to do so can edit the form value by simply editing the property of the file in the SharePoint form library.

InfoPath Browser-Capable Forms

The major limitation in InfoPath 2003 was that to fill in an InfoPath form, the user had to have the InfoPath client installed on their desktop.

InfoPath 2007, in combination with Microsoft Office SharePoint Server 2007, introduces the ability to build InfoPath forms that will run in a browser. While the set of functionality in the browser-based form is a subset of the rich client–based forms, browser-capable forms are still a very rich, powerful platform.

■**Note** Browser forms are compatible with IE 6.0+, Firefox, Mozilla, Safari, and Netscape.

The great power of InfoPath in this scenario is that you only need to design a form once. The same form can be published as a rich InfoPath client and also consumed by a browser from Microsoft Office SharePoint Server. The end-user experience is absolutely similar with minimal effort on the part of the developer. You can also have a single form that has a rich form-only view, and then a browser view that has a subset of the form data (see Figure 6-6).

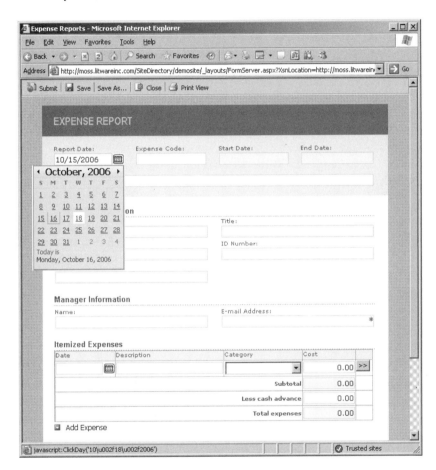

Figure 6-6. *An InfoPath form in a browser*

Browser-capable forms have a limited subset of functionality. If you design a browser-capable form, you'll note that you have a small selection of controls (see Figure 6-7).

Figure 6-7. *The restricted control options in a browser-capable form*

Other restrictions on browser-capable forms include the following:

- Any embedded code must be managed code.

- The form cannot submit directly to database connections.

- The form cannot submit form data using custom code.

- Digital signatures can only be applied to a section, not the entire form.

- The form cannot have custom task panes.

- You cannot merge forms using custom code.

Browser-capable forms are best used to extend the reach of richer forms used internally. As an example, consider a job application or a customer feedback form. The public-facing form would be a relatively simple web-based form. Then once the form is filled out and submitted, the organization could use a more complex, rich client form to route it internally.

Creating a Browser-Capable Form

It's pretty straightforward to create a browser-capable form. When you select options in the Design a Form dialog, there is a check box at the bottom labeled "Enable browser-compatible features only" (see Figure 6-8).

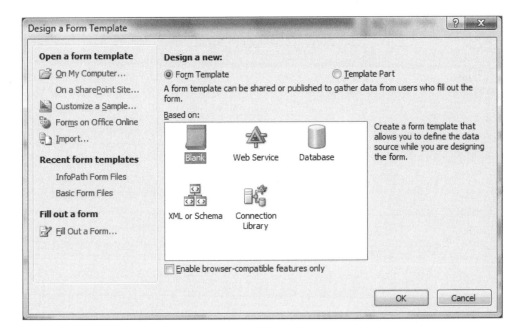

Figure 6-8. *Enabling browser-capable forms*

If you have an existing form you want to enable for browser forms, open the task pane by selecting Tools ➤ Design Checker. On the Design Checker task pane, click the Change Compatibility Settings link. This will open the Form Options dialog to the Compatibility tab. On this tab, simply checking the box for "Design a form template that can be opened in a browser or InfoPath" will enable browser compatibility for the form.

Once the form is enabled for InfoPath Forms Services, the design checker will also list features in the current form that are not compatible with a browser-capable form (unsupported controls, database connections, script, etc.). This will also enable the Browser tab in the Form Options dialog (Figure 6-9).

Figure 6-9. *The Browser page in the Form Options dialog*

Views

Browser-capable forms can also have multiple views. Any view you add to the form will be available in the browser (see Figure 6-10), with the exception of views you mark for InfoPath only. To mark a view as rich client only, select the view in the Views task pane and click the View Properties button. In the View Properties dialog, check the box labeled "Allow InfoPath-only features." In this view, you will now have full capabilities of the rich client, and the view will not be listed in the browser form.

■Tip Remember that views in an InfoPath form template are truly just "views" onto the underlying form data. Don't let the availability of multiple views confuse you into thinking there are multiple copies of form data underneath.

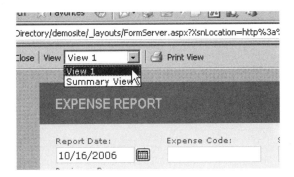

Figure 6-10. *Selecting views in a browser-capable form*

Forcing Forms to Open in a Browser

When a user opens an InfoPath form from a SharePoint form library (either by selecting New or clicking on an existing form), the form opens in InfoPath if it's installed; otherwise it will open in a browser. So, under the default behavior, if you have InfoPath installed, you can't open a form in a browser.

You can override this behavior, though. To do so, select the Settings menu in the form library, and then select Form Library Settings. You'll see the form library settings page (Figure 6-11).

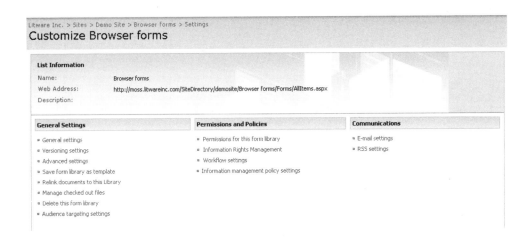

Figure 6-11. *Form library settings page*

Select "Advanced settings." The third option specifies how a browser-capable form should be opened if the InfoPath client is installed. Select "Display as web page" to force opening a browser-capable form in the browser. Scroll to the bottom of the page and click OK, and then use the breadcrumbs to return to the form library.

Browser-Specific Options

When you make a form browser-capable, the formatting options change for the controls on the form. There are two aspects to the changes: Some options are simply disabled, such as paragraph breaks and text wrapping in the text box control (Figure 6-12). Other options may be available, but not enabled in the browser form (but still operate in the InfoPath client). Examples of these include the placeholder text and the spelling checker.

Tip There is a browser plug-in, IESpell, that uses the Office dictionaries to run spell checking on the fields inside the browser. (Go to www.ieaddons.com and search for "spell" to find IESpell.) This can bridge the gap between the browser form and the dictionary.

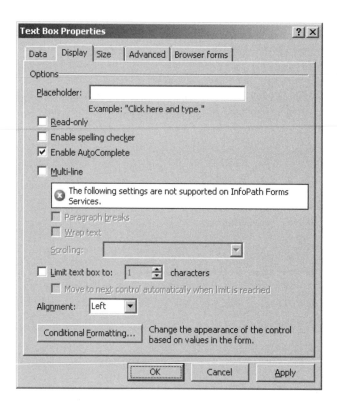

Figure 6-12. *Browser-capable forms have some options disabled*

Two other major control limitations are the repeating table (which cannot be used in a master/detail relationship in a browser form) and the rich text box (which doesn't allow paragraph breaks, has limited formatting options, and allows only embedded images). However, browser forms *do* offer rich text (see Figure 6-13)—albeit a limited version, compared to the InfoPath client.

Figure 6-13. *Rich text control on an InfoPath browser form*

The final change in the control options is a specific addition for browser-capable forms. In the properties for the control, you'll find a new tab titled "Browser forms." This tab has the option to control postback on the form when the user changes data. InfoPath Forms Services renders forms maximizing use of JavaScript to minimize round trips to the server. However, there are times when it may be necessary to contact the server for some type of update (e.g., adding a row to a repeating table). With this option, you have absolute control over whether or not the form is refreshed when data in the control changes.

You can set the control to never post back—perhaps a particular control is pretty busy and you don't want the form refreshing every time the user exits it. Alternatively, you can set the form to always post back. The most notable reason to do this would be if you have code in the form (which runs on the server) that you wish to run whenever a form value is changed.

Your final option is "Only when necessary for correct rendering of the form." Basically, this lets InfoPath Forms Services determine whether a control should post back when it's changed. As noted in the name of the option, this generally only happens when changing a value will change the appearance of the form.

Saving and Submitting

"Saving" a form from a browser provides the user with a browser dialog that allows the user to save to the current site, name the file, and indicate whether to overwrite the file if a file with the same name exists (see Figure 6-14). There is no way to save the XML file locally, which makes sense—the default option is that the form will only open in a browser if the user doesn't have InfoPath installed. If they don't have InfoPath installed, then the XML file isn't a lot of use to them.

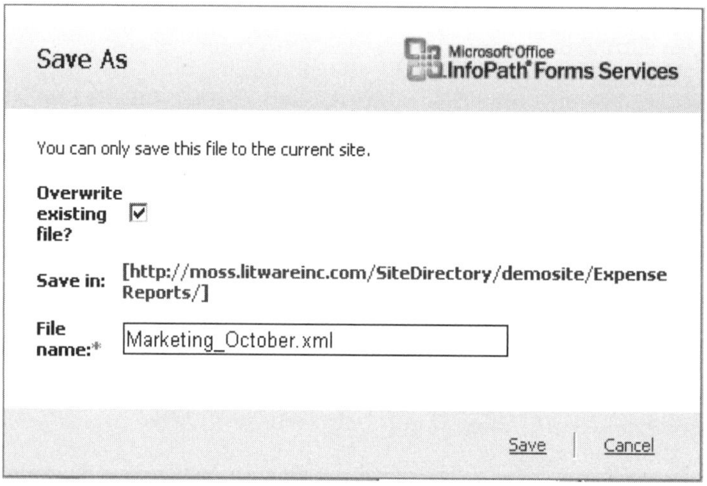

Save As   Microsoft Office
                                                         InfoPath Forms Services

You can only save this file to the current site.

Overwrite
existing   ☑
file?

Save in: [http://moss.litwareinc.com/SiteDirectory/demosite/Expense
            Reports/]

File
name:*   Marketing_October.xml

                                                    Save | Cancel

Figure 6-14. *The Save As dialog in a browser-capable form*

ALLOWING USERS TO SAVE FORM DATA

If you do have a business need to provide the user with a copy of the form data they submit, you have a number of options:

- You can provide a print view so that users can print the form as it is rendered.

- You can have the user provide their e-mail address, and then e-mail them the form data upon submit.

- Using SharePoint document conversion capability, you can render a conversion of the document and e-mail that to the user.

- You can use custom code to provide any other requirement you may have.

If you want to allow the user to submit a browser-capable form, you have a number of options available. However, they are somewhat complicated since the submission is performed at the server, not the browser. You set the options for submitting a form under Tools ➤ Submit Options; this opens the Submit Options dialog (shown in Figure 6-15).

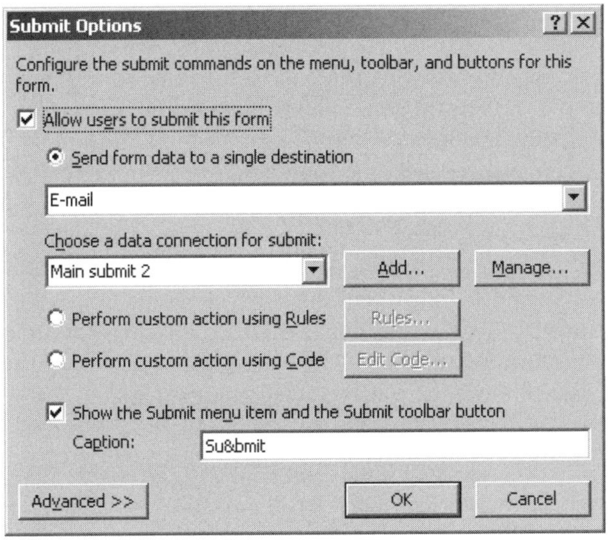

Figure 6-15. *The Submit Options dialog*

The first check box overrides the entire dialog. If it is unchecked, no submit actions will be available for the form, and it can only be saved. Checking the "Allow users to submit this form" option enables the other options: a set of radio buttons, an option to show the Submit menu item or toolbar button, and an advanced section for indicating what happens after a form is submitted.

The first option is the most straightforward—you can indicate where the form data goes when the user clicks the Submit button. Your options are as follows:

- *E-mail*: InfoPath will use the form user's local e-mail client to e-mail the form data as configured in the designated data connection. (If InfoPath "send mail" is not configured or is misconfigured, you can publish the form template, but the user will receive an error when they try to submit.)

- *SharePoint document library*: This allows you to designate a specific document library connection; the form data will be saved there as an XML file.

- *Web service*: This option allows you to submit to a SOAP-compliant web service connection.

- *Web server*: This option allows you to submit the form data to a web server using an HTTP POST command. It allows you to submit to an Office Server connection using the Microsoft Office SharePoint Server web service.

- *Hosting environment*: Use this option to submit the data to an environment that is hosting the InfoPath form (e.g., a .NET Windows or ASP.NET form with an InfoPath form embedded).

- *Connection from a data connection library*: This option provides a means of selecting a data connection from a data connection library (DCL).

Your next option for submitting forms is to perform a custom action using rules. The best reason for using rules is that you can have several actions defined with conditions specified. This provides an avenue for, say, submitting a copy of the form data to a specific admin clerk if the total amount on the form is in excess of a defined amount. In addition, you can provide other actions, such as setting a field's value or changing views before you submit the form.

Finally, you can run custom code when the user clicks the Submit button. If you select this option and click the Edit Code button, the Visual Studio Tools for Applications editor will open, and you can write custom managed code (C# or VB .NET) for the Submit event handler. (Remember that if you actually want to submit the form data somewhere, you need to provide for that in the code). Alternatively, if you design an InfoPath form using Visual Studio Tools for Office, then you will be designing the form inside Visual Studio; in this case, clicking Edit Code will simply insert a handler and flip to the form's code view.

I'll cover managed code forms (stand-alone and browser-capable) in Chapter 9.

Note If you enable e-mail or custom code submissions, your form will have to be published by an administrator on the SharePoint server. More on this in Chapter 9.

The next option indicates whether you want the Submit button displayed on the toolbar and in the File menu. You may ask, "Why wouldn't I want the Submit button to show?" One main reason would be that you don't want the submit functionality visible until the user completes the form. There's no easy code to make the Submit button hidden; but you can put your own button on the form and hide it with conditional visibility or code. You may also want submit performed as part of some other action or validation in the form.

For whichever reason, if you want submit functionality, but don't want to distract the user with a Submit button that will only error-out if they click it, this is where you can turn it off.

The Advanced tab provides the option to show the user messages when the user submits the form (success or failure), and what action to take after the form is submitted (close the form; open a new, blank form; or leave the form open).

E-mail Enabling Document Libraries

A side note worth pointing out is that document libraries (as well as form libraries, and in fact any list in SharePoint) can be e-mail enabled. This means that a form or document library can be assigned an e-mail address, and any e-mail to that address will automatically create an item in the library. Obviously, this can be a great way to enable users to submit forms to a library even when they're not connected to the intranet.

■Tip It's probably best not to use a main form library as the incoming destination for e-mailed forms. Apart from spam and security concerns, you can't be sure how a form gets mailed in. With some InfoPath options, you may actually get the e-mail body, a form template, and the form data showing up as three items in the form library. Best bet is to have an incoming "staging" area where inbound e-mailed forms are received and reviewed before posting to the main form library.

SharePoint Workflow

There's a story about two workers in an office.

They sat across from each other for years—one fellow was always clearing his desk early and heading home; the other was always stuck at his desk well into the night. Finally, one day, the overloaded worker stopped his coworker while he was heading out of the office.

"What's your secret?" he asked.

"Sorry?" the speedy worker replied.

"Every day I'm here until 10:00 p.m. trying to get caught up, while you're always out of here by 3:00. We have the same job—how do you do it?"

"Oh, that's easy," he whispered conspiratorially. "Everything that hits my desk I simply refer to 'John Smith.' I figure that somewhere in this huge company there's gotta be a John Smith, and he'll probably take care of it."

"I see," said the first. "You know, we've never formally met. I'm John Smith . . ."

"Workflow" is what most office workers really want when they talk about a paperless office or "getting rid of all this paper." The paper isn't actually the problem—the problem is the process (or lack thereof) around moving the paper from one place to another. Paper sitting in piles is virtually invisible and unfindable. Any kind of "process" is generally ad hoc with regard to who's supposed to get a document next (John Smith), what kind of information they need, and what actions need to be taken.

A good workflow solution will be flexible and robust—it will give the ability to change routing when necessary without the need to rewrite entire pieces of the engine; but it will also enforce routing rules such that one worker can't arbitrarily route everything to the desk of the guy who's on vacation.

Windows Workflow Foundation

SharePoint (both Windows SharePoint Services and Microsoft Office SharePoint Server) are built on Windows Workflow Foundation (WF), part of the .NET Framework 3.0. WF is a framework and set of services that provide a uniform method for building workflows. As designed, WF requires a hosting container to run and sustain the workflows designed by developers. Happily, SharePoint provides that container.

Both Windows SharePoint Services 3.0 and Microsoft Office SharePoint Server 2007 have the same workflow engine under the hood. The main difference is that Microsoft Office SharePoint Server provides four predefined workflows out of the box, while Windows SharePoint Services will require you to create workflows to have them available for use with document libraries.

Designing a Workflow

There are two ways to create a workflow for WF: using Visual Studio 2005 and the Workflow Designer, and using SharePoint Designer. The Visual Studio route is obviously more suited for developers, while SharePoint Designer is suitable for power users, providing an interface similar to the e-mail rules designer in Outlook. (I'll cover designing workflows in depth in Chapter 11.)

InfoPath and SharePoint Workflows

"That's nice, but what does this have to do with InfoPath?"

Workflows and InfoPath are thoroughly intertwined in several ways:

- InfoPath forms in a form library can have workflows attached to them. This is a powerful capability—any form submission is going to be routed, and will require a workflow. In SharePoint 2003, this required additional products or development. In 2007, it's out of the box.

- Office 2007 documents can use embedded InfoPath forms as part of a content type definition to interact with the workflow (see Chapter 8).

- InfoPath forms can be used to interact with the workflow for other documents.

- InfoPath forms can be generated by workflows.

Exercise 6-1. Assigning a Workflow

1. Take a form library you created earlier. (If you don't have a form library, use the Expense Report template and publish it to a SharePoint site using the directions in Exercise 5-3.)

2. From the document library, open the Settings menu and click Form Library Settings (see Figure 6-16).

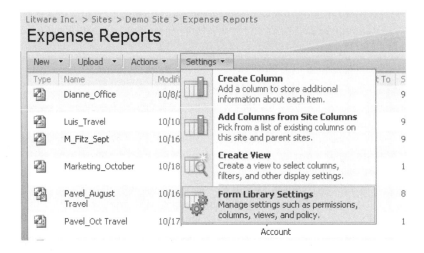

Figure 6-16. *Opening the form library settings*

3. From the Customize page, click "Workflow settings."

4. Microsoft Office SharePoint Server provides four workflows out of the box—for this exercise, select Approval.

5. Give this workflow the name "Expense Report Workflow."

6. SharePoint workflows can generate tasks in a task list when steps require action. Use the drop-down task list to either select an existing list or indicate that you want to create a new one.

7. In addition, SharePoint workflows can track their history using a special history list (a customized SharePoint list). Leave the default of Workflow History (new).

8. The next options govern how the workflow is initiated—whether it's started automatically when an item is added to the library, or only when one is changed. You can also allow form users to start a workflow manually. Check "Allow this workflow to be manually started," and clear the other check boxes.

9. Click Next.

10. In defining the workflow, you can choose serial or parallel. Leave the default of serial.

11. Leave both the Reassign and "Request a change" check boxes checked.

12. Add approvers to the list. These need to be people in the SharePoint directory (add alternate accounts if you need to). Separate multiple names with semicolons.

13. Enter **5** in the text box next to Day(s) for "Give each person the following amount of time."

14. Leave Notify Others blank.

15. You can define what conditions will indicate that the workflow is complete (e.g., if someone rejects an expense report, you could consider that submission complete and resubmit a new workflow). If you leave all the options blank, the workflow will be completed when it has run through all its tasks.

16. Leave Workflow Activities blank.

17. Click OK.

18. This returns you to the workflow settings for the form library. Note that your workflow is now listed as an available workflow, with no active workflows in progress.

19. Click the library name in the breadcrumbs to return to the form library.

20. In the form library, note that the context menu now has an option for "Workflows" (see Figure 6-17).

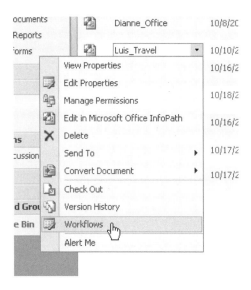

Figure 6-17. *The context menu on a form library item*

21. Select the Workflows option. This takes you to the form item's workflow page. You should see the workflow you created listed. Click the name or the icon.

22. This takes you to the "Start workflow" page (see Figure 6-18). Note that you can adjust the routing, due date, and notifications of the workflow. Click Start.

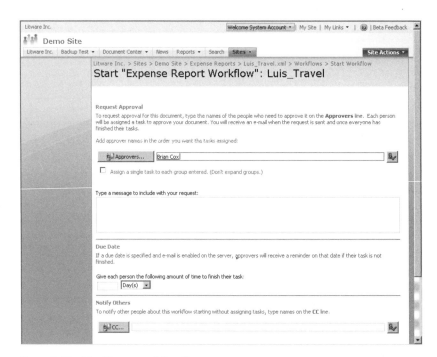

Figure 6-18. *The "Start workflow" page*

23. Once the workflow has processed, you will be returned to the form library. Note that you have a new column—Expense Report Workflow—with the document you used indicated as "In Progress."

24. Go to the tasks list that you designated for the workflow tasks. Make sure that the view (in the top-right corner) is set to All Tasks. You should see a task for your recipient to approve the file.

25. The task in the task list is what governs the next step. When it is marked "completed," the workflow will move on. (Outlook 2007 has an integrated task editor, so it's possible to review a workflow item and approve or reject it from within Outlook).

    That's all there is to using the basic SharePoint workflows. Chapter 8 will cover how to build your own.

Summary

Hopefully, you can see by now that the integration of InfoPath and SharePoint make the pair a compelling solution for electronic forms. The ease with which you can create a form, make it browser-capable with no additional design, publish to a form library, and leverage the workflow and publishing capabilities (PDF, XPS, TIFF) make the InfoPath/SharePoint combination a powerful one. Also remember that if InfoPath, InfoPath Forms Services, and SharePoint don't solve your problem out of the box, each are richly extensible with .NET for a robust, scalable, maintainable solution.

CHAPTER 7

∎∎∎

Data Connections

Electronic forms are somewhat pointless if you don't actually put the data anywhere. Fortunately, InfoPath has rich capabilities for "doing stuff" with the form data once the user has entered it. In addition, you have to consider the various aspects of getting data out of somewhere and into the form (to populate both form data and lookup lists, among other uses).

In this chapter, I'm going to go over the various ways to get data into and out of an InfoPath form from various data sources.

Overview

There are various types of data connections in InfoPath—all are connections that you can use to read or write data, but some allow you to design a form based on their schema. Table 7-1 has a breakdown of the types of connections.

Table 7-1. *Data Connections and InfoPath*

Connection Type	Receive	Submit	Design Form
SQL Server	X		X
Web service	X	X	X
XSD			X
XML	X		X
Data connection library (DCL)			X
E-mail		X	
SharePoint document library	X	X	

You can design a form based on a SQL Server table or query, a web service, an XML document or XSD schema, or a connection from a SharePoint connection library. Once the form is designed, you can use other connection types to retrieve data for use in the form (drop-down lists being the most notable example), or to submit form data to once the user is finished with the form.

AUTHENTICATION ISSUES

With data connections, you start to enter a world of authentication complexity. Whether you're designing a rich client form that will post to a database or a browser form that posts to a web service, you need to be aware of how authentication works, and especially the "double-hop" problem.

When a user posts to a web page, web service, or any kind of server, they are passing their credentials from the authenticated client to the server. Once at the server, the process that receives the credentials (in the case of a web service, this is IIS) can pass them to any other service *on the same machine* (SQL Server, for example). However, the service holding the credentials cannot, by default, forward those credentials to another server. This is referred to as the "double-hop" problem—there's one hop from the user console to the web server, and another hop from the web server to the database server (see Figure 7-1).

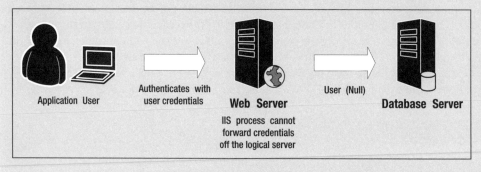

Figure 7-1. *Architecture of the "double-hop" problem*

Developers always encounter this problem when they develop on a single machine running all their services (and therefore, no double-hop), and then deploy to an n-tier architecture. The application stops working, and they get the fateful "Login failed for user (null)" (null because no credentials were passed). This is why you should *always* develop on an architecture that mirrors the production architecture.

There are four ways to address the double-hop problem:

- *Embedded credentials in the connection string:* You can encode a username and password in the connection string. This is generally a bad practice, but sometimes you do what you have to. If you must go this route, do not use a real user's account—create a limited-rights user account specifically for the connection. (For help with connection strings, see www.connectionstrings.com/.)

- *Kerberos authentication:* With Windows Server 2003 and Kerberos, you can grant permission to either a server or a set of services on a server to forward user credentials. This way, the user uses their credentials to authenticate against the server, and then the server can use those same credentials to authenticate against other servers. For information on implementing Kerberos, visit www.microsoft.com/windowsserver2003/, and click the Technology Centers link on the left pane. Scroll down and click the Kerberos Authentication link.

- *SharePoint single sign-on:* SharePoint Office Server offers single sign-on capabilities that you can leverage to basically map the user's credentials based on the data store the form is trying to access.

- *UDC from a DCL:* Microsoft Office SharePoint Server also offers a new type of library for data connections. You can store data connection files (with the extension UDC or ODC) in a DCL so that they can be centrally managed. The same caveats apply here as with embedded credentials in a connection string—don't use an existing user account in a connection. The benefit is that since they're centrally managed, it's easier for an administrator to maintain usernames and passwords on the connections (instead of having to open every form).

Data Connections

InfoPath uses data connections to get data into and out of a form. You can have a collection of connections for various purposes—populating lookup lists, looking up data for form rules, or submitting form data to multiple destinations.

Data connections are managed in the Data Connections dialog (Tools ➤ Data Connections, as shown in Figure 7-2). From here you can add new data connections, modify existing connections, or convert existing connections to use a data connection file.

Figure 7-2. *The Data Connections dialog*

The Convert button is new to InfoPath 2007—it allows you to convert an existing data connection to use a data connection file stored in a SharePoint DCL. This is an easy way to take forms that have embedded connection strings and export the connection to a centrally managed library. When you click Convert, you'll get the Convert Data Connection dialog, which will simply prompt you for a network location for the data file. If the file exists, InfoPath will simply map to it, overriding the connection information in the form. If the file doesn't exist, InfoPath will create a file at the location indicated and copy the connection information out to that file.

When you click Add, you will be presented with the first page of the Data Connection wizard (Figure 7-3). Notice that you're given options to create a connection for submitting data, create a connection for receiving data, and look for an existing connection on Microsoft Office SharePoint Server. Your selection here will govern where the wizard goes next.

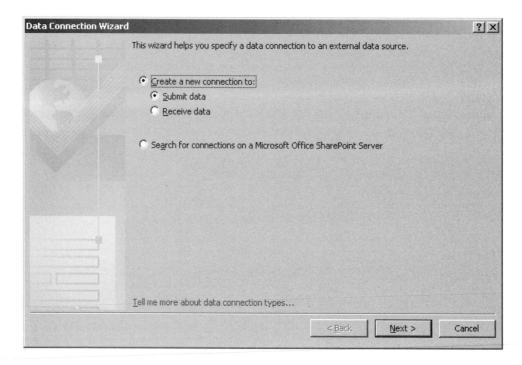

Figure 7-3. *The Data Connection wizard*

If you choose "Submit data," your options on the next page will be as follows:

- Web service

- SharePoint document library

- As an e-mail message

- To the hosting environment

If you choose "Receive data," then your options will be as follows:

- XML document

- Database (SQL Server only)

- Web service

- SharePoint library or list

I'll cover these options in depth throughout the rest of the chapter.

If you choose "Search for connections on a Microsoft Office SharePoint Server," then you will be prompted to select a SharePoint site from a list of sites (you can add sites directly from the dialog). After selecting a site, you will be presented with a list of data connections on that site to choose from (remember that those connections are the same as the other connection options here—the difference being that they are published on a SharePoint site and are therefore easier to manage). You will then be prompted to give the connection a name and finish the wizard.

Data Source

Data connections are simply that—connections. They are "windows on the world" from your form. However, the data source (or "main submit") *defines* your form—this dictates the underlying structure of the form itself. The best way to do this is to designate the data source when you create the form (Figure 7-4).

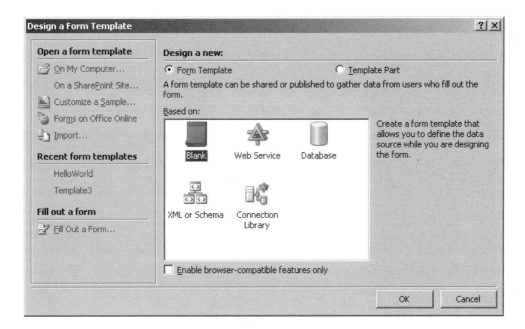

Figure 7-4. *Designing a form based on a data source*

When you assign a data source to the form, it becomes the underlying data structure for the form (Figure 7-5).

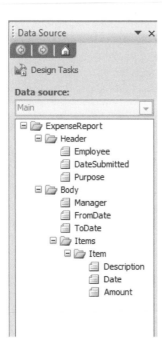

Figure 7-5. *The data structure for a form designed from an XML file*

As described in Chapter 3, your options for a main data source are a database connection, web service, or XML schema. When you define a form based on a database connection or web service, the data source is locked into the form—you cannot edit it in the data source task pane.

■**Tip** InfoPath can infer a schema from an XML document. However, this has significant drawbacks, as every element will be assigned a String data type (you can change it later in the data source pane). In addition, you may miss out on data structures such as optional or repeating fields if they are not represented in the sample document. The best approach is to design a proper XSD schema using a tool like Visual Studio or XMLSpy (see Appendix C).

Now let's review the types of data connections and how to best use them.

SQL Server

You can read and write data from SQL Server 2000 or 2005 (or an Access MDB file, but I won't be covering that here explicitly—the concepts are similar). Moreover, you can use a table or view from SQL Server as the data structure for a form. However, an important point to note is that you can *only* use SQL Server (not Oracle, MySQL, Sybase, etc.). It's because of this restriction, and the security implications of opening your database to a form to be filled out by "anyone," that I always recommend using web services instead of direct database access.

Note InfoPath uses the ODBC connection dialog from the host operating system to build a new data connection. As a result, when you first start building a connection, you may see options for other database connections if you have the client connectivity drivers installed. You will be able to walk through building a connection, since you're in the OS wizard. Once you try to finish, however, InfoPath will warn you that it only accepts SQL Server and Access data connections.

To create a form based on a SQL Server schema, you start by designing a form template (Figure 7-6). This will allow you to connect to either an Access MDB or a SQL Server database. The wizard will walk you through connecting to a database and selecting data, and then creating a data connection for the form, as well as generating a data schema for the form. When you create the connection, InfoPath will actually create two connections (one for retrieving data and one for submitting data).

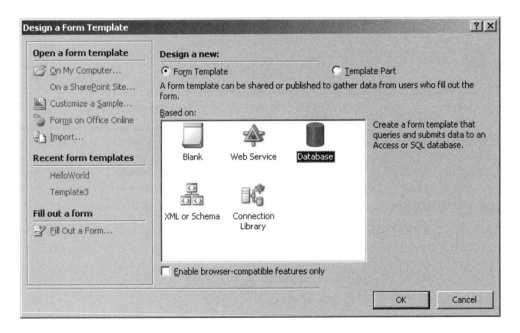

Figure 7-6. *Creating a form based on a database schema*

Exercise 7-1 will walk you through creating a form template based on a SQL Server connection. While the exercise takes a very easy (and appealing) path through creating a data-bound form, I do not want to mislead you as to the level of effort required to create electronic forms. Any e-forms initiative is going to require heavy analysis of the business uses, common use cases, workflows, data sources, and so on. InfoPath is a very powerful tool, and eases the implementation of an e-forms effort, but that effort still has a high demand for business analysis.

■**Note** Exercise 7-1 uses the pubs database in SQL Server. If you do not have the pubs database installed, you can download both the pubs and the Northwind sample databases from www.microsoft.com. The download indicates SQL Server 2000, but it can be used for either SQL Server 2000 or 2005.

Exercise 7-1. Creating a New Form Based on a Database Connection

1. Open InfoPath. In the Getting Started dialog, click the Design a Form Template link.

2. In the Design a Form dialog, select Database. Make sure that "Enable browser-compatible features only" is *not* checked.

   Note that if you leave "Enable browser-compatible features only" checked, then your form will not have submit enabled, as browser-capable forms cannot submit to a database connection. They can submit to a web service connection.

3. Click OK.

4. In the Data Connection wizard, click the Select Database button.

5. In the Select Data Source dialog, double-click NewSQLServer Connection.odc.

6. You'll get the Data Connection wizard—in the Server name box, enter the server name. The DNS name or IP address will suffice, and "localhost" will work if you're working on a dev box.

7. Select "Use Windows credentials," and click Next.

8. Select the pubs database and the Titles table, and then click Next.

9. On the Save Data Connection File and Finish screen, you can accept the defaults or give a specific file name, description, and friendly name to the ODC file that's being created.

10. Click Finish. You should now see the Titles table in the Data Connection Wizard, as shown in Figure 7-7.

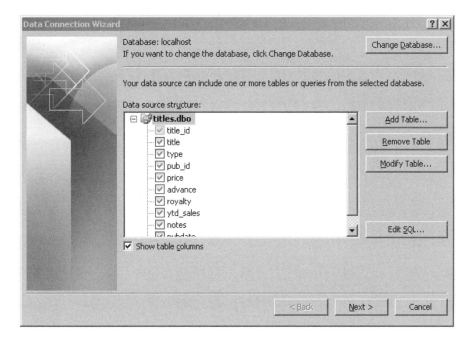

Figure 7-7. *The Data Connection wizard with a database table populated*

11. Click Next.

12. On the final page of the Data Connection wizard, there are some pretty important things going on (see Figure 7-8). For a database connection, InfoPath creates two connections: one to retrieve data (using a select query), and one to submit data (using insert and update queries). Uncheck "Enable submit for this connection," and note the changes in the Summary box—the form becomes retrieve-only, and submit is disabled.

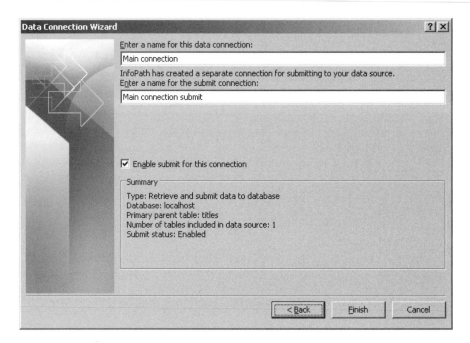

Figure 7-8. *Final page of the Data Connection wizard*

13. Ensure that the "Enable submit for this connection" check box is checked, and then click Finish. Once you're back in InfoPath, you'll have a form template with two areas: one labeled "Drag query fields here" and one labeled "Drag data fields here" (see Figure 7-9).

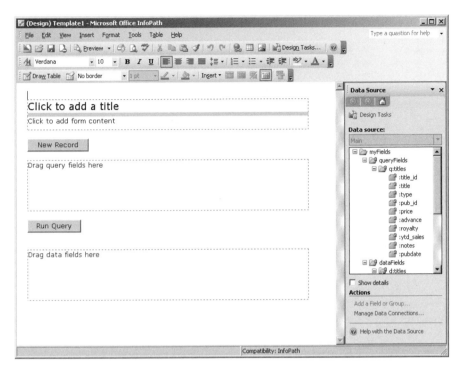

Figure 7-9. *New form template with database query logic*

14. Open the queryFields element in the task pane, and then the q:titles element.

15. Drag the :title_id element into the box labeled "Drag query fields here."

16. Scroll down in the data source pane, and then select and drag the d:titles element into the box labeled "Drag data fields here," as shown in Figure 7-10.

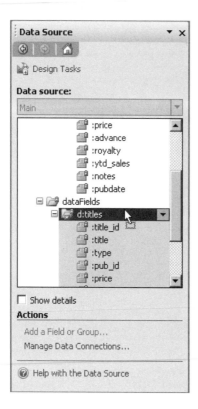

Figure 7-10. *Selecting the d:titles element*

When you release the element in the target box, you'll get a context menu on the drop point asking how to add the elements in the tree. Select "Repeating Section with Controls" (Figure 7-11).

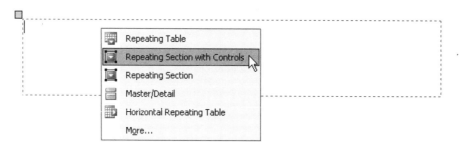

Figure 7-11. *The dialog presented when dropping an element tree into an InfoPath form*

Note that InfoPath parses Pubdate as a date and uses a date control.

17. Expand the Notes text box horizontally and vertically, and then double-click it to open the Properties dialog. Click the Display tab and put a check in the "Multi-line," "Paragraph breaks," and "Wrap text" boxes.

18. The form is now completely functional. Try it out—click the "Preview" button in the toolbar. Once the form is open, enter **MC2222** as the title ID and click the Run Query button. You'll get a warning about crossing the domain boundary—click OK. You'll see the record for that book returned.

19. If you want to add a record, you can enter the information in the fields below the Run Query button and click Submit.

20. Click the Close Preview button when you are finished experimenting with the form.

Web Services

But what if you need to submit data to an Oracle database? Or a mainframe? How else can InfoPath move data around?

Web services are a W3C-defined method of interoperating across server boundaries. A web service is a mix between an API and a web page—it's a structured way for a process to make a call using HTTP to a web server and get a result formatted as XML. The protocol for interacting with a web service is the Simple Object Access Protocol (SOAP), which can be encoded over an HTTP transport. Web services can also be self-defining—a web service can provide an XML document that defines the web service methods. Since the language for this description is the Web Service Description Language, the descriptive document is named (and referred to as) WSDL.

Since the interfaces for web services are defined with HTTP, XML, and W3C standards, it is possible for languages and servers to interoperate—you don't need to learn yet another API or get some hard-to-find client software to enable connecting to the server.

InfoPath can talk natively to web services—either for the schema of a form or as an additional data connection. When you set up the form or data connection, InfoPath queries the WSDL of the web service and allows you to pick the methods you want, and then presents the resulting data structure of the method (parameters for calling the method and the structure returned).

Note There are two "contracts" a web service can comply with: document or RPC. In addition, a web service can be encoded as either *literal* or *encoded*. InfoPath only supports web services that are document/literal. If you have to interact with a web service that is RPC/encoded, you will have to either write a .NET proxy service (a web service that calls the web service—watch your authentication!) or custom code in the form to communicate with the service natively.

When you design a form against a web service, it's similar to designing against a database, except that you have to create two connections: one to receive data and one to post the data (the wizard walks you through them both). The first connection is to read data—this will define the data structure for the form. The next step lets you select the web method to write the data, and map the form structure to the web service parameters.

Next, you'll create a form based on a web service. Actually, it will be based on a number of web service methods: one for reading data, one for submitting data, and a third as a data connection for a lookup list.

Exercise 7-2. Create a Form Based on a Web Service

This exercise uses a custom .NET web service written against the Northwind sample database. The web service is discussed in Appendix B.

1. Open the InfoPath form design wizard (File ➤ Design a Form Template).

2. Under "Design a new," select the Web Service option, and then click OK.

3. In the Data Connection wizard, indicate that the form is to receive and submit data, and then click Next.

4. On the next page, paste the URL for the web service (it should end in asmx). Alternatively, if you have UDDI enabled, you can use the UDDI wizard to discover the service. (Any organization investing in web services should set up a UDDI server.)

5. The next page of the wizard lists the methods available in the web service you selected. Select the method you will use to read data from, and then click Next.

6. The final page of the first half of the wizard (Figure 7-12) lets you name the connection (I recommend leaving "Main query" as the default name), summarizes the web method entered, and prompts you to click Next to enter the information for the Submit web service.

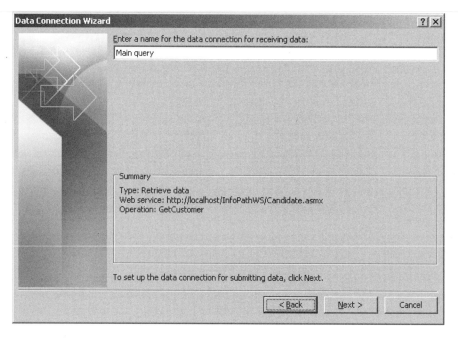

Figure 7-12. *The final page of the data retrieval wizard*

7. For the submit data web service, again enter the URL of the web service you want to use, and then click Next.

8. Select the web method you will use to submit the form data back, and click Next.

9. This next screen is where you map the form structure (defined by the web service you're using to retrieve the data) (see Figure 7-13).

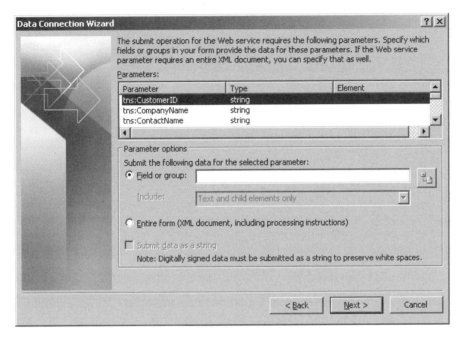

Figure 7-13. *Mapping data in the Data Connection wizard*

10. For each element in the form you want to post back to the web service, you will have to map it to a parameter in the web service you are posting to. Select a parameter in the list, and then click the element list button next to the "Field or group" field.

Note that you have the option to submit the entire form as an XML document—if you choose to process the XML behind your web service, or if you might be using one web service to receive XML from multiple locations, then you can just submit the form wholesale without mapping every element.

11. You will see the Select a Field or Group dialog (Figure 7-14). Select the appropriate field under the dataFields node. Repeat this for each required parameter of the web service. (Leave the Include option set to "Text and child elements only" for each parameter, as shown in Figure 7-13.)

Figure 7-14. *Selecting an element to map to a web service parameter*

12. Once you have finished populating every parameter, click Next.

13. The final page in the wizard allows you to give the submit connection a name. Click Finish.

14. You'll see the familiar skeleton form with data fields and query fields on the Data Source task pane.

15. To build the form, open the dataFields node down until you see the data fields. Click and drag the parent node of the data fields to the form and drop it in the area labeled "Drag data fields here." When you release the mouse, you will get a context menu with options—select Controls in Layout Table (Figure 7-15).

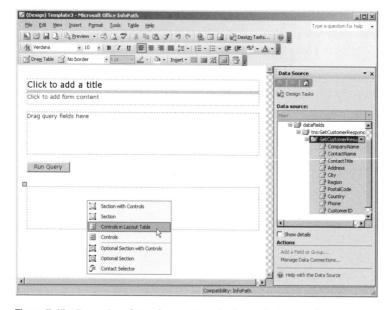

Figure 7-15. *Dragging data elements to the form design surface*

16. Next, open the queryFields node in the Data Source pane to find the parameters for the web service you're using; drag the parameters to the area labeled "Drag query fields here."

17. The form is now completely functional—you can preview the form and try some queries—enter a customer ID and click Run Query. If you make changes, click Submit to post those changes back.

E-mail

E-mail only serves as a "write-to" data connection—InfoPath doesn't read from it, nor can you design a form against it. If you need to design a form against incoming e-mail, then your best solution is either customization on your mail server, or BizTalk Server, which posts the e-mail into a database.

Having said that, you can have "post-to" e-mail connections to submit form data via e-mail. The great aspect of this option is that it's network independent. That is to say, you don't have to worry about the user being on the intranet, or sending through a firewall, or authenticating across the Internet; when the user submits the form, it is queued to their default e-mail client as an attachment and submitted the next time they sync their mail.

Configuring an e-mail adapter is very straightforward. For the most part, the settings you care about are on the first page of the wizard (Figure 7-16). Note that you have To, Cc, Bcc, and Subject fields, just as a normal e-mail. However, you also have the function buttons next to each field—these enable you to dynamically generate any of the fields based on various aspects of the form. In the figure, I have written the subject field such that it pulls the employee's name and the date of the report into the field.

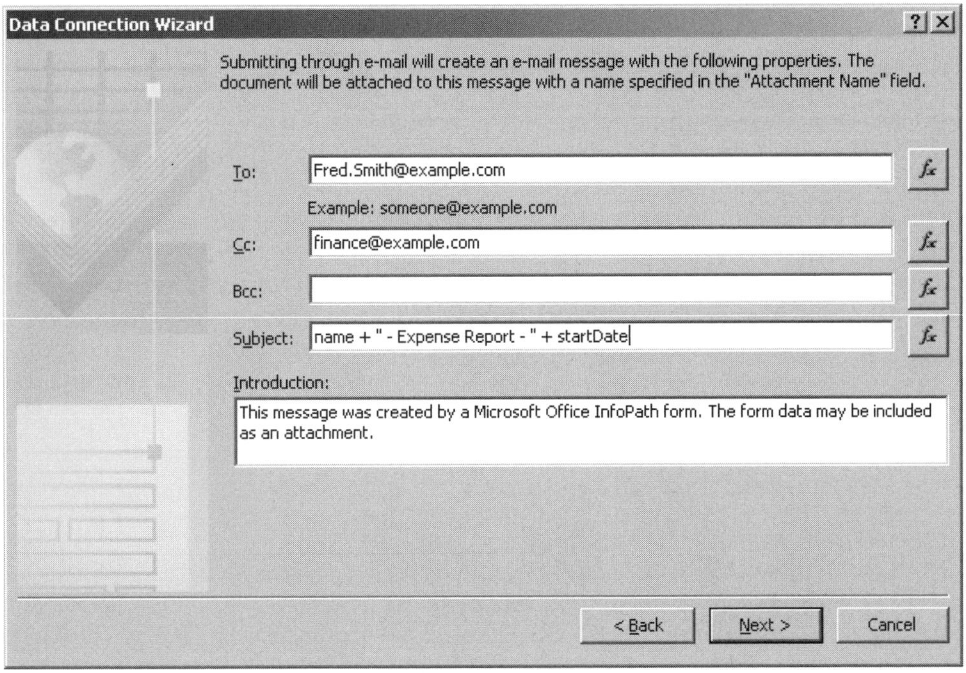

Figure 7-16. *First page of the e-mail form in the Data Connection wizard*

The second page of the wizard (Figure 7-17) governs how the form is sent in the e-mail. On this page, you can indicate whether to send the active view of the form (only supported in Outlook 2007, as detailed in Chapter 2) or to send the form data as an attachment. You can also send the form template as an attachment—however, this is only supported with restricted security forms (since domain security forms must be opened from a specific published location and full trust forms must be installed by the end user).

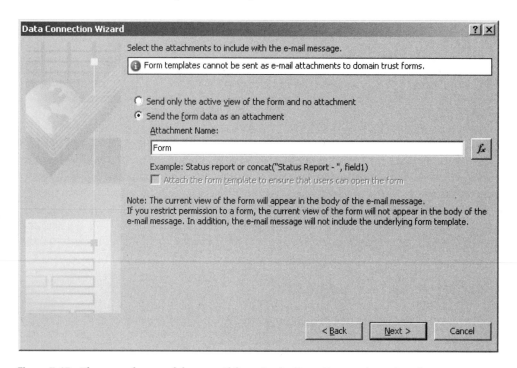

Figure 7-17. *The second page of the e-mail form in the Data Connection wizard*

You can give the form attachment a name, as well as the dynamic capabilities of our friend the formula box. InfoPath will render the current view of the form into the body of the e-mail upon submission as a static HTML view.

Once you have finished setting up the e-mail connection, on the final page you simply enter the name of the data connection and click Finish.

Now that you've set up the data connection, if you want to use it for submitting the form, you still have to designate it as the e-mail connection for your form (Tools ➤ Submit Options), as shown in Figure 7-18.

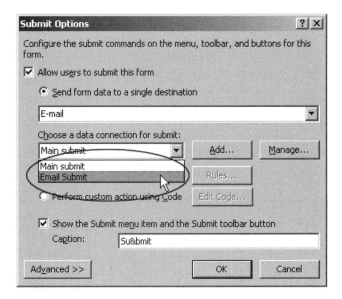

Figure 7-18. *Setting the submit data connector for e-mail*

Hosting Environment

Another new feature in InfoPath 2007 is that InfoPath forms can be hosted by another .NET application—you can have an InfoPath form embedded in your WinForm application. Of course, if you're going to have a form embedded in your application, you need a way to pass data back and forth.

There are no settings for a hosting environment connection—a standard API enables pushing the data in the schema of the data properties. The real work is done in the hosting environment.

I'll cover embedding InfoPath in a hosting environment in Chapter 9.

SharePoint

I discussed SharePoint integration with InfoPath in Chapter 6. This section is just going to build on those concepts, adding in what you've learned about data connections.

Lists

InfoPath has the capability of reading data from SharePoint lists. The great thing about this is that it gets developers out of having to either write code to maintain lookup lists or maintain the lists themselves. Now, for lookup data, you can simply create a SharePoint list (or hook to an existing one if it exists) and populate the list with the lookup items. Voilà—you have a web-based interface for managing your lookup data.

Adding a connection to a SharePoint list or library is very straightforward: add a new data connection in the usual way, select the option to add a connection to receive data, and then select "SharePoint library or list." Enter the URL of the site you want to use a list from, and you will get a list of lists or libraries in the site that you can use for a data connection (Figure 7-19).

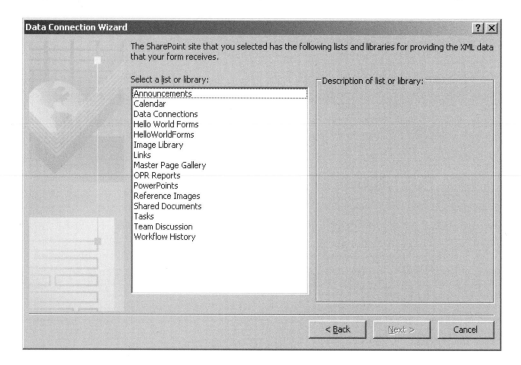

Figure 7-19. *Selecting a list or library for a data connection*

Select a list or library from the list and click Next. On the next page will be a list of fields that you can use for the data connection (Figure 7-20). Select the fields you want kept in the data connection, and click Next.

■**Tip** InfoPath caches lookup data for offline use. As a result, if you select more fields than you need, you bloat the form template. Keep the fields you select to the minimum necessary.

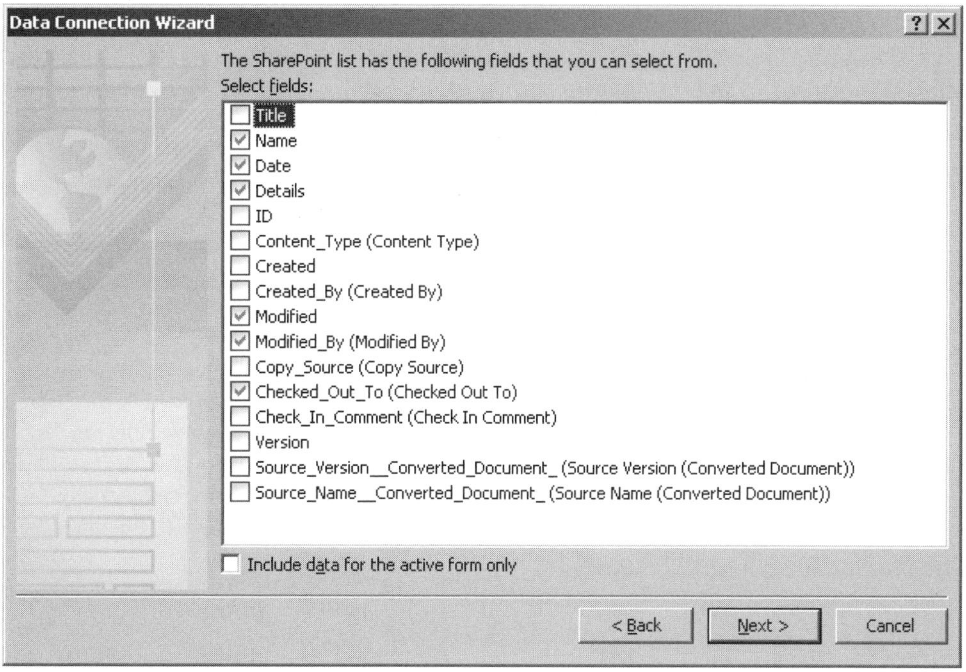

Figure 7-20. *Selecting fields from a SharePoint list*

The final page of the wizard has a check box to load the lookup data into the form template. As noted in the preceding tip, InfoPath caches lookup data when a form is opened for use offline. The check box on the final page can preload the lookup data so that it will be available the first time the form is opened.

Data Connection Library (DCL)

SharePoint can store data connections in a DCL. This makes it easier to manage connections—credentials, paths to database servers, permissions, and so on. A DCL is simply a type of SharePoint library—it's one of the options available when you go to create a list/library on a SharePoint site.

The easiest way to get a connection into a DCL is to create the connection in an InfoPath form, and then use the Convert function in the data connections manager to publish it to a SharePoint DCL. Once it has been published, an administrator will have to go to the library and approve the connection before it can be used.

Single Sign-On

One of the features of Microsoft Office SharePoint Server 2007 is the single sign-on capability. This is a "credential mapping" feature that can take a user's current credentials and map them to the appropriate credentials for other enterprise systems. For example, if Sally has an active directory logon that she uses to access an InfoPath form that is hosted on a site with integrated authentication, those credentials are available to the single sign-on service. By mapping her active directory credentials to those of the other systems, she gets the appropriate authentication, roles, and privileges on those other systems.

Summary

InfoPath's data connection capabilities are part of its true power. By being able to talk to web services natively and providing an easy-to-use designer interface, it allows developers to work on standard data interfaces, while business users can focus on designing their interfaces. Hopefully, this will help get developers out of the form design and maintenance business.

However, there are still complexities in InfoPath—I'll cover some of those in the next few chapters.

CHAPTER 8

■ ■ ■

Advanced InfoPath Topics

Now that the basics of the client and designer have been covered, I'm going to dive into some advanced topics with InfoPath forms. The "basics" cover most of what you need to build a robust line of business forms. However, there are still some aspects of InfoPath that need to be covered to round out the "out of the box" features available to a form designer.

This is a fairly eclectic collection of features, so bear with me as I hop from topic to topic—this chapter covers a grab bag that includes the following:

- *Importing Word forms*: InfoPath 2003 had the interfaces for importing forms, but did not include any actual importers. In InfoPath 2007, importers for Excel and Word are included.

- *Cascading drop-down lists*: One of the main questions about drop-down lists is "How can I filter the options in one list based on the selection in another?" This chapter will cover some of the issues around cascading drop-down lists.

- *Content types*: Microsoft Office SharePoint Server 2007 introduces the concept of reusable content templates, called *content types*. This chapter will look at how to use InfoPath forms as content types, as well as an interesting new way of enabling metadata in other Office applications.

- *Custom task panes*: Just like the task panes in the form designer, you can offer a custom task pane to your form users, perhaps for help information, form metadata, or additional form capabilities.

- *SharePoint site form library policies*: Microsoft Office SharePoint Server adds information management policies that allow an administrator to define policies governing auditing, expiration, and other aspects of managing form data.

- *Merging forms*: When you have a number of form data files, you may want to create an aggregated report. InfoPath gives you some powerful features to manage how to merge form data files.

After reading this chapter, you'll be able to take an existing form written in Word, import it into InfoPath, tweak it as necessary (including drop-down lists that filter other lists), and create a custom task pane for context-specific information. Then you can publish the form to Share-Point and designate it as a content type (reusable forms) and set information management security policies for the form library.

Finally, you'll be able to designate how to merge form data files and embed the form into your own applications if you choose to—a veritable cornucopia of powerful form template features!

■**Note** It takes a special kind of sense of humor to use "cornucopia" in a technical book.

Importing Word/Excel Forms

Most existing forms that are already in digital format will be in Word, Excel, or PDF format. InfoPath 2007 ships with importers for Word and Excel so that you can take your existing electronic forms and import them into InfoPath form templates.

■**Tip** If you need to import forms that are in PDF or other formats, you can either design your own importer or buy an add-in. I highly recommend FormBridge® by Texcel Systems (www.texcel.com)—they have been converting e-forms for over 15 years and their form converter produces InfoPath forms with incredible fidelity.

A comment about importing forms: don't ever expect 100 percent full fidelity from form translation. The vast variety of possibilities in form layout and the number of different ways forms can be annotated to show where data belongs leaves a lot of room for ambiguity that has to be resolved by the person reading the form. Any forms migration should plan for every form to be reviewed by a real live human after any type of bulk conversion.

After the form is reviewed, allocate development resources to correct translation problems. Budgeting here should be fairly straightforward, even if you have a lot of forms. Simply run ten forms through the conversion process and estimate the accuracy and time to fix each form on a "time per form" average basis. For example, let's say you have to convert 500 forms. You run ten forms through and find the conversion errors (layout problems, data entry misassignments, conversions of picklists to drop-down lists, etc.). You determine each form will take 15 minutes to fix. As such, with 500 forms at .25 hours per form, you can calculate that it will take 125 hours to correct all the forms.

Importing Forms

Importing a form is done by creating a new form template. You'll start from the familiar starting point—the Getting Started dialog. Click Import a Form to start the import (Figure 8-1).

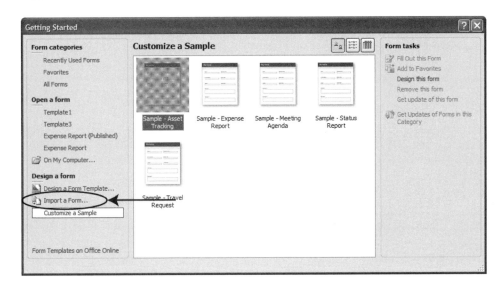

Figure 8-1. *Beginning a form import*

The next dialog offers a list of exporters installed in InfoPath. (Also note the link to search for additional converters on the Office Marketplace.) The next page in the wizard asks for the location of the file to import, and has a button for advanced options. I'll review the options in the following sections.

WRITING A CUSTOM IMPORTER

You may need to implement some form of custom import functionality—for example, if you have a large batch of forms that are built on a standard that the installed importers don't handle, but that you can automate in a fairly straightforward manner. This is the standard developer cost/benefit evaluation—if you have to convert a small number of forms, it may be easier to just design them by hand. On the other hand, if you have a large library of forms to import, it may be worth building your own custom importer.

Details on how to build a custom importer are in the InfoPath SDK, which can be downloaded from `http://msdn.microsoft.com/office/program/infopath`. A custom importer is a .NET DLL that is registered in `HKEY_LOCAL_MACHINE\SOFTWARE\Microsoft\Office\InfoPath\Converters\Import` to make the importer available in the list in InfoPath.

Word Forms

The Word Import Options dialog offers three main options, as shown in Figure 8-2 and described in the following list.

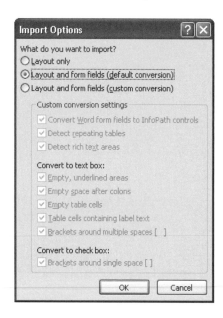

Figure 8-2. *The Import Options dialog for the Word importer*

- *Layout only*: Only imports the layout elements of the form; this option won't try to parse form data elements (underlines, check boxes, etc.)

- *Layout and form fields (default conversion)*: Imports the layout elements of the form and will try to "best guess" the data elements of the form (underlines to text boxes, empty table cells to text boxes, multi-row tables to repeating tables, and other estimations)

- *Layout and form fields (custom conversion)*: Similar to the default conversion, except that you can select the conversions that best reflect your needs

Once you select your options, click OK, and then click Finish. InfoPath will run the converter, relay any errors, and present the finished form in design mode. Figure 8-3 shows an example of a Word form, and Figure 8-4 shows the results of importing it into InfoPath.

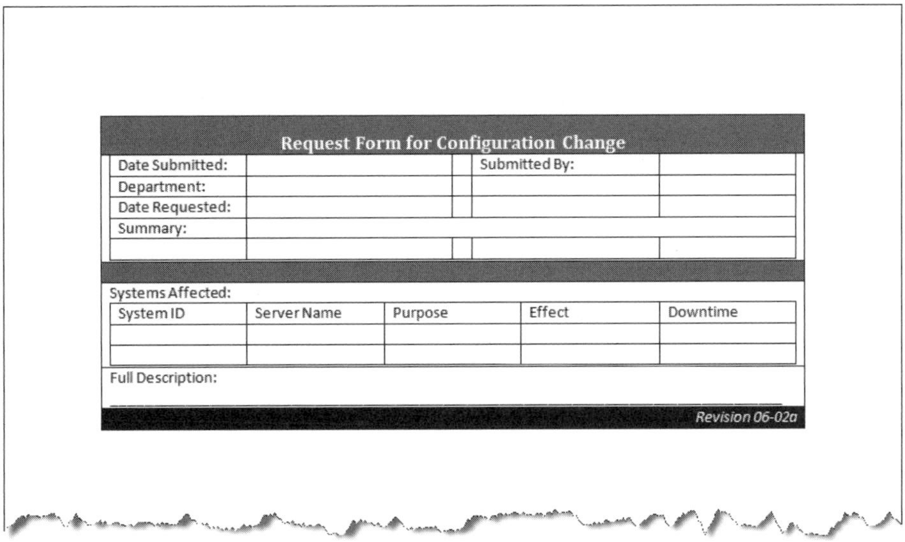

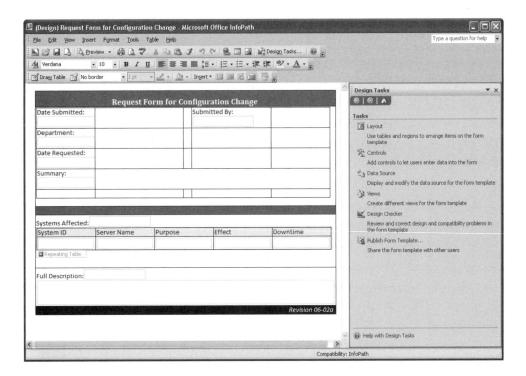

Figure 8-3. *A Word form to be converted*

Figure 8-4. *The resulting imported InfoPath form*

Note that the imported form isn't 100 percent perfect—the text boxes are below the labels instead of in the next column. You could address this by selecting the option to convert empty cells to text boxes, but then you would have new text boxes in every empty cell. It's easier to simply go through the form and drag the text boxes to where you want them.

The converter created a repeating table where the table was in the Word form—everything looks fine there. There are two entry points for "Full Description"—a text box (because of the trailing colon on the label) and a rich text box (as a result of the long underline in the form). You can either convert the named control to a rich text box, or delete the text box and rename the rich text box.

But you should see that not every form will be imported perfectly. Always budget time to review and correct forms after any form conversion effort. Form converters are time-savers, but they don't do the whole job!

Excel Forms

Importing Excel forms is somewhat different, and will probably take a bit more preparation to get the form to import properly. The trick is making sure that the InfoPath importer can tell what parts are part of the form, what parts are to be filled in, and what's just empty spreadsheet.

If you take a basic form that looks like the form in Figure 8-5 and import it into InfoPath, the importer won't be able to tell where to put text boxes, and you'll end up with something like what you see in Figure 8-6.

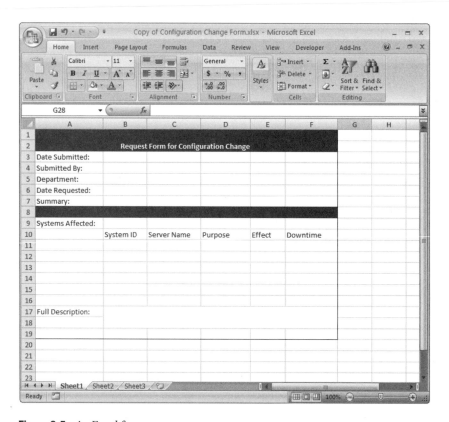

Figure 8-5. *An Excel form*

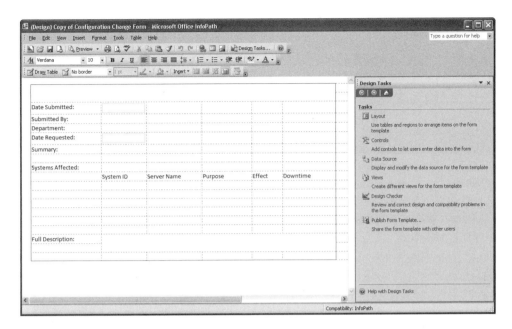

Figure 8-6. *The resulting imported form*

All you get as a result of the import is a large layout grid. What you need to do is indicate where the data entry points are. In Excel, you can do this by putting outlines on the cells you want to fill in. Outlining a cell has the same effect as using an underline or brackets in a Word form. Next, add some outlines, as shown in Figure 8-7, and import the spreadsheet again.

If you now run this spreadsheet through the importer, you'll get the form shown in Figure 8-8. Note that you now have text boxes and a repeating table. However, you've lost some formatting, and it's still not as clean an import as the Word import. But you should see that for a more complex form, this could be a real time-saver.

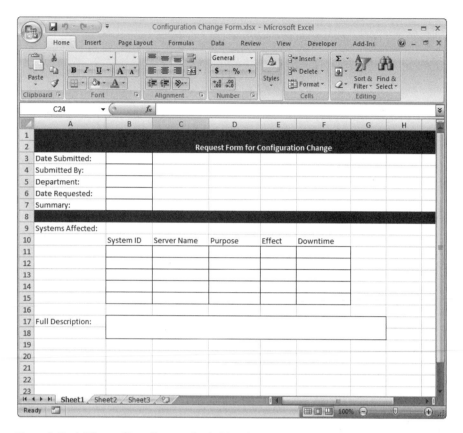

Figure 8-7. *Adding cell outlines to the fields where a user would enter data*

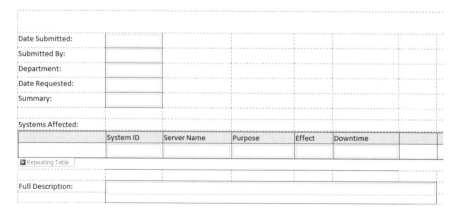

Figure 8-8. *The resulting InfoPath form*

However, remember that this is only the starting point. Now that you have your form in InfoPath, you can add validations, custom formulas, and other form logic. Once you've finished your form, you can publish the form template to SharePoint for easy user access, and then submit the form using any one of the data connection methods you learned about earlier.

Cascading Drop-Down Lists

This is a pretty basic concept, and once you understand how to do it in InfoPath, it's pretty straightforward. However, figuring out the "how" can often be a bit confusing.

What you want to do is have two drop-down lists. The value selected in one will filter the other list such that only related values are shown. The most common reason to do this is to narrow a fairly long list down to a manageable number of items.

For an example, let's take two custom lists in SharePoint—one lists a number of departments (Figure 8-10), and the other lists personnel and includes a field indicating which department each person is from (Figure 8-9). You want both of these lists to populate drop-down lists in an InfoPath form, and when the user chooses a department, you want to filter the personnel list to those persons in that department.

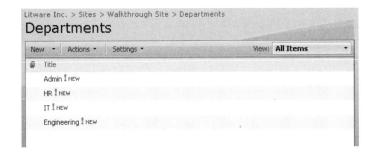

Figure 8-9. *A contact list in a SharePoint list*

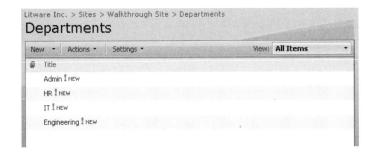

Figure 8-10. *The list of departments in a SharePoint list*

So next you build an InfoPath form with two drop-down lists—one using the Departments list as a data source; the other using the Contacts list. These will be the two connected lists—when you select a department, the list of employees will be filtered to those employees in the selected department.

So how do you do the filtering? This is the tricky bit. Open the properties of the drop-down list that's going to be filtered, and then click the XPath button (Figure 8-11). This will open the dialog to select the field or group the list is bound to. At the bottom of the dialog is a button labeled "Filter Data." Click it and you will be taken to the Filter Data dialog.

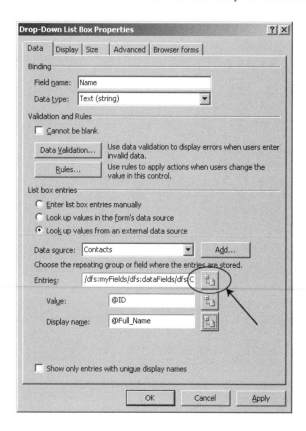

Figure 8-11. *The XPath selection button in the Drop-Down List Box Properties dialog*

The Filter Data dialog allows you to add filters that will filter the data in the drop-down list. In this case, you can filter employees by those whose departments match the selected department. You could add other filters—perhaps filtering by some user criteria (e.g., people who work in your department, or people who work for you) or filtering by workflow criteria. The concepts and interfaces are fairly straightforward for setting up the filtering.

Content Types

While in SharePoint 2003 you had custom lists, form libraries, and so on, you were somewhat limited in that you could put a lot of effort into customizing a list or library, only to have to repeat the work if you wanted another one on another site. SharePoint 2007 adds even richer customization features—and obviously, it would have been even more problematic to implement a highly customized list or library if you had to reinvent it every time you wanted to reuse it.

SharePoint 2007 introduces the idea of content types—if you publish a form template, build a list, or create a column as a content type, it becomes available on the site as a template for users to reuse as necessary.

CUSTOM COLUMNS IN A DOCUMENT LIBRARY

Besides the document itself, you can also designate a column as a content type to reuse in other libraries. If you consider some complex data types (perhaps a lookup to another list, or a long list of data that has to be maintained), this makes sense. It makes even more sense when you find out that in SharePoint 2007, it's a fairly straightforward development effort to create a custom column—you can have custom validations, custom formatting, or a unique data entry format (Figure 8-12).

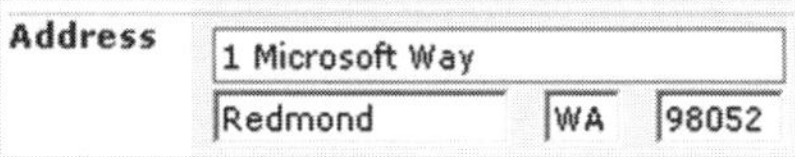

Figure 8-12. *A custom data entry field for a custom column*

Looking at that field, you can easily see why you would want this as a reusable feature in a SharePoint site.

Exercise 8-1 will walk through what it takes to publish an InfoPath form as a content type in a SharePoint site and then consume that content type in a library.

Exercise 8-1. Publishing a Form As a Content Type

1. Design a new form. For this exercise, you'll customize the sample Expense Report form template.

2. Start the Publishing wizard (File ➤ Publish). Save the form template when prompted.

3. For the publishing location, select "To a SharePoint server with or without InfoPath Forms Services."

4. Paste the URL from the site you want to publish the form to into the URL box, and then click Next.

5. On the page for "What do you want to create or modify?" select Site Content Type, and then click Next.

6. Select "Create a new content type," and then click Next.

7. Enter a name and description for the content type, and then click Next.

8. The next page of the wizard asks for a location to publish the template to. You will need a document library on the site to map to. I recommend having a separate document library for content type templates with appropriate access permissions. Select that library, enter a file name for the template, and click Next.

9. The next page is your familiar location to promote form columns to the library. Select the columns you want to promote, and then click Next.

10. The final page is a summary information page—verify the details shown, and then click Publish.

11. Now you have a content type on your site—you need to associate it with a document library to use it. On the SharePoint site, click View All Site Content on the left-hand navigation pane.

12. On the All Site Content page, click the Create link near the top of the page.

13. Click the Form Library link.

14. On the New page, you only need to give the library a name, and then click the Create button at the bottom of the page.

15. Now you have a document library. You need to add your content type to it. In the document library, click Settings, and then click Form Library Settings.

16. Under General Settings, click Advanced Settings.

17. For "Allow management of content types?" select Yes, and then click the OK button at the bottom of the page.

18. Back on the form library customization page, note that you have a Content Types section (see Figure 8-13).

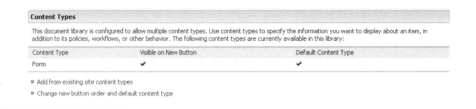

Figure 8-13. *The Content Types section of a form library customization page*

19. Click the "Add from existing site content types" link. This takes you to the Add Content Types wizard (Figure 8-14).

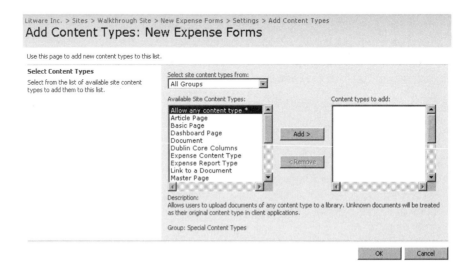

Figure 8-14. *The wizard page for adding content types to a form library*

20. Note the list of default content types, including the wildcard "Allow any content type *" at the top. You can add any number of content types to the form library.

21. For now, just select Expense Report Type (for the type you created), and then click Add >.

22. Click OK.

23. You're back at the customization page. Click the library name in the breadcrumbs to return to the form library.

24. Note that the New button in the toolbar has a drop-down arrow. Clicking this will show the content types that are available for this site. You should see your expense report form there (Figure 8-15).

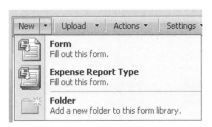

Figure 8-15. *Adding a new form from a content type*

One of the biggest problems with trying to attach metadata to documents in an intranet scenario is getting users to enter and update the data. SharePoint 2003 addressed this to some degree by having a pop-up form when a user saved a document to a SharePoint site. However, this was a two-step process and somewhat invasive (when you click the Save button, you just want the document to get saved and go away).

With SharePoint 2007 and Office 2007, a new feature called the *document information panel* makes it easier than ever for an end user to maintain metadata. The Office 2007 applications (Word, Excel, PowerPoint, etc.) are again "metadata aware" and will recognize the embedded metadata fields within a document. However, instead of presenting a dialog when the document is saved, they present an embedded InfoPath form within the application itself for the user to view and edit the document metadata.

The most powerful part of this solution is that the document information panel form is an InfoPath form that a developer can edit, so you can add branding graphics or color schemes to the panel, hook up lookup drop-down lists, add validations, and so on.

Exercise 8-2 shows you how easy it is to modify the document information panel.

Exercise 8-2. Modifying the Document Information Panel

1. Create a document library based on a Microsoft Office Word document.

2. Add a custom column for dates—click Settings, and then click Create Column.

3. Give the column the name **Due Date**.

4. Select Date and Time as the data type.

5. For "Require that this column contains information," select Yes.

6. Click OK.

7. Add another column, name it **Priority**, and give it a Choice data type.

8. For the choices, enter **High**, **Medium**, and **Low** on separate lines. Click OK.

9. Finally, add a column of type Multiple Lines of Text, title it **Description**, and Click OK.

10. Now you'll see the cool part. Open Word 2007 and type some text into the document.

11. Click File ➤ Save As. In the dialog, paste the URL of the document library you've created (minus the `/Forms/AllItems.aspx` part). This will navigate the dialog to the SharePoint document library (see Figure 8-16).

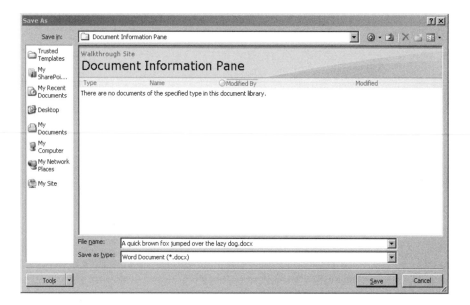

Figure 8-16. *Saving a document to a SharePoint document library*

12. Give the document a name and click Save.

13. You will get a warning because the properties are missing (Figure 8-17). This may seem a bit similar to the process in SharePoint 2003, but it is only happening at this step because you created the document outside SharePoint and saved it into the document library. To see what the document will look like when it's opened from the SharePoint library, click the Go to Document Information Panel button.

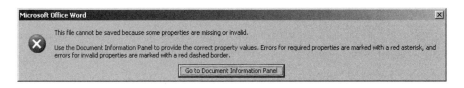

Figure 8-17. *Missing properties warning*

14. Once the document information panel is open, you'll see your metadata fields at the top of the Word document (Figure 8-18).

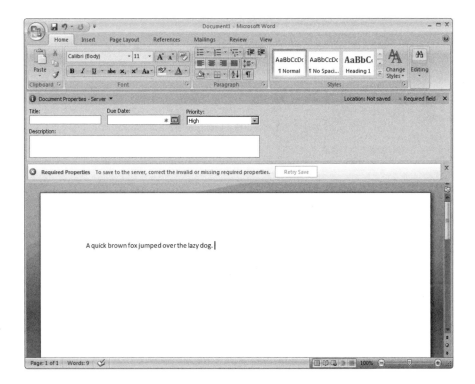

Figure 8-18. *The document information panel in Word 2007*

15. At this point, you may be wondering if you picked up a SharePoint book by mistake—why am I talking about Word? Well, that document information panel is . . . an InfoPath form!

16. Note that you have controls that match the data types of the columns you created (date, multiple choice, multi-line text, etc.).

17. To edit the form, go to the Settings menu and select Document Library Settings.

18. Go to Advanced Settings.

19. For "Allow management of content types?" select Yes.

20. Click OK at the bottom of the page.

21. You'll now have the content types editor on the customization page. Click the link for the Document content type.

22. On the List Content Type editing page, click the "Document Information Panel settings" link.

23. You'll see two settings: the template options and a Show Always option. The latter always opens the document information panel in the client application. From the template options, you can upload a new form template or edit the existing one.

24. Click the "Create a new custom template" link.

25. On the InfoPath dialog that pops up, click Finish.

26. Now you'll see the form that represents the document information panel in your friendly InfoPath form template editor (Figure 8-19).

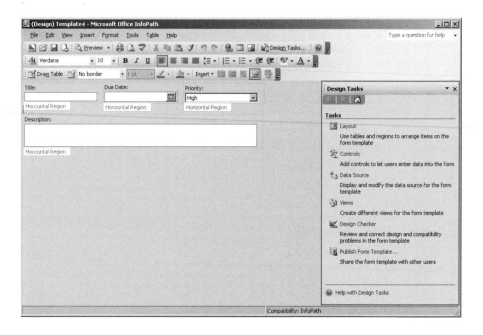

Figure 8-19. *A document information panel opened in InfoPath for editing*

27. Note that every control is in a region control. These are used by the Office applications to reflow the controls as necessary based on the size of the client window.

28. You can edit the form from here. When you are done, you can publish the form back (File ➤ Publish).

29. In the publishing wizard, you should now see a new option: "As a Document Information Panel template." Ensure that this option is selected, and then click Next.

30. Click Publish, and then click Close. Voilà—you've updated the document information panel.

Custom Task Panes

The InfoPath designer provides a way for you to associate a custom task pane with an InfoPath form. A custom task pane is basically a file or URL that renders HTML for the InfoPath form to render in the task pane.

Note You cannot use a custom task pane in a browser-enabled form running in the browser.

You can obviously just use an HTML file for the task pane. You can also show or hide the task pane in code, or change the file that is shown in the task pane. For example, you might want to show a different task pane when the view changes, or show context-sensitive help that changes when different controls are selected.

If you designate an HTML file for the task pane, you can hook the HTML window from code behind the form and execute JavaScript calls. This allows you to manipulate the task pane based on actions from the form.

Another alternative is that you can actually dynamically set the task pane to point to a URL-based ASP or ASP.NET page. This could pull dynamic content from a web server—perhaps a parameterized page showing some amplifying data.

Custom task panes are detailed more thoroughly in the InfoPath SDK.

Policies

Microsoft Office SharePoint Server 2007 allows administrators to set information management policies on the forms in a form library by setting the policies on the library. Policies are defined by site collection and applied to a form library. The types of policies you can apply include the following:

- *Labels*: Designate one or more mandatory labels that users must enter or that are automatically defined; these are then printed on every form.

- *Auditing*: Specify events related to the form that will be audited, such as opening or downloading items from the library, editing items, checking in or out, and deleting.

- *Expiration*: Assign an expiration date to all content in the library based on some event regarding the form. You can also specify what actions SharePoint should take when the content expires.

- *Barcodes*: Assign a barcode to every form in the library.

To set policies, go to the settings of the form library, and then click the link for "Information management policy settings." From the next page, you will see the default of "no policy assigned." Alternatively, you can select an existing policy from the site collection if one is available. Finally, you can define a policy on the fly by selecting "Define a policy" and clicking OK.

On the Edit Policy page (see Figure 8-20), there are some basic settings and four check boxes. Each check box enables one of the policies summarized in the preceding list. Checking a policy option displays the options for the policy.

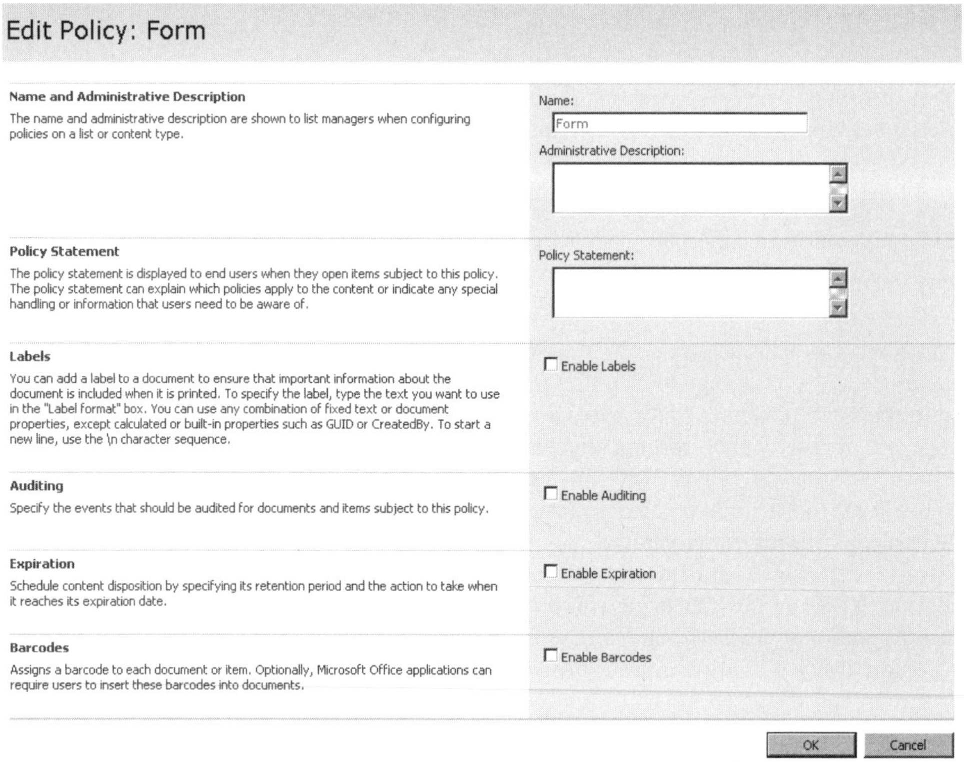

Figure 8-20. *The Edit Policy form*

Labels

Labels describe metadata that will be produced with each form when it is printed. The options are to prompt the user to insert the label, and to fix the label so that it can't be changed once it's added. You can also set the text formatting of the label and what data is in the label.

Labels are made up of raw text and can also include metadata—by putting a field name in curly braces, like {Employee Name}, the data from that field will automatically be inserted in the label. You can use "\n" to add a new line. You'll have to print labels separately with the form and attach it if necessary.

Auditing

Checking the box to enable auditing will display the auditing options (Figure 8-21). These are fairly straightforward—checking the boxes will enable audit logging for the actions indicated.

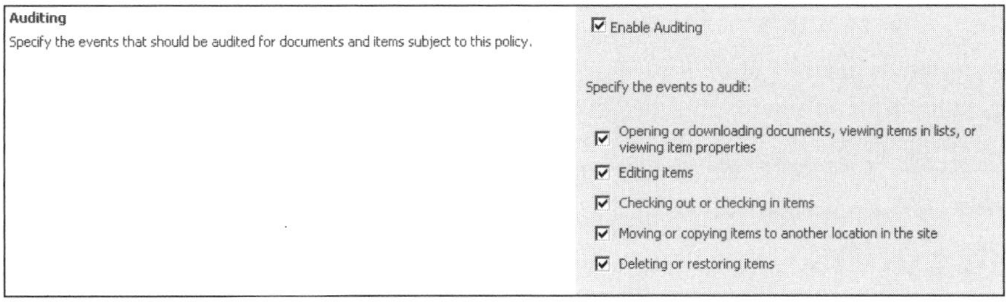

Figure 8-21. *Auditing options*

The tricky part is finding the audit log. Go to the site settings of the *root site* for the site collection. Then, under Site Collection Administration, click the link for "Audit log reports"—this will take you to the audit log reporting page. From here you can download a number of Excel spreadsheets that have reports on the audit reports (as well as expiration reports, audit reports on changes to audit policy, and settings reports).

Expiration

Checking the box for enabling expiration will, as I'm sure you've figured out by now, display the options for expiring content in the form library (see Figure 8-22).

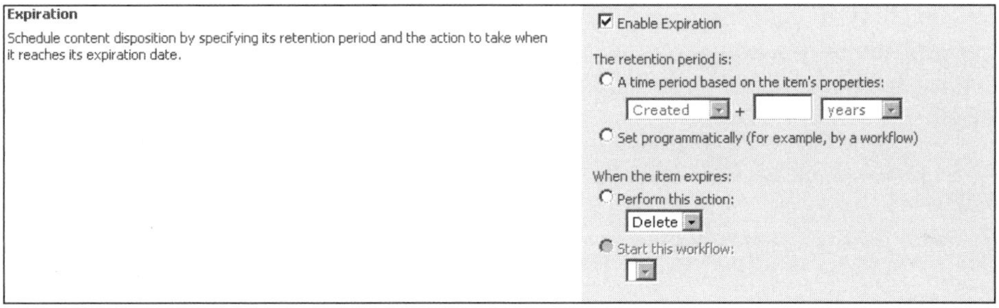

Figure 8-22. *Content expiration options*

These options are pretty straightforward—you can have an expiration date automatically assigned for every document in the form library, or allow one to be set by a workflow or custom code. Then you indicate what should happen to the document upon expiration—a specific action (delete by default) or the start of a particular workflow (e.g., an audit, archive, approval, and shredding workflow). Again, reports for document expiration are available in the same location as the audit logs.

Barcodes

Barcodes are similar to labels, except that SharePoint will generate a unique ID and matching barcode. This barcode can then be physically attached to an Office document or embedded in the document using an image.

Merging Forms

Once you have a number of forms in a document library, you may want to produce an aggregated report of some form—either a summary of the forms in the library, or perhaps an aggregate report. InfoPath has a built-in feature that allows users to merge form data into a single file.

You must enable form merging in the form options (Tools ➤ Form Options, on the Advanced tab). Here you can also enable merging forms using custom code (to perform parsing, specific types of aggregations, lookup data, etc.).

■**Note** Merging forms using custom code is not supported in form templates that are browser-enabled.

Merging forms successfully is all about design. If you anticipate that the forms you're designing might be merged later, ensure that the information you want aggregated properly is in repeating tables or sections. Simple controls have a Merge Settings option (Figure 8-23) on the Advanced tab of the Properties dialog.

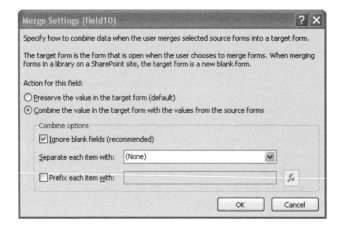

Figure 8-23. *The Merge Settings dialog for a text box control*

The Merge Settings dialog is powerful because it allows you to aggregate data into a single control. You can specify the delimiter for the merged data, indicate whether to skip blank fields, and, if necessary, prefix data with fixed values (or other values from the same form).

To merge forms, you need to have one form open. From there, going to File ➤ Merge Forms will open a dialog for you to select forms to merge *into* the current form. As you can see from the default value in the Merge Settings dialog, the value in any nonrepeating controls will be preserved in the current form unless configured otherwise. Repeating tables and repeating sections will be aggregated together. And due to the structured nature of the control, there are no options for controls like date pickers—you will either have to nest them in repeating controls or accept the values in the current form.

Summary

As I promised, this chapter has been an eclectic journey around some aspects of InfoPath that simply don't fit into other areas. You can see how adding additional capabilities from SharePoint 2007 truly empowers InfoPath to be an enterprise-level solution for forms and data collection.

CHAPTER 9

■■■

Writing Code in InfoPath

InfoPath's user interface is incredibly powerful—you've seen how to use rules, validations, dynamic sections, and views to create very robust forms. However, there will be things that you cannot do with the standard interface. When you find that the features of the InfoPath form designer aren't enough, you can write script or managed code (C# or VB .NET) behind the form.

■**Tip** While Jscript is supported for coding, it is incredibly limiting—neither browser-compatible forms nor secure forms implementations can use Jscript. In addition, managed code gives you additional options (plug-ins with VSTO, VSTO form solutions, etc.). It's really just better to stick with managed code for your InfoPath solutions.

There are three ways to write code behind an InfoPath form template: the Microsoft Script Editor (MSE) (for Jscript), Visual Studio Tools for Applications (VSTA), or Visual Studio 2005 Tools for Office (VSTO), Second Edition. Both the MSE and VSTA can be installed with InfoPath 2007; VSTO is a separate product that installs templates and provides interoperability assemblies for building Word, Excel, or InfoPath templates with code, or plug-ins for Word, Excel, or Outlook.

Visual Studio Tools for Applications (VSTA)

VSTA is a new lightweight coding platform Microsoft developed for software developers to include with their applications as a customization platform. VSTA enables you to create, build, and run add-in projects that are attached to existing applications. This provides an embeddable scripting platform and SDK so that application developers don't have to write their own scripting engines.

■**Note** VSTA does not have the ability to create or build stand-alone applications. It is solely for editing and building add-ins.

The reason you might be interested in it is that it's included with InfoPath as the design environment for writing code associated with the form. In InfoPath 2003, if you wanted to embed managed code in an InfoPath form, you had to use the InfoPath Visual Studio templates and create the InfoPath project from scratch in Visual Studio. Now if you want to add code to an InfoPath form, you have access to VSTA to write your managed code (Figure 9-1).

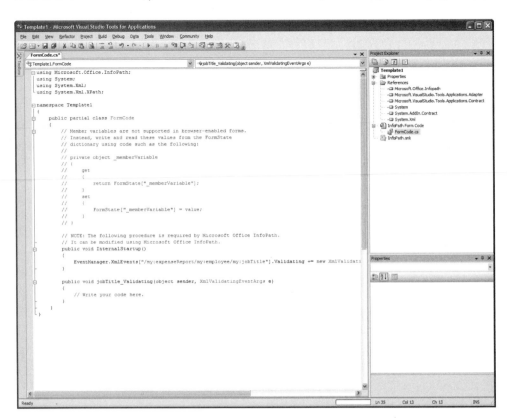

Figure 9-1. *The VSTA window*

There are three ways to access VSTA from the InfoPath designer:

- Press Alt+Shift+F12.

- Select Tools ➤ Programming ➤ Microsoft Visual Studio Tools for Applications.

- Right-click a control, select Programming, and then select an event to open in VSTA.

■Note If you don't see VSTA in any of those options, there are two potential problems. First, the form must be set to use managed code. To set it, go to Tools ➤ Form Options, and select Programming in the Category pane on the left of the Form Options dialog. In the "Programming language" section, if JScript or VBScript are selected, VSTA will not be available.

Alternatively, you may not have VSTA installed. To install it, open the Add or Remove Programs applet in the Control Panel, select Microsoft Office 2007, and then click the Change button. Select Add or Remove Features, and then select Continue. Navigate to Microsoft Office InfoPath ➤ .NET Programmability Support ➤ .NET Programmability Support for .NET Framework version 2.0 ➤ Visual Studio Tools for Applications. Drop down the selector and choose "Run from my computer." Finish the wizard.

You can use VSTA to write incidental code related to a form in event handlers. However, you can't use it to write add-ins for the form or task panes (or stand-alone .NET projects). For those, you need Visual Studio.

InfoPath and Visual Studio

InfoPath 2003 was released without any managed code capabilities or integration with Visual Studio. Service Pack 1 added .NET integration, but it was very awkward—you had to write code in Visual Studio, but manage the form in the InfoPath client. VSTO 2005 integrated the form with the design environment so that form designers had a unified design experience.

With InfoPath 2007, you have two options: VSTO 2005 SE (Second Edition) updates VSTO 2005 to work with Office 2007 (Figure 9-2). The next edition of Visual Studio (code named "Orcas") will have a new edition of the VSTO with native Office 2007 support.

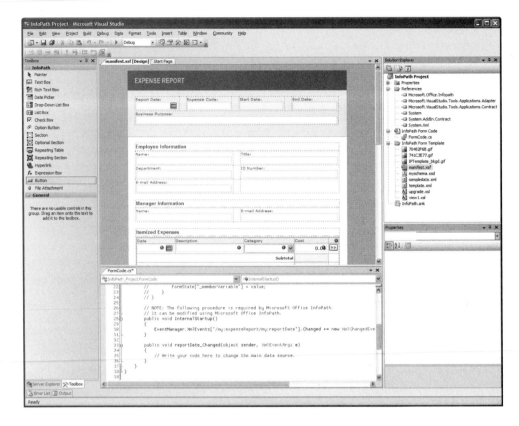

Figure 9-2. *An InfoPath solution in Visual Studio 2005 with VSTO 2005 SE*

In addition to working with the form template and the associated code, you can also use the XML features of Visual Studio to work with the schema and XML files, as well as add other assemblies or projects to the solution. With VSTO, you can also create InfoPath add-ins, which can enable document task panes (more on this in Chapter 10).

From Visual Studio, you have full access to the InfoPath features covered so far. The InfoPath Tools menu is merged into the Visual Studio Tools menu (Figure 9-3).

Figure 9-3. *The InfoPath Tools menu merged into the Visual Studio Tools menu*

You can also open all the InfoPath task panes you've come to know and love by selecting them from the View menu. (Note that the task panes will open as Visual Studio tool panes, so you can switch between them using the tabs at the bottom, or you can rearrange them to suit your taste—see Figure 9-4.) The Publish menu item is under the Build menu. When you select Build ➤ Publish, Visual Studio will build the project (and generate any compiler errors), and then open the familiar InfoPath publishing wizard.

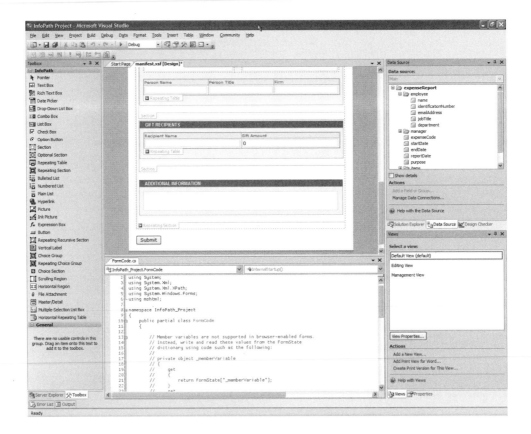

Figure 9-4. *An InfoPath project in Visual Studio with InfoPath task panes open*

So now let's take a look at the InfoPath object model, where most of your coding rubber will meet the application road.

Understanding the InfoPath Object Model

The InfoPath managed object model is self-descriptive and fairly straightforward. I'm going to review the major parts of the object model; additional information is available online at the Visual Studio Tools for the Microsoft Office System pages on MSDN (www.microsoft.com/downloads/details.aspx?FamilyID=771AEB45-9D27-4D1F-ACD1-9B950637D64E&displaylang=en).

The programming model for InfoPath varies based on whether a form template is for the InfoPath rich client only, or is marked as a browser-compatible form. Various classes, properties, methods, and events won't be available in a browser-compatible form. The IntelliSense in Visual Studio and VSTA will provide appropriate guidance based on the style of form template selected.

■**Tip** You can get a full illustration of the InfoPath 2007 managed object model as a download from MSDN. Search on "InfoPath 2007 object model" to find the "2007 Office System Document: Developer Posters" page.

Application

The root of the InfoPath object model is the `Application` class. This refers to the actual InfoPath application, not any facet of the form template. The `Application` class exposes a number of properties and methods that relate to the InfoPath application. I'm going to cover a few of the minor properties here, and then some more major properties following.

Environment

The `Environment` class (via `Application.Environment`) provides two Boolean properties that you should care about: `IsBrowser` (is the code running in a browser form) and `IsMobile` (is the code running in a mobile form). You can use these properties to adjust form behavior based on the platform the form is running on.

MachineOnlineState

The `MachineOnlineState` property returns an enum type (`MachineState`) with values of either `Online`, `Offline`, or `IEInOfflineState`. `Online` and `Offline` are taken from the state of the network connection; if IE is in an offline state, it will preempt checking the network connection.

User

The `User` property gives you access to the user's name and login ID, and also provides a method (`IsUserMemberOf`) that you can use to verify whether a user is a member of a specific security group.

Windows/ActiveWindow

In the rich client, the `Application` class has a property for enumerating windows (`WindowCollection` class), which is a collection of `Window` objects. The members of interest here are the `TaskPanes` property (for enumerating through task panes and interacting with them), the `MailEnvelope` property (if the window is for a mail item), and `WindowType`, which returns either `Editor` or `Designer` to indicate the current status of the InfoPath window.

XmlFormCollection/XmlForm Class

In either InfoPath-only or InfoPath and Forms Services forms, the `this` object refers to the current loaded form template. (In InfoPath-only forms, there is also an `XmlForms` collection object, which is a property of the `Application` class). For your form-based coding needs, this is where you will find most of the functionality of the InfoPath object model.

The `XmlForm` class gives you access to both the form template (controls, views, and data sources) and the form data (the underlying XML data). You also have a host of properties and methods associated with the form.

I'll cover some of the notable and important subordinate classes of the `XmlForm` class.

CurrentView

The `CurrentView` property returns a `View` object that describes . . . the current view of the form. This is how you access most aspects of interacting with the form from code. Managing different views is done through the `ViewInfos` collection (indexed with either the integer index or the `View` name as a string).

So, if you have multiple views, you can iterate through them with the `ViewInfos` collection, and use the `SwitchView()` method of the collection to switch between views. Once you have a specific view, you then use the `CurrentView` property of the `XmlForm` object to get a `View` object and interact with the form.

DataSources, DataConnections, MainDataSource, and QueryDataConnection

There's also a complex relationship between the `DataSources`, `DataConnections`, `MainDataSource`, and `QueryDataConnection` properties of the `XmlForm` class.

The `MainDataSource` property returns a `DataSource` object that refers to the underlying XML data of the form itself. So, while you can get all the data sources for a form template through the `DataSources` property, the `MainDataSource` property returns the `DataSource` for the form data directly.

Similarly, the `QueryDataConnection` property returns a `DataConnection` object that refers to the primary data connection used by the form (if it has one).

Errors

The `Errors` property returns a collection of `FormError` objects. The `FormError` class reflects data validation errors associated with the nodes in the underlying XML of the form. There are three types of data validation errors that a `FormError` object can indicate; the type can be determined from the `FormErrorType` property of the object.

The three types of errors are as follows:

- `SchemaValidation`: The form generated an error based on a schema requirement (data type is the most notable example).

- `SystemGenerated`: The form generated an error based on custom rules, validation, or custom code using the `ReportError()` method of the `XmlValidatingArgs` class.

- `UserDefined`: An error was created in code using the `FormErrorsCollection.Add()` method.

SignedDataBlocks

This property returns a collection of `SignedDataBlock` objects if a form has any. (If the form has no blocks set up for digital signatures, the collection is empty.) All the properties on the `SignedDataBlock` class are read-only, and the only method is the `Sign()` method, which invokes the UI for signing the data block.

Permission

The `Permission` class is for managing user permissions associated with the form. If the Windows Rights Management client is not installed or available, accessing this property raises an exception. The permission class gives you access to the rights management permissions set on the form, including policy information and rights by user.

XPathNavigator

In InfoPath 2003, you had to navigate the data sources by using the MSXML parser with an XML document and navigating nodes. In InfoPath 2007, you access the various parts of the data source and template using the XPathNavigator class (from the System.Xml.Xpath namespace), which provides a cursor-based model for navigating and editing the XML structures in an InfoPath form template.

You start by instantiating an XPathNavigator object, which you can create from any data source using the CreateNavigator() method. This method takes no arguments—it simply returns XPathNavigator for the data source. You can then use the XPathNavigator object to select various elements using a wealth of "move to" methods. The following list describes these methods:

- MoveToAttribute: Moves to the indicated attribute of the current element.

- MoveToChild: Moves the XPathNavigator to the child element indicated. You can designate the target element either with an element name and URI, or by indicating an XPathNodeType (attribute, comment, element, etc).

- MoveToFirst: Moves to the first sibling element of the current element (similar to resetting to the top of the current tree).

- MoveToFirstAttribute: Moves the XPathNavigator to the first attribute of the currently selected element (if the element has no attributes, it returns false and the position of the XPathNavigator isn't affected).

- MoveToFirstChild: Moves the XPathNavigator to the first child element of the currently selected element.

- MoveToFirstNamespace: Moves the XPathNavigator to the first namespace element of the current element.

- MoveToNext: Moves the XPathNavigator to the next sibling element of the current selection.

- MoveToNextAttribute: Moves the selector to the next attribute.

- MoveToNextNamespace: Moves to the next namespace.

- MoveToParent: Moves the XPathNavigator to the parent of the current element.

- MoveToPrevious: Moves to the previous sibling of the current element.

- MoveToRoot: Moves the XPathNavigator to the root element of the current document.

Note You must use the MoveToNextNamespace() method to navigate namespaces—MoveToNext() and MoveToPrevious() won't work; they will return false and not affect the location of the XPathNavigator. MoveToParent() will locate the navigator back on the parent element.

Once you've positioned the XPathNavigator where you want it, you can then act on the selected element—get or set the element's value, add an attribute, and determine information about the element (is it a node, is it empty, what is the URI of the element, does it have children, etc).

You can also use the XPathNavigator to select a collection of elements. The methods that provide this will return an XPathNavigator if they will only return a single element (e.g., SelectSingleNode()), or an XPathNodeIterator if the operation will return a collection of elements (e.g., SelectNodes()).

Once you have an XPathNodeIterator, you can navigate it just like any collection, or iterate through the members of its collection.

InfoPath Form Events

Most of your work in InfoPath code is going to be event-driven. Of course, you can do anything you want in managed code—fire off threads, manipulate images with GDI+, instantiate and load Windows forms, and so on. However, you will generally be working in event handlers, and the main way you'll access the code is by creating and attaching an event handler to an event. The following list describes the events available in the InfoPath object model.

■**Note** Not all events are supported in InfoPath Forms Services—the events supported in browser-compatible forms are indicated with an asterisk. In addition, if a form template is designed for rich and thin client forms, the rich client–only events won't be available, even in a "rich client–only" view.

■**Tip** When working with InfoPath in a VSTO solution (inside Visual Studio), the form level events are listed on the Insert menu.

- *Changed event**: Runs after a user changes the value in a control bound to a field (i.e., the value in the control has changed *and* the value in the underlying field has changed). Runs after the Validating event.

- *Changing event*: Runs after a user changes the value in a control bound to a field, but before the change has been committed to the underlying field. Runs before the Validating event.

- *Clicked event**: Runs when the user clicks a button.

- *Context Changed event*: Runs when the user changes their selection in the form. (The best use of this is to change the task pane to provide context-sensitive help.) This is a form-level event.

- *Loading event**: Runs when the form is first loaded.

- *Merge event*: Runs when the user merges a number of form data files. (Useful for providing some kind of final status—forms merged successfully, log details, etc.)

- *Save event*: Runs when the user selects to save the form.

- *Sign event*: Runs when the user selects to sign the form, but before the form has been completely signed. This gives you the opportunity to, for example, add some additional data to the form signature package (a valid time, additional certifying info, etc.).

- *Submit event**: Runs when the user submits the form. Note that this code will only run if the option for submitting a form has "Perform custom action using Code" selected. This code can cancel the actual Submit event by setting the `Cancel` property of `SubmitEventArgs.CancelableArgs` to `true`.

- *View Switched event**: Runs after the view of a form template has been successfully switched.

- *Validating event**: Runs after the value of the underlying XML document has been changed, but before the Changed event runs. Use this event to provide some custom validation or advanced validation and reporting.

- *Version Upgrade event*: Runs when the version number of the form data being opened is older than the version number of the currently installed form template. This event is available in case you need to provide some form of custom action to migrate data from an older form into a new form template data source.

Manipulating the Form

One of the first things you'll need code for is manipulating the controls on a form—handling optional sections, adding to a repeating section or table, dynamically working with choice groups, and so on.

Once again, remember that the form template is actually a representation of the underlying schema, so you will be restricted to what the underlying schema dictates—if a repeating node has a `maxoccurs` attribute of `1`, you won't be able to add more than one element to the node. Also be mindful of data types and when the `xsi:nil` attribute is in play.

DEALING WITH XSI:NIL ATTRIBUTES

Often when you try to set a value on a field, you will get a schema validation error. It's most likely that the element has the `nil` attribute set. Several value types (actually just about every value type with the exception of strings) use `nil` to indicate "no value"—for example, dates, whole numbers, decimals, and so on.

To set the value of an element, you first have to remove the `nil` attribute. The most efficient way to do this is to attempt to select the `nil` attribute, and if successful, delete it:

```
if (node.MoveToAttribute("nil", ➥
    "http://www.w3.org/2001/XMLSchema-instance"))
        node.DeleteSelf();
```

You can use this code in a function and simply call the function on the element you need to remove a `nil` attribute from. Once you've removed the attribute, you will be able to set the value of the element as needed.

The key to manipulating the InfoPath form template is the ExecuteAction() method. This enables you to act on the user interface elements of form components in various ways, such as inserting an optional section, adding instances to repeating sections, and so on.

■**Tip** Be very careful when coding the ExecuteAction() method—if you try to run an action that isn't possible (e.g., inserting an optional section that's already in the form or removing one that isn't there), then you will get various exceptions depending on the action. The key is to test the status of the control you intend to act on to ensure it's in an appropriate state for the action.

The ExecuteAction() method takes two arguments:

- ActionType: An enum type indicating what action to execute. For optional sections, you'll use either XOptionalInsert or XOptionalRemove.

- xmlToEdit: The control to act on. Note that there's a special control name you have to use for this argument—the property tag is displayed on the Advanced tab of the control's properties dialog as the "XmlToEdit for xOptional" (see Figure 9-5).

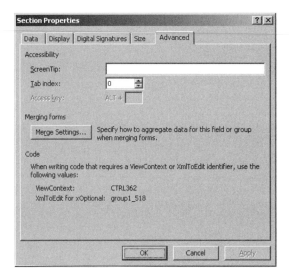

Figure 9-5. *The Advanced tab of the Section Properties dialog for an optional section*

Optional Sections

Optional sections may or may not be included in the form template by default, depending on the property you set in the section's options. However, you may want to insert or remove the optional section based on some conditions in the form (e.g., requiring additional information if a travel claim is over $500 total). While you can *hide* sections of a form template based on form values (using conditional formatting), hiding an optional section does not remove the section elements from the form data's XML, which may cause validation problems. It is likely in this case that you actually want to remove or insert the optional section, which you can't accomplish with the standard designer interface—you need to write either Jscript or managed code.

Exercise 9-1 will walk you through adding a data-driven optional section to a form.

Exercise 9-1. A Data-Driven Optional Section

1. Open the Expense Report sample in design mode.

2. Under the Itemized Expenses table, insert an optional section control.

3. Insert a text box control in the optional control; your form should look like Figure 9-6.

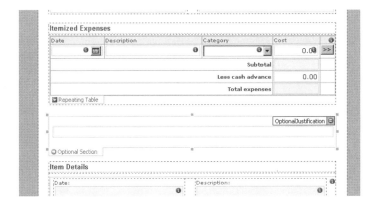

Figure 9-6. *Adding an optional section to the Expense Report sample form*

4. Select the style of managed code. Open the Form Options dialog (Tools ➤ Form Options).

5. Select the Programming tab.

6. Under "Programming language," you can select the language to be used for the form template project. If you've already created some code or opened VSTA, then this selection will be grayed out. You can change the language by clicking the Remove Code button, which will delete all the code in the project.

■**Caution** When you click the Remove Code button, all code in the form template will be deleted. You will not be prompted to save it.

---

7. Now select the Compatibility tab. Since `ExecuteAction()` isn't part of the object model under Forms Services, ensure that "Design a form template that can be opened in a browser or InfoPath" isn't checked.

8. Click OK to close the Form Options dialog.

9. Now you're going to set the optional section to appear when the total expenses are greater than $500, and go away if they're less than $500. Right-click the text box next to "Total expenses," and select Programming ➤ Changed Event.

10. This will open VSTA with a new event handler titled total_Changed.

11. Enter the code shown in Listing 9-1.

Listing 9-1. *Code for the total_Changed Event*

```
try
{
    string newValue = e.NewValue;
    decimal total = decimal.Parse(newValue);

    XPathNodeIterator optSect= MainDataSource.CreateNavigator() ➡
.Select("/my:expenseReport/my:OptionalJustification", NamespaceManager);

    if (total>=500 && optSect.Count==0)
    {
        this.CurrentView.ExecuteAction(ActionType.XOptionalInsert, ➡
            "group1_518");
    }

    if(total<500 && optSect.Count>0)
    {
        XPathNavigator node = MainDataSource.CreateNavigator() ➡
.SelectSingleNode("/my:expenseReport/my:OptionalJustification", ➡
NamespaceManager);
        CurrentView.SelectNodes(node, node, "CTRL362");
        CurrentView.ExecuteAction(ActionType.XOptionalRemove, ➡
            "group1_518");
    }
}
catch (NullReferenceException)
{
    //eat the "no currentview" exception
}
```

12. That's it—you can run the form from VSTA or preview it from InfoPath. If you enter a value greater than or equal to 500 in an expense item, the optional section will show up. Change the value to less than 500 and the optional section will be removed.

Let's review the code from the exercise to understand what it does.

First, since the Total field has a default value, it will fire the Changed event when the form is loaded. As the view hasn't finished loading at this point, you'll get a NullReferenceException on the call to the CurrentView, so you can wrap the whole thing in a try block and catch the exception.

```
string newValue = e.NewValue;
decimal total = decimal.Parse(newValue);
```

The e variable is an instance of the XmlEventArgs class. This class has a number of proper-ties relating to the element that prompted the event to fire:

- Match: Returns the XPath expression for the element that is currently being changed.

- NewValue: The value the element is being changed to.

- OldParent: Returns an XPathNavigator object for the parent of the elements being deleted.

- OldValue: The value of the element prior to the current change.

- Operation: Returns an XmlOperation enum type (Delete, Insert, None, and ValueChange), which indicates what type of change is being performed on the element.

- Site: Returns an XPathNavigator object pointing to the element being changed.

- UndoRedo: Returns a Boolean value that indicates if the current operation is part of an undo or redo operation.

So, you use the NewValue property to get the value that the total element is being changed to, and then you parse it to a decimal so that you can do the comparison to 500. In this case, you are relying on the InfoPath form template's data type specification to ensure that the value in NewValue is a decimal. Depending on how you use the form template, you may want to go with a "belt and suspenders" approach and add type checking to the NewValue property.

```
XPathNodeIterator optSect= MainDataSource.CreateNavigator() ➥
.Select("/my:expenseReport/my:OptionalJustification", NamespaceManager);
```

In the preceding line of code, you're selecting the optional section element in a way that won't fail in the event it's not there.

```
if (total>=500 && optSect.Count==0)
{
    this.CurrentView.ExecuteAction(ActionType.XOptionalInsert, "group1_518");
}
```

This group of code tests whether the value of the total is greater than or equal to 500. In addition, you test if the optional section is in the form template. If the optional section is already in place (count>0), then the if/then won't run (trying to insert the optional section if it's already in place will throw an error).

If the value is greater than or equal to 500 and the optional section isn't already in the form template, then you need to insert it. This is where the ExecuteAction line comes into play. You run ExecuteAction with the ActionType enumeration to insert an optional section. The second argument is the xmlToEdit—which control to act on. Again, I'll remind you that this tag comes from the Advanced tab of the control properties.

```
if(total<500 && optSect.Count>0)
{
    XPathNavigator node = MainDataSource.CreateNavigator() ➥
.SelectSingleNode("/my:expenseReport/my:OptionalJustification", NamespaceManager);
```

```
    CurrentView.SelectNodes(node, node, "CTRL362");
    CurrentView.ExecuteAction(ActionType.XOptionalRemove, "group1_518");
}
```

This final block of code is wrapped in the logical inverse of the first if/then. If the total is less than 500 *and* the optional section is in the form template (count>0), then insert it. The first two lines inside the block instantiate an XPathNavigator and use it to select the optional section in the form template. (Note that the SelectNodes() method uses the ViewContext tag for the optional section from the Advanced tab of the Section Properties dialog.)

The final line in the block runs the ExecuteAction() method, this time with the XOptionalRemove property of the ActionType enumerator.

Repeating Sections/Tables

With repeating sections or tables, there are some different options:

- XCollectionInsert: Inserts an element of the current collection at the end of the existing elements.

- XCollectionInsertAfter: Inserts an element of the current collection after the location of the current selection. If the current selection isn't within the indicated collection, an exception is thrown.

- XCollectionInsertBefore: Inserts an element of the current collection before the location of the current selection. If the current selection isn't within the indicated collection, an exception is thrown.

- XCollectionRefreshFilter: Refreshes the filtered view of the current collection (necessary if the filter criteria or the collection items change).

- XCollectionRemove: Removes the currently selected item from the collection.

- XCollectionRemoveAll: Removes all items in the current collection.

Note that the xmlToEdit argument requires the xmlToEdit tag from the Advanced tab of the Properties dialog of the repeating control you want to work with. If you want to execute an action depending on the selection of a specific item (XCollectionInsertBefore, XCollectionInsertAfter, XCollectionRemove, etc.), then you have to select a control to act on:

```
XPathNavigator node = MainDataSource.CreateNavigator() ➥
.SelectSingleNode("/my:expenseReport/my:group5/my:group6", NamespaceManager);
CurrentView.SelectNodes(node, node, "CTRL373");
```

File Attachments

The ExecuteAction()method also provides methods for interacting with a file attachment control:

- XFileAttachmentAttach: This will open the Attach File dialog box, prompting the user to select a file on their system to attach to the control.

- XFileAttachmentOpen: Opens the file attached to the control, which will execute in accordance with the file associations on the user's system. Note that the file template must be run in full trust for this operation to run.

- XFileAttachmentRemove: Removes the file attached to the control. Note that this removes the file from the control; it does not remove the control!

- XFileAttachmentSaveAs: Opens the Save As file dialog for the file attached to the selected file control.

One important note about the file attachment control is how InfoPath stores the file data within the form data. InfoPath takes the binary data and base64 encodes it, but InfoPath then adds a header to the encrypted chunk. Listing 9-2 shows how to parse the contents of a file attachment control in InfoPath.

Listing 9-2. *Uploading the Contents of a File Attachment Control*

```
string tmpData = xpi.Current.SelectSingleNode("my:ImageFile", ➡
    this.NamespaceManager).Value;

byte[] imgData=Convert.FromBase64String(tmpData);

int fileNameLength = imgData[20]*2;
byte[] fileName   = new byte[fileNameLength];
for (int i = 0; i < fileNameLength; i++)
{
    fileName[i] = imgData[24 + i];
}

char[] asciiName = UnicodeEncoding.Unicode.GetChars(fileName);
string stringName = new string(asciiName);
stringName = stringName.Substring(0, filename.Length - 1);

byte[] binaryFile = new byte[imgData.Length-(24+fileNameLenght)];
for (int i = 0; i < binaryFile.Length; i++)
{
    binaryFile[i] = imgData[24 + namebufferlen + i];
}

imgSvc.Credentials = System.Net.CredentialCache.DefaultCredentials;
imgSvc.Upload(imgLibrary, "", binaryFile, stringName, true);
```

■Note Listing 9-2 requires adding a web reference to the SharePoint imaging web service (`site/_vti_bin/ Imaging.asmx`, where `site` is the specific SharePoint site you want to use), and a reference to `using System.Text` added to the header.

Let's take a look at the first line of code:

```
tmpData = xpi.Current.SelectSingleNode("my:ImageFile", ➥
    this.NamespaceManager).Value;
```

`SelectSingleNode()` selects the file attachment control. Note the call to the `NamespaceManager` property of the current form (`this`). This is required because the reference to the control includes the namespace prefix `my`. After this line, `tmpData` contains the base64-encoded contents of the file.

Let's look at the next line of code:

```
imgData=Convert.FromBase64String(tmpData);
```

This line converts the base64-encoded file to binary. This still isn't the file—there is a header prepended to the beginning to define the file. Part of the file attachment header is the length of the embedded file name; this next line of code retrieves that length data from the binary data:

```
int fileNameLength = imgData[20]*2;
```

The next line pulls the file name from the binary file data into a binary variable, which is then converted to ASCII for the purpose of this code:

```
byte[] fileName  = new byte[fileNameLength];
```

This next section of code loops through the byte data to pull the file name into the byte array you created to hold the file name:

```
for (int i = 0; i < fileNameLength; i++)
{
    fileName[i] = imgData[24 + i];
}
```

These next lines of code convert the byte array to ASCII:

```
char[] asciiName = UnicodeEncoding.Unicode.GetChars(fileName);
string stringName = new string(asciiName);
stringName = stringName.Substring(0, filename.Length - 1);
```

The remainder of the byte array data is then looped through to pull it into your file variable:

```
byte[] binaryFile = new byte[imgData.Length-(24+fileNameLength)];
for (int i = 0; i < binaryFile.Length; i++)
{
    binaryFile[i] = imgData[24 + namebufferlen + i];
}
```

The final two lines set the credentials of the SharePoint imaging service and upload your file:

```
imgSvc.Credentials = System.Net.CredentialCache.DefaultCredentials;
imgSvc.Upload(imgLibrary, "", binaryFile, stringName, true);
```

■**Note** See the SharePoint 2007 SDK for more details on the SharePoint web services.

Working with Data Connections

There may be various reasons you want to interact with a data connection from code. You may want to perform an asynchronous submit action when certain conditions are met, or you may want to manipulate the data before submission (perhaps setting it to a different schema or format). Alternatively, you may want to pull some data from the data connection and use it in the form. In any event, let's look at how to write code to interact with a data connection.

One of the tasks a developer will want to perform is to dynamically change the items in a drop-down list with code. How to edit a list may seem perplexing at first—the temptation is to somehow edit the list binding, but it's not possible to change the underlying schema at run time.

The solution is that you need to create a data source for the drop-down list and edit that data source. Create an XML file similar to what you need the data source to look like. You'll need to add two empty nodes—otherwise, InfoPath won't interpret the node as a repeating node, and you won't be able to attach it as a data source for the drop-down list. Then, to manipulate the contents of the list, you simply manipulate the contents of the data source (based on the XML file).

Take a look at Listing 9-3, which pulls a list of image libraries from a SharePoint site and adds them to a drop-down list.

Listing 9-3. *Adding a List of SharePoint Lists to a Drop-Down List*

```
LitwareLists.Lists listService=new LitwareLists.Lists();
listService.Credentials = System.Net.CredentialCache.DefaultCredentials;
XmlNode node = listService.GetListCollection();

XPathNavigator lists=this.DataSources["ListsXML"].CreateNavigator();
lists.MoveToChild("Lists", "");
lists.MoveToChild("List", "");
lists.DeleteSelf();
lists.MoveToChild("List", "");
lists.DeleteSelf();

foreach (XmlNode listNode in node)
{
    if (listNode.Attributes["ServerTemplate"].Value == "109")
    {
        string title = listNode.Attributes["Title"].Value;
```

```
        XmlWriter xw= lists.AppendChild();
        xw.WriteStartElement("List");
        xw.WriteAttributeString("Title", title);
        xw.WriteEndElement();
        xw.Close();
    }
}
```

To work with this code, you will need to add a web reference to the lists web service on a SharePoint site (the URL is *sitename/_vti_bin/Lists.asmx*). You're also going to need a dummy XML file for your drop-down list (Listing 9-4).

■**Note** Again, note that the dummy XML file needs two dummy nodes so that InfoPath will infer a repeating group. If you only put one `List` element, InfoPath will infer it is a single element, and you won't be able to map the drop-down list to it as a data source.

Listing 9-4. *A Skeleton XML File for a Data-Driven Drop-Down List*

```
<?xml version="1.0" encoding="utf-8" ?>
<Lists>
    <List Title="" Type="" />
    <List Title="" Type="" />
</Lists>
```

Add the XML file as a data connection to receive data—then you will be able to map the drop-down list to the new data connection.

The first block of code instantiates the object referencing the SharePoint lists web service, sets the credentials for the web service to the current user's credentials, and gets the list of lists from the SharePoint site. The next block of code navigates the XML data source to remove the two empty elements that were added as placeholders.

The `foreach` block manipulates the data source to add any lists from the SharePoint site that are image libraries (`ServerTemplate` type 109). You get the value you need (the `Title` value), and then create an element on the data source and add and set the attributes as necessary. Once you're done updating the data source, you close the `XmlWriter` object you used to update it, and you're done.

Browser-Capable Forms

InfoPath browser-capable forms have a limited object model available. The best news is that the IntelliSense parser keeps track of the compatibility setting of the form, and only provides classes, methods, and properties that are available for the current compatibility setting. For example, the `ExecuteAction()` method is not available in browser-compatible forms, so you won't see it as an option.

Note From a code perspective, an InfoPath form template is "all or nothing." Setting specific views to "InfoPath client only" will not make the InfoPath-only code available.

The best way to think about code behind browser-capable forms is in terms of actions behind the scenes—you have very limited capability to manipulate the form itself.

Also note that forms with managed code will have to be set to Full Trust, and will have to be deployed as administrator-approved form templates using the Office Server Central Administration site. To upload a form template, do the following:

1. Open the SharePoint Central Administration site (Start ➤ All Programs ➤ Microsoft Office Server ➤ SharePoint 3.0 Central Administration).

2. Click the Application Management tab.

3. Under the InfoPath Forms Services section, click "Manage form templates."

4. Click the link for "Upload form template."

5. You'll see the Upload Form Template page (Figure 9-7).

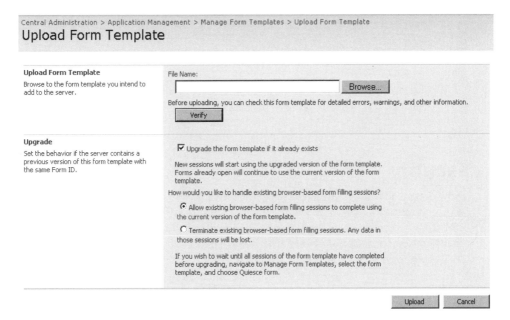

Figure 9-7. *The Upload Form Template page*

6. From this page, you can browse to the template (.xsn) file, verify it, and upload it.

█Note The Upgrade section gives you options on how to deal with overwriting the form template if it already exists on the site. In addition, you have to indicate how to handle the sessions for users that are currently filling out the form in a browser—either terminating their session (they will lose any data they've entered into the form), or allowing them to continue filling in the form, which will be submitted using the current template. A third option (noted at the bottom) is to choose to quiesce the form from the form template library—this will allow users currently filling in the form to finish, but nobody will be allowed to start a new form until the template is released.

---

7. Once you have uploaded the form, you will have to activate the template to a site collection (Figure 9-8).

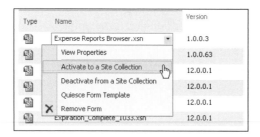

Figure 9-8. *Activating a form template*

8. The form template will now be available as a content type in the site collection you activated the template to—you can add the template as a content type to a form library to fill it out.

Security

If you've worked through the exercises in this book, you've already discovered some of the security implications of working with code behind InfoPath forms. Generally speaking, any InfoPath form that has managed code behind it will need to have the security level set to Full Trust (Tools ➤ Form Options ➤ Security and Trust tab).

Once a form is set to Full Trust, you have some restrictions on how you can work with it. For example, a form set to Full Trust must be installed by an administrator on a SharePoint site. For a form to be published via file share, it will have to be digitally signed or installed with an MSI distribution. In addition, browser-compatible forms cannot use database connections, and if web service connections cross domain boundaries, the form must be fully trusted.

Summary

Now that you've seen what's possible with basic managed code behind an InfoPath form, Chapter 10 will review some of the more advanced capabilities offered by Visual Studio.

CHAPTER 10

■■■

InfoPath Add-Ins and Task Panes

Now that I've covered basic coding with an InfoPath form template, I'm going to discuss two more advanced (and very useful) approaches to writing code: using Visual Studio Tools for Office (VSTO) 2005, Second Edition (SE) to write an add-in for InfoPath, and creating a custom task pane using Visual Studio.

Visual Studio, especially with VSTO 2005 SE, gives developers greater flexibility with InfoPath solutions. Visual Studio Tools for Applications (VSTA) allows you to add code behind an InfoPath form template, but that code is limited to a particular solution. If you want to create a utility or other solution for use across multiple form templates, your best option is to write an InfoPath add-in with VSTO.

VSTO add-ins also give you the ability to create custom task panes. You've seen the task pane InfoPath presents for use in building form templates; with VSTO, you can build your own task panes using Windows Forms custom controls. So you can have the power of using Visual Studio to build your add-ins coupled with the power of the InfoPath form engine (Figure 10-1).

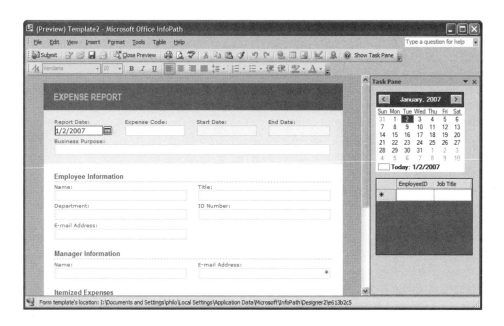

Figure 10-1. *A custom task pane in InfoPath*

I'll also show you how you can host an InfoPath form inside a Windows form (Figure 10-2).

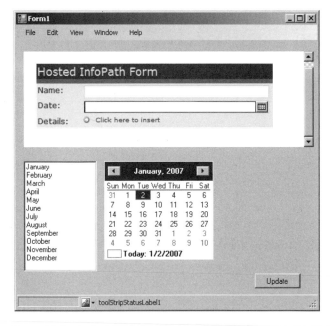

Figure 10-2. *An InfoPath form hosted in a Windows form*

By enabling the InfoPath form engine inside a Windows form control, a developer can allow a power user to work on the form design and encapsulate it inside an application. What's truly great is that with browser-based forms in InfoPath 2007 Forms Services, you can also host browser-based forms inside an ASP.NET web page (Figure 10-3).

This means you can provide the same "design-once" capability to application developers to design their forms. Consider an application that allows filling in and reviewing a large quantity of forms—an application developer can build the Windows Forms application for reviewing the forms internally, a web designer can build the harness for the forms to be posted to a web site, and an InfoPath form designer can build all the forms to be used (just once—the same form template can be used on the web site and the Windows form).

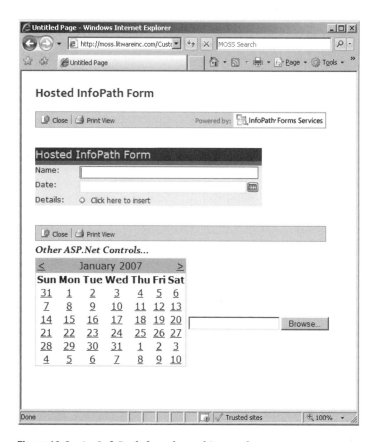

Figure 10-3. *An InfoPath form hosted in a web page*

Writing an InfoPath Add-In

To write an add-in for InfoPath 2007, you need Visual Studio 2005, and you need to download VSTO 2005 SE. After installing VSTO, you will have a number of new projects available in Visual Studio—the ones you're interested in are the InfoPath form template and the InfoPath add-in project.

InfoPath 2003 didn't offer an add-in capability. VSTO 2005 enables the building of COM add-ins for InfoPath 2007, but using COM to build add-ins (especially task panes) requires a lot of code and state management. VSTO 2005 SE provides a much simpler mechanism for creating and displaying custom task panes and interacting with the application.

You might ask when to write an add-in instead of simply writing managed code behind a form template. The simple answer is that you write managed code behind a form template when you need application-specific code for a particular form; you write an add-in when you need general functionality for all your InfoPath solutions.

Some examples of when you might write an add-in are as follows:

- To provide form utilities, such as a "clear all" or a currency converter

- To show the status of a workflow the form is using

- To automate archiving or auditing of form data entry

- To create geographic reference data, schematics, or other advanced visual assistance

Let's take the currency converter as an example—you could write a converter into your form template. However, if you're in a business where currency conversion comes up a lot in filling out forms (e.g., expense reports in various currencies, travel planners to various countries, dealing with client invoices from multiple nations, etc.), then it's probably a good idea to offer a currency converter as an InfoPath add-in so that it's available for all your forms.

Add-ins are code that's available from the host process (InfoPath). But how do you get to the code? In Word 2007, Excel 2007, and PowerPoint 2007, the new ribbon interface provides an easily extensible way of adding functionality to those applications. InfoPath 2007 didn't get the ribbon in this version, so you have to hook the command bar and add a custom button, as well as attach an event to the button so you can hook the event and call your code.

MANAGING ADD-INS: THE TRUST CENTER

InfoPath 2007 has new features that pull together the security and privacy options for the application called the Trust Center (Figure 10-4). This brings together user interfaces for managing digital certificates, add-ins, and InfoPath's privacy options.

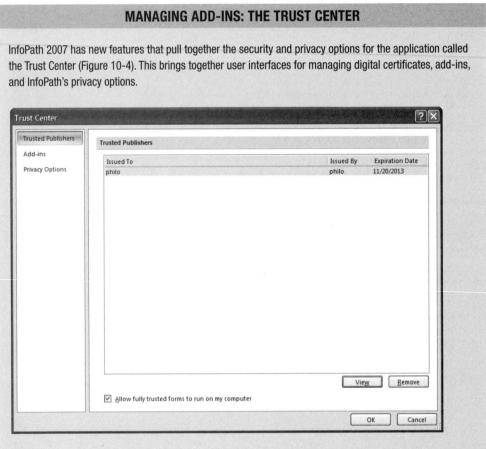

Figure 10-4. *The InfoPath Trust Center*

As you can see from Figure 10-4, the Trusted Publishers tab lists certificates you've installed—these govern the ability to open forms that are fully trusted. From here you can review the certificates you have installed or remove them. Also note the check box at the bottom to grant permission for fully trusted forms to run (if they are signed by a trusted publisher).

What you're more interested in here is the Add-ins manager (Figure 10-5). This lists all the installed add-ins, active, inactive, and disabled. The following list describes each:

- *Active*: The add-in is installed and functional.

- *Inactive*: The add-in has been disabled by the user.

- *Disabled*: The add-in has been disabled by InfoPath (generally after a program exception—disable and reenable an add-in to get it functioning again).

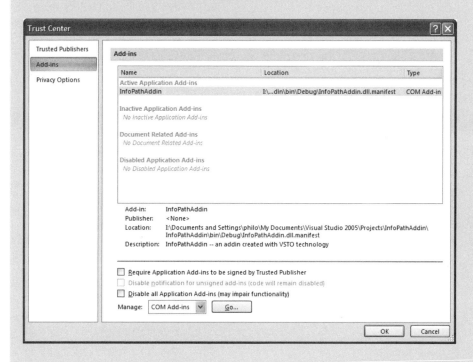

Figure 10-5. *Add-ins in the Trust Center*

Below the add-in list is a details pane that gives information about the add-in: name, publisher, path, and description. Below that are options that apply to all add-ins (requiring that add-ins be signed or disabling all add-ins). The final part of the dialog allows you to actively manage the installed add-ins—to enable or disable them.

When you create a new add-in, the template will add a number of references to the project, including the VSTO runtimes, Office tools, `Windows.Forms`, `System.Drawing`, and `System.XML` assemblies. Like most templates, it also adds a number of `using` statements, two of which are worth pointing out:

```
using InfoPath = Microsoft.Office.Interop.InfoPath;
using Office = Microsoft.Office.Core;
```

The great thing about making the using statement reference is that you can now use IntelliSense to browse the namespaces—just type Office or InfoPath and the dot gives you the pop-up list box to browse what members are available.

The only two members of the add-in class you have to worry about are ThisAddIn_Startup and ThisAddIn_Shutdown—these will be called when the add-in is started and when it shuts down (whether being removed by the user or as a result of the application exiting). Startup is where you can add to the command bars, customize them, instantiate program variables, and so on. Shutdown is where you should observe good behavior and put everything back as you found it (remove toolbar buttons, remove toolbars, etc).

Also created with your add-in project is the setup project you will need to distribute to install your add-in. Note that it's prepopulated with the necessary dependencies and will capture the DLL from your add-in project in the "Primary output from" item. This project will build your add-in to an MSI file in the appropriate directory (indicated in the properties for the project).

Exercise 10-1 will walk you through building a basic InfoPath add-in. The add-in will pop up a Windows form for currency conversion (using a public web service to do the conversion).

Exercise 10-1. Building an InfoPath Add-In

1. Open Visual Studio. Select the InfoPath Add-in project template (Figure 10-6). Name it **PopupConverter**.

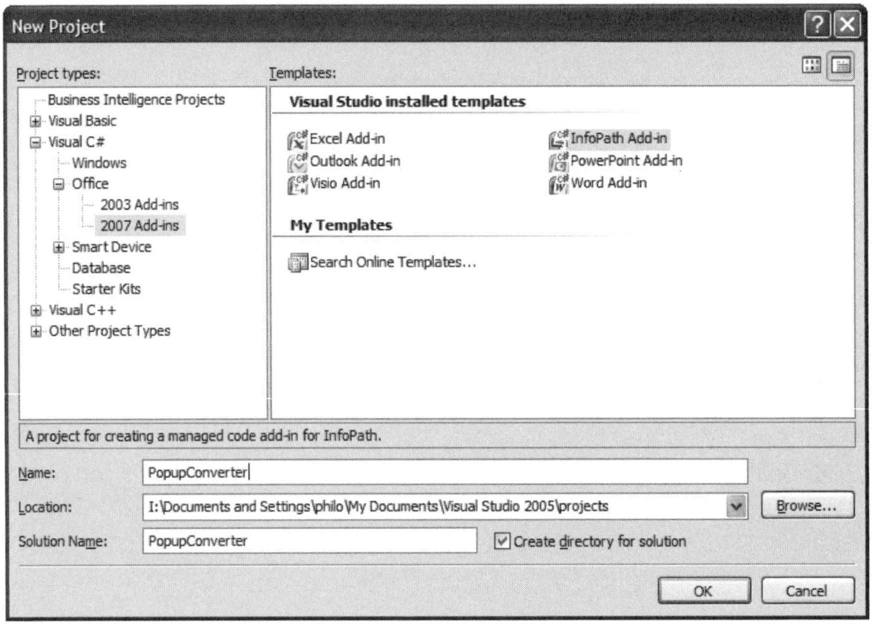

Figure 10-6. *The New Project dialog in Visual Studio 2005*

First you'll add a reference to a web service for currency conversion. There are a lot of ways to get daily changing currency conversion rates—this example is going to use a currency conversion web service. I'm using calcExcRate from `www.webcontinuum.net/webservices/ccydemo.asmx`.

■**Note** This web service is just for demonstration purposes.

---

2. Right-click the project and click Add Web Reference. You'll see the Add Web Reference dialog. Paste your web service URL into the URL box, and then click Go (see Figure 10-7).

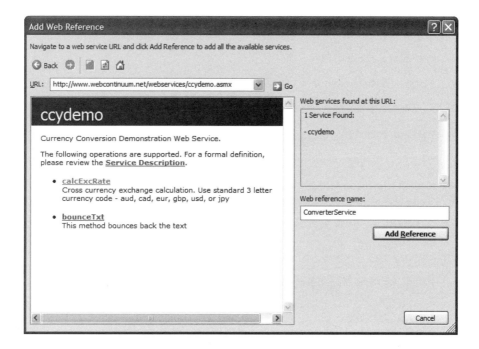

Figure 10-7. *The Add Web Reference dialog*

3. Name the web reference **ConverterService**, and then click Add Reference. Next, you'll lay out the form.

4. Right-click the PopupConverter project, and click Add ➤ Windows Form.

5. Name the form **Converter.cs**, and click OK.

6. Add four labels, two list boxes, two text boxes, and a button to the form. Lay it out similarly to that shown in Figure 10-8.

Figure 10-8. *Laying out the pop-up form*

7. Name the controls as follows:

   • *List box*: **lstFromCurrency**

   • *List box*: **lstToCurrency**

   • *Text box*: **txtFromAmount**

   • *Text box*: **txtToAmount**

I set the items collection for each list box to a simple string list—for a real-world application, you'd definitely want to feed it from a data source. Follow the next two steps for each list box.

8. Click the Items property, and then click the Builder button next to (Collection). The String Collection Editor will open (Figure 10-9).

Figure 10-9. *The String Collection Editor for the list boxes*

9. Enter the list of currency codes and countries as shown in Figure 10-9, and then click OK.

10. Double-click the button to create and attach the click event handler.

11. Add the following code to the event handler:

```
string fromCurrency = (string)lstFromCurrency.SelectedItem;
string toCurrency = (string)lstToCurrency.SelectedItem;

fromCurrency = fromCurrency.Substring(0, 3);
toCurrency = toCurrency.Substring(0, 3);

string fromValue = txtFromAmount.Text;
float sendValue = float.Parse(fromValue);

ConverterService.ccydemo conversionSvc = ➡
    new PopupConverter.ConverterService.ccydemo();
float rtnValue = conversionSvc.calcExcRate(fromCurrency, ➡
    toCurrency, sendValue);

this.txtToAmount.Text = rtnValue.ToString();
```

The code is fairly straightforward—it pulls the currency code from the selected item, instantiates the web service, and calls its exchange rate method. So let's set up the add-in to call it.

12. Open `ThisAddIn.cs`.

First you're going to add your event handler that your plug-in will call. All this code is going to do is instantiate and show your converter form.

13. Add the following code to the `ThisAddIn` class:

```
private void openConverter_Click( ➡
    Office.CommandBarButton src, ref bool Cancel)
{
    Converter converter = new Converter();
    converter.Show();
}
```

14. Now to add your command button—the first thing you have to worry about is the Getting Started dialog—when that is open, there is no `ActiveWindow` object to check for command bars. So you start by checking to see if you have an `ActiveWindow`. Add the following code to the `ThisAddIn_Startup()` method:

```
if (this.Application.ActiveWindow!=null)
{
}
```

15. Next, you get the `CommandBars` object from the `ActiveWindow` object and hook the Standard bar, if it's available. Add the following code inside your `if` block:

```
Office.CommandBars commandBars = Â    .
    (Office.CommandBars)this.Application.ActiveWindow.CommandBars;
Office.CommandBar standardBar = commandBars["Standard"];
```

16. If the Standard command bar isn't open, then the `standardBar` variable will be null, so you test for it. Add the following code after the line instantiating `standardBar`:

```
if (standardBar != null)
{
}
```

17. Now you create your new button from the control collection of the command bar. Add the following code inside the `standardBar` `if` block:

```
Office.CommandBarButton converterButton = ➡
    (Office.CommandBarButton)standardBar.Controls.Add ➡
    (Office.MsoControlType.msoControlButton, ➡
    Type.Missing, Type.Missing, Type.Missing, true);
```

18. Then you set the properties of the command button. Add the following code after the `Controls.Add` line:

```
converterButton.Caption = "Convert";
converterButton.Visible = true;
converterButton.Enabled = true;
converterButton.Style = Office.MsoButtonStyle.msoButtonCaption;
```

19. Finally, you attach the event handler for the command button. Add the following code, and you're done:

```
converterButton.Click += ➡
    new Office._CommandBarButtonEvents_ClickEventHandler ➡
    (openConverter_Click);
```

20. Test the add-in by pressing F5. Visual Studio will compile the project and launch InfoPath.

21. The Getting Started dialog will be showing—double-click any of the forms in Customize a Sample.

22. The form opens in design mode, and you have no add-in. Click the Preview button.

23. You should see the Convert button on the far right side of the toolbar, as shown in Figure 10-10.

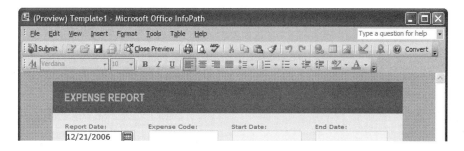

Figure 10-10. *The Convert add-in button on the InfoPath toolbar*

24. Click the button and you should get the conversion form, which you can use to convert currency.

Now that you've built a basic add-in, let's look at how you can use it to add a more complex user interface—a custom task pane.

Creating and Using a Custom Task Pane

With VSTO 2005 SE, InfoPath developers have access to programmable task panes—this gives you a very powerful user interface for your add-ins. In VSTO 2003, action panes had to be built in code—there was no visual designer. VSTO 2005 adds programmable task panes that utilize user controls for building its interface, leveraging the great layout capabilities of Visual Studio's designer.

To create a custom task pane, you design a .NET user control and lay out any controls you want. Once you have the design you need, you use the InfoPath add-in to load the task pane. Since Office standards don't guarantee having a task pane open or closed, the best design is to add a button to the toolbar and use the button event to load the task pane.

You can access the InfoPath form template from the task pane as well use the `Globals.ThisAddIn.Application` object. For the most part, you are probably going to be interacting with the form data, so you probably want to work with the application `ActiveWindow.XDocument.DOM` and go from there using XPath selectors against the DOM.

■**Note** The object model seems incomplete from this approach. I found several odd gaps, and the only real way I could interact with the form was through the DOM.

■**Tip** Be wary when designing your code here. Remember you are designing a form template–agnostic solution, so you cannot rely on having specific namespaces, schemas, or elements in the form. Any code you write will have to be very broadly focused.

Exercise 10-2 demonstrates a simple sample task pane: a find-and-replace add-in.

Exercise 10-2. Find-and-Replace Task Pane

1. Open Visual Studio, and create a new InfoPath add-in project.

2. First you need to add a reference to `Microsoft.Office.Interop.InfoPath.Xml`. Right-click the project, and click Add Reference.

3. On the .NET tab, scroll down to Microsoft.Office.Interop.InfoPath.Xml and double-click it.

4. If that assembly is not in the list, click the Browse tab and browse to `$program files$\Microsoft Office\Office 12`.

5. Find `Microsoft.Office.Interop.InfoPath.Xml.dll` and double-click it.

6. Now you'll add the user control to be used for your task pane. Right-click the project, and click Add ➤ User Control. Name the user control **TaskPane.cs**, and click OK.

7. Add two labels, two text boxes, and a button control to the user control so that it looks something like Figure 10-11.

Figure 10-11. *The user control layout*

8. Name the first textbox **txtFind**, and the second **txtReplace**.

9. Double-click the button to open the button's click event.

10. Add the following code to the click event:

```
string find = txtFind.Text;
string replace = txtReplace.Text;

InfoPath.Application app = Globals.ThisAddIn.Application;
IXMLDOMNodeList nodes = ➥
    app.ActiveWindow.XDocument.DOM. ➥
        documentElement.selectNodes("/descendant::*");

foreach (IXMLDOMNode node in nodes)
{
    if (node.nodeType == DOMNodeType.NODE_ELEMENT)
    {
        if (node.childNodes.length == 1)
        {
            string tmpValue = node.text;
            if (tmpValue.Length > 0)
                node.text = tmpValue.Replace(find, replace);
        }
    }
}
```

Most of this code is fairly straightforward. You get the find and replace values from the text box controls. You then get the application object from the Globals.ThisAddIn object. The following line is of the most interest—you use the DOM to select all the descendant nodes from the parent in the DOM. From there, it's a matter of filtering out the nodes you need and iterating through them to do a replace on each text node.

11. Now that your task pane is ready, you just need to rig the add-in to call it. Open ThisAddIn.cs.

12. Add a global variable for your task pane just after the partial class declaration:

```
private TaskPane tp;
```

13. Use the code from Exercise 10-1 to add a button to the standard command bar.

14. In the button's event handler, you simply need the following code to attach the task pane and show it:

```
tp = new TaskPane();
CustomTaskPanes.Add(tp, "Task Pane");
CustomTaskPanes[0].Visible = true;
```

15. Now if you run your solution, InfoPath should open to the Getting Started dialog.

16. Double-click a sample, and then preview the form template.

17. You should see the button for your task pane—click it to show the task pane (Figure 10-12).

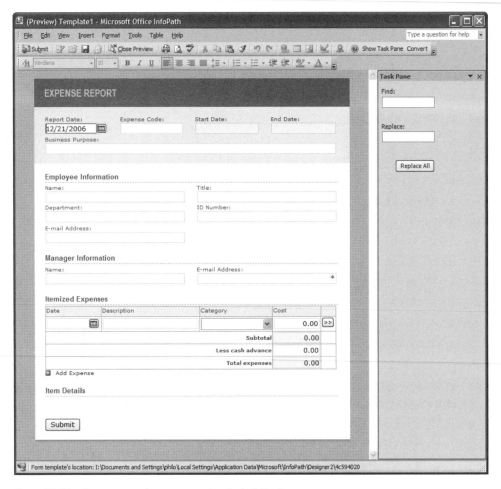

Figure 10-12. *A custom task pane running in InfoPath*

Those are the basics of InfoPath add-ins. Obviously, you can get much more complex, both in the program code in the add-in and how you manipulate the InfoPath form template. Just remember that if you want a solution for a *specific* form, the code should probably be in that form template. Add-ins work across form solutions, and need to be form template–agnostic.

Hosting InfoPath Forms

A common request with InfoPath 2003 was to be able to use the InfoPath designer and InfoPath form templates in custom .NET solutions. InfoPath 2007 answers these requests; it introduces controls that developers can use on a Windows form designer or an ASP.NET form designer to load an InfoPath form template into their applications at run time.

There are a number of benefits to hosting InfoPath forms in your own applications:

- Reusing existing InfoPath form templates

- Having non-developers design your form interfaces using InfoPath's powerful design interface

- Designing a form once, after which it can be used in the InfoPath client, on the Web, in your application, or on a custom web page

The key to hosting InfoPath forms in Visual Studio designers is the availability of new controls to host the forms.

Hosting an InfoPath Form in a Windows Form

To host an InfoPath form in a Windows application (Figure 10-13), you simply need to use the InfoPath FormControl control. This control renders empty during design time—at run time, you use the NewFromFormTemplate() or Open() methods to populate the control with a form.

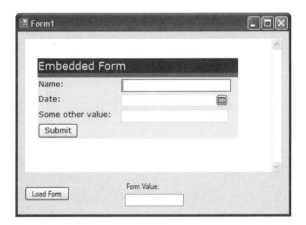

Figure 10-13. *A Windows application with an embedded InfoPath form*

You can interact with the embedded form by accessing the XmlForm object through the form control—this gives you access to both the underlying data and a thorough collection of IOLECommand objects to automate the form application itself. In addition, by implementing the ISubmitToHostEventHandler interface, you can catch when a user submits data to the host environment from the form template.

Exercise 10-3 shows you how to build an interactive embedded form.

Exercise 10-3. Hosting an InfoPath Form in a Windows Application

First, you'll design an InfoPath form to embed.

1. Open InfoPath, and design a form template based on a blank form.

2. Lay out a form similar to the embedded form in Figure 10-13.

3. Right-click the Submit button, and select Button Properties.

4. Click the Rules button.

5. Click Add.

6. Click the Add Action button.

7. Under Action, select "Submit using a data connection."

8. Click the Add button next to "Data connection."

9. Ensure that "Create a new connection to" and "Submit data" are selected. Click Next.

10. Select "To the hosting environment." Click Next.

11. Click Finish. Close all remaining open dialogs.

12. Publish the form (File ➤ Publish). Select "To a network location."

13. Select a location on your local system that will be easy to remember (such as `C:\temp\ embeddedform.xsn`).

14. Finish the publishing wizard. Close InfoPath.

15. Open Visual Studio 2005. Create a new Windows application.

16. Now you need the InfoPath FormControl control. Odds are it's not in your toolbox. If it isn't, right-click the toolbox and select Choose Items.

17. If the FormControl control is not listed on the .NET Framework Components tab, click Browse.

18. Browse to `%program files%\Microsoft Office\Office12\`.

19. Find `Microsoft.Office.InfoPath.FormControl.dll` and double-click it.

20. Click OK in the Choose Toolbox Items dialog.

21. Drag the FormControl control to the Windows form.

22. Add a button, label, and text box control, similar to the layout in Figure 10-14.

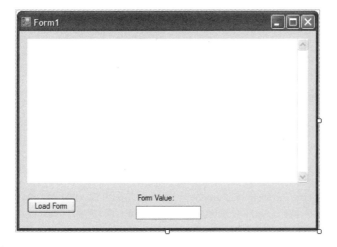

Figure 10-14. *The Windows form you'll load the InfoPath form into*

23. Double-click the Load Form button to open the click event handler.

24. In the event handler, add the following line of code, using the location of your InfoPath form template:

```
formControl1.NewFromFormTemplate(@"c:\temp\embeddedform.xsn");
```

25. Now you'll wire the form to accept the Submit event from the embedded form. Add the following after the partial class declaration to add the interface to your form:

```
Microsoft.Office.Interop.InfoPath.ISubmitToHostEventHandler
```

26. Right-click the interface and select "Implement interface" to add the SubmitToHostEventHandler handler to your code.

27. Add the following line to the Form_Load event (double-click the form surface to generate the event handler if you don't have a Form_Load event):

```
formControl1.SetSubmitToHostEventHandler(this);
```

28. Add the following using statements to the top of the class module:

```
using System.Xml;
using System.Xml.XPath;
using Microsoft.Office.InfoPath;
```

29. Finally, add your code to handle the Submit event in the Windows form:

```
XPathNavigator xnav= formControl1.XmlForm.MainDataSource.CreateNavigator();

xnav = xnav.SelectSingleNode("/my:myFields/my:SomeOtherValue", ➥
    formControl1.XmlForm.NamespaceManager);
```

```
textBox1.Text = xnav.InnerXml;

errorMessage = "";

return 1;
```

Most of this should look fairly familiar after Chapter 9. An `XmlNavigator` is created from the `XmlForm` object of the form control. Then, a node is selected based on the navigator. Note the `NamespaceManager` as the second argument of the `SelectSingleNode()` method—this resolves the "my" namespace references.

Then, the text box control is set to hold the inner XML value. The `errorMessage` return value is set to an empty string and returns a success value of `1`.

30. That wraps it up—you can use the same XPathNavigator methods to push data into the form. Run the application—you should be able to click the button to load the InfoPath form, and then put a value in the form and submit it to populate the text box control on the Windows form.

Hosting an InfoPath Form in an ASP.NET Form

Hosting an InfoPath form in a custom ASP.NET form is somewhat different in that you don't quite have the simple freedom you do with your Windows application. With an ASP.NET form, the ASP.NET page must be hosted on the same IIS server that InfoPath Forms Services is available on. InfoPath offers the XmlFormView control for ASP.NET pages to host InfoPath form templates.

Note You can only have one XmlFormView control on an ASP.NET page.

There is a thorough walkthrough of how to work with a hosted InfoPath form control on MSDN at `http://msdn2.microsoft.com/en-us/library/aa701078.aspx`.

Summary

You've broadened your horizons here somewhat, exploring template-agnostic InfoPath add-ins, task panes, and hosting InfoPath form templates in your own applications. There is one more area to cover, and it's the most powerful aspect of Microsoft Office SharePoint Server 2007: workflow.

CHAPTER 11

■ ■ ■

Workflow

One of the most exciting new features in Microsoft Office SharePoint Server 2007 is the integration of Windows Workflow Foundation (WF). By building WF into SharePoint at the framework level, human workflow is available and seamlessly integrated into a powerful collaboration engine.

InfoPath plays into this workflow scenario in two ways: First of all, many aspects of the workflow interface leverage InfoPath for their interface. Second, the workflow capabilities are available to SharePoint form libraries so that users can leverage the workflow for forms applications.

Note that WF is not an engine in and of itself—it is only a framework. To actually have a running workflow, you need to have a host. Generally in WF solutions, providing a host is part of the problem—it's about building workflow into your server application, web application, business process management, or other solution. While you can use InfoPath with WF in a custom workflow host, I'm going to focus on using SharePoint as the workflow host process. I covered implementing an "out of the box" workflow for an InfoPath form library in Chapter 6; here, you're going to look more in-depth at two other aspects of InfoPath interacting with WF:

- Building a custom workflow using SharePoint Designer for handling InfoPath forms

- Building a custom workflow using Visual Studio with custom InfoPath forms for the workflow interface

But first, let's learn more about WF itself.

Windows Workflow Foundation (WF)

A great aspect of SharePoint workflow is that there is a continuous spectrum of capability vs. implementation complexity. At one end is the "out of the box" capability of SharePoint workflow—basic routing and approval systems to cover a lot of routine scenarios with no modification necessary. At the other end is the full capability of WF—managed code that can leverage all aspects of the .NET framework (web services, threading, database access, GDI+, XML management, etc.).

WF provides a number of standard component concepts and interfaces to make building workflows across Microsoft platforms a standard process. Whereas before you had any number of chunks of custom code built to manage work processes, human interaction, human/machine interaction, and routing, now you can use a standard framework of components to create these processes and workflows in a way that maximizes interoperability.

The components that make up WF include the following:

- *Activity*: The basic functional units in WF, these are the building blocks of workflows, and standardization of their interfaces is what makes WF so powerful. Activities are meant to be functional representations of human actions, so they can be anything from simple tasks such as "set a value" or "send an e-mail" to very involved, complex tasks such as adjusting values in a mainframe database or running a piece of machinery.

- *Workflow*: A workflow is simply a collection of activities connected together with values and options to implement a complete business process.

- *Windows Workflow Foundation Runtime Engine*: This is the framework responsible for providing the semantic operation of a workflow. This operates as the interpretive layer between the workflow and the host process.

- *Host process*: This is a Windows application that is responsible for executing the WF engine and its workflows.

I already mentioned the host process. WF is a framework just as .NET is a framework— just as you cannot leverage the .NET Framework without something to "run it on" (whether it be a console application, a Windows Forms app, an ASP.NET process, or another host)—you need to have something to run the workflow. The host process needs to be able to manage workflows—instantiate the proper workflows when necessary, persist their state and unload them if necessary, handle transactions, and perform other functions. As you have SharePoint at your disposal, I won't mention the host process again.

Activities are the core concept in WF. There are a number of activities that are packaged with WF (called the *base activity library*). These include activities such as WebServiceInput and WebServiceOutput for interacting with web services, IfElse for switching, While for looping, Delay for pausing a workflow for a specific period of time, and Listen for pausing the workflow until externally triggered. You can also install packages of activities from other sources (a collection of SharePoint WF activities will be covered later in the chapter), and you can design your own custom activities in Visual Studio (which is outside the scope of this book).

Once you have a library of activities, you'll want to hook them together in some fashion. There are two fundamental ways to create a workflow: with markup (in a workflow-oriented XML syntax called XAML) or with managed code. With markup, the workflow is statically defined through the XML rendered in the markup file. With managed code, the code creates the workflow dynamically in the workflow constructor, so the workflow can change based on specific circumstances.

There is a third, hybrid way of creating a workflow, in which XAML files define the workflow and "code-beside" is used to define any extra logic necessary for the workflow implementation (this is the method you'll use later to create a custom workflow in Visual Studio).

Now let's take a look at using SharePoint Designer to implement a basic custom workflow.

SharePoint Designer and Workflow

Microsoft Office SharePoint Server 2007 offers several ad hoc workflows that you can attach to lists and libraries. However, what if you need something a little more specific? As I noted earlier, it is possible to build a custom workflow in managed code using Visual Studio. However, if you consider an enterprise implementation, this puts the site administrator in the position of having to review a lot of fairly complex code that people will want to run on the site's server. Luckily, there's another option: SharePoint Designer (see Figure 11-1).

■**Note** SharePoint Designer grew out of the FrontPage family of products. FrontPage 2003 was actually a very powerful tool for editing SharePoint sites, in addition to its web design capabilities. With the 2007 versions, the SharePoint editing capabilities have been split off into a wholly separate product: SharePoint Designer 2007.

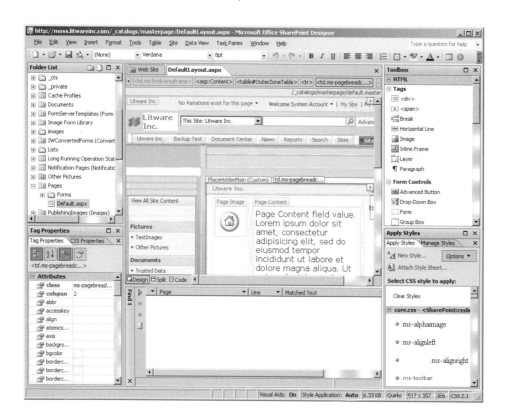

Figure 11-1. *SharePoint Designer*

Why should you care about SharePoint Designer? Well, if you'll recall, one of the options for composing workflows is using XAML—this takes defined activities, assembles them into a workflow, sets values where necessary, and so on. Most importantly, it makes it easy to create a visual designer for workflows, one of which is incorporated into SharePoint Designer (Figure 11-2).

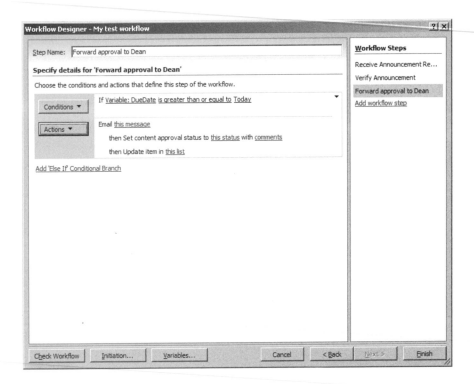

Figure 11-2. *Workflow design in SharePoint Designer*

Designing workflows in SharePoint Designer has a number of advantages and drawbacks. The advantages include the following:

- The interface is very straightforward to use. If a user can create rules in Outlook, they can use this designer.

- Workflows can run on Windows SharePoint Services or Microsoft Office SharePoint Services.

- Because only standard and approved activities are listed, there is a minimal security risk regarding deploying workflows.

- The workflow capabilities are fairly robust, including the ability to look up items in other lists or prompt the user for values.

The drawbacks, however, include the following:

- The forms capabilities are limited to basic ASP.NET forms automatically generated to capture user input.

- There are no advanced code capabilities.

- Workflows are attached to a specific list or library—you cannot reuse them.

- Workflows are static—they cannot change based on contextual requirements.

■**Note** SharePoint Designer is a separate product from the Microsoft Office suite, so you may not have it installed. It is available for online trial at `http://office.microsoft.com/sharepointdesigner/` or through your MSDN subscription.

Despite the drawbacks, this is still a powerful way to make a custom workflow available via SharePoint, and if it meets the needs of the organization, there's no need to build a workflow in Visual Studio. Let's walk through a basic scenario for building a workflow in SharePoint Designer (and a reminder—the importance to InfoPath is that you can attach these workflows to an InfoPath form library, not that you can use InfoPath forms in the workflow).

Exercise 11-1 shows you how to take the Expense Report sample form and build a workflow based on it to set up an approval process embodying the following rules:

- The finance department must be notified of all expense reports for which the total is greater than $1,000.00.

- Expense reports less than $100.00 are automatically approved.

- All other expense reports go to the manager for approval.

Exercise 11-1. Implementing a SharePoint Workflow

1. Open InfoPath, and under Customize a Sample, select the Expense Report sample.

2. Publish the Expense Report form to a SharePoint site, promoting the fields for Start Date, End Date, Department, Manager Email Address, and Total.

3. Open the form library you published the expense report to.

4. You need a column to store the status of your form—click "Settings," and then click "Create Column."

5. On the Create Column page, enter **Status** for the Column name, and **Choice** for the type of information.

6. For the choices, enter **Submitted**, **Rejected**, **Approved by Manager**, and **Approved**.

7. Click OK.

8. Open SharePoint Designer.

9. Click File ➤ Open Site.

10. In the Open Site dialog, enter the URL for the site you want to open. You must include the `http://`, but not the `default.aspx` at the end (see Figure 11-3).

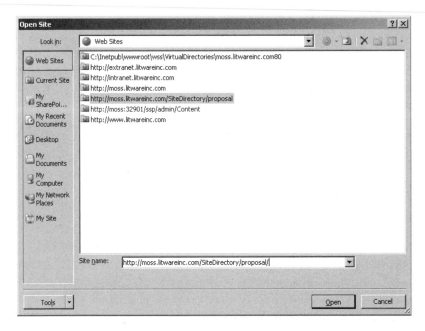

Figure 11-3. *The Open Site dialog in SharePoint Designer*

11. Click Open.

12. Click File ➤ New ➤ Workflow to open the Workflow Designer (Figure 11-4).

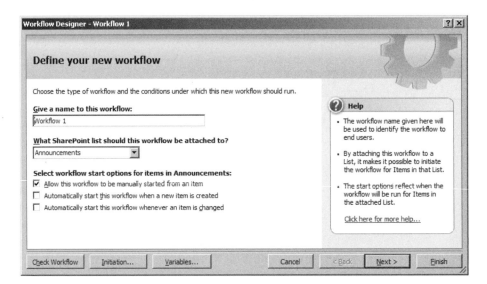

Figure 11-4. *Starting the Workflow Designer*

13. Enter **ExpenseReptWF** for the name (Figure 11-4 shows Workflow 1 as the default name).

14. Select the form library you published the Expense Report form template to.

15. Click Next; and you'll see the Workflow Designer step editor (Figure 11-5).

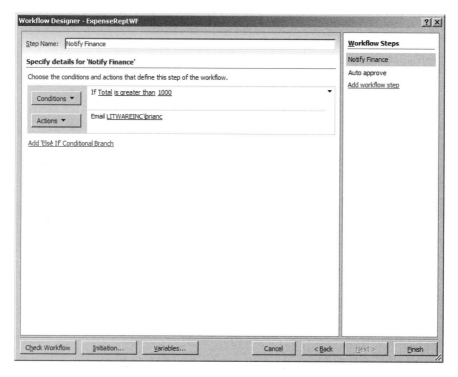

Figure 11-5. *The Workflow Designer step editor*

16. Name this step **Notify Finance**.

17. Click the Conditions button and select "Compare Expense Reports field"—this will insert the boilerplate rule text "if field equals value."

18. Click "field" and select Total.

19. Click "equals" and select "is greater than."

20. Click "value," and type **1000** into the text box. You're done with the condition.

21. Click the Actions button, and select "Send an email"—this will insert the "Send this email" boilerplate text.

22. Click "this email" to open the e-mail editor (Figure 11-6).

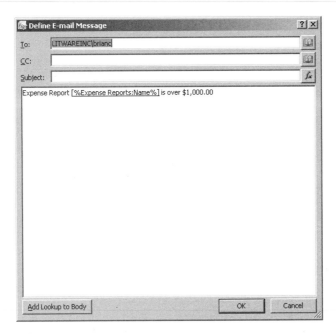

Figure 11-6. *The Workflow Designer e-mail editor*

23. Address the e-mail as necessary, and add some text in the body area. Note that you can use the Add Lookup to Body button at the bottom of the form to insert tokens for values from the current workflow item.

24. Click OK.

25. This finishes this step. Click "Add workflow step" in the right-hand pane to add the next step.

26. Rename step 2 to **Auto Approve**.

27. For the condition, select "Compare Expense Reports field."

28. Set the condition to be "If Total is less than 100."

29. Select the Set Field in Current Item action, and change it to Set Status to Approved.

30. Click the Add 'Else If' Conditional Branch link.

31. Leave the condition blank; add an action to e-mail the submitter's manager.

32. Add the Wait for Field Change in Current Item action and change it to Wait for Status to Equal Approved by Manager. (Note that the value gives you a drop-down list populated with the choices you entered in the custom column.)

33. Click the Finish button. If everything went well, your workflow will be published to the site.

If you fill out a form and add it to the site, select Workflows from the item's context menu and you will see your ExpenseReptWF workflow here, ready to be started. That's all there is to it!

You'll see that the editor is fairly straightforward as to how it works. However, you should also be able to see from the use of the Status column you created that any kind of intricate workflow is going to require additional design on the form, the library, and the workflow to keep track of status and approvals. If you need to deal with things like, "If Joe hasn't approved it in ten days, forward to Mary," or calculations on form values, the SharePoint Workflow Designer quickly becomes insufficient for the task.

The next section will move on to developing a workflow with code-behind in Visual Studio.

Designing Workflow in Visual Studio

The WF Workflow Designer for Visual Studio gives a more flowchart–oriented graphical designer for laying out workflows (see Figure 11-7). Of course, you can always just write the whole workflow in code if you choose to, but I won't cover that here. You can design some pretty advanced workflows in the designer, as well as manipulate them from code.

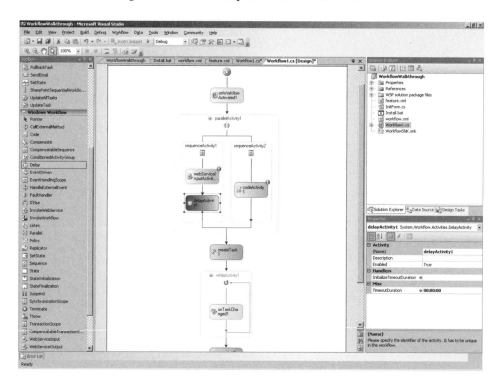

Figure 11-7. *The Workflow Designer in Visual Studio*

To design workflows in Visual Studio 2005, you will need to get Visual Studio 2005 Extensions for Windows Workflow Foundation, which you can download from www.microsoft.com/downloads. This will provide the assemblies, activities, and project templates you need to build workflows. Once you install the extensions, you will have a number of workflow project templates available. However, the templates of interest for this book will be listed under SharePoint Server. They are as follows:

- *SharePoint Sequential Workflow Library*: Sequential workflows are like flowcharts, as shown in Figure 11-7—one activity follows another. There may be branching or looping, but the workflow essentially follows a path from start to finish.

- *SharePoint State Machine Workflow Library*: State machine workflows operate by maintaining the state of various aspects of the workflow. When an event acts on the workflow, how the workflow reacts is based on the current state of the workflow. For example, a document review may be implemented as a state machine—the document will have a state at any given moment (submitted, under review, pending executive approval, etc.). Any action can operate on the document at any moment (open, check-in, edit, etc.). How the document reacts to the action depends on the state. The action may change the state of the document, cause some other action, throw an error, and so on.

The activities available will depend on whether you choose a sequential workflow or a state machine. In this chapter, you're going to be working with sequential workflows, so let's look at the activities in the Windows Workflow toolbox for a sequential workflow (Figure 11-8).

Figure 11-8. *The Windows Workflow activities toolbox*

I'm not going to go through every activity here—that's a topic for a more in-depth workflow book. However, I'll hit some of the important ones:

- `CallExternalMethod`: This is an activity that allows calling to a method in associated code.

- `Code`: This executes a block of managed code.

- `Delay`: This is a simple time delay on the workflow sequence. Note that this activity can be enabled or disabled and the delay time can be set programmatically.

- `Listen/EventDriven/EventHandlingScope/HandleExternalEvent`: These provide a "wait for something to happen" stage in your workflow. The `Listen` activity holds the workflow until one of the events configured in a `HandleExternalEvent` activity acts on it—the workflow then proceeds down the path indicated.

- `IfElse`: This is a simple branching activity where you can set condition criteria to choose between alternate sequences to execute.

- `InvokeWebService/WebServiceInput/WebServiceOutput`: These activities allow you to interact with external web services, allowing your workflow to reach across server boundaries.

- `Parallel`: This allows you to execute multiple simultaneous paths in a workflow (such as requesting multiple reviewers to review a document at once). The parallel activity will only complete when all the child activities are complete.

- `Policy`: This hosts a set of rules to be executed in the current sequence, and is a good way of grouping similar sets of business rules that need to be part of a workflow.

- `Replicator`: This runs a set of activities a specified number of times—similar to a `ForEach`-type construct in many languages.

- `SetState/State/StateInitialization/StateFinalization`: This can provide a state machine–type aspect to your procedural workflow.

- `Suspend`: This temporarily halts execution of a workflow.

- `Terminate`: This stops execution of a workflow.

- `Throw`: This allows you to throw an exception out of the workflow (for error reporting in the host process).

- `While`: This is a looping activity container that allows you to define a "while" condition to continue executing the contained activities.

Those are just the activities from the base activity library that WF offers. You can also write custom activities—for example, let's say you have a mainframe payroll processing system with a complex interface, and a common task is to submit an update to the number of hours an employee has billed. You could write the appropriate logic and encapsulate it (while creating the appropriate parameters for number of hours, employee number, contract number, etc.) in an activity. Now you can reuse this activity in any number of workflows that involve adjusting employee-billable hours.

You can also install additional collections of activities. I expect as the partner ecosystem grows around WF, we'll see more WF activity libraries commercially available. One collection of activities that is notable is the collection of SharePoint Workflow activities that are made available when you install Windows SharePoint Services. Many of them are similar to the WF base activity library, but many of them are SharePoint-centric and designed to work with SharePoint lists and libraries natively (most notably interacting with task lists). You'll see some of the SharePoint activities following.

Creating a Workflow Project

Many of the user interface elements you see in SharePoint are in fact InfoPath forms. Just as Office 2007 renders InfoPath forms as document information panels, Microsoft Office SharePoint Services 2007 uses web-based forms rendered with InfoPath Forms Services in many of the stages of running a workflow.

To use custom InfoPath forms with a workflow, you have to learn how to build a workflow in Visual Studio. Let's create a new SharePoint Sequential Workflow Library project:

1. In Visual Studio, click File ➤ New Project.

2. In the New Project dialog, open Visual C#, then SharePoint Server, and then SharePoint Sequential Workflow Library.

3. Name it **MySharePointWorkflow**.

4. Click OK.

The template has created a number of files for you; let's walk through them and see what they do.

- `feature.xml`: You are going to bundle your workflow solution and install it as part of a SharePoint feature. `feature.xml` defines the packaging for a SharePoint feature—the definition of the feature itself within SharePoint, the manifest for the feature (in this case, you'll use `workflow.xml`), and properties associated with the feature.

- `install.bat`: The template creates a utility batch file you can use to load your workflow feature into SharePoint—this has the command lines necessary to copy the files into their proper locations, load the assembly into the global assembly cache (GAC), verify the InfoPath forms on the server, and activate the workflow for use on the server.

- `workflow.xml`: This file defines the aspects of the workflow necessary for it to run inside Office SharePoint Server. There are the defined metadata elements for the workflow, and a collection of other tags that you'll use to specify your InfoPath forms.

- `Workflow1.cs`: This is where it all happens—the workflow designer and code. You'll see when you start out that you only have one activity: `onWorkflowActivated`.

Now let's talk about what workflow you want to implement. You're going to use a variation of the example from the earlier part of the chapter. If you recall, you designed a workflow for processing expense reports, with the following business rules:

- The finance department must be notified of all expense reports for which the total is greater than $1,000.00.

- Expense reports less than $100.00 are automatically approved.

- All other expense reports go to the manager for approval.

Let's add a few criteria that would have been very problematic to deal with in SharePoint Designer (I know, because I was going to do them in that exercise and decided not to):

- Expense reports covering more than 30 days must go to your manager's manager for approval.

- Any expense report your manager has not approved in ten days goes to your manager's manager for approval.

It turns out that in the Visual Studio Workflow Designer, once you climb the mountain of building a custom workflow, working with conditions such as these becomes *very* straightforward and intuitive. Let's start by laying out a workflow on the designer, and then I'll walk you through the details of getting everything working.

First, you'll handle your first criterion: "The finance department must be notified of all expense reports for which the total is greater than $1,000.00."

1. Drag an IfElse activity from the toolbox to the workflow after onWorkflowActivated1. Change the name to IsTotalOverOneThousand. You'll set this later to check the total from the InfoPath form.

2. There are two branch activities—name them NotifyFinance and ElseDoNothing.

3. Drag a SendEmail activity to the NotifyFinance branch. Change its name to NotifyFinanceByEmail.

That will handle the "If it's over $1,000.00, notify the finance department" part. Now notice that you have a branch for which the value is under $1,000. Notice the next criterion:

- Expense reports less than $100.00 are automatically approved.

Well, since $100 is less than $1,000, you can probably handle that here, right?

1. Drag another IfElse activity to the ElseDoNothing branch. Change its name to IsTotalUnderOneHundred.

2. Label one branch AutoApprove, and the other ElseContinue.

3. Drag a code activity to the AutoApprove branch, and rename it ApproveItem.

4. Drag a terminate activity to the AutoApprove branch after the code activity, and name it ExitWorkflow.

Now you've handled the first two conditions—your workflow diagram should look like Figure 11-9. You'll have a number of validation errors in the designer (the exclamation mark icons on the activities) because you haven't set various required properties throughout the workflow. I'll show you how to take care of those in a little while.

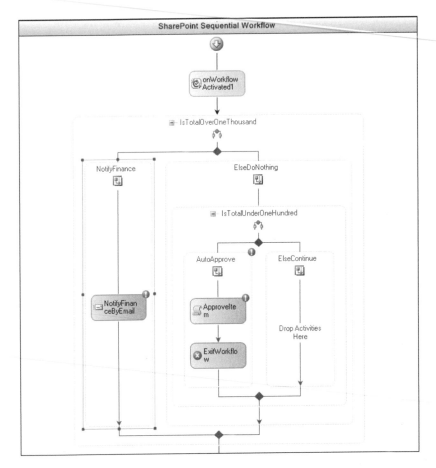

Figure 11-9. *Workflow for the first two conditions*

Now you're going to take care of the rest of your workflow—everything coming out of your workflow here goes to the manager for approval; if the manager takes more than 10 days to approve, or the expense report covers more than 30 days, it goes to the manager's boss (I'll call this person the "director") for approval.

First, you'll handle the manager's approval:

1. Drag a CreateTask activity to the bottom of the IsTotalOverOneThousand activity. Name it TaskForManagerApproval.

2. Drag a While activity under the TaskForManagerApproval activity. Name it WhileWaitingApproval. This will pause the workflow until specified criteria are met. In this case, you'll be specifying until the manager approves the task or ten days have passed.

3. An OnTaskChanged activity goes inside the WhileWaitingApproval activity. Change the OnTaskChanged activity's name to ManagerApprovedTask. This will pause the workflow until a specific task is changed—you'll customize this to set a flag if the manager approves the task.

4. Drag a `CompleteTask` activity underneath the `WhileWaitingApproval` activity. Rename it `MgrApprovedTask`. This will close out the task for the workflow.

5. Next you need an `IfElse` task. Change its name to `NeedsDirectorApproval`. This will test whether either of the director approval criteria occurred. Change the name of the branches to `IfDirAppCreateTask` and `NoDirectorApprovalDoNothing`.

6. Drag a `CreateTask` activity to the `IfDirAppCreateTask` branch, name it `DirectorApproval`, and you're done—the second half of the workflow should look like Figure 11-10.

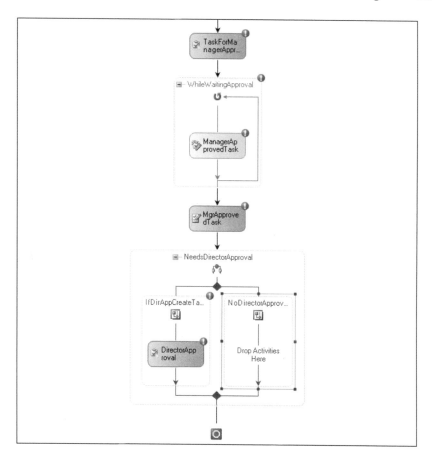

Figure 11-10. *Workflow to handle the remaining criteria*

Now I'll show you how to design the custom InfoPath forms you're going to use when someone submits an expense report for approval, and also when they are editing a task to indicate approval (or rejection). So you're going to need two InfoPath forms, and they're going to need some special configuration to work well with the workflow.

Creating the Form Library

Pretty basic stuff here, but you need to create the form and library you'll use for the workflow. Here's how:

1. Open InfoPath, and select Customize a Sample.

2. Double-click the sample expense report.

3. Now, publish the form template to a SharePoint site. Click File ➤ Publish.

4. Save the form template.

5. On the Publishing wizard, choose "To a SharePoint server," and then click Next.

6. Enter the location of your SharePoint site, and click Next.

7. Leave "Enable this form to be filled out by using a browser" checked, select Document Library, and click Next.

8. Leave "Create a new document library" selected, and click Next.

9. Give your document library a unique name and a description if you like, and then click Next.

10. This is the key step here—promote the following fields; these are the fields you are going to use to interact with the form from the workflow. (Names in parentheses are what they should be promoted as):

    - startDate (Start Date)

    - endDate (End Date)

    - purpose (Purpose)

    - items/item/total (Total)

    - manager/managerName (Manager Name)

    - employee/name (Name)

11. Click Next.

12. Click Publish, and then once the form is published, close the publishing dialog.

13. Now go to the form library you just created—you need a status column.

14. In the form library, click Settings, and then click Create Column.

15. Make the column name **Status** and select Choice for the type.

16. For the choices, enter **Submitted**, **Processing**, **Approved**, and **Rejected**.

17. Click OK.

Creating an InfoPath Workflow Initiation Form

First you're going to create a basic form to kick off the workflow—this example will keep it simple, but you could use a fairly complex form to gather whatever information you need to start a business process. The important part is covering what is necessary for the form to interact properly with the workflow.

First you'll build the kickoff form—this is most likely the form a user will be presented with when they submit an expense report for approval. Ideally, all the necessary information is in the expense report itself—but this example will show you how to offer a chance to make some comments and grab the current date.

1. Open InfoPath. Select Form Template, and then select Blank. Ensure "Enable browser-compatible features only" is checked. Click OK.

2. Select "Layout" from Design Tasks, and then insert a table with a title.

3. Change the title to **Submit Expense Report**.

4. Click the table cell labeled "Click to add form content," and insert a table with two columns and three rows.

5. Lay out the form as shown in Figure 11-11.

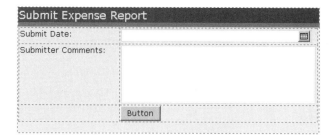

Figure 11-11. *The workflow initiation form*

6. Name the date picker control **SubmitDate** and set it to have a default value of today.

7. Name the text box **SubmitComments** and make it multiline.

8. In the task pane, select the Data Source view.

9. Right-click myFields and select Properties.

10. The form schema root needs a unique name within the workflow, so change it to **SubmitExpenses**. Click OK.

11. Now you'll add the rules to the button you'll need for SharePoint to successfully use the form in a workflow—right-click the button, and select Button Properties.

12. Click the Rules button.

13. Click Add to add a rule.

14. In the Rule editor, click Add to add an action.

15. For the action, select "Submit using a data connection."

16. Next to "Data connection" (which should be disabled), click Add.

17. In the Data Connection wizard, select "Create a new connection to," and then ensure that "Submit data" is selected. Click Next.

18. On the destination page, select "To the hosting environment," and then click Next. This submits your data to the workflow that is hosting the form.

19. Leave the default name, and then click Finish.

20. Click OK.

21. In the Rule editor, click Add Action.

22. For the action, select "Close the form." The dialog will note that you can't prompt the user to save (because the form is browser-capable).

23. Click OK. Continue to close all the open dialog boxes.

24. To work in the workflow, the form must be set to domain security—click Tools ➤ Form Options.

25. Select Security and Trust for the category to show the security level settings.

26. Uncheck "Automatically determine security level."

27. Select "Domain," and then click OK.

28. Save the form somewhere convenient as SubmitExpenseReports.xsn, and then publish it, using the "To a network location" option, to the directory in which your workflow project is located.

■**Caution** By default, the Publishing wizard puts the form location in the "If all form users can access the location" field. Delete the location—this control should be blank.

The final step to take is generating the object model to use in the workflow so that you can pull the values from the initialization form. To do this, you're going to pull the schema from the form by extracting the form files, and then using the xsd.exe tool to generate the class hierarchy from the schema.

1. Open the `SubmitExpenseReports.xsn` form template from the Visual Studio project directory.

2. Click File ➤ Save as Source Files. Save the files to an easy-to-find location (such as `C:\temp\formfiles`).

3. Open the Visual Studio command prompt (Start ➤ All Programs ➤ Microsoft Visual Studio 2005 ➤ Visual Studio Tools ➤ Visual Studio 2005 Command Prompt).

4. Navigate to the directory you used in step 2. In that directory, you should find a file named `myschema.xsd`. You're going to use the `xsd` tool to generate your classes with the following command:

```
xsd myschema.xsd /c
```

■**Note** You must have the InfoPath form template closed when you run this, otherwise the `myschema.xsd` file will be locked by InfoPath.

---

5. This will generate a file named `myschema.cs`—copy this file back to the Visual Studio project directory.

6. Add the `myschema.cs` file to the project by going to the Solution Explorer in Visual Studio (with your workflow project open). Click the Show All Files button (shown in Figure 11-12).

Figure 11-12. *The Show All Files button in Visual Studio's Solution Explorer*

7. When you click the button, all files in the directory are shown—you should see `myschema.cs` there. Right-click it and select Include in Project.

8. Click Show All Files again to deselect it, and you're done with this form.

Creating an InfoPath Task Editing Form

Now you need to create a form that the manager will use to edit the task assigned and approve or deny the expense report. This is a similar process to the initiation form, except that you're going to need to load data from the workflow into the form.

1. Create a form similar to the last form, as shown in Figure 11-13.

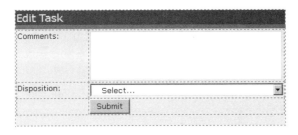

Figure 11-13. *The Edit Task form in InfoPath*

2. Give the text box the name **approveComments** and give the drop-down list the name **disposition**. Manually populate the drop-down list with two values: Approve and Reject.

3. Add the same rules as in steps 11 through 23 of the previous exercise (including creating the data connection) to the button.

4. Now you need to add the data connection that will populate your comments for you. You're going to create a separate schema that will conform to the way the XML data is passed to the form when the workflow instantiates it. You'll use the data connection capability and a default value in InfoPath to move the data into the Comments field of the form. Open Notepad and enter the following:

```
<z:row xmlns:z="#RowsetSchema" ows_instructions="" />
```

The only part you have to worry about here is the last section—ows_instructions. This is the ows_ prefix followed by the name of the property of the task you want passed in.

5. Save the file somewhere handy as task.xml.

6. Back in your InfoPath form, you're going to create a data connection based on that XML file. Select Tools ➤ Data Connections.

7. Click the Add button.

8. Select "Create a new connection to," and then Receive Data. Click Next.

9. Ensure that "XML document" is selected; click Next.

10. Browse to where you saved the XML file you just created in Notepad and select it; click Next.

11. You don't want to be dependent on the file system of this machine—you want your XML file included so that the form is self-containing. Ensure that "Include the data as a resource file in the form template or template part" is checked, and then click Next.

12. Click Finish, and then click Close.

13. Finally, you need to set the default value of the instructions control to the data connection you just hooked up—open the properties of the Comments text box.

14. Click the "fx" button next to the Default Value text box; this will open the Insert Formula dialog.

15. Click the Insert Field or Group button.

16. In the Select a Field or Group dialog (Figure 11-14), drop down the "Data source" drop-down list and select the data source you created with the XML file.

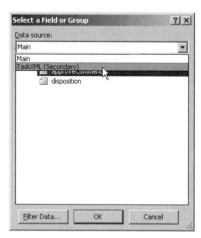

Figure 11-14. *Selecting the secondary data source*

17. Select the :ows_instructions node, and then click OK and close all the dialog boxes.

18. Ensure that the form security level is set to Domain.

19. Publish this form exactly as you published the previous form. You don't need the object model of this form, so extracting the form files and converting to .cs isn't necessary.

Wiring Up the Workflow

Now that you have all the InfoPath bits and pieces you need, you can get your workflow hooked up so that you can publish it and take it for a test spin! You need to add the event handlers to the activities you're using. I'm going to walk through the workflow activities you've laid out and explain the configuration necessary for each one.

onWorkflowActivated1

1. Click in the Invoked handler, type **onInvoked**, and then press Enter to create the handler for this event.

2. Add class variables for your instructions by adding the following code before the workflow constructor:

```
private string instructions=default(String);
private DateTime submitDate = default(DateTime);
```

3. You're going to get the values for these from the initialization form that kicked off this workflow. The data is passed as a serialized XML string from your InfoPath form, so you can use the object model you generated to break down the serialized XML string for you. Add the following code to the onInvoked event handler:

```
XmlSerializer xs = new XmlSerializer(typeof(SubmitExpenses));
XmlTextReader xtr = new XmlTextReader( ➥
    new System.IO.StringReader(workflowProperties.InitiationData));
SubmitExpenses expenses = (SubmitExpenses)xs.Deserialize(xtr);

instructions = expenses.SubmitComments;
if(expenses.SubmitDateSpecified)
    submitDate = (DateTime)expenses.SubmitDate;

workflowProperties.Item.Properties["Status"] = "Processing";

workflowId = workflowProperties.WorkflowId;
```

IsTotalOverOneThousand

This requires no additional configuration.

NotifyFinance

1. Set the Condition property to Code Condition.

2. In the Condition property underneath, type **ifTotalGreater** and press Enter, which will take you to the event handler for the Condition event.

3. Enter the following code in the event handler:

```
if ((int)workflowProperties.Item.Properties["Total"] > 1000)
    e.Result = true;
```

This tests the designated property of the underlying item, and shows why you needed to promote the total from the InfoPath form. If the total is in fact greater than 1,000, you return a value of true to the Boolean result.

NotifyFinanceByEmail

1. For the CorrelationToken property, drop down the list and select "workflowToken."

2. Fill in the properties for the e-mail (To, From, Subject) as you see fit.

ElseDoNothing

This requires no additional configuration.

IsTotalUnderOneHundred

This requires no additional configuration.

AutoApprove

1. For the `Condition` property, select Code Condition. Expand the Condition property.

2. For the `Condition` property under `Condition`, type **AutoApproveCondition**, and then press Enter.

3. Similar to the previous condition, you're going to test the total, so enter the following code:

```
if ((int)workflowProperties.Item.Properties["Total"] < 100)
    e.Result = true;
```

ApproveItem

1. In the `ExecuteCode` property, type **FinishWorkflow**, and then press Enter.

2. You're going to annotate the form and set the status before closing out the report. Add the following code:

```
string tmpPurpose = (string)workflowProperties.Item.Properties["Purpose"];
workflowProperties.Item.Properties["Purpose"] = ➥
    tmpPurpose + ", Approved Automatically.";
workflowProperties.Item.Properties["Status"] = "Approved";
```

ExitWorkflow

This requires no additional configuration.

TaskForManagerApproval

Now you'll wire up the manager approval section of the workflow.

1. Set the `CorrelationToken` property to **mgrTaskToken**. (It's not in the drop-down list, so you'll have to type this in.)

2. Once you type it in, open out the `CorrelationToken` property and select Workflow1 as the `OwnerActivityName` property.

3. Click in the `TaskId` property, and then click the ellipses button at the end. This opens the "Bind 'TaskId' to an activity's property" dialog (Figure 11-15).

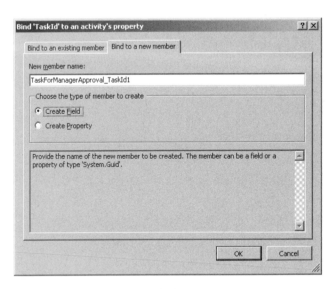

Figure 11-15. *Binding the TaskId to a property*

4. Click the "Bind to a new member" tab, leave the default member name, and select Create Field. Click OK.

5. Click in the `TaskProperties` property, and then click the ellipses button to open the Bind dialog again.

6. Select the "Bind to a new member" tab, accept the default name, and select Create Field. Click OK.

7. Type **CreateMgrTask** in the `MethodInvoking` handler, and press Enter.

8. In the resulting event handler, add the following code:

```
TaskForManagerApproval_TaskId1 = Guid.NewGuid();
TaskForManagerApproval_TaskProperties1.Title = "Approve Expense Report";
TaskForManagerApproval_TaskProperties1.AssignedTo = ➥
    (string)workflowProperties.Item.Properties["Manager Name"];
TaskForManagerApproval_TaskProperties1.Description = instructions;
TaskForManagerApproval_TaskProperties1. ➥
    ExtendedProperties["comments"] = instructions;
```

WhileWaitingApproval

1. For the condition, select CodeCondition.

2. Open out the CodeCondition property. In the Condition property underneath, type **MgrApproved** and press the Enter key.

3. You need to add a flag to test whether the manager has approved the report—add the following line *above* the MgrApproved event handler:

```
private bool mgrApproved = false;
```

4. Now add the following code to the handler. You're testing whether the manager has approved the report and also if it's been more than ten days since the report was submitted. If the logic looks off, remember that you want to keep looping while these are true.

```
TimeSpan nbrDays=DateTime.Now.Subtract(submitDate);
e.Result = !((mgrApproved) || ( nbrDays.Days > 10));
```

ManagerApprovedTask

1. Set the CorrelationToken property to "mgrTaskToken."

2. For the AfterProperties and BeforeProperties properties, bind to a new member— ensure that Create Field is selected.

3. For the TaskId, bind to existing member TaskForManagerApproval_TaskId1.

4. In the Invoked event handler, type **ManagerApproved**, and then add the following code to the event handler created (this simply takes the isFinished property of the task item from the SharePoint list and maps it into your internal Boolean for the While loop).

```
mgrApproved = bool.Parse(ManagerApprovedTask_AfterProperties1 ➥
.ExtendedProperties["isFinished"].ToString());
```

MgrApprovedTask

1. Set the CorrelationToken property to "mgrTaskToken."

2. For the TaskId, bind to existing member TaskForManagerApproval_TaskId1.

NeedsDirectorApproval

Since you've created enough workflow for you to get a taste of the configuration, you can reduce the complexity (and potential bugs) by deleting the NeedsDirectorApproval activity— select it and delete it. With that, you've finished wiring up your workflow, and you should really be getting a feel for how powerful the workflow editor can be. Now you can get your solution ready for deployment.

Deploying the Workflow

Before you deploy your workflow, you need to edit the `feature.xml`, `workflow.xml`, and `install.bat` files to provide for your solution. Before you start into these, you need to ensure that your project is strongly named and build it.

1. In the Solution Explorer, right-click the project and select Properties.

2. Select the Signing tab.

3. Make sure "Sign the assembly" is checked.

4. If you don't have a key file already, select <New . . .> from "Choose a strong name key file."

5. Put the key file in a place you'll remember, like `wfsnk.snk`. Uncheck "Protect my key file with a password" for now.

6. Now build the solution—you shouldn't receive any errors.

feature.xml

When you open `feature.xml`, you'll be in for a bit of a surprise, as you'll see this:

```
<?xml version="1.0" encoding="utf-8"?>
<!-- _lcid="1033" _version="12.0.3111" _dal="1" -->
<!-- _LocalBinding -->

<!-- Insert feature.xml Code Snippet here.  To do this:
1) Right click on this page and select "Insert Snippet" (or press Ctrl+K, then X)
2) Select Snippets->SharePoint Workflow->feature.xml Code -->
```

"What do I do with this?" you might ask. Simply follow the instructions—use Visual Studio's snippets to paste in the framework of the `feature.xml` file.

■**Note** If you don't see the snippets, my first suggestion is to save everything, close Visual Studio completely, and then reopen it—it seems to need a "kick" for them to show up. If you still don't see them, go to Tools ➤ Code Snippets Manager, change the language to XML, and add `C:\Program Files\Microsoft Visual Studio 8\Xml\1033\Snippets\SharePoint Server Workflow` to your snippets.

In the `feature.xml`, you only need to change the title and description, and generate a unique GUID for the feature ID.

To create a unique GUID, do the following:

1. Open a Visual Studio 2005 command prompt.

2. Type **guidgen**, and then press Enter.

3. Click the New GUID button.

4. Select "4. Registry Format," and then click Copy.

5. Paste the result where it says "GUID" in the `feature.xml` file, and then delete the curly braces.

The end result of your `feature.xml` should be similar to this:

```
<?xml version="1.0" encoding="utf-8"?>
<!-- _lcid="1033" _version="12.0.3111" _dal="1" -->
<!-- _LocalBinding -->

<Feature  Id="7EA40C1C-0AE9-46df-A456-DCD328CF5A8B" ➥
        Title="Expense Report Approval Feature" ➥
        Description="Manager and Director approval of expense reports." ➥
        Version="12.0.0.0" ➥
        Scope="Site" ➥
        ReceiverAssembly="Microsoft.Office.Workflow.Feature, Version=12.0.0.0, ➥
        Culture=neutral, PublicKeyToken=71e9bce111e9429c" ➥
        ReceiverClass="Microsoft.Office.Workflow. ➥
            Feature.WorkflowFeatureReceiver"
        xmlns="http://schemas.microsoft.com/sharepoint/">
    <ElementManifests>
        <ElementManifest Location="workflow.xml" />
        <ElementFile Location="SubmitExpenseReports.xsn"/>
        <ElementFile Location="TaskEdit.xsn"/>
    </ElementManifests>
    <Properties>
        <Property Key="GloballyAvailable" Value="true" />
        <Property Key="RegisterForms" Value="*.xsn" />
    </Properties>
</Feature>
```

workflow.xml

`workflow.xml` also has a snippet to plug in. Once you've done that, you've got a bit of work to do here.

1. Give your workflow a unique name.

2. The Description field is wholly optional.

3. For the ID field, you need another unique GUID—use the same process you used for `feature.xml`.

4. Change the project name in the CodeBesideClass element. If you changed your workflow name from Workflow1, be sure to update that as well.

5. You shouldn't need to update the ContentTypeId or Urls elements.

6. Under MetaData, you need to get the URNs for your InfoPath forms. The URN is located in the Form Template Properties dialog (under File ➤ Properties), as shown in Figure 11-16. The URN for the SubmitExpenseReports form goes in the Instantiation_FormURN and Association_FormURN elements, while the URN for the TaskEdit form goes in the Task0_FormURN element.

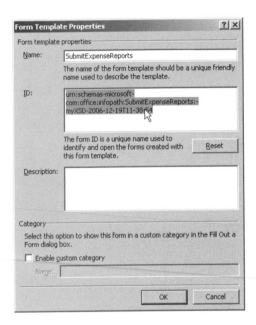

Figure 11-16. *The URN of an InfoPath form*

7. Delete the Modification URN fields.

8. You also need the public key token for the assembly. To get this, you need to install the assembly into the Global Assembly Cache (GAC)—then you can get the key from the assembly name in C:\WINDOWS\assembly. To install the assembly into the GAC, use this command from the Visual Studio 2005 command prompt:

```
gacutil.exe -if bin\Debug\MySharePointWorkflow.dll
```

9. Once you have the public key token, paste it where indicated in the CodeBesideAssembly line.

The final file should look similar to this:

```
<?xml version="1.0" encoding="utf-8" ?>
<!-- _lcid="1033" _version="12.0.3015" _dal="1"   -->
<!-- _LocalBinding   -->

<Elements xmlns="http://schemas.microsoft.com/sharepoint/">
    <Workflow ➡
        Name="Expense Report Approval Workflow" ➡
```

```
         Description="Provides routing for expense reports" ➡
            Id="81D38D1E-DADF-4cae-97D3-07DCF72A50C5" ➡
         CodeBesideClass="MySharePointWorkflow.Workflow1"  ➡
         CodeBesideAssembly="MySharePointWorkflow, Version=3.0.0.0, ➡
            Culture=neutral, PublicKeyToken=d0759da3a8953e71" ➡
         TaskListContentTypeId="0x01080100C9C9515DE4E24001905074F980F93160"
         AssociationUrl="_layouts/CstWrkflIP.aspx" ➡
         InstantiationUrl="_layouts/IniWrkflIP.aspx" ➡
         ModificationUrl="_layouts/ModWrkflIP.aspx">

      <Categories/>
      <MetaData>
         <Association_FormURN>urn:schemas-microsoft-com:office:infopath: ➡
            SubmitExpenseReports:-myXSD-2006-12-19T11-38-54 ➡
            </Association_FormURN>
         <Instantiation_FormURN>urn:schemas-microsoft-com:office:infopath: ➡
            SubmitExpenseReports:-myXSD-2006-12-19T11-38-54 ➡
            </Instantiation_FormURN>
         <Task0_FormURN>urn:schemas-microsoft-com:office:infopath: ➡
            TaskEdit:-myXSD-2006-12-19T12-36-18</Task0_FormURN>
         <StatusPageUrl>_layouts/WrkStat.aspx</StatusPageUrl>
      </MetaData>
   </Workflow>
</Elements>
```

install.bat

Updating install.bat is actually fairly pleasant, because it is very well documented. The five changes you need to make are listed at the top, and since you didn't change the names of feature.xml or workflow.xml, you can ignore steps (d) and (e) from the list at the header of the template. The final result should look like this:

```
echo Copying the feature...
echo.
rd /s /q "%CommonProgramFiles%\Microsoft Shared\ ➡
    web server extensions\12\TEMPLATE\ ➡
    FEATURES\MySharePointWorkflow"
mkdir "%CommonProgramFiles%\Microsoft Shared\ ➡
    web server extensions\12\TEMPLATE\ ➡
    FEATURES\MySharePointWorkflow"

copy /Y feature.xml  "%CommonProgramFiles%\Microsoft Shared\ ➡
    web server extensions\12\ ➡
    TEMPLATE\FEATURES\MySharePointWorkflow\"
copy /Y workflow.xml "%CommonProgramFiles%\Microsoft Shared\ ➡
    web server extensions\12\ ➡
    TEMPLATE\FEATURES\MySharePointWorkflow\"
xcopy /s /Y *.xsn "%programfiles%\Common Files\Microsoft Shared\ ➡
```

```
         web server extensions\12\ ➥
         TEMPLATE\FEATURES\MySharePointWorkflow\"


echo.
echo Adding assemblies to the GAC...
echo.
gacutil.exe -uf MySharePointWorkflow
gacutil.exe -if bin\Debug\MySharePointWorkflow.dll

echo.
echo Verifying InfoPath Forms...
echo.
"%programfiles%\common files\microsoft shared\ ➥
    web server extensions\12\bin\stsadm" ➥
     -o verifyformtemplate -filename SubmitExpenseReports.xsn
"%programfiles%\common files\microsoft shared\ ➥
    web server extensions\12\bin\stsadm" ➥
     -o verifyformtemplate -filename TaskEdit.xsn

echo.
echo Activating the feature...
echo.
pushd %programfiles%\common files\microsoft shared\web server extensions\12\bin

stsadm -o installfeature -filename MySharePointWorkflow\feature.xml -force
stsadm -o activatefeature -filename MySharePointWorkflow\feature.xml -url ➥
    http://moss.litwareinc.com


echo Doing an iisreset...
echo.
popd
iisreset
```

That's it—once you've finished this edit, run install.bat from a command line, and with any luck, you'll be able to see your workflow in action!

1. Go to your Expense Reports form library.

2. Select the Settings menu, and then select Form Library Settings.

3. Under Permissions and Management, click the "Workflow settings" link.

4. On the Add a Workflow page, you should find your workflow in the "Select a workflow template" list.

5. Give this workflow instance a unique name, and then click Next.

6. You should now see your workflow kickoff form (see Figure 11-17). Here you can set default values for the form. Note that the Submit Date field is populated with today's date!

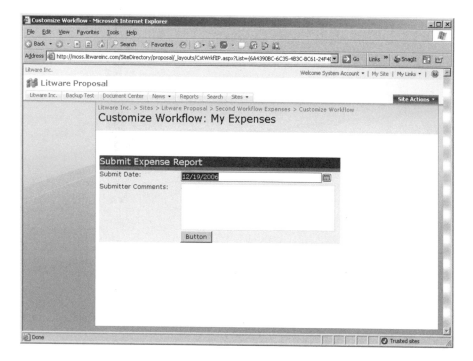

Figure 11-17. *Custom InfoPath form in the workflow instantiation*

7. Click the button to close the form, and your workflow will be attached to the form library.

8. I'll now leave you to explore the remainder of the workflow for yourself. Enjoy!

Summary

It may seem a bit odd to delve so deeply into workflow in an InfoPath book, but I hope you can see how tightly InfoPath is woven into workflow in SharePoint. Not only can InfoPath form libraries leverage the workflows that you create, but InfoPath is also a part of the workflow process and provides a rich, powerful capability for customizing workflows and presenting users with well-designed forms to manage their business processes.

Understanding the Manifest

An InfoPath form is completely dictated by the `manifest.xsf` file found in the form template XSN file. There are two ways to get to the manifest:

- Open the form template in design mode in InfoPath, and then select File ➤ Save as Source Files. This will prompt you for a directory to save the files in.

- Rename the XSN file to a CAB file, and then use Windows Explorer or WinZip to open the CAB file.

The manifest is just an XML file—you can use any XML tool to open it (or IE to open it read-only and Notepad to open it for editing). Due to the complexity of the file, I recommend opening it in Visual Studio 2005 or XMLSpy (see Figures A-1 and A-2).

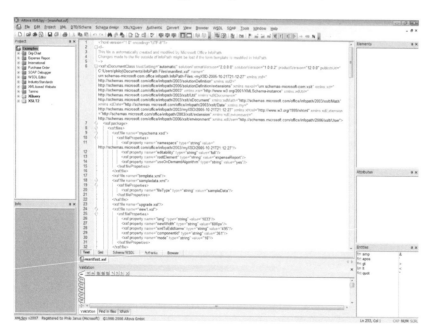

Figure A-1. *Raw XML in XMLSpy*

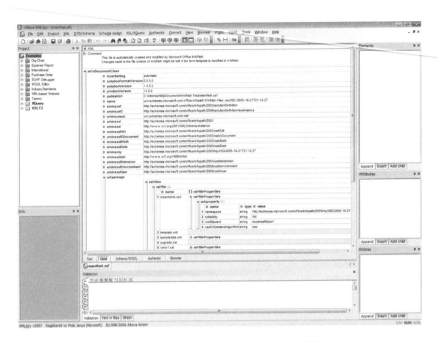

Figure A-2. *XMLSpy showing manifest.xsf in a structured XML view*

The schema for manifest.xsf is available in the InfoPath 2003 Software Development Kit (SDK), a free download from www.microsoft.com. Having the schema is vitally important if you plan to edit the manifest, as you can then use it to validate your edits using an XML/schema validation tool.

xDocumentClass

xDocumentClass is the root element of the manifest. This is the container for all the other document elements, and has a number of attributes that describe the form as a whole. Most of the attributes are optional and metadata-type information. The most notable required attributes are version information, namespace, view definitions, and package data (defining the physical files in the form package).

The xDocumentClass element will also contain elements for application parameters, rule sets, submit adapters, data adapters, calculations, event handlers, and validations.

Package

The Package element simply consists of a complex element listing the files in the solution. Each file will have some basic metadata describing both the physical file and the contents of the file.

DataAdapters

The DataAdapters element contains a list of elements describing each data adapter in the form solution. The full description of the data adapters is located here, in structured XML. Be advised that manifest.xsf is not encrypted and is fairly easy to access from the XSN file.

Note Since data adapters are stored in a relatively easily accessible file in plain text, let me reiterate that any data access from InfoPath should leverage integrated authentication so that usernames and passwords are not stored in this file.

FileNew

FileNew is simply a pointer to the XML file used to store and load default data into a form when the user creates a new form by any means. It may be easier to edit default data via this route than using InfoPath's editor if you have a lot of data to populate by default.

Repackaging an XSN

Once you've finished editing or simply examining the form, you have two options for repackaging it into an XSN file:

- Open the template in InfoPath. If your file associations are intact, you should be able to double-click the manifest.xsf file and have InfoPath open the whole package. You can then save it to an XSN file.

- Use the makecab tool, found in the C:\WINDOWS\system directory.

To use the makecab tool, you need a CAB definition file, which should look something similar to this:

```
; directives for <YourFormTemplate>.xsn
.Set CabinetNameTemplate=<FormName>.xsn

;** These files will be stored in cabinet files

.Set Cabinet=on
.Set Compress=off

manifest.xsf
myschema.xsd
sampledata.xml
template.xml
view1.xsl
Invoice.xsd
; Replace this line with other files that should be included in the xsn

; end of directives
```

Then run makecab /f settings.txt to package the files into an XSN file.

Summary

This appendix is only meant to be a rough introduction to "take the fear out of" the manifest and make it approachable. Do note that when possible, you'll want to work through the design interface to modify InfoPath form templates; editing `manifest.xsf` (or opening the XSN file at all) should be reserved for troubleshooting or very on-the-edge manipulations.

Should you need more background on the manifest file and documentation on its elements and attributes, download the InfoPath 2003 SDK (search for "InfoPath SDK" at `http://download.microsoft.com/`), which has full documentation of the innards of an InfoPath form template.

Note As of publication, only the InfoPath 2003 SDK is available online, and it is not clear whether an updated version will be released. However, the schema in the 2003 SDK should be very close to the 2007 schema.

APPENDIX B

■ ■ ■

Web Services

The W3C defines a web service as "a software system identified by a URI, whose public interfaces and bindings are defined and described using XML. Its definition can be discovered by other software systems. These systems may then interact with the web service in a manner prescribed by its definition, using XML based messages conveyed by Internet protocols" (www.w3.org/TR/2002/WD-ws-arch-20021114/#whatisws).

Web services are becoming an industry standard method of interoperating between servers. Traditionally when processes had to interact, developers would use the proprietary API and hard-code an interface between the systems. The problem was that these connections were fragile—upgrading a version, changing a schema, and even adding additional data to an interface could break the whole system. Web services have evolved to create platform-agnostic interfaces between these systems. You may hear the term "service-oriented architecture" (SOA)—this is referring to the idea of using web services as APIs for integrating loosely coupled systems.

Hundreds of organizations have contributed to the standardization of web services and web service protocols. The overarching coordination for these efforts has been through the World Wide Web Consortium (W3C, www.w3.org), the Web Services Interoperability Organization (WS-I, www.ws-i.org), and the Organization for the Advancement of Structured Information Standards (OASIS, www.oasis-open.org).

Web services have a number of benefits:

- SOAP and WSDL are W3C standards, which makes them vendor-agnostic.

- Web services communicate on port 80, which minimizes firewall and routing complications.

- Web services can leverage SSL for secure communications.

- There are already authentication standards for HTTP-based protocols.

- The web service definition only places requirements on the interface; the internal implementation is open to whatever the developer needs to do.

This isn't intended to be a full study of HTTP web services, just an overview and introduction to demystify them to some degree. For a more in-depth study of web services, I recommend *Beginning ASP.NET 2.0 Web Services in C#: From Novice to Professional*, by Adam Freeman.

Next, I'll review some basic terms and concepts you'll hear in dealing with web services.

Simple Object Access Protocol (SOAP)

SOAP is one of the most popular communications protocols for XML web services. SOAP describes the XML format of a web service call and response. In addition, it describes how a SOAP message should be bound to the HTTP protocol. For the most part, if you are using a toolkit or IDE (such as Visual Studio 2005) to produce web services, you can be almost wholly spared dealing with SOAP—the toolkit or development environment produces the SOAP interface for you.

SOAP is simply the XML wrapper for the call and results so that you can make web service calls between vendor implementations. As mentioned in the introduction, a Java application can make a web service call to a .NET web service because the intervening communications are all XML. Listing B-1 shows an example of a SOAP envelope.

Listing B-1. *An Example SOAP Envelope*

```xml
<?xml version="1.0" encoding="utf-8"?>
<soap:Envelope xmlns:xsi=http://www.w3.org/2001/XMLSchema-instance ➥
 xmlns:xsd="http://www.w3.org/2001/XMLSchema" ➥
xmlns:soap="http://schemas.xmlsoap.org/soap/envelope/">
  <soap:Body>
    <GetCustomerResponse xmlns="http://www.microsoft.com/">
      <GetCustomerResult>
        <CompanyName>string</CompanyName>
        <ContactName>string</ContactName>
        <ContactTitle>string</ContactTitle>
        <Address>string</Address>
        <City>string</City>
        <Region>string</Region>
        <PostalCode>string</PostalCode>
        <Country>string</Country>
        <Phone>string</Phone>
        <CustomerID>string</CustomerID>
      </GetCustomerResult>
    </GetCustomerResponse>
  </soap:Body>
</soap:Envelope>
```

Given a specific web service that is going to expect a call to a specific method, encoded in SOAP, and the return of some specific result, also encoded in SOAP, how do you determine how to interact with the web service? Web services in and of themselves are not self-describing—there is no way to examine a web service and intuit how to call it.

However, there is a related protocol that a web service can implement to document itself—this is WSDL. With WSDL, a web service can have an accompanying interface or file that does document the interface. Best of all, with Visual Studio .NET and IIS, the WSDL file is generated automatically—you don't have to deal with it at all!

Web Service Description Language (WSDL)

WSDL (pronounced *wiz-dell*) is the method of describing what the interface of a web service looks like. Basically, a WSDL file wraps the SOAP interface declarations in one package and makes it available for discovery. WSDL 1.2 has been submitted to the W3C (www.w3.org/TR/wsdl), and is expected to become a formal recommendation.

In ASP.NET web services, WSDL files can be dynamically rendered by querying the web service with a ?WSDL parameter. This will return the schema that defines the objects used by the web services, and the descriptions of the web service methods. The reason this is important is that InfoPath requires a WSDL file to hook a web service as a data connection, and not all web services will have a WSDL file.

■Note If you want to learn more about how ASP.NET implements WSDL and ways of extending the WSDL file, read the MSDN article "Extend the ASP.NET WebMethod Framework with Business Rules Validation," available at http://msdn.microsoft.com/msdnmag/issues/03/08/businessrules/.

Writing .NET Web Services Suitable for InfoPath

One of the great things about recommending web services for InfoPath is that they are so easy to write in .NET. In fact, it's possible that a web service is the easiest application to write in .NET, with the exception of a console application (and those are no fun). When you write a web service and associated web methods in Visual Studio, you simply have to focus on the application logic you need for the implementation of the web service. The .NET WebMethod class handles the SOAP encoding, and IIS generates the WSDL file, and even generates a test harness page for you upon publication.

Listing B-2 shows a basic web service. There are a few things worth pointing out before diving into the exercise. The first line designates a namespace—by default it is set to tempuri.org. It's best to change the namespace to something more meaningful for your needs. The namespace will be the root of the URI that can uniquely identify the nodes in the web service methods. (The URI plus the xpath to the node equals a globally unique location.)

The WebServiceBinding metadata tag describes interfaces for the web service. This, coupled with binding attributed on the web methods within the web service, allows various interfaces to be presented depending on how the service is called. ASP.NET 2.0 web services created with Visual Studio 2005 conform to the WS-I Basic Profile 1.1. This encompasses the implementation of SOAP 1.1, HTTP/1.1, the HTTP state management mechanism, and their interrelation. I'm not going to go into bindings in depth here.

The service has a default constructor. You can use the constructor for setup logic for the web service—establishing and opening database connections, instantiating objects, and so on. There's a commented line in the constructor to initialize the web service component. If you choose to use the designer (right-click the .cs or .vb file, and click View Designer) to add components to your web service, uncomment that line to ensure that they initialize properly.

Listing B-2. *A Basic ASP.NET Web Service*

```
[WebService(Namespace = "http://tempuri.org/")]
[WebServiceBinding(ConformsTo = WsiProfiles.BasicProfile1_1)]
public class Service : System.Web.Services.WebService
{
    public Service () {

        //Uncomment the following line if using designed components
        //InitializeComponent();
    }

    [WebMethod]
    public string HelloWorld() {
        return "Hello World";
    }

}
```

Within the web service class there is one default web method. The web method is tagged with the WebMethod attribute, which can have various properties associated, like so:

```
[WebMethod(Description="This is how to add a description to a web service.")]
```

The properties you can add to a web method consist of the following:

- BufferResponse: The default value of true indicates that ASP.NET will buffer the entire XML response package before sending it down to the client. When false, ASP.NET buffers the response in 16-KB chunks.

- CacheDuration: This sets how many seconds ASP.NET should cache the results (default value is zero).

- Description: The Description property is a free-text field that gives the developer a chance to add some narrative description of the web method beyond the interface and parameters.

- EnableSession: The default value of false disables the session state for the method. Enabling it allows the code in the method to access the session state collection directly (authentication, cookies, etc.).

- MessageName: The MessageName property allows you to overload methods in the web service class. Since every method must have a unique name, you can give the method a unique name in the MessageName property. The value defined in the MessageName property will be what is reflected in the SOAP envelope.

- TransactionOption: This property allows the method to initialize or participate in a transaction. The default value is Disabled.

Exercise B-1 will give you an example of how to write a web service—time to say hello to the world yet again!

Exercise B-1. Writing a Web Service

1. Open Visual Studio 2005.

2. Create a new web service project from File ➤ New ➤ Web Site, which opens the New Web Site dialog.

3. Select ASP.NET Web Service. Leave the Location as File System, and give the project a name by changing the project folder name. Choose the language you're most comfortable with (but note that this exercise will be in C#). Click OK.

   You'll end up with a web service project including a `Service.asmx` file (the file harness) and a `Service.cs` file (the code-behind file). The `Service.cs` file will be open in the editor.

4. Change the web service namespace (by default `http://tempuri.org`) to a suitable namespace. The best option is the domain you use for hosting development work (schemas, documentation, etc).

5. Change the web method signature to accept a string parameter, like this:

   ```
   public string HelloWorld(string MyName) {
   ```

6. Change the one line in the method to return a value with the string, such as the following:

   ```
   return "Hello, " + MyName;
   ```

7. Run the web service. If you've installed the components, Visual Studio 2005 will deploy to the local web server and open the web service test harness. You should get the asmx documentation page, as shown in Figure B-1.

Tip If you get a window with a warning that reads "This web service is using `http://tempuri.org/` as its default namespace," you need to change the default namespace.

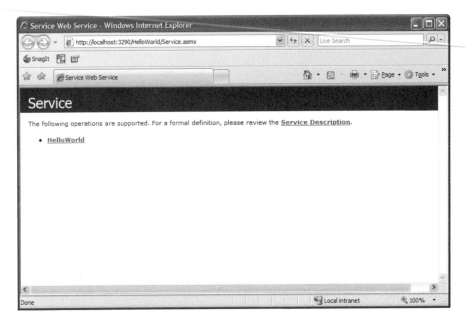

Figure B-1. *The asmx documentation page*

8. Clicking the Service Description link will show you what the WSDL file for this web service looks like.

9. Click the HelloWorld link to see the documentation page for the web method. You will see information about the method, a test harness, and sample SOAP calls for request and response.

10. Type your name in the text box, and then click the Invoke button.

11. You should get a response similar to this XML (as seen in the HTTP POST listing at the end of the test page):

```
<?xml version="1.0" encoding="utf-8" ?>
<string xmlns="http://www.microsoft.com/">Hello, Philo</string>
```

12. That's it—a simple web service that can be called across the Internet, through firewalls, and hooked by custom code or an InfoPath form. Implement integrated security on the directory where the web service resides and you have a secure web service. Add a standard IIS SSL implementation for an encrypted web service.

Tip If you want to edit the documentation page/test harness that ASP.NET generates for web services, there's a great article on doing so at www.15seconds.com/issue/040609.htm.

Posting and returning primitive value types is pretty straightforward—but what do you do if you have a more complex requirement for retrieving data? For example, if you need to retrieve a personnel record, invoice, or order form, how do you get the data back in a reasonable form?

And what about the input values? You may need to submit a large number of values or some kind of structured data into a web service as well.

For either posting or retrieving data, you always have the option of using XML—then you can post or retrieve any kind of complex data. Web services also allow you to designate the schema of the posted and returned XML schema.

For posting data, you can use a list of parameters (see Figure B-2), but that can get unwieldy if you end up with a long list of variables or some complex data you want to receive.

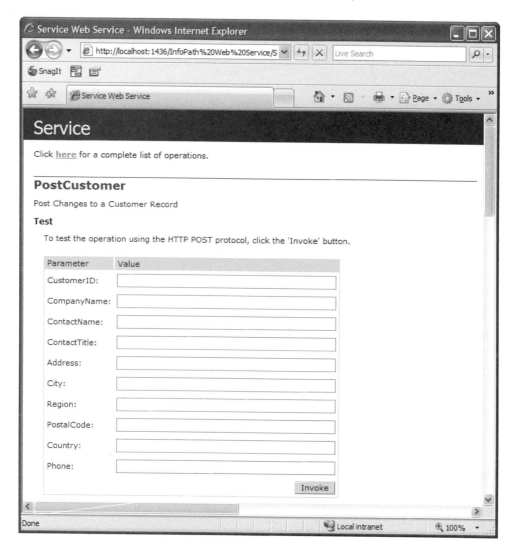

Figure B-2. *An asmx test harness for a large collection of input parameters*

However, a more structured way to move data is by declaring a public class in the web service and using that for your structured data. This has the benefits of being seen as a structure of discrete values by InfoPath and other .NET code, and providing a class structure inside your web service code. However, within the SOAP world, the structure is rendered as XML. The only minor downside to using a class for an input data type is that you can't use the default asmx test harness.

Listing B-3 shows a web service using a public class as a return type, and Listing B-4 shows the custom class used.

Tip Your custom class must use proper property encapsulation (getters and setters). Using public properties can yield unpredictable results.

Tip The custom class must also have a default constructor, even if you don't plan to use one. If you don't have a default (parameterless) constructor, an error will be thrown when you try to load the test harness.

Listing B-3. *A Web Method Returning a Custom Class*

```
[WebMethod(Description = "Get a Customer's Detail")]
public Customer GetCustomer(string CustomerID)
{
        Customer cust = new Customer(CustomerID);

        return cust;
}
```

Listing B-4. *A Custom Class for Use with a Web Service*

```
public class Customer
{
    public Customer()
    {
        //default empty constructor
    }

    public Customer(string CustomerID)
    {
        string connectionString = ConfigurationManager.ConnectionStrings ➥
["Northwind"].ConnectionString;

        SqlConnection cxn = new SqlConnection(connectionString);

        string sqlQuery = "SELECT [CustomerID] " +
            ",[CompanyName] " +
            ",[ContactName] " +
            ",[ContactTitle] " +
            ",[Address] " +
```

```csharp
            ",[City] " +
            ",[Region] " +
            ",[PostalCode] " +
            ",[Country] " +
            ",[Phone] " +
            ",[Fax] " +
            "FROM [Northwind].[dbo].[Customers] " +
            "WHERE CustomerID='" + CustomerID + "'";

    SqlDataAdapter da = new SqlDataAdapter(sqlQuery, cxn);
    DataTable dt = new DataTable();
    da.Fill(dt);

    this.m_CustomerID = CustomerID;
    this.m_CompanyName = dt.Rows[0]["CompanyName"].ToString();
    this.m_ContactName = dt.Rows[0]["ContactName"].ToString();
    this.m_ContactTitle = dt.Rows[0]["ContactTitle"].ToString();
    this.m_Address = dt.Rows[0]["Address"].ToString();
    this.m_City = dt.Rows[0]["City"].ToString();
    this.m_Region = dt.Rows[0]["Region"].ToString();
    this.m_PostalCode = dt.Rows[0]["PostalCode"].ToString();
    this.m_Country = dt.Rows[0]["Country"].ToString();
    this.m_Phone = dt.Rows[0]["Phone"].ToString();
}

private string m_CustomerID;
private string m_CompanyName;

public string CompanyName
{
    get { return m_CompanyName; }
    set { m_CompanyName = value; }
}
private string m_ContactName;

public string ContactName
{
    get { return m_ContactName; }
    set { m_ContactName = value; }
}
private string m_ContactTitle;

public string ContactTitle
{
    get { return m_ContactTitle; }
    set { m_ContactTitle = value; }
}
private string m_Address;
```

```
        public string Address
        {
            get { return m_Address; }
            set { m_Address = value; }
        }
        private string m_City;

        public string City
        {
            get { return m_City; }
            set { m_City = value; }
        }
        private string m_Region;

        public string Region
        {
            get { return m_Region; }
            set { m_Region = value; }
        }
        private string m_PostalCode;

        public string PostalCode
        {
            get { return m_PostalCode; }
            set { m_PostalCode = value; }
        }
        private string m_Country;

        public string Country
        {
            get { return m_Country; }
            set { m_Country = value; }
        }
        private string m_Phone;

        public string Phone
        {
            get { return m_Phone; }
            set { m_Phone = value; }
        }

        public string CustomerID
        {
            get { return m_CustomerID; }
            set { m_CustomerID = value; }
        }

    }
```

DATASETS AND WEB SERVICES

When you write a web service that's accessing data from a database, you might be tempted to simply return a dataset from a web method. This is a bad idea for a few reasons:

- Datasets carry a significant amount of metadata overhead. Remember that web services have to serialize and deserialize all data returned—constructs with large amounts of overhead can adversely affect scalability.

- Datasets are a .NET-only structure. Returning a dataset from a web service means your web service is not vendor-agnostic.

- Datasets are not structured data. That is to say, you cannot know in advance what is going to be in the dataset; it's effectively a "bag of objects." This makes for a weak contract at the interface, and makes designing to consume a web service problematic. It's much better to return structured data so that consumers of the web service can write appropriate code to consume what's being returned.

One way to leverage datasets and still provide an appropriate interface is to take advantage of strongly typed datasets.

So now you've seen how to build a web service, and how to build an InfoPath form based on a web service. But what if you have an InfoPath form and want to build a web service to post the form to? Exercise B-2 shows a neat trick that uses some Visual Studio sleight of hand to create a tailor-made web service based on an existing InfoPath form.

Exercise B-2. Creating a Web Service for an InfoPath Form

1. Customize the Expense Report sample template as your starting form.

2. Extract the form files from the form template (File ➤ Save as Source Files).

3. Open the Visual Studio 2005 command prompt by navigating to Start ➤ All Programs ➤ Visual Studio 2005 ➤ Visual Studio Tools ➤ Visual Studio .NET 2005 Command Prompt.

4. Switch to the directory you saved the InfoPath files to.

5. You're going to use a .NET utility called xsd.exe to generate a class library based on the schema of your form. Run this command in the window:

```
xsd.exe myschema.xsd /classes /l:cs /n:InfoPathService
```

6. In the project window of the web service project, right-click the App_Code folder and select Add Existing Item (Figure B-3).

Figure B-3. *Adding an existing item to the project*

7. Browse to the directory where you extracted the InfoPath files. You should find a file called `myschema.cs`—select it to add to the folder.

8. You now have access to a full object model matching the form. Add a WebMethod metadata tag like the following (note the namespace that resulted from the `/n` parameter in the XSD call):

   ```
   [WebMethod(Description="Submit an Expense Report form here")]
   public void PostExpenseReport(InfoPathService.expenseReport expenses)
   {
   }
   ```

9. Now you can type inside the web method and have full IntelliSense related to the form structure—try `expenses.employee.name`, for example.

10. Publish the web service.

11. Now you need to connect your InfoPath form to the web service. In the form designer, go to Tools ➤ Submit Options.

12. Check "Allow users to submit this form," and then "Send form data to a single destination."

13. Select "Web service" from the drop-down list.

14. Next to "Choose a data connection for submit," click Add.

15. Paste the URL for the web service in the text box. Click Next.

16. Select your web method, and then click Next.

17. On the next page, ensure that "Field or group" is selected, and then click the Modify button next to the text box.

18. Ensure that the root element (expenseReport) is selected, and then click OK.

19. Next to Include, select "XML subtree, including selected element," (shown in Figure B-4).

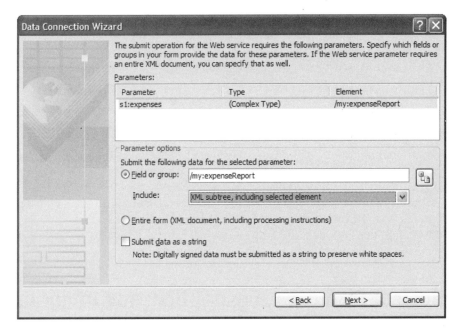

Figure B-4. *Configuring the web service adapter*

20. Click Next.

21. Give the connection a name, and then click Finish.

22. Click OK—your form should be ready to submit to your web service!

Web Services Enhancements (WSE)

While working with web services, you will probably run into mention of Web Services Enhancements (WSE). WSE is a series of add-ons for Visual Studio .NET and the .NET Framework 2.0 that allow you to build more robust web services—providing reusable components for security, scalability, long-running transactions, and more.

WSE 3.0 supports these WS-* specifications:

- XML, SOAP, and WSDL

- WS-Security

- WS-Trust

- WS-SecureConversation

- WS-Addressing

- Message Transmission Optimization Mechanism (MTOM)

InfoPath does not natively implement WSE—it only natively connects to standard SOAP web services. However, you can always use managed code behind an InfoPath form to implement anything managed code can do (including WSE). WSE is currently at version 3.0. Moving forward, WSE is being deprecated in favor of Windows Communication Foundation (WCF, previously code-named "Indigo") in the .NET Framework 3.0.

Windows Communication Foundation (WCF)

Windows Communication Foundation is a collection of formalized web services extensions that are part of the .NET Framework in version 3.0. WCF formalizes the web service framework, opening up the endpoints, schema definitions, enhancements, and other aspects of web services to a uniform framework that makes it easier to build robust, powerful web services that can interoperate with .NET web services and other platforms.

Again, InfoPath 2007 does not natively interact with WCF services, but it's possible to interoperate with them by writing managed code within the form.

Universal Discovery, Description, and Integration (UDDI)

UDDI services were first envisioned as massive catalogs of public web services on the Internet that users and developers could browse for web services to consume. That vision hasn't panned out, but UDDI can still be incredibly useful inside the firewall.

In a large organization, if business groups are cooperating and collaborating well, they should be interoperating with each other's data. Currently this means making arrangements with IT departments every time one department wants to access another department's data. However, in a very large organization, the collection of web services and methods would quickly become unwieldy.

Despite the failure of the initial vision of UDDI, it is still a viable and powerful technology for cataloging web services in an intranet, and InfoPath can utilize UDDI catalogs to find web services. Windows Server 2003 has native UDDI capabilities (Figure B-5). You can learn more about UDDI at www.microsoft.com/uddi/.

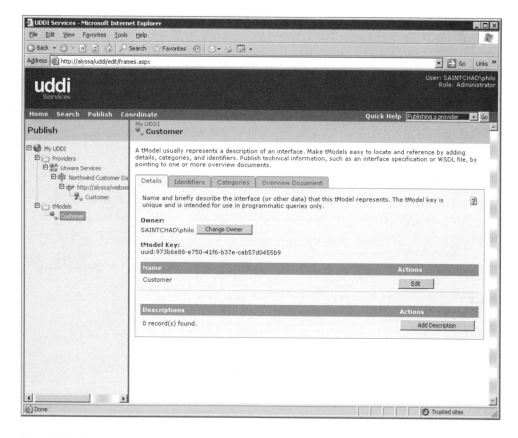

Figure B-5. *The UDDI management interface for Windows Server 2003*

Web Services and SQL Server

SQL Server 2005 introduced a native web service capability (or more accurately, a method of accessing database data over HTTP using SOAP). This means you can register a URL (port and path) on a SQL server and use it to execute stored procedures or bare T-SQL batch statements. In this section, I'm going to focus on executing a stored procedure via an HTTP endpoint.

■**Note** SQL Server must be running on Windows Server 2003 to run HTTP endpoints, since the capability relies on the kernel mode HTTP driver to register namespaces and endpoints.

To enable SQL Server to listen for SOAP requests, you have to register an HTTP endpoint with a unique URL. When you register the endpoint, SQL Server registers the URL with http.sys. When an HTTP call comes into the server matching the registered URL, http.sys intercepts the call and routes it to SQL Server to handle.

The really neat thing is that InfoPath can natively consume SQL Server 2005 web services. Exercise B-3 gives you a glimpse at how.

Exercise B-3. Creating a SQL Server Web Service

1. You'll need the Northwind sample database if you haven't already installed it. Search for "Northwind sample database" on www.microsoft.com to find the free download (it will be tagged for SQL Server 2000, but it runs fine on SQL Server 2005).

   You're going to use the CustOrderHist stored procedure that's part of the Northwind database.

2. First, you need to reserve the namespace you're going to use for your HTTP endpoint. From SQL Server Management Studio, execute the following stored procedure with an unused path for your server:

   ```
   sp_reserve_http_namespace N'http://[servername]:80/sql/demo'
   ```

3. Now you're going to create the endpoint that hooks to the stored procedure. Use the following listing:

   ```
   CREATE ENDPOINT get_Customer_History
   STATE=STARTED
   AS HTTP(
       SITE = '[servername]',
       PATH = '/sql/demo',
       AUTHENTICATION = ( INTEGRATED ),
       PORTS = ( CLEAR )
   )
   FOR SOAP (
       WEBMETHOD
           'http://[servername]/'.'CustOrderHist'
           (NAME='Northwind.dbo.CustOrderHist'),
           BATCHES = ENABLED,
           WSDL = DEFAULT
   )
   ```

4. After executing this, your web service will be running on the database server. Open InfoPath.

5. Choose to design a new form template off a web service.

6. Choose "Receive data," and then click Next.

7. Paste the URL of your web service into the address box.

8. Select the CustOrderHist operation, and then click Next.

9. Put a sample value in for @CustomerID (in Northwind, "CHOPS" is a valid value).

10. Click OK to the warning about multiple datasets, and then click Next.

11. Click Finish.

12. In the form, drag the CustomerID element from the data source task pane to the Query Fields area of the form.

13. Open the dataFields element, s1:CustOrderHistReponse, CustOrderHistResult, and then (Choice). Note the options in the result set of elements.

14. Click and drag the SqlRowSet element to the data fields area. When you drop the selection, choose "Repeating Section with controls" from the context menu that comes up.

15. The form should work now—preview it and run a query on CHOPS to get a result of the order history of this customer.

Summary

This appendix has given a high-speed overview of web services. As you can see, it's a very broad field. However, I wanted to demystify the subject to encourage you to embrace web services as a way to interoperate between servers and services.

■■■

Using XMLSpy with InfoPath

Since InfoPath is completely XML-based, it makes sense that to work with form templates, you should probably have a good XML tool in your back pocket. If you're using Visual Studio 2005 anyway, it offers a lot of strong XML capabilities, but it can be a bit of overkill simply as an XML tool. Altova's XMLSpy (www.altova.com/), on the other hand, is a great fit because it is simply an XML tool. Admittedly, it's a very powerful XML tool—an XML Swiss army knife, if you will.

In this appendix, I'm going to go over some scenarios in which XMLSpy can make your life working with InfoPath form templates easier.

About XMLSpy

XMLSpy is a stand-alone XML editing and management tool that provides both text-based and graphical editing for XML files, XSL transform (XSLT) files, XML schemas (XSD), and other aspects of working with XML. Generally when you're working with XML, you will have to work with it in Notepad or another text editor (see Figure C-1).

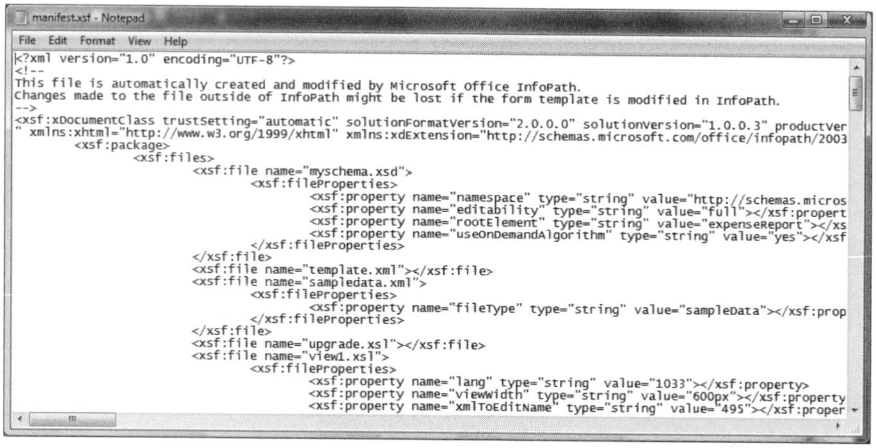

Figure C-1. *Editing XML in Notepad*

Due to the structured nature of XML, this presents a number of problems. First, even though whitespace is not recognized by XML parsers, failing to follow whitespace conventions can quickly present real problems in reading and working with the XML. Second, XML is a structured and strongly typed markup language, especially XML that is bound to a schema. Every entry must be syntactically and semantically correct, or else the file will be corrupted. Trying to read a schema and work with an XML file to keep compliant with the schema can quickly become daunting.

Finally, simply trying to navigate a large XML document can be painful—an XML document can contain hundreds or thousands of lines of markup text that are defined by their position in the document (e.g., Employee/Name is different than Manager/Name). This assumes you know the structure of the document—if you are trying to parse an unknown document, then following the structure through opening and closing tags can be tortuous.

This is where XMLSpy comes in—it can provide a graphical view that makes reading and navigating XML files much, much easier to manage. Note how just at a glance the XML file in Figure C-2 is easier to read, parse, and understand.

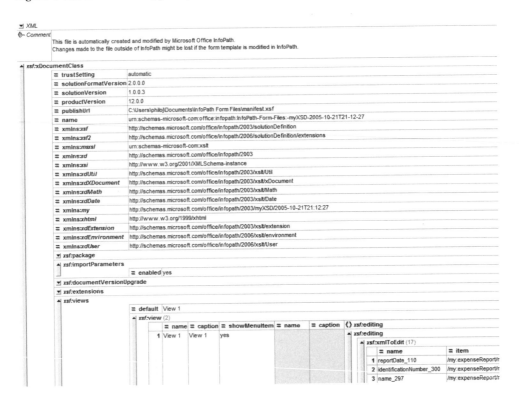

Figure C-2. *The same XML document opened in XMLSpy's grid view*

In addition, XMLSpy can parse XML files and report on whether they are well-formed. XML files must follow the W3C conventions regarding file formation (every opening tag must have a matching closing tag, tag names cannot have spaces, etc). If any of these conventions are not followed, the document is not well-formed XML, and XMLSpy will report an error.

Beyond checking for well-formed documents, XMLSpy can validate XML files against a schema. So, if you have the schema for a given XML file, XMLSpy will help you edit the file and also be able to report if the file does not comply with the schema (Figure C-3).

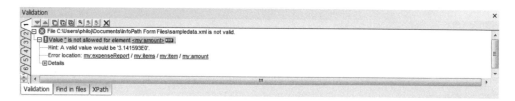

Figure C-3. *An example of schema validation in XMLSpy*

Another benefit you get from having a schema associated with an XML file is that XMLSpy will suggest valid options when you are typing (see Figure C-4). As well as being a convenience, this helps you discover the options that are available from the underlying schema.

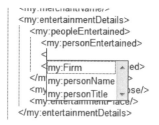

Figure C-4. *XMLSpy suggesting nodes in an XML document based on the attached schema*

XMLSpy will also perform XSL transforms for you if you have an XML file and the corresponding XSL file. This allows you to take an XML file, select the XSL transform file, and apply it, rendering the results appropriately (XML view for an XML output, browser view for HTML output, etc.).

You can also use XMLSpy to determine and parse XPath expressions. XPath is an XML query language that gives you a specific element or group of elements within the document. InfoPath is very dependent on XPath queries for selecting elements, so this is a handy tool to have around.

The final aspect of XMLSpy I'll discuss (but by no means the end of its features) is its ability to group your files into projects. This may seem somewhat simplistic, but when you really have to bang on an InfoPath project, you'll be going from one file to another, tweaking and hacking to make it work. Being able to have those files at hand in an easily managed structure makes life much easier. XMLSpy's projects are great because they are, once again, XML-oriented.

XMLSpy and XML Files

Exercise C-1 will walk you through using XMLSpy to work with an XML file.

■Note You can download a free trial version of XMLSpy from www.altova.com/.

Exercise C-1. Using XMLSpy

1. You'll use InfoPath to create an XML document and a schema. Open InfoPath.

2. Select "Customize a sample," and then select the expense report to customize.

3. Click the Preview button to preview the form.

4. Fill in the form. I recommend adding several expenses and using the >> button to add expense details (Figure C-5).

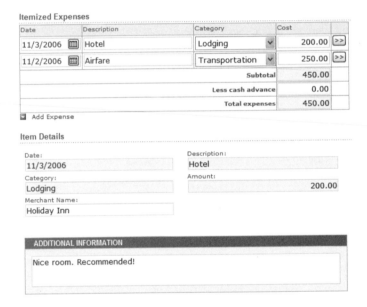

Figure C-5. *Filling in the Expense Report form*

5. Once you've filled in the form, save it (File ➤ Save As). When prompted to save or submit, select Save As.

6. Close the preview (you won't be able to open the XML file while it's open in InfoPath).

7. Open XMLSpy, and then open the XML file in XMLSpy (File ➤ Open). You'll see the XML in text view (Figure C-6).

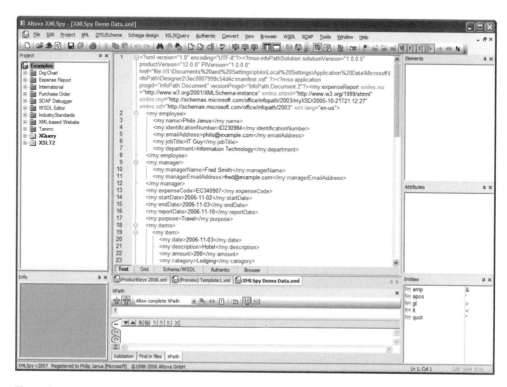

Figure C-6. *An XML file open in XMLSpy*

8. Note the panes open to either side—you can hide those by selecting Window ➤ All on/off (select this option again to show them).

9. Now click the Grid selector at the bottom of the XML window to switch to the grid view of the file.

The initial view you see may not seem like much help (see Figure C-7). Let's open it up and make it easier to see.

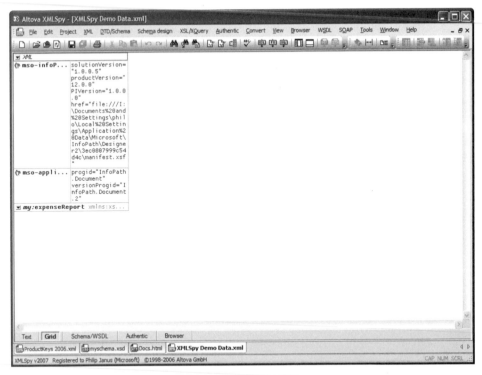

Figure C-7. *An XML file in XMLSpy's grid view*

10. Click the small down arrow next to my:expenseReport (▾).

11. This expands the element, showing the various namespaces and attributes for the document. Near the bottom, you will see elements for my:employee, my:manager, and my:items. Expand each of these as well.

12. Now you have a number of elements open, but lots of ellipses and line wrapping. Let's fix that. Select the Optimal Widths tool (View ➤ Optimal Widths)—this will resize the columns of the grid view to provide a more readable layout, as shown in Figure C-8.

Note The file is completely editable here—you can click in a data field and change the value. You can also change the element labels, which will change both the opening and closing tags in the underlying XML. However, if you do this, note that the form won't open in InfoPath, since it won't match the schema anymore.

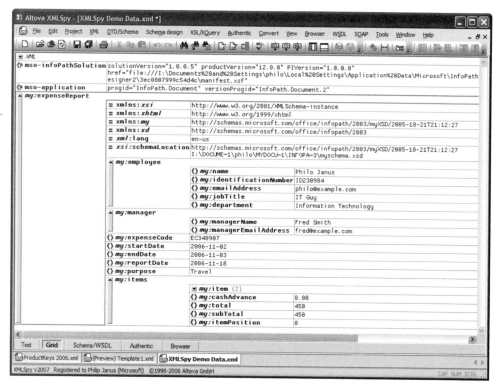

Figure C-8. *The same XML file with elements opened and optimal widths selected*

13. Close XMLSpy.

Schemas

There are two powerful aspects of schemas that XMLSpy presents—working with schemas, and using schemas to validate XML documents.

Note The precursor to XSD was the document type declaration (DTD). DTD was fairly more limited than XSD in that it didn't support namespaces, and that certain aspects of an XML document couldn't be enforced with DTD. XMLSpy supports using DTD, but I won't cover those aspects here.

XMLSpy makes working with schemas fairly straightforward by presenting them in a graphical editor view (Figure C-9). Again, instead of having a large, unwieldy list of text with interrelationships to track, you can work in a GUI that presents contextual options and maintains the semantically correct forms that the W3C schema standard requires.

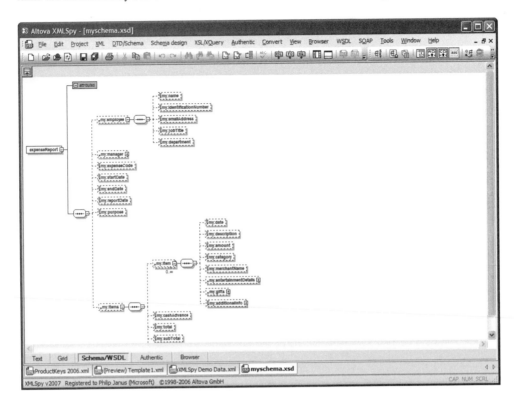

Figure C-9. *An XML schema in XMLSpy*

For general XML use, XMLSpy makes creating schemas very straightforward, including proper representations of element references, attributes, validations, data types, namespaces, and so on. However, for the purposes of this appendix—looking at using XMLSpy with InfoPath—I'm only going to describe viewing schemas and using them to validate XML files.

You can view a schema in XMLSpy in the text view, a grid view similar to what you used in Exercise C-1, or a special schema view (shown in Figure C-9). XMLSpy offers other capabilities as well:

- Generating documentation of a schema

- Managing namespaces more easily (Figure C-10)

- Generating program code matching the schema

- Generating a sample XML file matching the schema

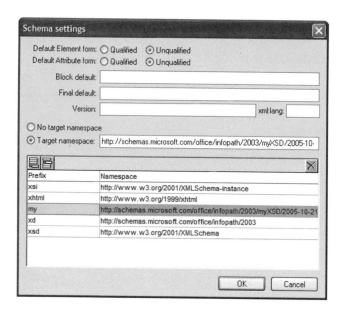

Figure C-10. *Managing namespaces and prefixes with XMLSpy*

The best part of using XMLSpy with schemas and XML files is being able to validate an XML file against a schema. Exercise C-2 will show you how that works.

Exercise C-2. Schemas in XMLSpy

1. If you don't still have the form design open from Exercise C-1, customize the Expense Report form again.

2. Select File ➤ Save as Source Files to extract the files that make up the form.

3. Select a folder to save the files to, and click OK.

4. Close InfoPath.

5. Open XMLSpy, and then open the XML file you created in Exercise C-1.

6. With the XML file selected, click DTD/Schema ➤ Assign Schema.

7. The Browse dialog offers the options of browsing to an XSD file or selecting a schema from an open window. Browse to myschema.xsd from the location you saved the files to in step 3.

8. Click OK.

9. Once you have assigned the schema, you can validate the XML file against the schema by selecting XML ➤ Validate (or pressing F8).

10. The schema can also guide editing the file—right-click any element and select Insert Element.

> **Note** XMLSpy provides you with a drop-down list to select the elements that are valid for that location. It also provides contextual assistance for attributes and values based on the schema.

Using Projects

XMLSpy uses projects to group files, similar to Visual Studio projects. If you're working on a complex InfoPath form solution, this can be a real time-saver in opening related files, keeping track of them, and grouping them by type. Creating a project in XMLSpy is very straightforward—just choose New Project from the Project menu. This will create a new project in the XMLSpy project pane. From there you can add files to the project and have them logically grouped and easy to find when you are working on the project (Figure C-11).

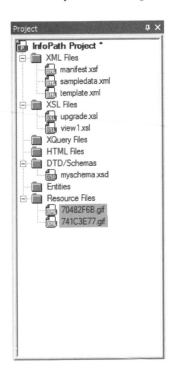

Figure C-11. *Files organized in an XMLSpy project*

> **Note** As shown in Figure C-11, I've put the `manifest.xsf` file under XML Files because it is an XML file. When you add it, you'll have to change the file filter to "All files (*.*)" to see it.

Summary

The goal of this appendix has been to show that XMLSpy is more than just a glorified XML editor—it's literally a Swiss army knife for all things XML. Beyond simply pretty-printing XML and verifying well-formed files, you can also use it to validate schemas, validate XML against schemas, generate a schema from an XML file (and vice versa), and generate program code from a schema. XMLSpy is also a great tool for *learning* more about XML requirements and how schemas work.

Index

HARCOURT
· T R O P H I E S ·

A HARCOURT READING/LANGUAGE ARTS PROGRAM

BANNER DAYS

SENIOR AUTHORS
Isabel L. Beck ◆ Roger C. Farr ◆ Dorothy S. Strickland

AUTHORS
Alma Flor Ada ◆ Marcia Brechtel ◆ Margaret McKeown
Nancy Roser ◆ Hallie Kay Yopp

SENIOR CONSULTANT
Asa G. Hilliard III

CONSULTANTS
F. Isabel Campoy ◆ David A. Monti

Harcourt

Orlando   Boston   Dallas   Chicago   San Diego

Visit *The Learning Site!*

www.harcourtschool.com

Acknowledgments appear in the back of this book.

Printed in the United States of America

ISBN 0-15-339783-7

12 13 14 15 16 17 18   032   12 11 10 09 08

Dear Reader,

Did you ever want to visit a cowboy? Have you ever thought about traveling on the high seas? Have you ever had to solve a mystery?

In **Banner Days,** all days are great days for reading. You will read about people and story characters who use their imaginations, travel to faraway places, and work with their neighbors to solve problems.

There are so many things to discover. Read on!

Sincerely,

The Authors

The Authors

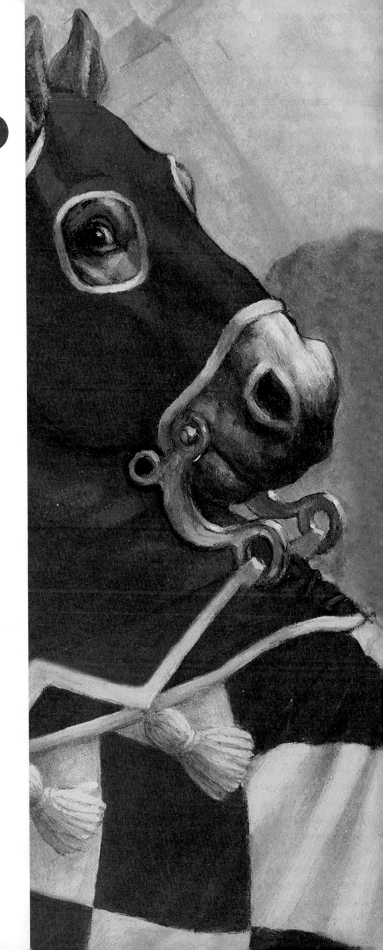

Imagine That!

CONTENTS

Reading
Across
Texts

Reading
Across
Texts

Reading
Across
Texts

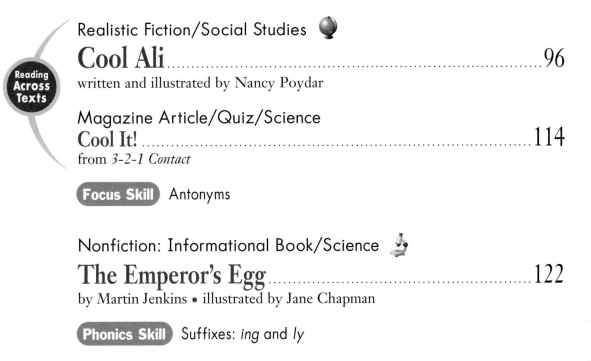

Neighborhood News

CONTENTS

Travel Time

CONTENTS

Reading Across Texts

Using Reading Strategies

A strategy is a plan for doing something well. You can use strategies when you read to help you understand a story better. First, look at the title and pictures. Then, think about what you want to find out. Using strategies like these can help you become a better reader.

Look at the list of strategies on page 11. You will learn how to use these strategies as you read the stories in this book. As you read, look back at the list to remind yourself of the strategies good readers use.

- Use Decoding/ Phonics
- Look at Word Bits and Parts
- Self-Correct
- Read Ahead
- Reread Aloud

- Make and Confirm Predictions
- Sequence Events/Summarize
- Create Mental Images
- Use Context to Confirm Meaning
- Make Inferences

Here are some ways to make sure you understand what you are reading:

✔ Copy the list of strategies onto a piece of construction paper.

✔ Fold it and use it as a bookmark as you read.

✔ After you read, talk with a classmate about the strategies you used.

11

Imagine That!

CONTENTS

Vocabulary Power

boring

ducked

sense

suppose

tractor

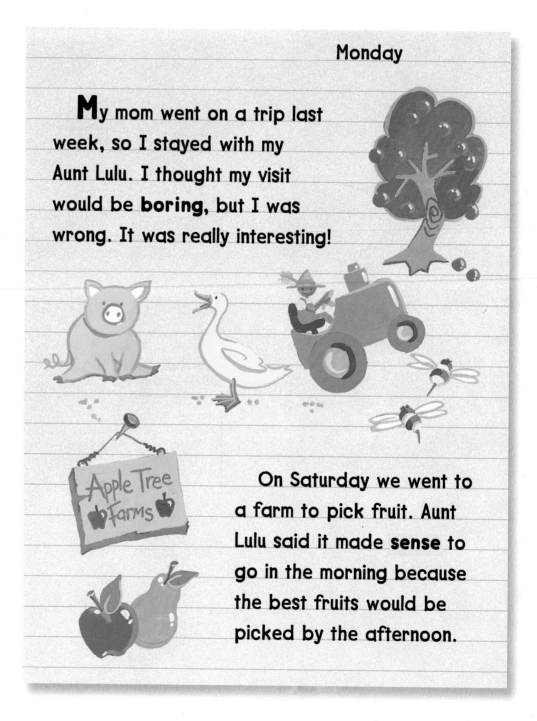

Monday

My mom went on a trip last week, so I stayed with my Aunt Lulu. I thought my visit would be **boring**, but I was wrong. It was really interesting!

Apple Tree Farms

On Saturday we went to a farm to pick fruit. Aunt Lulu said it made **sense** to go in the morning because the best fruits would be picked by the afternoon.

When I was putting our fruit in a basket, I heard a loud noise. I **ducked** down behind Aunt Lulu and peeked around her. The noise came from an enormous **tractor**! Its back wheels were taller than I was!

The man on the tractor was a friend of Aunt Lulu's. He gave me a long ride all over the farm. I had a great time! I **suppose** I should write a thank-you note to Aunt Lulu right away!

Vocabulary-Writing CONNECTION

Have you ever thought something would be **boring** but it turned out to be fun? Write in your journal about what you did.

The Day
Jimmy's Boa
Ate the Wash

ALA
Notable Book

Children's
Choice

HAKES NOBLE
EVEN KELLOGG

Fantasy

A fantasy is a story about events that can not happen in real life.

Look for

- animals that do things real animals can not do.

- a setting that may be different from the real world.

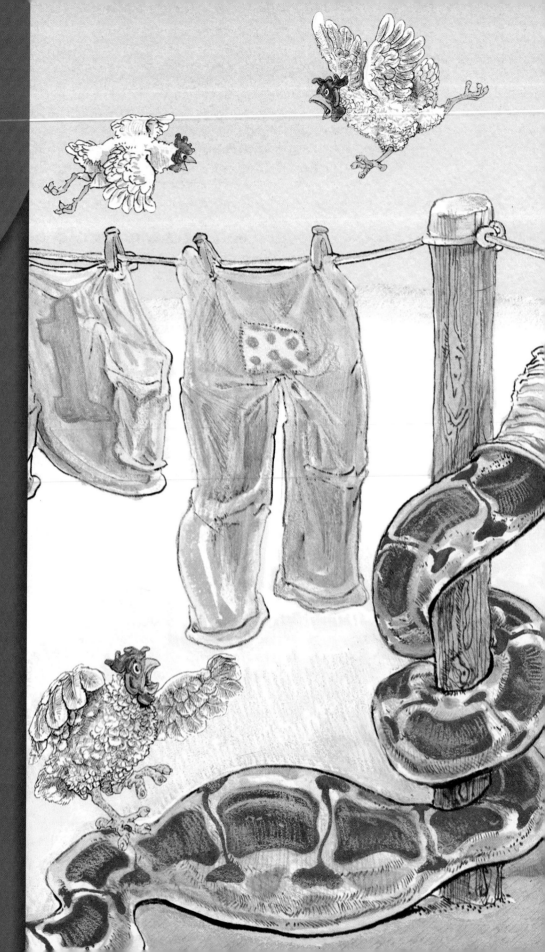

The Day Jimmy's Boa Ate the Wash

by Trinka Hakes Noble   pictures by Steven Kellogg   17

"How was your class trip to the farm?"
"Oh . . . boring . . . kind of dull . . .
until the cow started crying."

18

"A cow . . . crying?"
"Yeah, you see, a haystack fell on her."
"But a haystack doesn't just fall over."

"It does if a farmer crashes into it with his tractor."

"Oh, come on, a farmer wouldn't do that."

"He would if he were too busy yelling at the pigs to get off our school bus."

"What were the pigs doing on the bus?"

"Eating our lunches."

"Why were they eating your lunches?"

21

"Because we threw their corn at each other, and they didn't have anything else to eat."
"Well, that makes sense, but why were you throwing corn?"

22

"Because we ran out of eggs."
"Out of eggs? Why were you throwing eggs?"

"Because of the boa constrictor."

"THE BOA CONSTRICTOR!"

"Yeah, Jimmy's pet boa constrictor."

"What was Jimmy's pet boa constrictor doing on the farm?"

"Oh, he brought it to meet all the farm
animals, but the chickens didn't like it."
"You mean he took it into the hen house?"
"Yeah, and the chickens started squawking
and flying around."
"Go on, go on. What happened?"

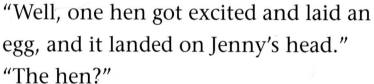

"Well, one hen got excited and laid an egg, and it landed on Jenny's head."

"The hen?"

"No, the egg. And it broke—yucky—all over her hair."

"What did she do?"

"She got mad because she thought Tommy threw it, so she threw one at him."

"What did Tommy do?"

"Oh, he ducked and the egg hit Marianne in the face.

26

"So she threw one at Jenny but she missed and hit Jimmy, who dropped his boa constrictor."

"Oh, and I know, the next thing you knew, everyone was throwing eggs, right?"

"Right."

"And when you ran out of eggs, you threw the pigs' corn, right?"

"Right again."

"Well, what finally stopped it?"
"Well, we heard the farmer's wife screaming."
"Why was she screaming?"
"We never found out, because Mrs. Stanley
made us get on the bus, and we sort of left in
a hurry without the boa constrictor."

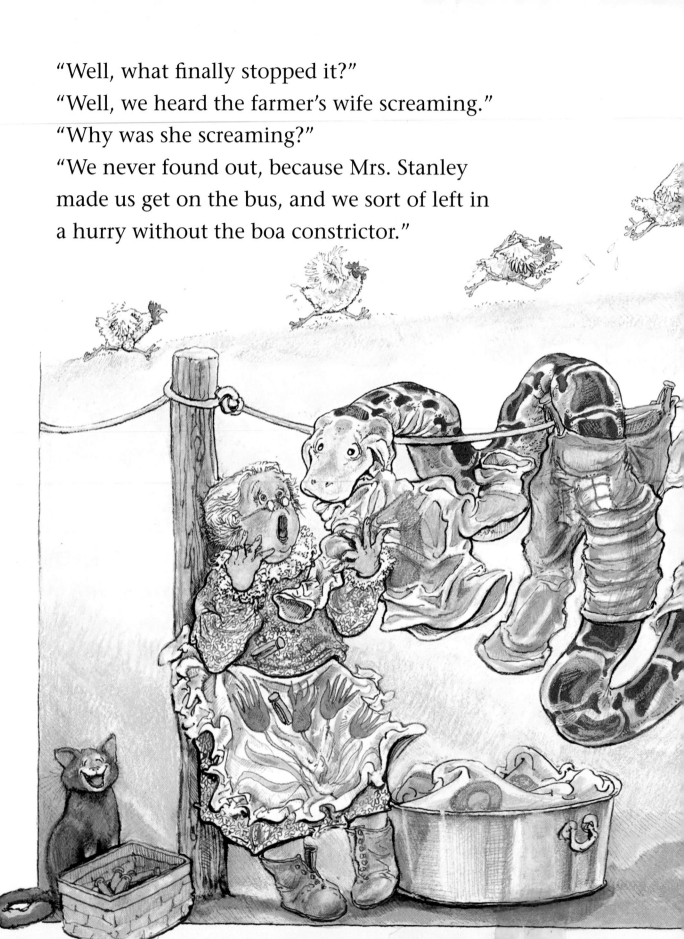

"I bet Jimmy was sad because he left his
pet boa constrictor."
"Oh, not really. We left in such a hurry
that one of the pigs didn't get off the bus,
so now he's got a pet pig."

"Boy, that sure sounds like an exciting trip."
"Yeah, I suppose, if you're the kind of kid
who likes class trips to the farm."

Think and Respond

1. What kinds of trouble does the class get into on the trip to the farm?

2. How is the setting important to this story?

3. How would the story be different if the author did not have Jimmy bring his boa to the farm?

4. Do you think a class trip to a farm would be **boring** or exciting? Why?

5. How did thinking about what might happen next help you read this story?

Meet the Author

Trinka Hakes Noble

Trinka Hakes Noble grew up on a small farm in Michigan. She went to a school that had only one room. In fact, she was the only person in her grade. Trinka Hakes Noble was an art teacher before she began writing and illustrating children's books. For "The Day Jimmy's Boa Ate the Wash," however, she wanted an illustrator with a style different from her own.

Meet the Illustrator

Steven Kellogg

Before Steven Kellogg illustrates a story, he reads the author's words carefully. He likes to picture the events in his head like a movie. Then he thinks of drawings that will show things the words don't tell. "Putting the words and pictures together is like a puzzle," he says. "That's the thing I like best about making children's books."

Visit *The Learning Site!* www.harcourtschool.com

Snakey

*by Katy Hall and
Lisa Eisenberg*

**How did the boa
constrictor sign his
letter to the goat?**

"With lots of hugs..."

**In what river are you
sure to find snakes?**

The Hississippi!

RIDDLES

pictures by
Simms Taback

What do snakes put on their kitchen floors?

Rep-tiles!

Why did the second-grade snakes get into trouble in school?

They were always hiss-pering!

Making Connections

Compare Texts

1 Imagine That! is the title of this theme. Why do you think "The Day Jimmy's Boa Ate the Wash" is part of this theme?

2 Think about the plot of this story. Which story events could be real? Which are made-up?

3 How are the snakes in "Snakey Riddles" like Jimmy's boa constrictor?

Write a Riddle

Write a riddle about a snake. First, think of a word that has the "hiss" sound in it. That word should be the answer to your riddle. Then write a question with your "hiss" word as the answer. Share your riddle with classmates.

Writing CONNECTION

What do you call a snake that knows about the past?

A hisstory buff.

Compare Soils

Farmers need to know about different kinds of soil. Gather soil from three different places. Then make a chart like this one. Talk with classmates about how the soils are alike and how they are different.

Science CONNECTION

Soils	What color is it?	How does it feel?	Is it sticky or not?
SOIL 1	light brown		
SOIL 2	black		
SOIL 3			

We Need Farms

Think about the foods and other products that people get from farms. Then work with others to make a "We Need Farms!" poster. Include words and pictures to show the many different things we get from farms and why those things are important.

Social Studies CONNECTION

37

Cause and Effect

Focus Skill

In "The Day Jimmy's Boa Ate the Wash," many strange things happen. What makes each thing happen? Read this sentence.

Jimmy was sad *because* he left his boa constrictor at the farm.

The first part of the sentence tells that Jimmy was sad. This is the **effect**. It tells what happened *because of* something else.

The second part of the sentence tells why Jimmy was sad. This is the **cause**.

Cause and effect can help you understand why story events happen and why characters act the way they do.

Cause	→	Effect
The haystack falls over.	→	The cow cries.
The farmer is busy yelling at the pigs.	→	The farmer crashes into the haystack.
	→	The pigs eat the children's lunches.

What caused the pigs to eat the children's lunches?

Test Prep
Cause and Effect

Read the story. Then complete the sentences.

The Big Game

Saturday was the day of the big game. As the home team ran onto the field, dark clouds began to cover the sky. In a few minutes, raindrops began to fall. Soon everything in the stadium was soaked. The umpire canceled the game. Everyone was disappointed.

1. **The game was canceled because—**
   - Suzie had her mitt
   - the coach was late for the game
   - the baseball stadium was open
   - rain soaked everything in the stadium

Tip

Read all the answer choices carefully before you choose one.

2. **Everyone was disappointed because—**
   - the game was in the stadium
   - the game was canceled
   - Jim was not a good baseball player
   - the home team was playing

Tip

Often, the cause happens right before the effect.

captured
imagination
manners
matador
plains
relax
vacation

Vocabulary Power

I had a great **vacation** last summer at the Grand Canyon. My dad said we should **relax** after a year of hard work.

Mom asked us to behave and use our best **manners** in the car. We spent a lot of time together!

We drove across flat **plains** to get to the Grand Canyon. It was much bigger than I had pictured it in my **imagination**!

One day we went on a nature walk. We saw many different plants and animals. I **captured** a beautiful butterfly, but of course I let it go.

At a local fiesta, we saw a clown dressed as a **matador**. He was waving a red cape at a fake bull. We had a great vacation at the Grand Canyon!

Vocabulary–Writing CONNECTION

Make a list of **manners** to use when traveling with other people in a car or bus.

How I Spent

Parents'
Choice

Mark Teague
How I Spent My
Summer Vacation

Genre

Fantasy

A fantasy is a story
that could not really
happen.

Look for

- characters who do
  things real people
  can not do.

- a setting that may
  be different from
  the real world.

42

My Summer Vacation

written and illustrated
by Mark Teague

When summer began, I headed out west.
My parents had told me I needed a rest.
"Your imagination," they said, "is getting too wild.
It will do you some good to relax for a while."
So they put me aboard a westbound train
to visit Aunt Fern in her house on the plains.

How I Spent
My Summer
Vacation
By Wallace Bleff

But I was captured by cowboys,
a wild-looking crowd.
Their manners were rough
and their voices were loud.

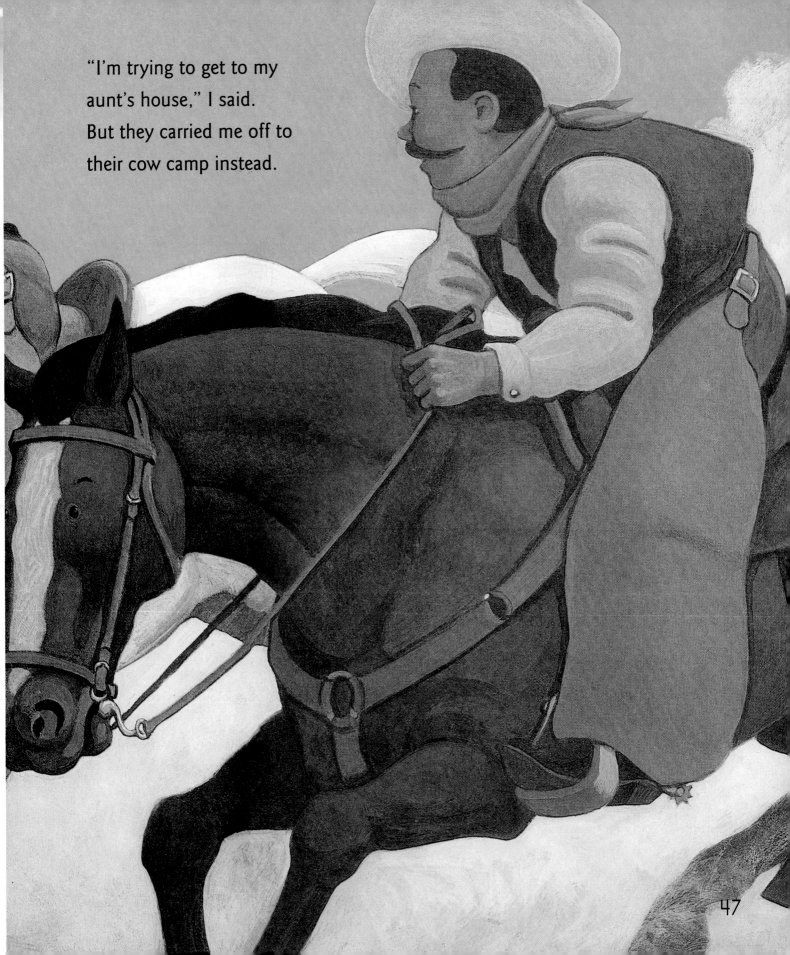

"I'm trying to get to my aunt's house," I said. But they carried me off to their cow camp instead.

47

48

The Cattle Boss growled, as he told me to sit,

"We need a new cowboy. Our old cowboy quit.

We could sure use your help. So what do you say?"

I thought for a minute, then I told him, "Okay."

Then I wrote to Aunt Fern, so she'd know where I'd gone.

I said not to worry, I wouldn't be long.

Dear Aunt,
Captured by
Cowboys. Don't
Worry. See
You soon.
Love,
Wallace

Aunt Fern
P.O. Box 5
Prairie
Tumblewe

That night I was given a new set of clothes.

Soon I looked like a wrangler from my head to my toes.

But there's more to a cowboy than boots and a hat,

I found out the next day

and the day after that.

Each day I discovered
some new cowboy
tricks.
From roping
and riding

to making fire with sticks.
Slowly the word spread
all over the land:
"That wrangler 'Kid Bleff'
is a first-rate cowhand!"

51

The day finally came when the roundup was through.
Aunt Fern called: "Come on over. Bring your
cowboys with you."
She was cooking a barbecue that very same day.
So we cleaned up (a little) and we headed her way.

52

The food was delicious. There was plenty to eat.
And the band that was playing just couldn't be beat.

53

54

But suddenly I noticed a terrible sight.
The cattle were stirring and stamping with fright.
It's a scene I'll remember till my very last day.
"They're gonna stampede!" I heard somebody say.
Just then they came charging. They charged right at *me!*
I looked for a hiding place—a rock, or a tree.

What I found was a tablecloth spread out on the ground.
So I turned like a matador
and spun it around.
It was a new kind of cowboying, a fantastic display!
The cattle were frightened and stampeded . . . away!

Then the cowboys all cheered, "Bleff's a true buckaroo!"
They shook my hand and slapped my back,
and Aunt Fern hugged me, too.

And *that's* how I spent my summer vacation.

57

I can hardly wait for show-and-tell!

Think and Respond

1. How does Wallace use his **imagination** in his report?

2. What words would you use to describe Wallace? Why?

3. Why do you think the author shows the animals in the classroom at the end of the story?

4. Which part of this story do you like the best? Why?

5. Which strategies did you use to help you read this story? Why?

Meet the Author and Illustrator

Mark Teague

W hat does Mark Teague do during *his* summer vacations? He spends most summers—and falls, winters, and springs—writing and illustrating children's books.

Mark Teague began making children's books while working at a bookstore in New York City. The children's books in the store reminded him of how much he enjoyed writing and illustrating his own stories when he was young.

Visit *The Learning Site!*
www.harcourtschool.com

59

Caldecott
Honor

June

The sun is rich
    And gladly pays
In golden hours,
    Silver days,

And long green weeks
    That never end.
School's out. The time
    Is ours to spend.

There's Little League,
    Hopscotch, the creek,
And, after supper,
    Hide-and-seek.

The live-long light
    Is like a dream,
And freckles come
    Like flies to cream.

by John Updike
illustrated by Trina Schart Hyman

61

Making Connections

Compare Texts

1. Is Wallace using his imagination when he tells this story? How do you know?

2. How is Wallace like the girl telling the story in "The Day Jimmy's Boa Ate the Wash"?

3. Does "How I Spent My Summer Vacation" or does the poem "June" tell more about what you might really do on your summer vacation? Give examples.

Write a Postcard

Wallace sends Aunt Fern a postcard. Make a postcard to send to one of your classmates. On an index card, draw a place you would like to visit. On the other side of the card, tell where you are and what you are doing. Include an address.

Writing CONNECTION

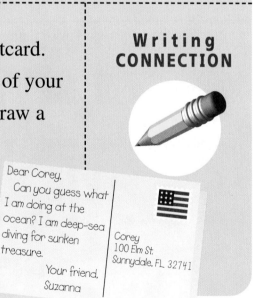

Dear Corey,
   Can you guess what I am doing at the ocean? I am deep-sea diving for sunken treasure.
      Your friend,
      Suzanna

Corey
100 Elm St.
Sunnydale, FL 32741

Home on the Range

Find out more about how cowboys and cowgirls live. Then write three interesting facts, and draw pictures to go with your facts. Share what you learn with your classmates.

Sources of Heat

"Kid Bleff" learns to make fire with sticks. What other ways do people get heat to cook or to stay warm? Make a chart to show your ideas. Present your chart to classmates.

Sources of Heat

Heat for cooking	Heat for staying warm
fire	fire
	sun

▲ How I Spent My
Summer Vacation

Words with
oi and *oy*

Phonics
Skill

Read these sentences from the story.

But I was captured by **cowboys**, a wild-looking crowd.
Their manners were rough and their **voices** were loud.

Say the underlined words, *cowboys* and *voices*.
Listen for a sound that is the same in these words.
The letters *oi* and *oy* stand for that sound.

Now look at the two words below. What is the
same about these two words that is also the same
about *cowboys* and *voices*?

choice   **enjoy**

Here are some longer words. Use what you know
about word parts to help you read these words.

asteroid   **employed**   **disappoint**

> **Use these tips to read a longer word.**
> - Look for word parts you know.
> - Break the word into parts.
> - Say each part. Then blend the parts and say
>   the word.

64

Test Prep

Words with *oi* and *oy*

Find the word with the same sound as the underlined letters in the first word.

Example: t<u>oy</u>

● noise

○ sock

○ dog

Tip

Look at the underlined letters closely. Be sure you know the sound they make.

1.   p<u>oi</u>nt

○ mouth

○ remove

○ joy

2.   r<u>oy</u>al

○ voice

○ house

○ soap

Tip

Skip over choices that don't make sense.

3.   ann<u>oy</u>

○ stay

○ address

○ choice

▲ Dear Mr. Blueberry

details

disappoint

forcibly

information

oceans

stroke

Vocabulary Power

Goldie is my pet goldfish. Before I got her, I read a lot of books to get **information** about goldfish. I wrote down **details** about how to care for her.

One of my first jobs was to feed Goldie. The lid on her food was hard to open. My father had to open it **forcibly**.

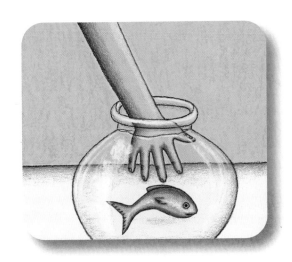

One time I tried to **stroke** Goldie. Mom said she was sorry to **disappoint** me, but this could harm a fish. I would not want to hurt Goldie!

Now I take care of Goldie all by myself. I know there are millions of fish swimming in the Earth's **oceans**, but my favorite fish is Goldie!

Vocabulary–Writing CONNECTION

What animal would you like to have as a pet? Write **details** about how you would care for it.

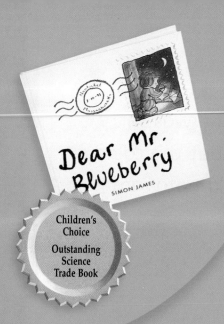

Dear Mr.
Blueberry

SIMON JAMES

Children's
Choice

Outstanding
Science
Trade Book

Genre

Informational
Story

An informational
story gives facts
about a topic
through a story plot.

Look for

- characters that
  tell facts.

- a plot with a
  beginning, a middle,
  and an end.

Dear Mr. Blueberry

story and pictures by SIMON JAMES

Dear Mr. Blueberry,
    I love whales very much and
I think I saw one in my pond
today. Please send me some
information on whales, as
I think he might be hurt.

Love
Emily

Nantucket
June 18
Massachusetts

70

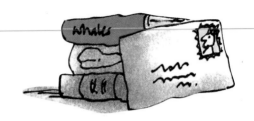

Dear Emily,

Here are some details about whales. I don't think you'll find it was a whale you saw, because whales don't live in ponds, but in salt water.

Yours sincerely
Your teacher,

Mr. Blueberry

73

Dear Mr. Blueberry,

I am now putting salt into the pond every day before breakfast and last night I saw my whale smile. I think he is feeling better.

Do you think he might be lost?

Love
Emily

Dear Emily,

Please don't put any more salt in the pond. I'm sure your parents won't be pleased.

I'm afraid there can't be a whale in your pond, because whales don't get lost, they always know where they are in the oceans.

Yours sincerely,

Mr. Blueberry

Dear Mr. Blueberry,

Tonight I am very happy because I saw my whale jump up and spurt lots of water. He looked blue.

Does this mean he might be a blue whale?

Love
Emily

P.S. What can I feed him with?

Dear Emily,

   Blue whales are blue and they eat tiny shrimplike creatures that live in the sea. However, I must tell you that a blue whale is much too big to live in your pond.

   Yours sincerely,

Mr. Blueberry

P.S. Perhaps it is a blue goldfish?

Dear Mr. Blueberry,

   Last night I read your letter to my whale. Afterward he let me stroke his head. It was very exciting.

   I secretly took him some crunched-up cornflakes and bread crumbs. This morning I looked in the pond and they were all gone!

   I think I shall call him Arthur. What do you think?

Love
Emily

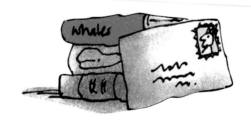

Dear Emily,

I must point out to you quite forcibly now that in no way could a whale live in your pond. You may not know that whales are migratory, which means they travel great distances each day.

I am sorry to disappoint you.

Yours sincerely,

Mr. Blueberry

Dear Mr. Blueberry,

   Tonight I'm a little sad. Arthur has gone. I think your letter made sense to him and he has decided to be migratory again.

Love
Emily

Dear Emily,

Please don't be too sad. It really was impossible for a whale to live in your pond. Perhaps when you are older you would like to sail the oceans studying and protecting whales.

Yours sincerely,

Mr. Blueberry

Dear Mr. Blueberry,

It's been the happiest day! I went to the beach and you'll never guess, but I saw Arthur! I called to him and he smiled. I knew it was Arthur because he let me stroke his head.

I gave him some of my sandwich and then we said good-bye.

I shouted that I loved him very much and, I hope you don't mind . . .

I said you loved him, too.

Love
Emily (and Arthur)

Think and Respond

1. What **information** does Emily learn about whales?

2. Who are the characters in this story? How are they alike and different?

3. How would this story be different if Emily had seen a goldfish in her pond instead of a whale?

4. Would you like to have a whale for a pet? Why or why not?

5. What strategies did you use to read this story?

Meet the Author and Illustrator
Simon James

Simon James used to be a farmer. He was also a salesperson, a restaurant manager, and a police officer. In fact, Simon James has had fourteen different jobs! Now he makes children's books and teaches at a school near his house. He likes to show children how to have fun making a mess and showing their ideas at the same time.

 Visit *The Learning Site!* www.harcourtschool.com

A Whale Scale

A male narwhal grows a long tusk. This tusk is really an enormous tooth!

Baby killer whales are born black with yellow markings. As they grow, their yellow spots turn white like their parents'.

Humpback whales make noises that sound like songs.

0   10   20   30   40   50   60

Length in Feet

Right whales have no teeth. They eat by swimming with their mouths wide open through large groups of tiny animals and plants.

The blue whale is bigger than the biggest dinosaur was. It can live for about 80 years.

In "Dear Mr. Blueberry," Emily finds out that a blue whale is much too big to live in her pond. Read about whales of all sizes on this "whale of a scale."

Think and Respond

How are all these kinds of whales alike?

|70 |80 |90 |100

Making Connections

Compare Texts

1 Why do you think this selection is part of the Imagine That! theme?

2 Compare Emily's whale to the boa in "The Day Jimmy's Boa Ate the Wash." What is imaginary about each animal?

3 Reread Mr. Blueberry's letters and "A Whale Scale." What facts about whales did you learn?

Write a Letter

Imagine that you have found an unusual animal living near your home. Write a friendly letter to your teacher to tell about the animal. Be sure your letter has a heading, a greeting, a body, a closing, and your signature.

Writing
CONNECTION

92

As Big as a Blue Whale?

Blue whales can grow to be more than 30 meters long! Go outside with your class. Use a measuring stick to find out how long 30 meters is. Then make a chart like the one below. Which things are smaller than a blue whale? Which things are bigger? What makes you think so?

Objects	Smaller than a blue whale	Bigger than a blue whale
a car	✔	
your classroom		
your school		
a very large dog		
a school bus		

Which Way to the Beach?

Find North America on a map. Then find the state where you live. Which ocean is closest to your state? With your finger, trace how you might travel to get to the ocean. Share your information with a classmate.

▲ **Dear Mr. Blueberry**

Make Inferences

Focus Skill

When you **make inferences**, you use what you already know to fill in ideas that a story doesn't tell you. To make inferences, look for word and picture clues as you read.

Here are some inferences you might make when reading "Dear Mr. Blueberry." What inference might go in the last box?

Clues from the Story	+ What You Know	= Inference
Mr. Blueberry knows about whales.	There are a lot of books that tell about whales.	Mr. Blueberry must have read a book about whales.
Emily tries hard to take care of Arthur.	People who have pets should take good care of them.	Emily might make a good pet owner.
Emily lives near a pond.	Whales do not live in ponds.	?

Visit *The Learning Site!*
www.harcourtschool.com

See *Skills* and *Activities*

94

Test Prep
Make Inferences

Read the paragraph. Then answer the questions.

Spilled Milk

Curtis walked into the kitchen. A milk carton was on its side, and milk was spilled on the table. Curtis's cat, Sophie, was drinking the spilled milk. Curtis quickly grabbed a sponge from the sink.

1. **It is most likely that—**
   - ○ Curtis spilled the milk
   - ○ Sophie spilled the milk
   - ○ Sophie's cat spilled the milk
   - ○ no one spilled the milk

Tip
Reread the story carefully to be sure you have the important information.

2. **What do you know about cats that helps answer the first question?**
   - ○ Cats have nine lives.
   - ○ Cats make good pets.
   - ○ Cats like to drink milk.
   - ○ Cats should not stand on tables.

Tip
Think about cats you have seen and read about.

▲ Cool Ali

Vocabulary Power

admired

fussed

haze

mimicked

notice

pale

We went to the art museum yesterday. My mom said it was a good place to escape the dusty **haze** and heat of summer.

First we **admired** some statues. We thought they were beautiful. Then we looked at paintings. My dad liked one of a man on a mountaintop. He **mimicked** the face the man made in the cold wind.

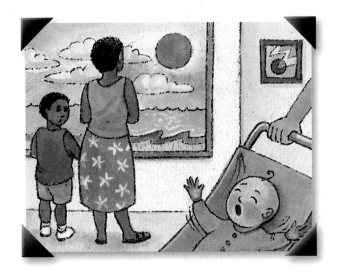

Mom's favorite painting was of the sun setting over a beach. She liked the **pale** colors of the clouds more than the bright orange of the sun. A baby in a stroller next to us must have liked the painting, too. He **fussed** when he had to leave.

My favorite painting was so small, I almost didn't **notice** it. It showed a turtle swimming in a pond. I wished I could splash with it in the cool water!

Vocabulary-Writing CONNECTION

Write about a painting, a statue, or another piece of art you have **admired**. Tell how it made you feel.

COOL ALi
written and illustrated by Nancy Poydar

Genre

Realistic Fiction

Realistic fiction is a story that shows characters as they are in real life.

Look for

- **a setting that could be real.**
- **events that could really happen.**

98

cool

written and illustrated
by Nancy Poydar

99

Ali loved to draw.
She drew all the time.

One summer day, her mother said, "Ali, Ali, it's just too hot to be indoors!"

That's when Ali took her box of fat chalk outside.

It hadn't rained in weeks, so Ali drew grasses and flowers on the sidewalk. She was so busy she didn't notice other people coming out of the hot building. Some complained about the temperature. Some made newspaper fans.

The babies fussed. No one could get their mind off the heat.

Then, Ali drew a little lake
around Mrs. Frye's chair.
"My!" sighed Mrs. Frye as
she kicked off her sandals
and wiggled her toes.
"My, my!"

"Cool," piped up Ira Baker,
squinting in the sunlight.

That was when Ali drew the beach umbrella over Ira's head. "Cool!" he said again.

Mr. Boyle put down his newspaper fan and looked around to see what was so cool on such a hot day.

There was no more room in the lake or under the beach umbrella.

Mr. Boyle looked into the hot haze and complained, "Not even a breeze, not even a breeze."

103

That was when Ali drew the North Wind.
Mr. Boyle's teeth began to chatter. "Brrr," he said.
"Brrr," mimicked the babies. "Brrr, brrr!"
    Ali drew a polar bear with pale yellow fur.
"Grrr," he seemed to say. "Grrr, grrr!"
    "Wheee," squealed the babies as they took
turns riding on his back. "Wheee!"

"What a day," said Ali's mother, finally coming out of the hot building. "What a day!" she said when she saw what Ali had done! Then, she tested the water, admired the beach umbrella, bowed before the North Wind, and stayed out of the polar bear's way.

"Ali, soon you'll have everything covered!" she cried.

That was when Ali got the coolest idea of all.

She began by drawing little
snow dots on the wall and
the sidewalk, little snow dots
around the big feet and little
feet . . .

. . . little snow dots all over the
lake and the beach umbrella.
She drew polar bear paw prints
and icicles, too.
　　She drew and
she drew and she drew.

106

"My, my!" sighed Mrs. Frye.
"Cool!" said Ira Baker.

"Brrr!" chattered Mr. Boyle.
"Wheee!" squealed the babies.
"OOOO!" said the gathering crowd,
thrilled to be chilled to the bone!

108

No wonder no one noticed a little breeze rippling the haze and turning the leaves inside out. No wonder no one noticed the darkening sky or the first big drops of cold rain.

No one noticed until it pinged on the porches, drummed on the mailbox at the curb, and hissed off the hot sidewalk.

Then, it poured. Mrs. Frye did a jig with Mr. Boyle. The babies opened their mouths to catch the rain, and Ira Baker splashed in the first puddles that formed.

Only Ali noticed the sidewalk pictures blotch,
dribble, and stream brightly into the rushing gutter.

Raging blizzard, polar bear, North Wind, beach
umbrella, and little lake all washed away.

"Oh, no," Ali moaned. "Oh, no!"

But the crowd noticed Ali, whose drawing beat
the heat.

They clapped, they cheered, and they lifted
her onto the tallest shoulders.
"Ali, Ali!" they chanted.

Ali loved to draw. She drew all the time. Sometimes it was just too wet to draw outdoors.

Think and Respond

1 How does Ali's imagination help her neighbors beat the **haze** and heat?

2 How might the story have been different if the setting were in winter instead of summer?

3 What do you think Ali might do if it rains for a long time?

4 What would you have drawn to make the neighbors feel cool? Why?

5 How did picturing the story in your mind help you understand what you read?

Meet the Author and Illustrator
Nancy Poydar

When she is not illustrating her own stories, Nancy Poydar likes to illustrate the stories of other well-known children's authors. She illustrated *The Adventures of Sugar and Junior*, by Angela Shelf Medearis.

Before she began making children's books, Nancy Poydar was a teacher. She lives in Massachusetts with her husband, her cat, Sunny, and her dog, Coco.

Nancy Poydar

Visit *The Learning Site!*
www.harcourtschool.com

113

Cool It!

by Lynn O'Donnell

Take This HOT Animal Quiz

When things heat up, these animals know how to cool down! Like humans, animals need to maintain a stable body temperature. If they overheat, their bodies might shut down.

We've listed three possible ways each of these animals keeps cool in the summer. Only one of the answers is true. Can you guess the right answer for each animal?

The answers are on page 117.

1. Rabbits

A. take cold showers.
B. eat lots of lettuce.
C. let outside air cool blood flowing through their ears.

2. Bees

A. drink iced tea.
B. produce less honey.
C. collect water and pour it over their honeycombs.

3. Dogs

A. bark a lot.
B. shed their top coats.
C. pant.

4. Prairie Dogs

A. curl up in underground burrows.

B. stand under large mammals to shade themselves.

C. wear grass hats.

5. Birds

A. open their beaks and flutter their throats.

B. flap their wings wildly.

C. fly above the clouds.

6. Roadrunners

A. go to a spa.

B. sit still.

C. hang out on cactus branches.

7. Ground Squirrels

A. sleep during the day.
B. shade their bodies with their tails.
C. fan themselves with big oak leaves.

8. Pigs

A. eat ice cream.
B. roll around in mud.
C. lose weight.

Think And Respond

How are the ways animals keep cool the same as ways humans do?

Hot Animal Quiz Answers

1. C
2. C. The water prevents the beeswax from melting.
3. C. Panting makes air flow over the dog's wet mouth and tongue, whisking away moisture and body heat.
4. A. It's cooler underground!
5. A
6. C. Roadrunners hang out on cactus branches when the sand gets too hot to walk on.
7. B
8. B. Rolling around in mud keeps moisture in a pig's skin.

Making Connections

Compare Texts

1. Why is "Cool Ali" part of the Imagine That! theme?

2. Compare Ali to Emily from "Dear Mr. Blueberry." How are the girls alike? How are they different?

3. How is the quiz "Cool It!" different from the story "Cool Ali"? What purposes did the authors have for writing these selections?

Write a Paragraph

Ali is special. She draws pictures that make people feel cooler. You are special, too. No one can do things the way you do. Write a paragraph that tells the ways you are special. Use a web to plan your paragraph.

Writing
CONNECTION

Why I Am Special

I make my baby sister laugh.

What's the Temperature?

Ali and her neighbors felt the heat in the air.
They could have used a thermometer to measure
how hot it was. Measure the temperature outside
each day for one week. Write down all the
temperatures. Compare them to those in the
newspaper or on the TV news.

Monday	Tuesday	Wednesday	Thursday	Friday	Saturday	Sunday

Big Cities and Small Towns

Ali lives in a city. How are big cities different
from small towns? Find out about the biggest
cities in your state. Then find out about some
small towns. Make a chart to show how they are
different.

Big Cities	Small Towns
• have many elementary schools	• have one elementary school

Antonyms

Antonyms are words with opposite meanings. Look at the chart below. It shows some words from "Cool Ali" and their antonyms.

Words from "Cool Ali"	Antonyms
fat	skinny
hot	cold
little	big
North	South

Now look at these words. Give an antonym for each one.

wet   good
summer   heavy
tall   soft
first   large

Visit *The Learning Site!*
www.harcourtschool.com

See *Skills* and *Activities*

Test Prep

Antonyms

Read the story. Then complete the sentences.

Alexa's Room

Alexa heard her mom's footsteps on the stairs. Her mom was home from work. Alexa knew she was in trouble. She should have cleaned up her room, but she <u>forgot</u>. She had spent all afternoon drawing. Her mom was going to be <u>angry</u>.

1. **An antonym for <u>forgot</u> is—**
   - ○ lost
   - ○ worked
   - ○ thought
   - ○ remembered

Tip

Remember that when you are looking for antonyms, you must find words with opposite meanings.

2. **An antonym for <u>angry</u> is—**
   - ○ pleased
   - ○ mad
   - ○ silly
   - ○ afraid

Tip

When looking for an antonym, do not choose words that mean the same as the question word.

▲ The Emperor's Egg

Vocabulary Power

flippers

hatch

horizon

miserable

slippery

waddled

The Fillmore Times

Sunday, August 11, 2002 — 50 cents

New Baby Joins Penguin Family

Yesterday, a baby penguin was born at Fillmore Zoo. Zookeeper John Gordon said, "I knew the chick was about to **hatch** when I saw a crack in the egg. The other penguins **waddled** over to watch."

The chick came out just as the sun was setting on the **horizon**. That's why the workers at the zoo decided to name her "Sunny."

Many people came to see Sunny. "I rushed over as soon as I heard," said visitor Lila Lewis. "I had to see a penguin chick take its first steps on the **slippery** ice."

Seven-year-old Kenny Stuart also came to see Sunny. "Waiting in line for two hours was **miserable**," he said. "Then I saw Sunny's tiny beak and long **flippers**. The wait was worth it. She is so cute!"

Vocabulary–Writing CONNECTION

Imagine that you are watching a baby penguin **hatch**. Write about your thoughts and feelings.

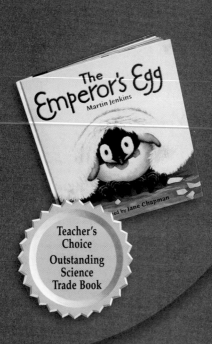

Genre

Nonfiction: Informational Book

An informational book gives facts about a topic.

Look for

- information that helps you learn more about our world.

- captions that give more information about the pictures.

The Emperor's Egg

written by Martin Jenkins

illustrated by Jane Chapman

Down at the very bottom of the world, there's a huge island that's almost completely covered in snow and ice. It's called Antarctica, and it's the coldest, windiest place on Earth.

Antarctica

The weather's bad enough there in summer, but in winter it's really terrible.

It's hard to imagine anything actually living there.

But wait . . .
what's that shape over there?
It can't be.

Yes!

It's a penguin!

It's not just any old penguin either. It's a male Emperor penguin (the biggest penguin in the world), and he's doing a Very Important Job.

He's taking care of his egg.

He didn't lay it himself, of course.

Male Emperor penguins are about 4 feet tall.

The females are a little smaller.

His mate did that
a few weeks ago.

But very soon
afterward
she turned around
and waddled off
to the sea.

That's where female Emperor penguins
spend most of the winter — swimming about,
getting as fat as they can,
eating as much as they can,
and generally having a very nice time
(as far as you can tell)!

Emperor penguins eat mainly fish, squid
and tiny shrimplike animals called krill.

Which leaves the father penguin stuck on the ice with his egg.

Now, the most important thing about egg-sitting is to stop your egg from getting cold.

That means it has to be kept off the ice and out of the wind.

And what better way to do that than to rest it on your feet and tuck it right up under your tummy?

Which is just what the father penguin does.

Inside the egg, a penguin chick is starting to grow.
If the egg gets cold, the chick will die.

And that's how he'll stay for two whole months, until his egg is ready to hatch.

Can you imagine it?
Standing around in the freezing cold
with an egg on your feet
for **two whole** months?

*Female Emperor penguins lay one egg in May or June,
which is the beginning of winter in Antarctica.*

What's more, there's nothing for
the father penguin to eat on land.

And because he's egg-sitting,
he can't go off to the sea to feed.

So that means two whole
months with an egg on your feet **and no dinner!**

Or breakfast

or lunch

or snacks.

I don't know about you
but I'd be **very, very** miserable.

Luckily, the penguins don't seem to mind too much. They have thick feathers and lots of fat under their skin to help keep them warm.

And when it gets really cold and windy, they all snuggle up together and shuffle over the ice in a great big huddle.

Most of the time, the huddle trundles along very, very slowly.

But **sometimes,**
when the penguins get to a particularly slippery slope ...

they slide down it on their tummies,
pushing themselves along
with their flippers,
always remembering
to take care of their egg —
and trying hard not to bump into each other.

Even though the males keep the egg tucked up tight under their tummies when they slide, it sometimes rolls out and breaks.

And that's how the father penguin spends the winter.

Until one day he hears a chip, chip, chip.

His egg is starting to hatch.
It takes a day or so, but finally the egg
cracks right open —

and out pops a penguin chick.

Now the father penguin
has two jobs to do.
He has to keep
the chick warm

and he has to feed it.

The chick is only about 6 inches tall at first,
and much too small to keep warm by itself.

But on what? The chick is too small to be taken off to the sea to catch food, and it can't be left behind on the ice.

Well, deep down in the father penguin's throat, there's a pouch where he makes something a little like milk. And that's what he feeds to his hungry chick.

The father penguin can make only enough of the
milky stuff to feed his chick for a couple of weeks.
But just as he's about to run out,
a dot appears on the horizon.

It gets closer
and closer
and yes!

It's mom!

She starts trumpeting **"hello"** and the father penguin starts trumpeting **"hello"** and the chick whistles.

The racket goes on for hours, and it really does sound as if they're extremely pleased to see each other.

Every adult penguin has its own special call, like a fingerprint. Chicks have their own special whistle, too.

142

As soon as things have calmed down, the mother penguin is sick — right into her chick's mouth!

Yuk,

you may think.

Yum,

thinks the chick,

and gobbles it all down.

It's the mother's turn to take care of the chick now, while the father sets off to the sea for a well-earned meal of his own.

About time, too!

Think and Respond

1 How do Emperor penguin fathers take care of their eggs before they **hatch**?

2 What kind of information does the author give in the captions?

3 How are Emperor penguin parents the same as human parents?

4 What did you learn about Emperor penguins that you did not know before?

5 Which strategies did you use to read this selection?

Meet the Author and Illustrator

Martin Jenkins

Martin Jenkins is a scientist who studies plants and animals. He admires the way Emperor penguin dads take care of their eggs because he doesn't like cold weather himself.

Jane Chapman

Jane Chapman always paints in her kitchen, where she can look out at her garden. She was happy to paint pictures of penguins. She had wanted to ever since she saw a penguin at the zoo.

Visit *The Learning Site!*
www.harcourtschool.com

145

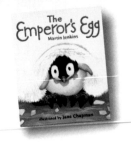

Making Connections

Compare Texts

1 Why do you think this selection is part of the Imagine That! theme?

2 Think about the problem Ali and her neighbors had in "Cool Ali." Explain why they might enjoy a visit to where the Emperor penguins live.

3 How is "The Emperor's Egg" different from the other stories in this theme?

Thanks, Dad

Write a paragraph to explain how the male Emperor penguin takes care of his chick. Use a web to plan your writing.

Writing CONNECTION

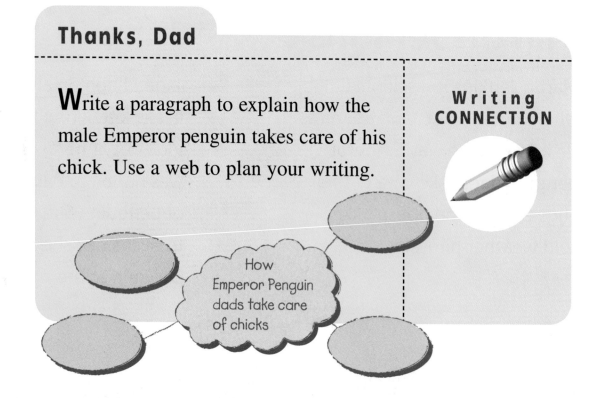

How Emperor Penguin dads take care of chicks

Going South

On a world map or globe, find where you live. Then find Antarctica. Name the areas of land and water you might travel over in a plane to get from where you live to Antarctica.

Social Studies CONNECTION

North America

Antarctica

Penguin Time

The male Emperor penguin takes care of an egg for about two months before it hatches. Use what you know about time to tell

- the number of weeks in two months.
- the number of days in two months.

Share your answers with classmates.

Math CONNECTION

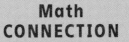

Suffixes: *-ing* and *-ly*

Phonics Skill

When you add *-ing* or *-ly* to a word, you add to the meaning of the word.

Word	+	Suffix	=	New Word
start	+	*ing*	=	starting
slow	+	*ly*	=	slowly

The chick is <u>starting</u> to walk.

The penguin waddled <u>slowly</u>.

Sometimes there are special rules to follow when you add *-ing*.

- To add *-ing* to a word that has a silent **e** at the end, drop the silent **e**.
  tak~~e~~ + *ing* = taking

- To add *-ing* to a word that ends in a vowel and a consonant, double the last letter.
  swim + m + *ing* = swimming

Use these tips to read a longer word.
- Look for word parts you know.
- Break the word into parts.
- Say each part. Then blend the parts and say the word.

Test Prep

Suffixes: *-ing* and *-ly*

Fill in the bubble next to the word with *-ing* or *-ly* correctly added.

Example: **get**

   ○ geting

   ● getting

   ○ geeting

Tip

Look at how each word is spelled. Think about the rules before you choose.

1.   **particular**

   ○ particularely

   ○ particularly

   ○ particularlly

2.   **freeze**

   ○ freezing

   ○ freezeing

   ○ freezzing

Tip

Say each choice aloud. Which seems best?

3.   **stand**

   ○ standding

   ○ standeing

   ○ standing

Neighborhood News

CONTENTS

▲ The Pine Park Mystery

caused

clasp

confused

cornered

objects

removes

typical

Vocabulary Power

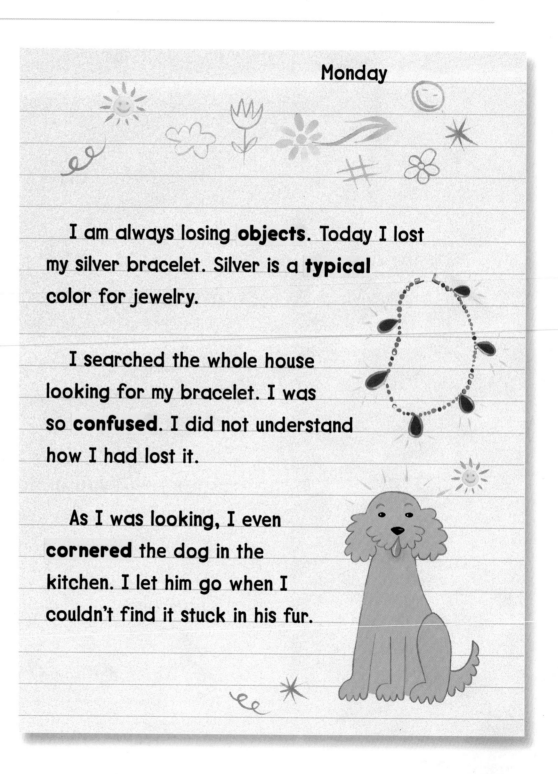

Monday

I am always losing **objects**. Today I lost my silver bracelet. Silver is a **typical** color for jewelry.

I searched the whole house looking for my bracelet. I was so **confused**. I did not understand how I had lost it.

As I was looking, I even **cornered** the dog in the kitchen. I let him go when I couldn't find it stuck in his fur.

Finally, I saw something shiny by my bed. It was my bracelet! The **clasp** had broken that held it closed. This had **caused** it to fall off while I was sleeping.

My mother always **removes** her jewelry before she goes to bed. From now on, I think I'll do that, too.

Vocabulary-Writing CONNECTION

Write about an **object** you once lost. Tell how you tried to find it.

The
PINE PARK
MYSTERY
by Tracey West
Illustrated by Myra GrandPré

Award-Winning
Illustrator

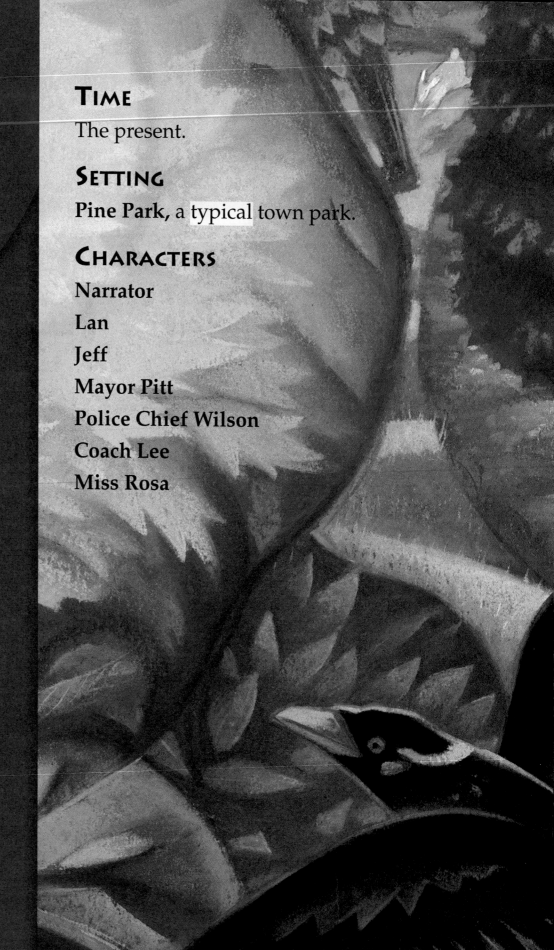

TIME

The present.

SETTING

Pine Park, a typical town park.

CHARACTERS

Narrator

Lan

Jeff

Mayor Pitt

Police Chief Wilson

Coach Lee

Miss Rosa

The
PINE PARK
MYSTERY

by Tracey West

illustrated by Mary GrandPré

SCENE ONE

Narrator: It is a beautiful afternoon in
Pine Park. The sun is shining, and the
birds are singing. It's just another ordinary
day... or is it?

(**Coach Lee,** *blowing his whistle, runs toward* **Mayor Pitt.**)

Mayor Pitt: Hello, Coach Lee. It's a great day for a walk in the park, isn't it?

Coach Lee: *(jogging in place)* It sure is, Mayor. Well, I've got to catch up with the team!

(**Coach Lee** *runs off.*)

Mayor Pitt: Coach Lee is always in a hurry!

(*She sits on a bench and removes her jacket.*)

Mayor Pitt: *(looking at her jacket, confused)* That's funny. I thought I wore my silver pin today. I wonder where it could be!

156

Narrator: In another part of the park, Lan and Jeff are playing catch.

Lan: I'm bored. Nothing exciting ever seems to happen around here.

(*Jeff* tosses the ball to *Lan*.)

Jeff: You're always bored. Isn't playing catch in the park enough fun for you?

(*Lan* catches the ball and then drops it suddenly, looking confused. She looks closely at her wrist.)

Lan: That's funny. My charm bracelet is missing. The clasp was loose. . . .

Jeff: Maybe it fell off near here. Let's look.

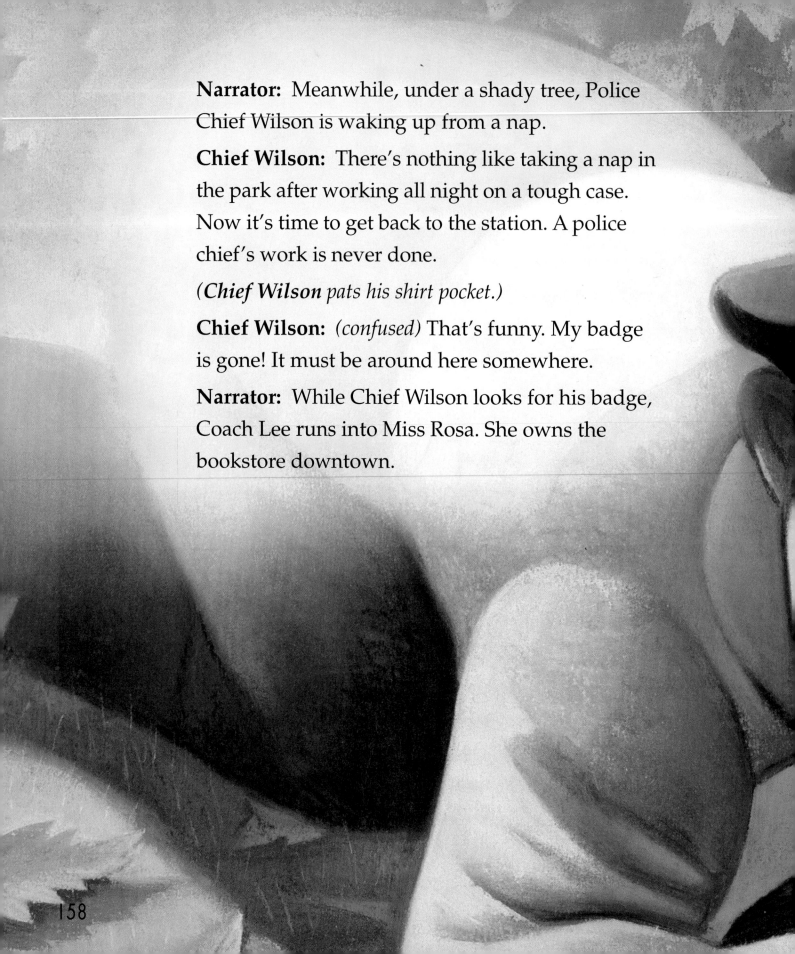

Narrator: Meanwhile, under a shady tree, Police Chief Wilson is waking up from a nap.

Chief Wilson: There's nothing like taking a nap in the park after working all night on a tough case. Now it's time to get back to the station. A police chief's work is never done.

(**Chief Wilson** *pats his shirt pocket.*)

Chief Wilson: *(confused)* That's funny. My badge is gone! It must be around here somewhere.

Narrator: While Chief Wilson looks for his badge, Coach Lee runs into Miss Rosa. She owns the bookstore downtown.

Miss Rosa: Hi, Coach. Where are you running to?

Coach Lee: I'm trying to find my whistle. I had it a few minutes ago, but now I can't find it anywhere.

Miss Rosa: That's funny—I'm looking for something, too.

Narrator: Is something mysterious happening in Pine Park? Lan and Jeff are about to find out.

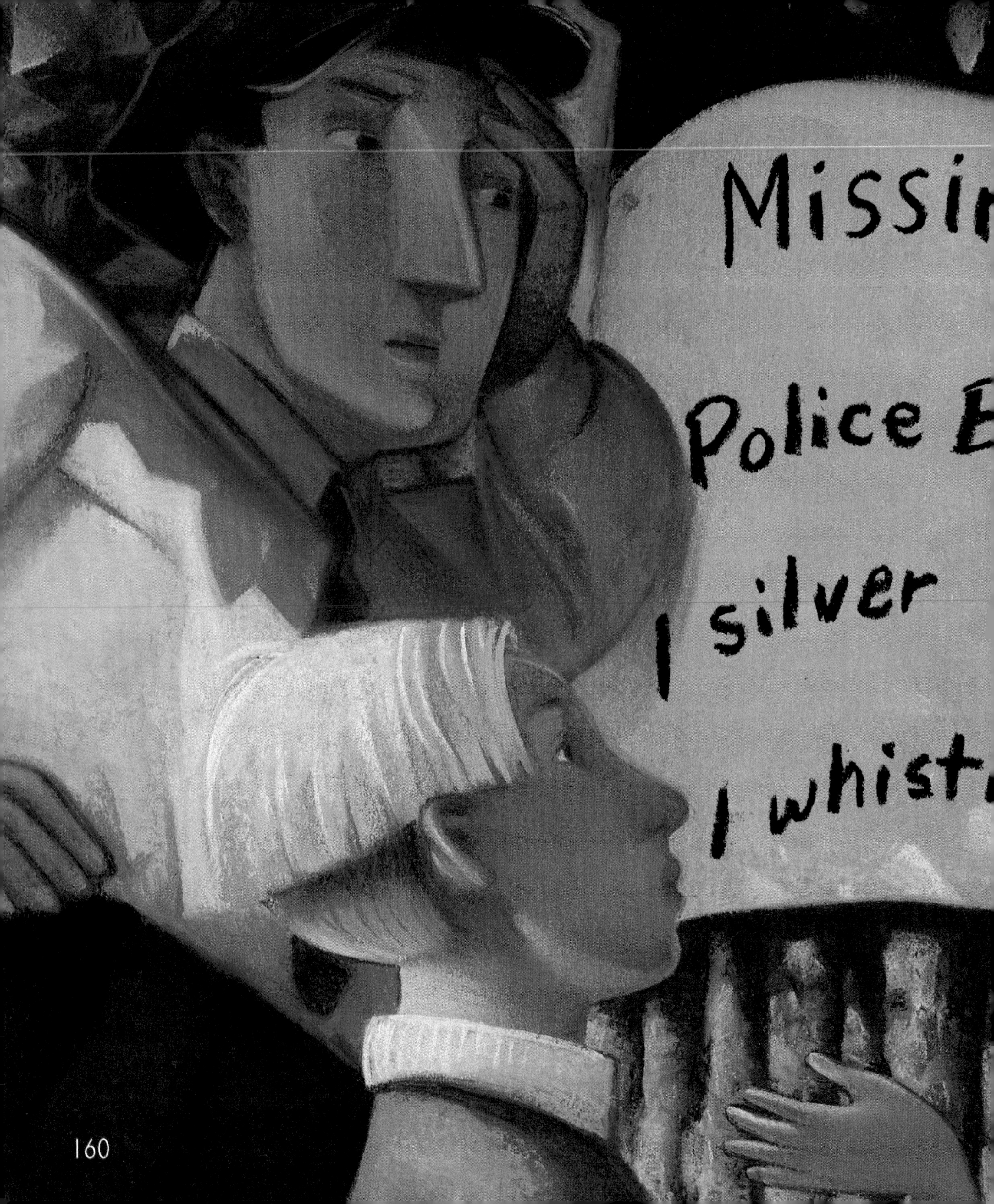
Missin
Police B
1 silver
1 whist

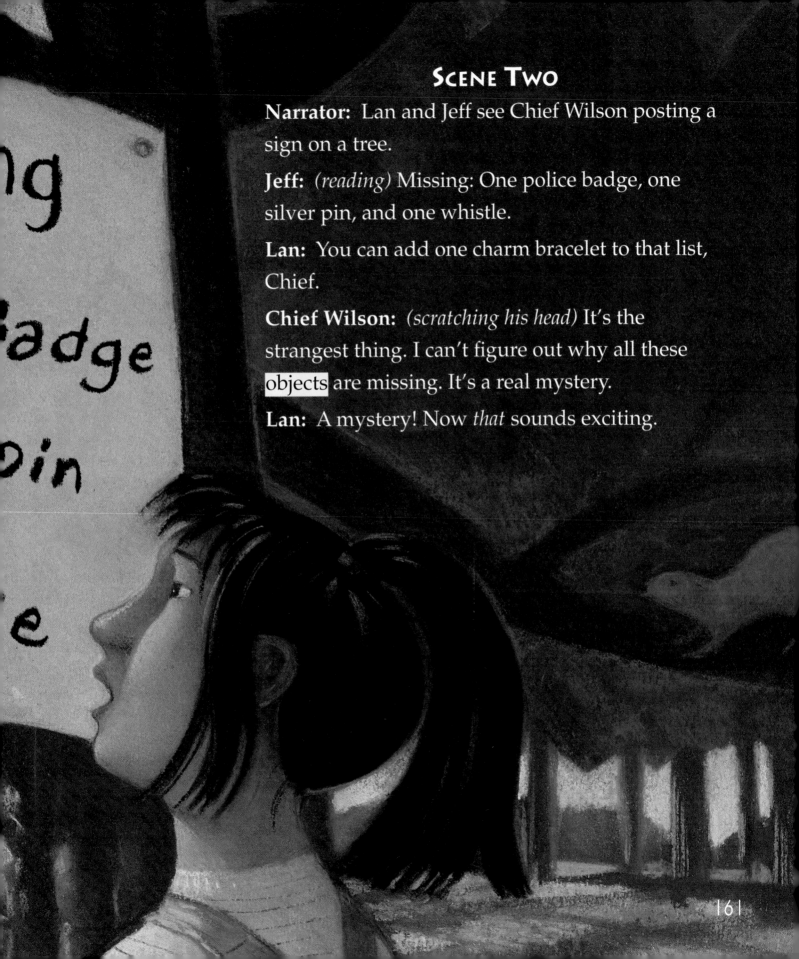

SCENE TWO

Narrator: Lan and Jeff see Chief Wilson posting a sign on a tree.

Jeff: *(reading)* Missing: One police badge, one silver pin, and one whistle.

Lan: You can add one charm bracelet to that list, Chief.

Chief Wilson: *(scratching his head)* It's the strangest thing. I can't figure out why all these objects are missing. It's a real mystery.

Lan: A mystery! Now *that* sounds exciting.

161

SCENE THREE

Narrator: Lan and Jeff are about to try to solve the case of the missing objects.

Lan: We have to think like real detectives, Jeff. Let's start by listing what we know about this case.

Jeff: Well, everyone noticed the objects were missing while he or she was in the park.

Lan: That's right. What else do we know?

Jeff: All of the objects were pretty small . . . they were all shiny, too.

Lan: I have an idea! Let's put another small, shiny object in the park. Then we can hide and see what happens to it.

Jeff: How about the key to my bicycle lock?

(*Jeff takes the key from his pocket and puts it on a nearby rock. Jeff and Lan hide behind a tree. A group of kids runs across the stage, blocking the audience's view of the key on the rock.*)

Narrator: There goes Coach Lee's team. But look! The key is gone!

SCENE FOUR

(*Lan leads* **Chief Wilson**, **Mayor Pitt**, **Coach Lee**, *and* **Miss Rosa** *to a tree in the park, where* **Jeff** *is waiting for them.*)

Lan: (*to Jeff*) Do you have the thief cornered?

Jeff: (*smiling*) She's up in that tree.

Coach Lee: (*jogging in place*) Thief? I don't see anybody in that tree.

164

Chief Wilson: *(peers into the tree and smiles)* The thief isn't any*body*, Coach. It's a bird!

Miss Rosa: *(gasps)* That's Dynah! She's my new pet mynah bird. She escaped from the bookstore this morning. I've been looking for her all day! *(looks at **Lan** and **Jeff**)* How did you two know Dynah was the thief?

165

Lan: Jeff figured out that all the missing objects were small and shiny, so we decided to set a trap. We put Jeff's bicycle key on a rock. Dynah flew by and picked it up.

Jeff: Then she flew into this tree.

Miss Rosa: Mynah birds do like to collect shiny objects. I'll bet you'll find all the missing things somewhere in the tree.

166

Narrator: Chief Wilson calls the Pine Park Fire Department. The firefighters use a ladder to get the objects and bring them down.

Chief Wilson: Here they are—one badge, one silver pin, one whistle, one charm bracelet, and one bicycle key.

167

Miss Rosa: *(holding a bird cage with Dynah in it)* I'm sorry Dynah caused so much trouble, Mayor Pitt. I'll try to keep a close eye on her from now on.

Mayor Pitt: *(laughing)* She certainly caused quite a stir! A day in Pine Park was never so exciting.

Lan: I can't wait to come back to the park tomorrow!

Jeff: To play catch?

Lan: No, I want to see if there's another mystery we can solve!

THINK AND RESPOND

1 What is the mystery in Pine Park?

2 Where in the play did you find out what **caused** this mystery? Why?

3 What clues helped you solve the mystery?

4 What part of the play did you like best?

5 What strategies helped you read this play?

Tracey West   _Mary GrandPré_

MEET THE AUTHOR

Tracey West loved reading so
much as a child that she decided
she wanted to be an author. She
writes at her home near New
York City, where she lives with
her husband, her dog, Tisha,
and her cat, Elvira.

MEET THE ILLUSTRATOR

Mary GrandPré has illustrated
many children's books and made
artwork for an animated film.
She lives in St. Paul, Minnesota.

169

Birds D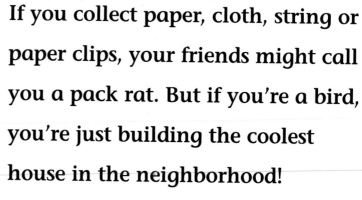 It! Recycle!

If you collect paper, cloth, string or paper clips, your friends might call you a pack rat. But if you're a bird, you're just building the coolest house in the neighborhood!

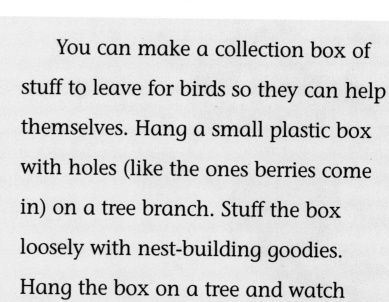

You can make a collection box of stuff to leave for birds so they can help themselves. Hang a small plastic box with holes (like the ones berries come in) on a tree branch. Stuff the box loosely with nest-building goodies. Hang the box on a tree and watch birds climb on board to pick through the junk to find their treasures.

170

Look and see how your old junk can help decorate and warm a bird's new home.

Worn-out shoelaces work well to keep a nest snug and warm.

Bits of cotton help keep a nest warm and cozy.

Birds like yarn. Make sure the strings are no longer than six inches. Otherwise, birds may get tangled up in them and get hurt.

Rags are great. Try to give birds strips of cloth made of natural fibers.

Think and Respond

What things can you do in your community to help nature?

Making Connections

Compare Texts

1 Why do you think "The Pine Park Mystery" is in a theme called Neighborhood News?

2 Think about two characters in "The Pine Park Mystery" who have community jobs. Tell how their jobs are alike and different.

3 In "Birds Do It! Recycle!" you read about things that birds collect for building their nests. How are the objects that Dynah picks up different?

Write a Scene

Jimmy: Hi, Dave. Do you want to go to the park?

Dave: Sure! What should I bring?

Jimmy: Bring a baseball and your glove.

Dave: Okay! Let's meet on the corner right away.

Think of a time you talked with a friend. Write what each of you said, as a scene in a play. With a classmate, read your scene with feeling.

Writing
CONNECTION

Bird-Watching

To find out about birds in your community, make a bird feeder to hang near your house or classroom. Draw and write about the kinds of birds that come to eat from your feeder.

Science CONNECTION

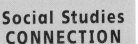

Meet the Mayor

You have a mayor in your city or town. Find out your mayor's name and write it. Then list the jobs you know about that your mayor does to help your community.

Social Studies CONNECTION

173

Narrative Elements

Every story has a setting, characters, and a plot. The **plot** is what happens during the beginning, middle, and end of a story. The beginning tells about a problem. The middle tells how the characters deal with it. The end tells how they solve it.

A story map shows the plot of a story. Look at this story map for "The Pine Park Mystery." What would you write in the last box?

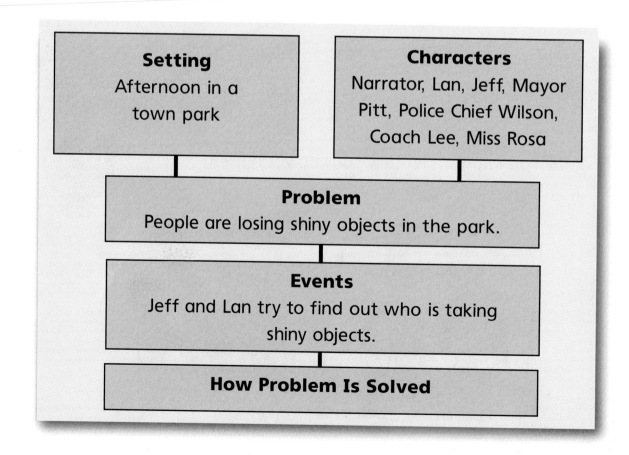

Setting	Characters
Afternoon in a town park	Narrator, Lan, Jeff, Mayor Pitt, Police Chief Wilson, Coach Lee, Miss Rosa

Problem
People are losing shiny objects in the park.

Events
Jeff and Lan try to find out who is taking shiny objects.

How Problem Is Solved

Test Prep

Narrative Elements

Read the story. Then answer the questions.

A Day at the Park

The town park was a mess. Jason wanted to clean it up, but he could not do it alone. He asked his friends and neighbors to meet at the park on Saturday. They all worked together to pick up trash, paint the benches, and trim the bushes. Now everyone can enjoy the park.

1. **In this story's plot, what is the problem?**
   - ○ The park is closed.
   - ○ The park is a mess.
   - ○ People clean the park.
   - ○ Jason needs a friend.

Tip

Reread the beginning of the story to help you find the answer.

2. **How is the problem solved?**
   - ○ Jason finds people to help clean the park.
   - ○ People stop using the park on Saturdays.
   - ○ The mayor cleans the park.
   - ○ Jason cleans the park alone on Sunday.

Tip

Carefully read each answer choice before you choose the correct answer.

▲ Good-bye, Curtis

addresses

clerk

grown

honor

pour

route

Vocabulary Power

Hundreds of letters **pour** into your post office each day.

The **clerk** who works at the post office sorts the letters by their street **addresses**.

Each letter has a stamp. Some stamps **honor** famous people by showing their faces.

Letter carriers deliver the letters to homes and businesses every day. The path they follow is called a mail **route**.

The United States Postal Service has **grown** very large. Now it is one of the biggest and best postal systems in the world.

Vocabulary-Writing CONNECTION

Only persons who are no longer alive are shown on stamps. Name someone you think deserves this **honor**. Tell why you feel as you do.

Good-bye, Curtis

KEVIN HENKES
ARISABINA RUSSO

Award-Winning
Author

Realistic Fiction

Realistic fiction is a story that can happen in the real world.

Look for

- story events that can happen in real life.

- characters that act in ways they might act in the real world.

FIRST CLASS

PARIS BX ARTS
18 H
93
1995
R DES ST PERES (7)

Good-

by Kevin Henkes

bye, Curtis

pictures by Marisabina Russo

Curtis has been a letter carrier

for forty-two years.

Today is his last day.

Everyone loves Curtis —

the old woman on the hill,

the baby in 4-C,

the clerk at the butcher shop,

and the crossing guard

at the corner of First and Park.

All of the mailboxes all over his route are filled

with all kinds of surprises. There is a chocolate

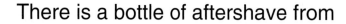

cupcake with sprinkles from Mrs. Martin.

There is a drawing from Debbie,

Dennis, and Donny.

There is a bottle of aftershave from

the Johnsons, and a box of nuts

from their dog.

There are cards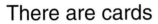

and candy and cookies.

 There are hugs and

handshakes and kisses.

There is a small, fat book from

Mr. Porter, and a pencil sharpener

in the shape of a mailbox from Max.

Boneless steaks   3.48
Boneless Pork Chops   3.49
Pork Tenderloin Fillets 4.99
Chicken Legs   .74
Turkey Breast   5.19

"We'll miss you, Curtis,"

say the old woman on the hill

and the baby in 4-C

and the clerk at the butcher shop

and the crossing guard

at the corner of First and Park.

The children Curtis met when

he first began his route have

grown up.

Some of them have children of their own.

Some of them have grandchildren.

Some of the children have had

dogs. Some of the dogs have had puppies.

Cats have had kittens, too.

Trees have grown from little to big.

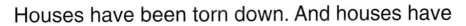

Houses have been torn down. And houses have

gone up. People have moved out.

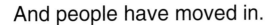

And people have moved in.

But everyone loves Curtis.
"We'll miss you," they all say.
The dogs and cats say so, too.

When Curtis gets to the last mailbox
at the last house on the last street . . .

Surprise! Surprise! Surprise!

Curtis's own family is waiting there.
Friends pour out the door and down the steps.
People from all over his route run out from
the backyard.

They have a party in Curtis's honor.
"We love you, Curtis," they all say.
"We'll miss you."

There is dancing and eating and
remembering. There are balloons and
streamers and tiny tin horns.

That night Curtis dreams of his party.
When he wakes up the next morning,
he begins writing thank-you notes to everyone.

And he knows all the addresses by heart.

Think and Respond

1 What changes has Curtis seen during his forty-two
years as a letter carrier?

2 How is the setting important in this story?

3 How do the author and illustrator show that the people
on Curtis's **route** care about him?

4 Would you like to live along Curtis's route? Why or
why not?

5 What strategies did you use to read this story?

Meet the Author
Kevin Henkes

Dear Readers,

When I was your age, I loved to go to the
library. I carried all my books home by myself,
no matter how many I had. I think my visits to the
library helped me decide to become an author.

I like to end my stories in a hopeful way.
Reading a story with a hopeful ending is like
coming home from school and putting on play
clothes. It feels good!

Kevin Henkes

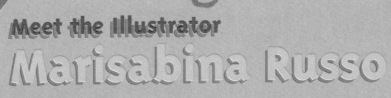

Meet the Illustrator
Marisabina Russo

Dear Readers,

When I was a child, I drew pictures all the time. I especially liked to draw pictures of children and dogs. Once I got into trouble for drawing on the bottom of a table. After that my mother gave me a new pad of paper every week.

Marisab Russo

Visit *The Learning Site!*
www.harcourtschool.com

195

Making Connections

Compare Texts

1 How is Curtis a special part of his neighborhood?

2 What is the setting of this story? Compare it to the setting of "The Pine Park Mystery."

3 Tell about some of the characters in this story besides Curtis. How do you think they feel about Curtis? How do you know?

Letter of Introduction

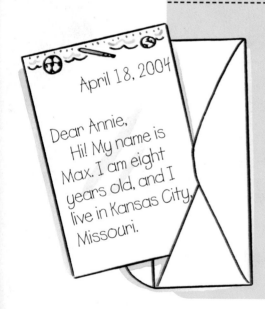

April 18, 2004

Dear Annie,
   Hi! My name is Max. I am eight years old, and I live in Kansas City, Missouri.

Imagine that you have just found a pen pal—a new friend to write to in a faraway place. Write a letter about yourself that Curtis could deliver with other mail. In your letter, give your name and tell what you like to do.

Writing CONNECTION

Personal Time Line

Social Studies
CONNECTION

Curtis has had a long and busy life. Make a time line of your own life. List important things that have happened in your life and the years when they happened. Show them in the right order.

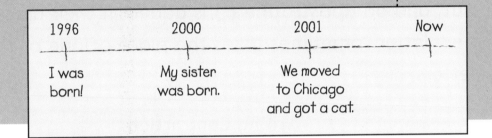

1996	2000	2001	Now
I was born!	My sister was born.	We moved to Chicago and got a cat.	

Stamp Sense

Math
CONNECTION

Find out how much it costs to buy one stamp for a letter. How much does it cost to buy two stamps? Three stamps? Share your information with the class. Explain how you found your answers.

▲ Good-bye, Curtis

Contractions:
'll, n't, 's

Sometimes, when you use two words together, you can make them into one word. These new words are called **contractions**. One or more letters are taken out, and an **apostrophe (')** is added in their place. A new letter sometimes takes the place of one or more letters.

Writing Contractions	
Contractions with 'll	**Contractions with n't**
we will ⟶ we'll they will ⟶ they'll	do not ⟶ don't can not ⟶ can't
Contractions with 's	**Contractions That Change Spelling**
let us ⟶ let's he is ⟶ he's	will not ⟶ won't

Make the contractions in each of these sentences.

<u>I am</u> going to the party.

They <u>will not</u> come with me.

<u>She is</u> going to the post office.

Test Prep

Contractions: 'll, n't, 's

Choose the word that is the correct contraction for the underlined words.

Example: <u>did not</u>

- ○ did'nt
- ○ didnt
- ● didn't
- ○ dident

Tip

Skip over any choice that does not have an apostrophe.

1. <u>they will</u>
   - ○ they'ill
   - ○ they"ll
   - ○ thell
   - ○ they'll

2. <u>she is</u>
   - ○ she'is
   - ○ she's
   - ○ she"is
   - ○ shee's

3. <u>will not</u>
   - ○ willn't
   - ○ will'nt
   - ○ wo'nt
   - ○ won't

Tip

Remember that the apostrophe comes between the *n* and the *t*.

199

Vocabulary Power

appeared

conductor

created

imitated

rhythm

startled

Alex waited with his father at the train station. He **created** a drum set from boxes to pass the time.

Alex could see the train coming. He listened to the **rhythm** in the sound of the wheels against the tracks. He **imitated** it on his boxes. *Rat-tat, rat-tat.*

Suddenly a loud whistle **startled** Alex. He jumped up in surprise.

The train **conductor** soon **appeared** at an open door. Alex and his dad gave him their tickets and climbed aboard.

Vocabulary-Writing CONNECTION

Write about a time that you **imitated** someone or something. Tell how you did it.

Genre

Realistic Fiction

Realistic fiction tells about events that could happen in real life.

Look for

- **characters that do things real people do.**

- **a setting that could be a real place.**

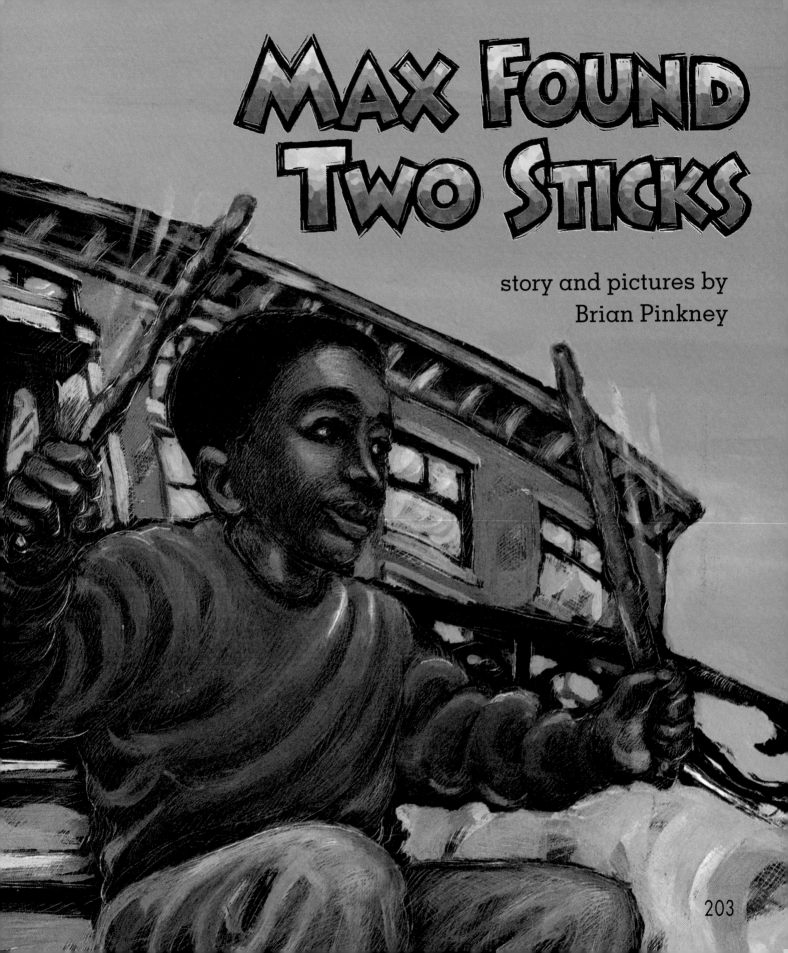

Max Found Two Sticks

story and pictures by
Brian Pinkney

It was a day when Max didn't feel like talking to anyone. He just sat on his front steps and watched the clouds gather in the sky.

A strong breeze shook the tree in front of his house, and Max saw two heavy twigs fall to the ground.

"What are you gonna do with those sticks?" Max's grandpa asked as he washed the front windows.

Not saying a word, Max tapped on his thighs, *Pat . . . pat-tat. Putter-putter . . . pat-tat.* His rhythm imitated the sound of the pigeons, startled into flight.

When Max's mother came home carrying new hats for his twin sisters, she asked, "What are you doing with Grandpa's cleaning bucket, Son?"

Max responded by patting the bucket, *Tap-tap-tap.*

Tippy-tip . . . tat-tat. He **created** the rhythm of the light rain falling against the front windows.

After a while the clouds moved
on and the sun appeared.
Cindy, Shaun and Jamal showed
up drinking sodas. "Hey, Max!
Whatcha doin' with those
hatboxes?"

Again Max didn't answer.
He just played on the boxes,
Dum . . . dum-de-dum.

Di-di-di-di. Dum-dum. Max
drummed the beat of the
tom-toms in a marching band.

211

"What are you up to with those soda bottles?" his dad asked as he brought out the garbage cans on his way to work.

Max answered on the bottles, *Dong . . . dang . . . dung.*

Ding . . . dong . . . ding!
His music joined the chiming of the bells in the church around the corner.

213

Soon the twins came out to show off their new hats. "Hey, Max," they asked, "what are you doin' with those garbage cans?"

Max hammered out a reply on the cans, *Cling . . . clang . . . da-BANG!*

A-cling-clang . . . DA-BANGGGG!
Max pounded out the sound of the wheels thundering down the tracks under the train on which his father worked as a conductor.

Suddenly Max heard *Thump-di-di-thump . . . THUMP-DI-DI-THUMP!* as a marching band rounded the corner.

Max watched the drummers with amazement as they passed, copying their rhythms. The last drummer saw Max. Then with a nod and a wink, he tossed Max his spare set of sticks.

"Thanks," called Max—and he didn't miss a beat.

Think and Respond

1. What things does Max tap on to create **rhythm**?

2. How might the story be different if Max lived in the country instead of in the city?

3. How does Max feel at the beginning of the story? How does he feel at the end?

4. What is your favorite part of the story? Why?

5. What strategies helped you read this story?

Meet the Author and Illustrator
BRIAN PINKNEY

What made you decide to write this book?

I wanted to write a book about drumming because I've played the drums most of my life. I almost made music my career. I had ideas about a book, but I didn't really have a story. I would jot down notes about a boy and how he liked to drum. It took me about four years to finish the book. I decided to start with the pictures. I would draw a little and then write a little. Most of the words came to me when I was just waking up in the morning or when I was away from my studio.

Brian Pinkney

Visit *The Learning Site!*
www.harcourtschool.com

Snap your fingers.
Tap your feet.
Step out a rhythm
down the street.

Rap on a litter bin.
Stamp on the ground.
City music
is all around.

Beep says motor-car.
Ding says bike.
City music
is what we like.

by Tony Mitton

Making Connections

Compare Texts

1 Think about the settings in "Max Found Two Sticks," "Good-bye, Curtis," and "The Pine Park Mystery." How do these settings fit into this theme?

2 Why might Brian Pinkney have written "Max Found Two Sticks" as a story rather than as a play?

3 How is the poem "City Music" like "Max Found Two Sticks"?

What Happens Next?

What do you think Max will do with his new drumsticks? Use a web to list your ideas. Then write a story to tell what Max does next.

Max has new drumsticks.

Writing
CONNECTION

Sounds All Around

Max made music with objects he found. You can, too. Find things you can use to make interesting sounds. You might use sticks with boxes, cans, and other things. As you make different sounds, compare their loudness, or *volume*.

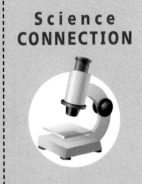

Science CONNECTION

All Aboard!

Imagine that you are a train conductor. Look at a map to find a place to travel to in your train. Will you travel to a city or the countryside? Brainstorm a list of the sights and sounds you might expect when you arrive.

Social Studies CONNECTION

Multiple-Meaning Words

**Focus
Skill**

Words that are spelled the same but have different meanings are called **multiple-meaning words.** Below is a multiple-meaning word from "Max Found Two Sticks." You can figure out its meanings from the ways it is used in the following sentences.

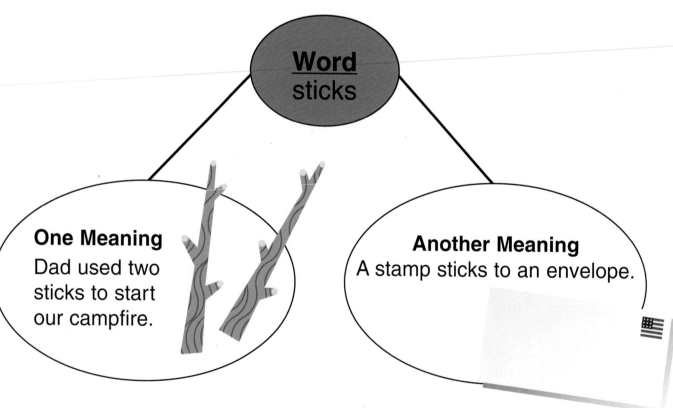

Word
sticks

One Meaning
Dad used two sticks to start our campfire.

Another Meaning
A stamp sticks to an envelope.

The word *saw* is another multiple-meaning word from the story. What are its two meanings?

Visit *The Learning Site!*
www.harcourtschool.com

See *Skills* and *Activities*

226

Test Prep

Multiple-Meaning Words

Read the paragraph. Then complete the sentences.

Last Weekend

We went to the fair last weekend. We went on rides, played games, and stood in lines with lots of people. What I liked best was the band. It played jazz music all day long.

---

1. **In the paragraph above, the word** *fair* **means—**

   ○ nice, warm weather

   ○ honest and even

   ○ an event with rides and games

   ○ not too bad

Tip

Choose the answer that goes with the meaning in the paragraph.

2. **In this story, the word** *band* **is —**

   ○ a piece of rubber used to hold things together

   ○ a group of people who play music together

   ○ a stripe of bright color

   ○ a group of people who live together

Tip

Think about the meaning in the paragraph before you choose an answer.

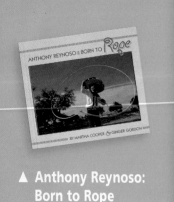

▲ Anthony Reynoso:
Born to Rope

Vocabulary Power

dappled

exhibition

landscape
business

ranch

thousands

Each year, my family goes to the county fair. It is crowded with **thousands** of people. They come to look at animals, see arts and crafts, and eat delicious food.

My dad takes a day off to take us to the fair. He works for a **landscape business**. His job is to care for people's lawns and keep them looking good!

When we go to the fair, the first thing we do is look at the horses. They come from a nearby **ranch** that raises horses and cattle.

This is my favorite horse, Daisy. She has a beautiful **dappled** coat with brown spots on white. I come to see her every year.

A great part of the day is the talent **exhibition**. We watch people show off their special skills.

Vocabulary-Writing CONNECTION

Have you ever been to a place where there were **thousands** of people? Tell about the place and why so many people were there.

Genre

Nonfiction: Personal Narrative

A personal narrative is a true story about something important to the narrator.

Look for

- information about the narrator's life.

- first-person words such as *I*, *me*, and *my*.

Anthony Reynoso:
BORN TO ROPE

by Martha Cooper & Ginger Gordon

My name is Anthony Reynoso. I'm named after
my father, who is holding the white horse, and my
grandfather, who is holding the dappled horse.
We all rope and ride Mexican Rodeo style on my
grandfather's ranch outside of Phoenix, Arizona.

As soon as I could stand, my dad gave me a rope. I had my own little hat and everything else I needed to dress as a *charro*. That's what a Mexican cowboy is called. It's a good thing I started when I was little, because it takes years to learn to rope.

I live with my mom and dad in the little
Mexican-American and Yaqui Indian town of
Guadalupe. All my grandparents live close by.
This will help a lot when the new baby comes.
My mom is pregnant.

I've got a secret about Guadalupe. I know where there are petroglyphs in the rocks right near my house. My favorite looks like a man with a shield. People carved these petroglyphs hundreds of years ago. Why did they do it? I wonder what the carvings mean.

Every Sunday morning the old Mexican Mission church is packed. At Easter, lots of people come to watch the Yaqui Indian ceremonies in the center of town.

Some Sundays, we go to Casa Reynoso, my grandparents' restaurant. If it's very busy, my cousins and I pitch in. When there's time, my grandmother lets me help in the kitchen. Casa Reynoso has the best Mexican food in town.

235

On holidays, we go to my grandfather's ranch. Once a year, we all get dressed up for a family photo.

I've got lots of cousins. Whenever there's a birthday we have a piñata. We smash it with a stick until all the candy falls out. Then we scramble to grab as much as we can hold.

Best of all, at the ranch we get to practice roping on horseback. My dad's always trying something new . . . and so am I!

In Mexico, the Rodeo is the national sport. The most famous charros there are like sports stars here.

On weekdays, Dad runs his landscape business,
Mom works in a public school, and I go to school.
I wait for the bus with other kids at the corner
of my block.

I always come to school with
my homework done. When I'm
in class, I forget about roping
and riding. I don't think anyone
in school knows about it except
my best friends.

It's different when I get home. I practice hard with Dad. He's a good teacher and shows me everything his father taught him. We spend a lot of time practicing for shows at schools, malls, and rodeos. We are experts at passing the rope. Our next big exhibition is in Sedona, about two hours away by car.

After rope practice we shoot a few baskets. Dad's pretty good at that too!

On Friday after school, Dad and I prepare our ropes for the show in Sedona. They've got to be just right.

Everything's ready for tomorrow, so I can take a break and go through my basketball cards. I decide which ones I want to buy, sell, and trade. Collecting basketball cards is one of my favorite hobbies.

It's Saturday! Time for the show in Sedona. I get a little nervous watching the other performers. I sure wouldn't want to get messed up in my own rope in front of all these people! After the Mexican hat dance, we're next!

My dad goes first . . . and then it's my turn. While the mariachis play, I do my stuff. Even Dad can't spin the rope from his teeth like this!

Then Dad and I rope together, just like we practiced. It's hard to do with our wide charro hats on. When my dad passes the rope to me and I spin it well, he says he has passed the Mexican Rodeo tradition on to me. Now it's up to me to keep it going.

Mom is our best fan. She always comes with us. It makes me feel good to know she's out there watching.

Sometimes tourists want us to pose for pictures with them. It makes me feel like a celebrity.

After the show, boy, are we hungry! We pack up and eat a quick lunch. Then we go to a special place called Slide Rock. Slide Rock is a natural water slide where kids have played for hundreds, maybe even thousands, of years. It's cold today! I'd rather come back in the summer when it's hot. But Dad pulls me in anyway. Brrr!

Time to go home. Next time we come to Sedona, the baby will be with us. I wonder if it will be a boy or a girl. It's hard to wait! I'm going to love being a big brother. Pretty soon the baby will be wearing my old boots and learning how to rope from me.

THINK AND RESPOND

1. What does Anthony tell you about his life in a Mexican-American family?

2. Why do you think the authors wrote about Anthony Reynoso?

3. Why do Anthony and his father rope and ride Mexican Rodeo style?

4. What skill would you like to learn? What kind of **exhibition** might you give to show off your skill?

5. What strategies helped you read this selection?

244

MEET THE AUTHORS

Ginger Gordon is a first-grade teacher and a writer. She has written another book with Martha Cooper called *My Two Worlds.* That book is about an eight-year-old girl who lives in both New York City and the Dominican Republic. Ginger Gordon likes to show what life is like for children in different cultures.

Martha Cooper is a photographer. She likes to show how people from many different backgrounds live together in neighborhoods. Her photographs can be found in magazines, books, calendars, and museum shows. Martha Cooper lives in New York City.

Visit *The Learning Site!*
www.harcourtschool.com

245

Making Connections

Compare Texts

1   Why do you think "Anthony Reynoso: Born to Rope" is part of the Neighborhood News theme?

2   Who is speaking in this selection? How does this way of telling a story differ from "Max Found Two Sticks"?

3   How is the main character in this story like the main character in "Max Found Two Sticks"?

In the Family

Write a paragraph to tell what things Anthony's parents do to help him be a good roper. Make a list of examples from the story to help you plan your paragraph.

Writing
CONNECTION

Local Weather

The weather in your area can be very different from the weather in another place. Use a newspaper to keep track of the temperature in a city that is far away for two weeks. Use a thermometer to record your local temperature. Compare the temperatures by using a chart like this one.

Temperature

Place	May 18	May 23	May 28
Phoenix	70°	80°	88°
My Home	65°	70°	75°

Map Search

Use a map of North America to find Arizona, Anthony's home. Then find Mexico, the place where Anthony's family came from. Find the names of the states closest to Arizona. Then share your information with the class.

▲ Anthony Reynoso:
Born to Rope

Words with
gh and *ph*

Read these sentences about Anthony Reynoso.

Anthony gets dressed up for a <u>photo</u>.
He <u>laughs</u> when his dad pulls him into the water.

Say the underlined words, *photo* and *laughs*. Listen for the "f" sound in each word. In these words, the letters **gh** or **ph** stand for the "f" sound.

Look at the next two words. What do you notice about *graph* and *cough* that could help you read the words?

graph   cough

Here are some longer words. Use what you know about **gh** and **ph** to sound them out. What do all these words have in common?

toughen	**coughing**	**graphed**
alphabet	**photographer**	**laughing**

> **Use these tips to read a longer word.**
> - Look for word parts you know.
> - Break the word into parts.
> - Say each part. Then blend the parts and say the word.

Test Prep

Words with *gh* and *ph*

Find the word that has the same sound as the underlined letters in the first word.

Example: **p̲h̲oto**

- ○ steep
- ○ post
- ● staff

Tip

Look at the underlined letters closely. Be sure you know the sound they make.

1.   **lau̲g̲h̲**
- ○ tricky
- ○ alphabet
- ○ grass

2.   **gra̲p̲h̲**
- ○ grin
- ○ pass
- ○ puffing

3.   **cou̲g̲h̲ing**
- ○ photograph
- ○ creak
- ○ gash

Vocabulary Power

▲ Chinatown

celebrations

develop

furious

graceful

grocery store

students

Baker Street Mall has many stores. Mom goes to Jack's Market. It is a **grocery store** that sells all kinds of food.

Grandpa and I watch the dance **students** practice. They are learning to be **graceful** as they move in beautiful ways. They practice to **develop** and build strong legs.

250

Dad is **furious** with himself. He is angry because he forgot to bring along the sweater he wanted to return.

My sister likes the party store. She looks at the things people use for birthdays and other **celebrations**.

Vocabulary-Writing CONNECTION

Write a short description of your favorite **celebration**. Tell when it is, what you do, and why you like it.

251

CHINATOWN
WRITTEN AND ILLUSTRATED BY
WILLIAM LOW

Genre

Realistic Fiction

Realistic fiction is a story with characters and events that are like people and events in real life.

Look for

- a setting that is a real place.

- story events that could really happen.

252

253

CHINESE AMERICAN

I live in Chinatown with my mother, father, and grandmother. Our apartment is above the Chinese American grocery store.

Every morning Grandma and I
go for a walk through Chinatown.
We hold hands before we cross
the street. "Watch out for cars,
Grandma," I tell her.

258

Most days the tai chi class has already begun by the time we get to the park. Students, young and old, move in the sunlight like graceful dancers.

259

We always stop and say hello to Mr. Wong, the street cobbler. If our shoes need fixing, Mr. Wong can do the job.

"Just like new, and at a good price, too," says Mr. Wong.

Chinatown really wakes up when the delivery trucks arrive. Men with handcarts move quickly over the sidewalks and into the stores.

Every day Grandma and I walk past the Dai-Dai Restaurant. Roasted chicken is my favorite, but Grandma likes duck best.

When it gets cold outside and
Grandma needs to make medicinal soup,
we visit the herbal shop. Inside it is dark
and smells musty. The owner, Mr. Chung,
is bagging dried roots and herbs.

"Winter is here," says Grandma. "We
must get our strength up."

Sometimes Grandma and I go for lunch at a seafood restaurant. I like to watch the fish swim in the tank. Grandma says, "You won't find fresher fish than those in Chinatown."

The kitchen in the restaurant is a noisy place. Hot oil sizzles, vegetables crackle, and woks clang and bang. The cooks shout to be heard.

At the outdoor market I can barely move. But we go there because Grandma likes to buy fresh snapping crabs for dinner. When the crabs seem furious, Grandma is pleased. "The angrier the crabs, the tastier the meat," she says.

265

On Saturdays I take lessons at the kung fu school. Master Leung teaches us a new move each week. "To develop your body *and* your mind," says Master Leung, "you must practice every day."

My favorite holiday
is Chinese New Year.
During the celebrations
the streets of Chinatown
are always crowded.
"Be sure to stay close
by," Grandma says.

267

On New Year's Day the older kids from my kung fu school march to the beat of thumping drums. Grandma and I try to find a good place to watch, and I tell her that next year I'll be marching, too.

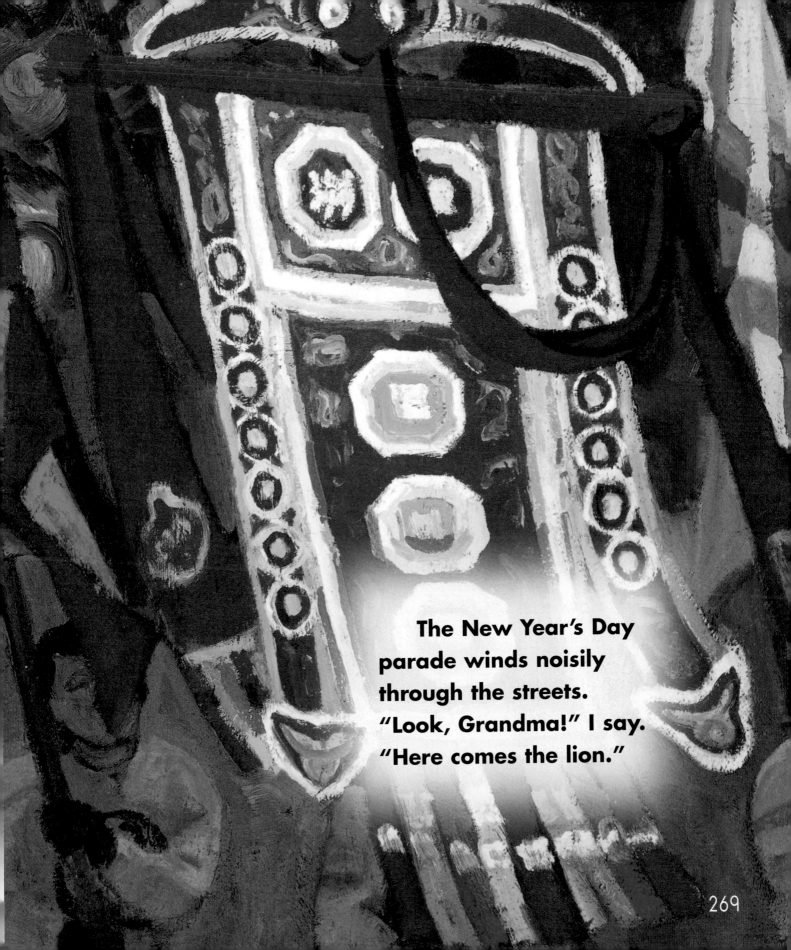

The New Year's Day parade winds noisily through the streets. "Look, Grandma!" I say. "Here comes the lion."

269

Firecrackers explode when the lion dance is over. I turn to Grandma, take her hand, and say, "Gung hay fat choy, Grandma."

She smiles at me. "And a happy new year to you, too."

Think and Respond

1 What do the boy and his grandmother see and do on their walk through Chinatown?

2 How does the author write about the setting?

3 How do you think the boy feels about Chinatown? Tell why you think as you do.

4 What **celebrations** do you enjoy most? Why?

5 What did you picture in your mind as you read this story?

MEET THE AUTHOR AND ILLUSTRATOR
WILLIAM LOW

William Low was born in New York City, but he never lived in Chinatown. He grew up in the Bronx and Queens, which are other parts of the city. When he was older, William Low climbed onto the roof of his parents' house and painted pictures of nearby buildings. Today, he teaches art at a school near Chinatown.

 Visit *The Learning Site!*
www.harcourtschool.com

Look What Came From
CHINA

by Miles Harvey

Children practicing kung fu

Tai Chi

Chinese acrobats

Sports and Exercise

Many of China's physical arts have made their way to the United States. One very famous Chinese sport is a special type of boxing known as *kung fu*. This sport is very difficult. To become good at it, you have to practice for many years.

A popular kind of exercise in China is known as *tai chi*. It is very good for you. It is also very interesting to watch. People who do tai chi sometimes look as if they are dancing in slow motion.

For more than 2,000 years, people in China have been doing a sport called *acrobatics*. People who are acrobats perform amazing tricks. Some of them juggle things in the air. Others pile objects up very high and then balance themselves on top of these objects. No wonder people love to go see acrobats at the circus!

273

Making Connections

Compare Texts

1 In this theme, which communities are most alike? Why?

2 How is the ending of "Chinatown" like the ending of "Max Found Two Sticks"?

3 Compare "Chinatown" to "Look What Came From China." Which selection gives more information about *kung fu* and *tai chi*?

Write About Your Neighborhood

The boy in "Chinatown" tells about the sights, sounds, and smells of his community. In your journal, write about the things you see, hear, and smell in your own neighborhood. Use describing words to add details.

Writing
CONNECTION

April 21, 2003
Yesterday I went to the park with Grandpa. We saw Miss Perez playing with her dogs. The smallest dog jumped and barked.

274

Exercise Your Muscles

The boy in "Chinatown" says that people in the *tai chi* class move "like graceful dancers." Think about the steps to a dance or exercise that you like to do. Write notes. Then have a partner listen to your directions and follow them. Use words such as *up, down, around,* and *under*.

Health CONNECTION

Getting What You Need

Think about the different kinds of stores where you live. Make a list of the ones your family needs. Then tell why each of these stores is important.

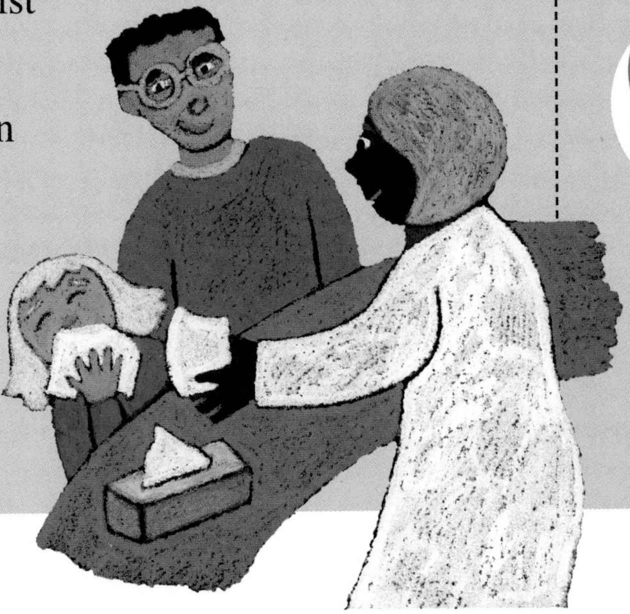

Social Studies CONNECTION

Details

Focus
Skill

Details are bits of information in a story or in other writing that tell more about something. Details help you picture what you read. They also make what you read more interesting.

Read the sentences below. How did the author use details to help you know more about each topic?

TOPIC	TOPIC + DETAILS
The kitchen in the restaurant is a noisy place.	The kitchen in the restaurant is a noisy place. Hot oil sizzles, vegetables crackle, and woks clang and bang. The cooks shout to be heard.
I live in Chinatown.	I live in Chinatown with my mother, father, and grandmother. Our apartment is above the Chinese American grocery store.

Chinatown

Read page 262 again. What details do you find?

Visit The Learning Site!
www.harcourtschool.com

See *Skills* and *Activities*

276

Test Prep
Details

Read the story. Then answer the questions.

Annie's New Hat

Annie bought a new hat. It was white with a yellow ribbon around it. On the ribbon were white daisies. The ribbon matched her new yellow dress perfectly.

1. **Annie's hat was—**
   - ○ yellow
   - ○ white
   - ○ curly
   - ○ old

Tip

As you read the story, note any details that are important.

2. **What kind of flowers were on Annie's hat?**
   - ○ yellow daisies
   - ○ white daisies
   - ○ yellow tulips
   - ○ white tulips

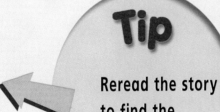

Tip

Reread the story to find the answer.

CONTENTS

▲ Abuela

Vocabulary Power

flock

glide

harbor

soared

swooping

I live by a large harbor. A **harbor** is a place by the sea where boats can dock. It's also a great place to watch birds!

This morning I saw a **flock** of seagulls flying together. There must have been hundreds of them. They were **swooping** through the air, moving up and down and side to side.

I saw one seagull **glide** above the waves for a long time. The bird looked calm and peaceful as it flew.

Finally the bird **soared** up high and joined the others. I watched them fly away and wished that I could fly, too!

Vocabulary-Writing CONNECTION

Think about the way birds **glide** through the air. Write a short poem about how you think they feel.

ALA
Notable Book

Notable Social
Studies Trade
Book

Genre

Fantasy

A fantasy is a
story about events
that can not happen
in real life.

Look for

- characters who do
  things that real
  people can not do.

- a setting that may
  be different from
  the real world.

by Arthur Dorros

illustrated by Elisa Kleven

Abuela takes me on the bus. We go all around
the city.

Abuela is my grandma. She is my mother's mother.
Abuela means "grandma" in Spanish.
Abuela speaks mostly Spanish because that's what
people spoke where she grew up, before she came to
this country. Abuela and I are always going places.

Today we're going to the park.
"El parque es lindo," says Abuela.
I know what she means. I think the park is beautiful too.

"Tantos pájaros," Abuela says
as a flock of birds surrounds us.
So many birds. They're picking up the bread we brought.

What if they picked me up
and carried me
high above the park?
What if I could fly?
Abuela would wonder where I was.
Swooping like a bird, I'd call to her.

Then she'd see me flying.
Rosalba the bird.
"Rosalba el pájaro," she'd say.
"Ven, Abuela. Come, Abuela," I'd say.
"Sí, quiero volar," Abuela would reply
as she leaped into the sky
with her skirt flapping in the wind.

We would fly all over the city.
"Mira," Abuela would say, pointing.

And I'd look, as we soared
over parks and streets, dogs and people.

We'd wave to the people waiting for the bus.
"Buenos días," we'd say.
"Buenos días. Good morning,"
they'd call up to us. We'd fly
over factories and trains . . .

286

and glide close to the sea.
"Cerca del mar," we'd say.
We'd almost touch the tops of waves.

Abuela's skirt would be a sail.
She could race with the sailboats.
I'll bet she'd win.

We'd fly to where the ships are docked,
and watch people unload fruits
from the land where Abuela grew up.
Mangos, bananas, papayas—
those are all Spanish words.
So are rodeo, patio, and burro.
Maybe we'd see a cousin of Abuela's
hooking boxes of fruit to a crane.
We saw her cousin Daniel once,
unloading and loading the ships.

Out past the boats in the harbor
we'd see the Statue of Liberty.
"Me gusta," Abuela would say.
Abuela really likes her.
I do too.

We would circle around Liberty's head
and wave to the people visiting her.
That would remind Abuela of when
she first came to this country.

"Vamos al aeropuerto," she'd say.
She'd take me to the airport where
the plane that first brought her landed.
"Cuidado," Abuela would tell me.
We'd have to be careful
as we went for a short ride.

Then we could fly to *tío* Pablo's
and *tía* Elisa's store.
Pablo is my uncle, my *tío*,
and Elisa is my aunt, my *tía*.
They'd be surprised when we flew in,
but they'd offer us a cool *limonada*.
Flying is hot work.
"Pero quiero volar más,"
Abuela would say.
She wants to fly more.
I want to fly more too.

We could fly to *las nubes*, the clouds.
One looks like a cat, *un gato*.
One looks like a bear, *un oso*.
One looks like a chair, *una silla*.
"Descansemos un momento,"
Abuela would say.
She wants to rest a moment.
We would rest in our chair,
and Abuela would hold me in her arms,
with the whole sky
our house, *nuestra casa*.

We'd be as high as airplanes,
balloons, and birds,
and higher than the tall buildings downtown.
But we'd fly there too
to look around.

We could find the building where my father works.
"*Hola, papá,*" I'd say as I waved. And Abuela would
do a flip for fun as we passed by the windows.

"*Mira,*" I hear Abuela say.
"Look," she's telling me.
I do look,
and we are back in the park.

We are walking by the lake.
Abuela probably wants to go for a boat ride.
"*Vamos a otra aventura,*" she says.
She wants us to go for another adventure.
That's just one of the things I love
about Abuela.
She likes adventures.

Abuela takes my hand.
"*Vamos,*" she says.
"Let's go."

Think and Respond

1 What adventures do Rosalba and Abuela have in the city?

2 Why do you think the author uses Spanish words in the story?

3 How would this story be different if Rosalba and Abuela were walking instead of **swooping** through the air?

4 Would you like to travel with Rosalba and Abuela? Explain your answer.

5 How did looking for smaller words and word parts help you read long words that you didn't know?

Glossary

The capitalized syllable is stressed in pronunciation.

Abuela (ah-BWEH-lah)   Grandmother

Buenos días (BWEH-nohs DEE-ahs)   Good day

Cerca del mar (SEHR-kah dehl mahr)   Close to the sea

Cuidado (kwee-DAH-doh)   Be careful

Descansemos un momento (dehs-kahn-SEH-mohs oon moh-MEHN-toh)   Let's rest a moment

El parque es lindo (ehl PAHR-kay ehs LEEN-doh)   The park is beautiful

Hola, papá (OH-lah, pah-PAH)   Hello, papa

Las nubes (lahs NOO-behs)   The clouds

Limonada (lee-moh-NAH-dah)   Lemonade

Me gusta (meh GOO-stah)   I like

Mira (MEE-rah)   Look

Nuestra casa (NWEH-strah CAH-sah)   Our house

Pero quiero volar más (PEH-roh key-EH-roh boh-LAR mahs)   But I would like to fly more

Rosalba el pájaro (roh-SAHL-bah ehl PAH-hah-roh)   Rosalba the bird

Sí, quiero volar (see, kee-EH-roh boh-LAR)   Yes, I want to fly

Tantos pájaros (TAHN-tohs PAH-hah-rohs)   So many birds

Tía (TEE-ah)   Aunt

Tío (TEE-oh)   Uncle

Un gato (oon GAH-toh)   A cat

Un oso (oon OH-soh)   A bear

Una silla (OON-ah SEE-yah)   A chair

Vamos (BAH-mohs)   Let's go

Vamos al aeropuerto (BAH-mohs ahl ah-ehr-oh-PWEHR-toh)   Let's go to the airport

Vamos a otra aventura (BAH-mohs ah OH-trah ah-behn-TOO-rah)   Let's go on another adventure

Ven (behn)   Come

Meet the Author
Arthur Dorros

Dear Readers,

"Abuela" is about my New York grandmother and about imagining flying. When I was in the second grade, I liked to fly kites. I watched my kite rise until it was just a tiny dot in the sky. I imagined what it would be like to soar in the sky like a bird.

Later, I could see much of New York City from the apartment building I lived in. The city appeared below, as it did for Rosalba and Abuela in the story. Imagine how your home might look from high above!

Your friend,

Arthur Dorros

Meet the Illustrator
Elisa Kleven

Visit *The Learning Site!*
www.harcourtschool.com

Dear Readers,

I enjoyed making the pictures for "Abuela." I did not know New York City very well, so Arthur Dorros drew a map to show me the places where Rosalba and Abuela would fly.

When I made the artwork for this story, I first drew pencil illustrations. Then I used pens, crayons, watercolors, and collage materials to finish the artwork. I even used some material from a blouse of mine to make Abuela's purse!

Your friend,

Elisa Kleven

Making Connections

Compare Texts

1. Why do you think "Abuela" is part of a theme called Travel Time?

2. Compare the setting of "Abuela" to the setting of another story you have read recently. How are the settings alike? How are they different?

3. Which parts of "Abuela" could happen in real life? Which parts could not happen?

Adventure in the Air

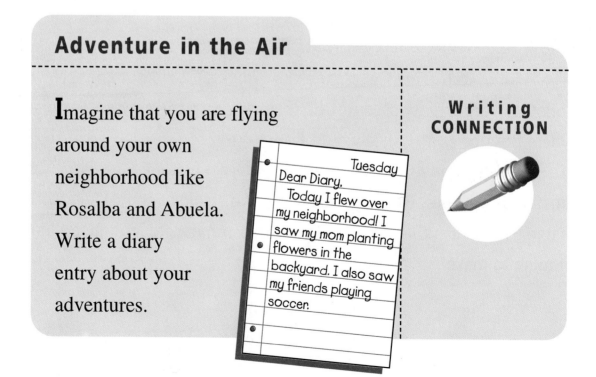

Imagine that you are flying around your own neighborhood like Rosalba and Abuela. Write a diary entry about your adventures.

Writing
CONNECTION

Tuesday
Dear Diary,
Today I flew over my neighborhood! I saw my mom planting flowers in the backyard. I also saw my friends playing soccer.

All About Birds

Science
CONNECTION

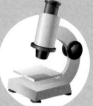

Find out more about the lives of birds. You can choose a bird from this list.

- robin
- sparrow
- eagle
- condor
- hummingbird

Write three facts about your bird. Then draw a picture of it.

Where Are You From?

Social Studies
CONNECTION

Rosalba's grandmother came to the United States from another country. Did members of your own family come from other countries? Find out where they lived before moving to this country. Show these places on a map. Share what you learn with classmates.

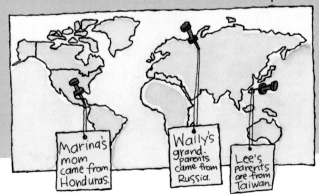

Marina's mom came from Honduras.

Wally's grandparents came from Russia.

Lee's parents are from Taiwan.

▲ Abuela

Words with
air and *are*

Read these sentences from "Abuela."

We'd have to be <u>careful</u> as we went.
We would rest in our <u>chair</u>.

Say the underlined words *careful* and *chair*. Listen for the sound in each word. The letters **are** and **air** in a word stand for the same sound, even though they are spelled differently.

Here are some more words with that sound. Look for the letter patterns **air** and **are**. Say each word aloud. Which words have the same letter pattern?

fairy	stare	repair
barely	hair	hare
dare	square	chairman

Use these tips to read a longer word.
- Look for word parts you know.
- Break the word into parts.
- Say each part. Then blend the parts and say the word.

304

Test Prep

*Words with **are** and **air***

Find the word that has the same sound as the underlined letters in the first word.

Example: **stair**
- ● square
- ○ store
- ○ car

1.   **repair**
- ○ appear
- ○ cheer
- ○ hare

2.   **hairy**
- ○ glare
- ○ heart
- ○ fear

3.   **prepare**
- ○ unfair
- ○ opera
- ○ steer

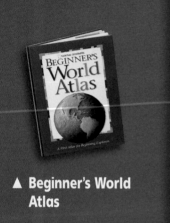

▲ Beginner's World
Atlas

connects

distance

features

mapmaker

peel

Vocabulary Power

This man is a **mapmaker**. His job is to make a flat picture of the round Earth.

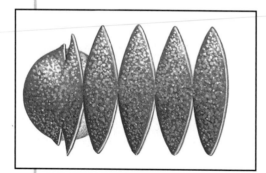 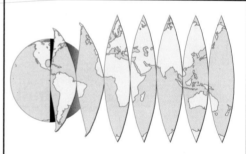

Find out how this works. First **peel** an orange in one piece. Then lay the orange piece flat. This is like a map of the Earth. The Earth is round like an orange. A map of the Earth is flat like an orange skin.

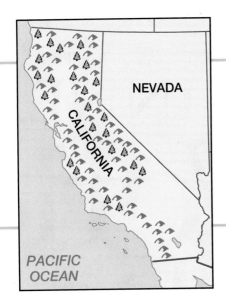

The mapmaker must show **features** of the land. The map will show deserts, forests, and mountains.

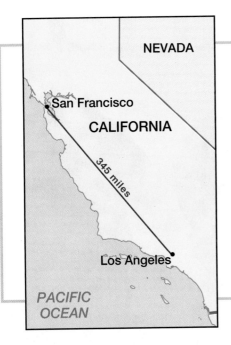

The mapmaker may also show cities on a map. If he **connects** two cities with a line, he can find out how far apart they are. He may write the **distance** beside the line to help travelers.

Vocabulary-Writing
CONNECTION

Make a list of other **features** that you might find on a map.

307

A First Atlas for Beginning Explorers

Genre

Nonfiction: Atlas

An atlas is a book of maps.

Look for

- **map keys that help you understand the information on the maps.**

- **scales that tell you about distance.**

NATIONAL GEOGRAPHIC

BEGINNER'S World Atlas

What Is a Map?

A map is a drawing of a place as it looks from above. It is flat, and it is smaller than the place it shows. A map can help you find where you are and where you want to go.

Mapping Your Backyard . . .

. . . from the ground

From your backyard you see everything in front of you straight on. You have to look up to see your roof and the tops of trees. You can't see what's in front of your house.

. . . from higher up

From higher up you look down on things. You can see the tops of trees and things in your yard and in the yards of other houses in your neighborhood.

. . . from a bird's-eye view

If you were a bird flying directly overhead, you would only see the tops of things. You wouldn't see walls, tree trunks, tires, or feet.

. . . on a map

A map looks at places from a bird's-eye view, but it uses drawings called symbols to show things like houses that don't move.

311

Finding Places on the Map

A **map** can help you get where you want to go. A map tells you how to read it by showing you a compass, a key, and a scale.

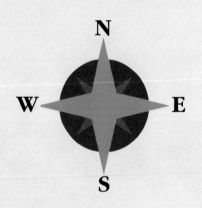

◀ A **compass** helps you travel in the right direction. It tells you where north (N), south (S), east (E), and west (W) are on your map. Sometimes it only shows where north is.

▼ A **scale** tells you about distance on a map. Look at the scale on the map at the right. The length of the top bars is the same as traveling a hundred yards.

| 0 | | 100 Yards |
| 0 | | 100 Meters |

	House
	Store
	School
	Library
	Play Area
	Water

◀ A **map key** helps you understand the symbols used by the mapmaker to show things like houses, play areas, and schools on the map.

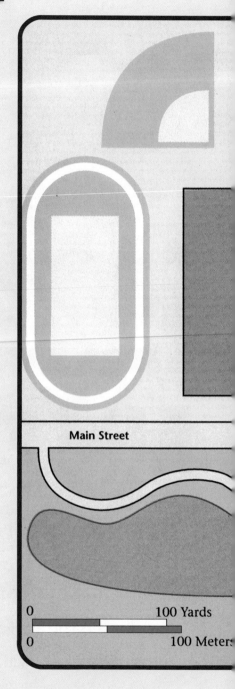

Main Street

0   100 Yards
0   100 Meters

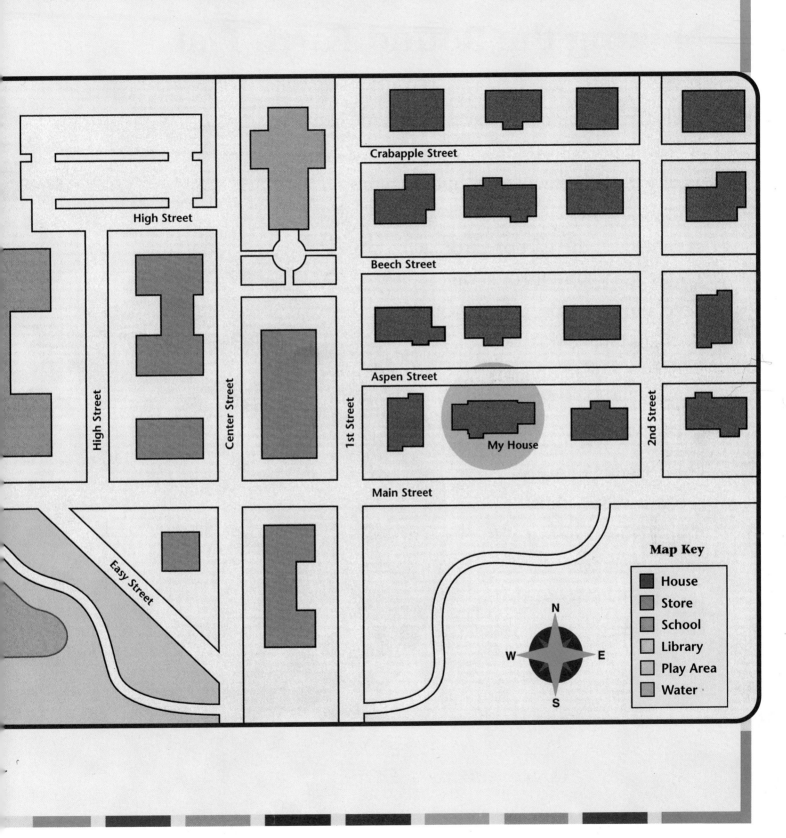

High Street

High Street

Center Street

1st Street

2nd Street

Easy Street

Crabapple Street

Beech Street

Aspen Street

My House

Main Street

Map Key

N
W — E
S

House
Store
School
Library
Play Area
Water

Making the Round Earth Flat

From your backyard the Earth probably looks flat. If you could travel into space like an astronaut, you would see that Earth is a giant ball with blue oceans, greenish-brown land, and white clouds. Even in space you can only see the part of Earth facing you. To see the whole Earth at one time you need a map. Maps take the round Earth and make it flat so you can see all of it at one time.

▶ Earth in Space

From space you can see that the Earth is round with oceans, land, and clouds. But you can see only half the Earth at one time.

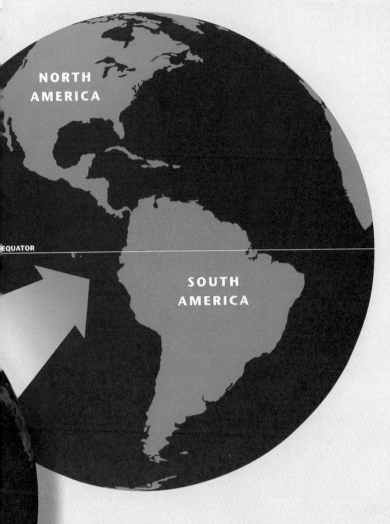

NORTH
AMERICA

EQUATOR

SOUTH
AMERICA

▲ Earth as a Globe

A **globe** is a tiny model of the Earth that you can put on a stand or hold in your hand. You have to turn it to see the other side. You still can't see the whole Earth at one time.

▼ Earth on Paper

If you could peel a globe like an orange, you could make the Earth flat, but there would be spaces between the pieces. Mapmakers stretch the land and the water at the top and bottom to fill in the spaces. This is how a **map** lets you see the whole world all at once.

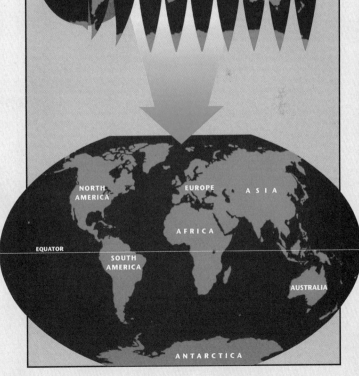

NORTH
AMERICA

EUROPE

ASIA

AFRICA

EQUATOR

SOUTH
AMERICA

AUSTRALIA

ANTARCTICA

The Physical World

A physical map uses symbols to show where mountains, deserts, forests, and other features of the land are. The map key tells what the symbols mean.

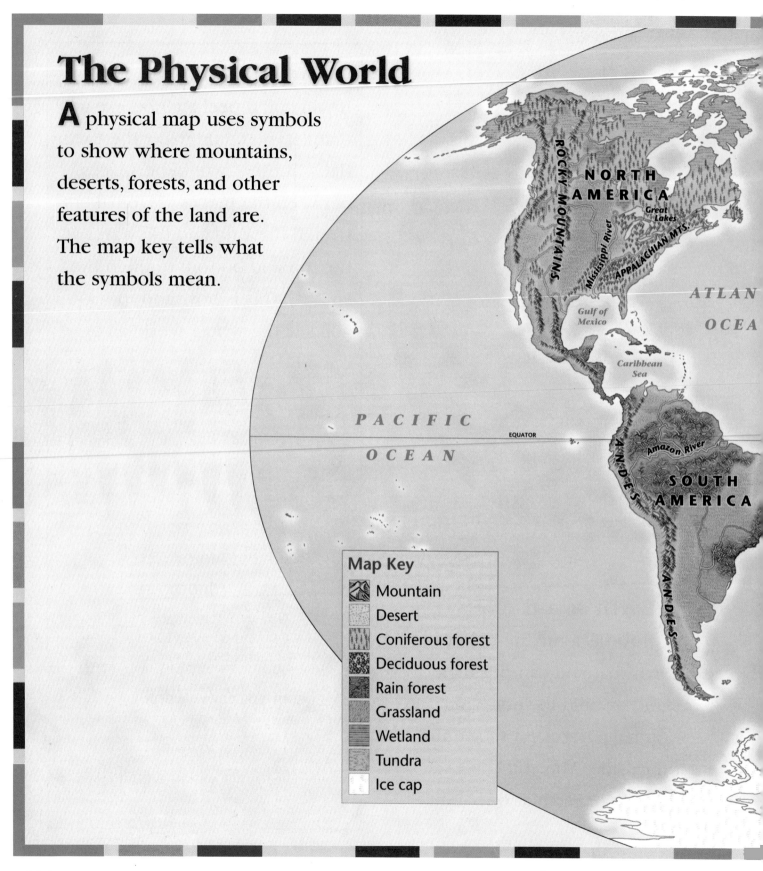

NORTH AMERICA

ROCKY MOUNTAINS

Great Lakes

Mississippi River

APPALACHIAN MTS.

Gulf of Mexico

ATLAN

OCEA

Caribbean Sea

PACIFIC

OCEAN

EQUATOR

Amazon River

ANDES

SOUTH AMERICA

ANDES

Map Key

Mountain

Desert

Coniferous forest

Deciduous forest

Rain forest

Grassland

Wetland

Tundra

Ice cap

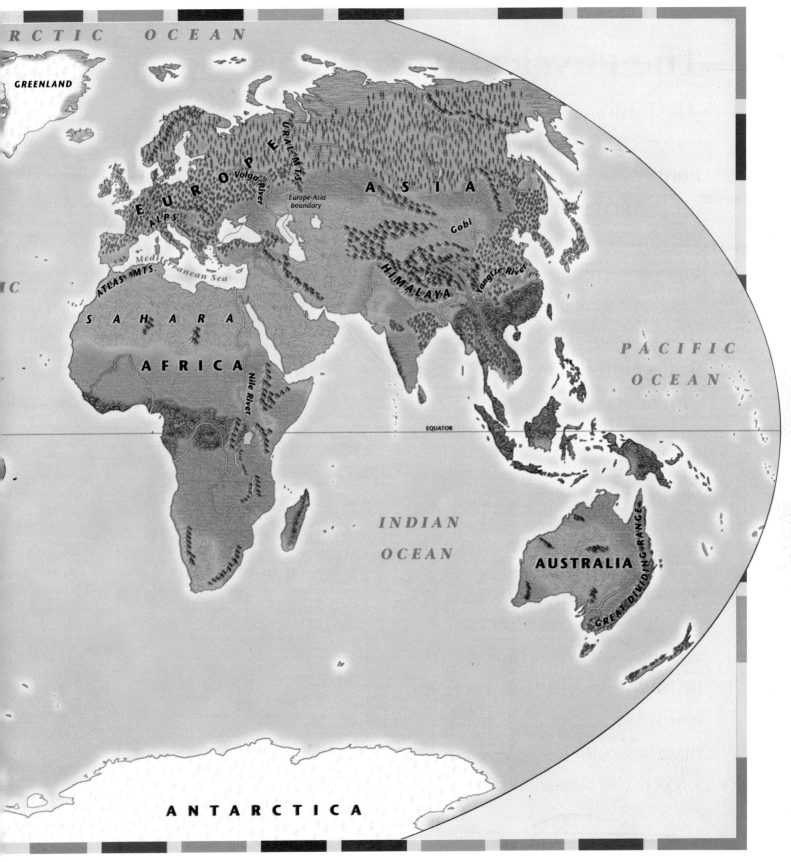

ARCTIC OCEAN

GREENLAND

EUROPE

URAL MTS.

Volga River

Europe-Asia boundary

ASIA

ALPS

Gobi

Mediterranean Sea

ATLAS MTS.

HIMALAYA

Yangtze River

SAHARA

AFRICA

Nile River

PACIFIC OCEAN

EQUATOR

INDIAN OCEAN

AUSTRALIA

GREAT DIVIDING RANGE

ANTARCTICA

317

The Physical World Close Up

The Earth's surface is made up of land and water. The biggest landmasses are called **continents.** All seven of them are named on this map. **Islands** are smaller pieces of land that are surrounded by water. Greenland is the largest island. Land that is nearly surrounded by water is called a **peninsula.** Europe has lots of them.

Oceans are the largest bodies of water. Can you find all four oceans? **Lakes** are bodies of water surrounded by land—like the Great Lakes, in North America. A large stream of water that flows into a lake or an ocean is called a **river.** The Nile is Earth's longest river.

ARCTI

GREENLAND

ROCKY MOUNTAINS

NORTH AMERICA

Great Lakes

Mississippi River

APPALACHIAN MTS.

ATLANTIC OCEAN

Gulf of Mexico

Caribbean Sea

PACIFIC OCEAN

EQUATOR

Amazon River

ANDES

SOUTH AMERICA

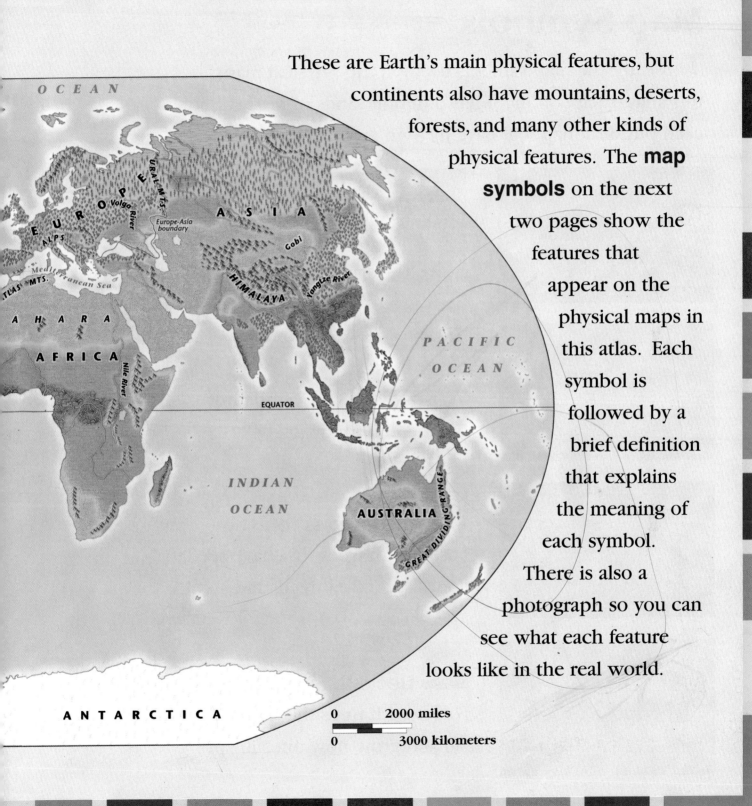

These are Earth's main physical features, but continents also have mountains, deserts, forests, and many other kinds of physical features. The **map symbols** on the next two pages show the features that appear on the physical maps in this atlas. Each symbol is followed by a brief definition that explains the meaning of each symbol. There is also a photograph so you can see what each feature looks like in the real world.

O C E A N

E U R O P E

URAL MTS.

Volga River

ALPS

Europe-Asia boundary

ATLAS MTS.

Mediterranean Sea

A S I A

Gobi

HIMALAYA

Yangtze River

S A H A R A

A F R I C A

Nile River

PACIFIC OCEAN

EQUATOR

INDIAN OCEAN

AUSTRALIA

GREAT DIVIDING RANGE

ANTARCTICA

0   2000 miles

0   3000 kilometers

Map Symbols

These are the map symbols used on the physical maps in this atlas. Each continent has different kinds of features, so each physical map will have its own map key.

 Mountain

Land that rises at least 1,000 feet above the surrounding land

 Desert

Very dry land that can be hot or cold and sandy or rocky

 Coniferous forest

Forest with trees that have seed cones and often needlelike leaves

 Deciduous forest

Forest with trees that lose leaves in fall and grow new ones in spring

 Rain forest

Forest with trees that keep their
leaves all year and need lots of rain

 Ice cap

A permanent sheet of thick ice that
covers the land, as in Antarctica

 Tundra

A cold region with low plants
that grow during warm months

 Wetland

Land, such as a marsh or swamp,
that is mostly covered with water

 Grassland

A grass-covered area with too little
rain for many trees to grow

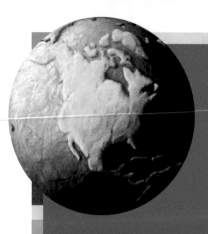

North America

North America is shaped like a triangle ▼. It is wide in the north. In the south it narrows to a strip of land so narrow that a Marathon runner could cross it in two hours. Ships make the trip on the Panama Canal. The warm islands in the Caribbean Sea are part of North America. So is icy Greenland in the far north. The seven countries between Mexico and South America make up a region commonly called Central America. It **connects** the rest of North America and South America.

Kha-hay! I'm from the Crow tribe in Montana. This beautiful valley is in Yosemite National Park, in California. It's in the Sierra Nevada mountains. Look for them on the map when you turn the next page.

North America

The Land

Land regions The Rocky Mountains run along the west side of North America through Mexico. There, the mountains are called the Sierra Madre Oriental. Lower mountains called the Appalachians are in the east. Grassy plains lie between the two mountain chains.

Water The longest rivers are the Mississippi and the Missouri. The Great Lakes are the world's largest group of freshwater lakes.

Climate The far north is icy cold. Temperatures get warmer as you move south. Much of Central America is hot and wet.

Plants North America has large forests where there is plenty of rain. Grasslands cover drier areas.

Animals There is a big variety of animals—everything from bears, moose, and wolves to monkeys and colorful parrots.

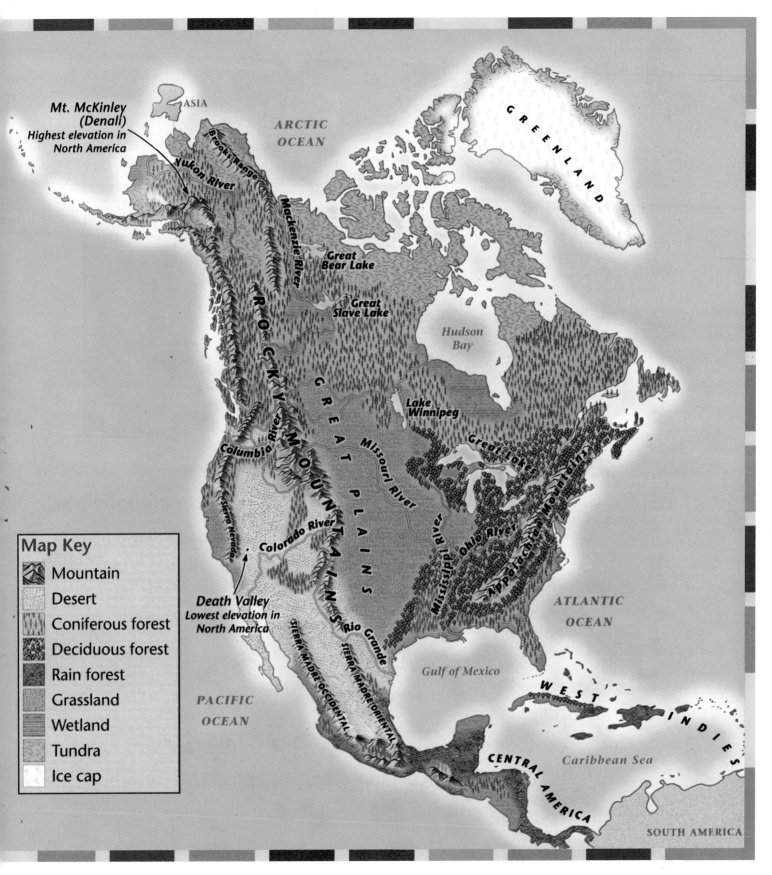

Mt. McKinley
(Denali)
*Highest elevation in
North America*

ASIA

ARCTIC
OCEAN

GREENLAND

Brooks Range

Yukon River

Mackenzie River

Great
Bear Lake

Great
Slave Lake

Hudson
Bay

R O C K Y

Lake
Winnipeg

Columbia River

Great Lakes

Sierra Nevada

Missouri River

G R E A T   P L A I N S

M O U N T A I N S

Colorado River

Mississippi River

Ohio River

Appalachian Mountains

Death Valley
*Lowest elevation in
North America*

Rio Grande

ATLANTIC
OCEAN

SIERRA MADRE OCCIDENTAL

SIERRA MADRE ORIENTAL

PACIFIC
OCEAN

Gulf of Mexico

W E S T

Caribbean Sea

I N D I E S

CENTRAL
AMERICA

SOUTH AMERICA

Map Key

- Mountain
- Desert
- Coniferous forest
- Deciduous forest
- Rain forest
- Grassland
- Wetland
- Tundra
- Ice cap

North America

▼ Palm trees grow along sandy beaches on islands in the **Caribbean Sea.** In this part of North America the weather is warm year-round.

▲ North America is famous for its **deciduous forests.** Leaves turn fiery colors each fall!

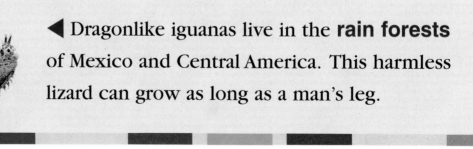

◀ Dragonlike iguanas live in the **rain forests** of Mexico and Central America. This harmless lizard can grow as long as a man's leg.

▶ This view from a plane shows that **Greenland** has high mountains and lots of snow and ice.

◀ A white-tail deer nuzzles her babies in a meadow near the **Great Lakes.** Deer live in almost every country on the continent.

▲ **Deserts** are found in the southwestern part of North America. The large rock formation on the right is called The Mitten. Can you guess why?

North America

The People

Countries Canada, the United States, Mexico, and the countries of Central America and the West Indies make up North America.

Cities Mexico City is the biggest city in North America. Next in size are New York City and Los Angeles. Havana, in Cuba, is the largest city in the West Indies.

People The ancestors of most people in North America came from Europe. Many other people trace their roots to Africa and Asia. Native Americans live throughout.

Languages English and Spanish are the main languages. A large number of people in Canada and Haiti speak French. There are also many Native American languages.

Products North America's chief products include cars, machinery, petroleum, natural gas, silver, wheat, corn, beef, and forest products.

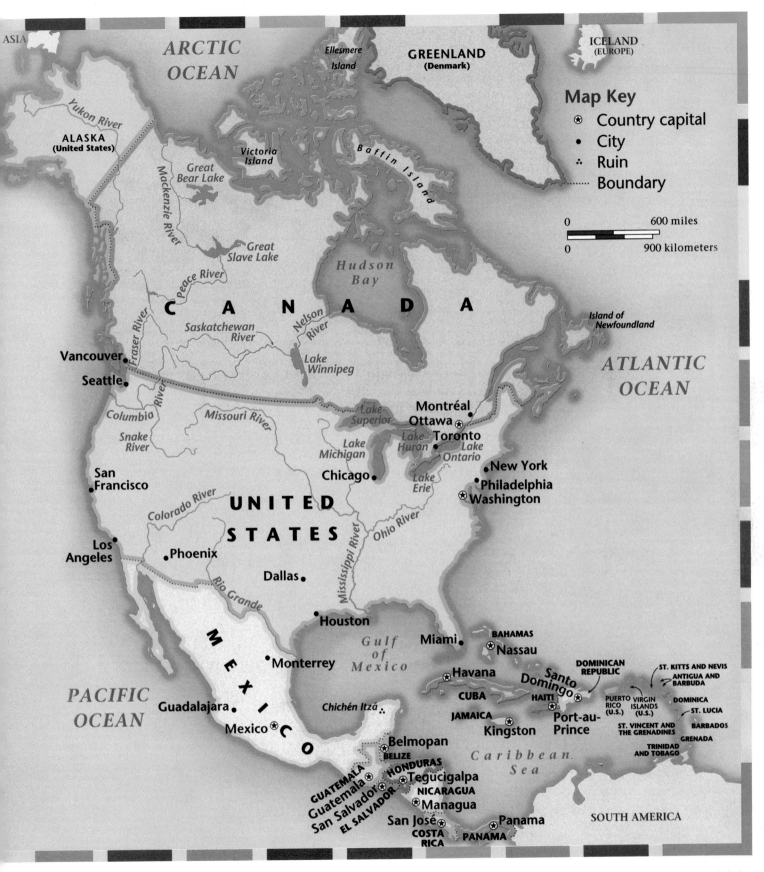

ASIA

ARCTIC OCEAN

Ellesmere Island

GREENLAND (Denmark)

ICELAND (EUROPE)

Yukon River

ALASKA (United States)

Victoria Island

Great Bear Lake

Baffin Island

Map Key
⊛ Country capital
• City
∴ Ruin
...... Boundary

Mackenzie River

Great Slave Lake

Peace River

C A N A D A

Hudson Bay

0   600 miles
0   900 kilometers

Fraser River

Saskatchewan River

Nelson River

Island of Newfoundland

Vancouver

Lake Winnipeg

Seattle

Columbia River

Missouri River

Lake Superior

ATLANTIC OCEAN

Snake River

Lake Michigan

Montréal
Ottawa ⊛
Toronto
Lake Huron
Lake Ontario

San Francisco

Chicago

Lake Erie

New York
Philadelphia
⊛ **Washington**

UNITED STATES

Colorado River

Ohio River

Los Angeles

Phoenix

Dallas

Mississippi River

Rio Grande

M E X I C O

Houston

Gulf of Mexico

Miami

BAHAMAS
⊛ **Nassau**

DOMINICAN REPUBLIC

ST. KITTS AND NEVIS
ANTIGUA AND BARBUDA

Monterrey

⊛ **Havana**

Santo Domingo

CUBA

HAITI

PUERTO RICO (U.S.)

VIRGIN ISLANDS (U.S.)

DOMINICA

PACIFIC OCEAN

Guadalajara

Chichén Itzá ∴

JAMAICA

Kingston

Port-au-Prince

ST. LUCIA

ST. VINCENT AND THE GRENADINES

BARBADOS

GRENADA

Mexico ⊛

Belmopan

BELIZE

Caribbean Sea

TRINIDAD AND TOBAGO

GUATEMALA
Guatemala ⊛
San Salvador
EL SALVADOR

HONDURAS
⊛ **Tegucigalpa**

NICARAGUA
⊛ **Managua**

San José ⊛
COSTA RICA

⊛ **Panama**
PANAMA

SOUTH AMERICA

329

North America

▶ Skiing and ski jumping are popular sports in the **Rocky Mountains.**

◀ This is **Mexico City.** More people live here than in any other city in North America.

▶ These red berries hold coffee beans. Many farmers in **Guatemala** make a living growing coffee.

◀ This pyramid at **Chichén Itzá** was built long ago by the Maya people.

◀ This boy is dressed like a jaguar for a celebration in **Mexico.** Many people admire the jaguar for its strength and courage.

◀ This farmer is harvesting wheat on a big farm in **Canada.** Canada and the United States grow much of the world's wheat.

▶ Ships travel across Panama on the Panama Canal. It is a shortcut between the Atlantic and the Pacific Oceans.

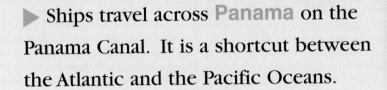

Think and Respond

1 What information do the maps and photographs in this selection give you?

2 How does a map key help you read a map?

3 Which map would you use to show where the biggest rivers of North America are located? Why?

4 If you drew a map of your school, what **features** would you include?

5 What strategies did you use to read longer words in this selection?

Making Connections

Compare Texts

1 Why do you think this selection is part of a theme called Travel Time?

2 How are the maps of North America on pages 325 and 329 different? In what ways are they alike?

3 How did the photographs in "Beginner's World Atlas" help you better understand the map information?

Make a Glossary

Make a glossary of map words. First reread the selection. Find five words in **bold** type. Then write each word and what it means.

Glossary

globe- a round model of the Earth

Writing
CONNECTION

332

Map a Room

Make a map of your classroom. On your map, show where the furniture is placed. Make a map key. Then write a title and share your map with classmates.

Make a Graph

Draw a map of your neighborhood. Then make a picture graph to show how many houses are on each street. Make a key for your picture graph.

Locate Information

Focus Skill

You can use a **table of contents** at the beginning of a book to help you find information. Many tables of contents list **chapters** in a book and the page number for the start of each chapter.

Look at this table of contents. What kinds of information does it show?

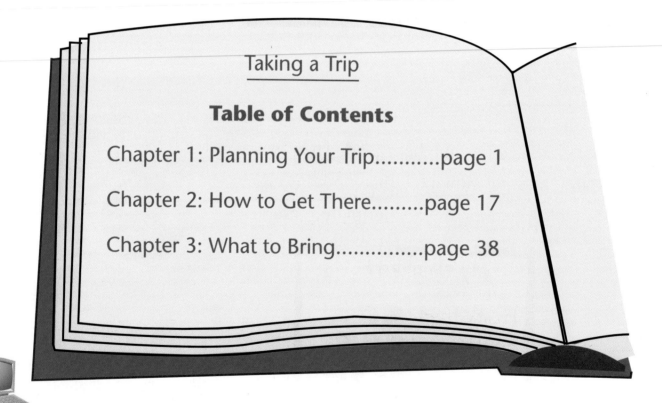

Taking a Trip

Table of Contents

Visit *The Learning Site!*
www.harcourtschool.com

See *Skills* and *Activities*

Test Prep

Read the table of contents. Then answer the questions below it.

The Perfect Bike

Table of Contents

---

1. **On which page would you begin to find information on bike safety?**

    ○ page 1

    ○ page 15

    ○ page 27

Tip

Use your finger to guide you as you read.

2. **Which chapter would tell you the most about a bike's wheels?**

    ○ Chapter 1

    ○ Chapter 2

    ○ Chapter 3

Tip

Read each chapter title. Think about the information you might find in each chapter.

▲ Dinosaurs Travel

Vocabulary Power

cassette

companions

luggage

relatives

sturdy

Hello! I am Amanda, and this is a picture of me with Mom and Dad. They were my **companions** on an airplane trip.

We visited Uncle Danny, Aunt Rose, and some other **relatives**.

336

Before we went to the airport, I packed my clothes in a strong, **sturdy** suitcase. My mom and dad packed their **luggage**, too.

We took along presents for Uncle Danny's birthday. I gave him a card. Dad and Mom gave him a **cassette** of his favorite music.

Vocabulary-Writing CONNECTION

Write a short description of a trip you have taken. Tell who your **companions** were and what you packed in your **luggage**.

Genre

Nonfiction: Informational Book

An informational book gives information about a topic.

Look for

- headings that tell you what a page is about.

- facts that are presented in a way that makes sense.

Laurie Krasny Brown
and
Marc Brown

Traveling

Do you ever wish you could climb a mountain,

fly through the air,

or ride around town in a long limousine?

Every time you leave home,
whether to travel

around the world,

or around the block,
get ready for an adventure!

Getting Ready for a Trip

Books and maps can help you learn about a new place before you go there.

You may not be able to take your pets with you, but someone else will take good care of them.

If you take the addresses of friends and relatives, you can write to them while you're away.

Find out about the weather where you're going and choose clothes that will be good to wear. Only pack a few toys, games, books, and tapes. Small, light, and sturdy things travel best.

Remember one or two favorite companions.

And don't forget these!

Getting From Place to Place

Wherever you're headed, getting there can be part of the fun!

On Foot

Walking lets you stop
and see the sights.

You may meet other travelers
along the way.

You can hike on a trail where
almost no one ever goes.

And your body is all that
you need!

Your Own Wheels

Bicycles and skateboards are faster than walking. You're the driver! It's up to you to know the rules of the road.

Keep your bike or board in good working order, so you're all set to ride anytime.

With your own set of wheels, you can go most anywhere!

You and your family can
go biking together.

Sometimes you have to pedal
hard to get where you're going,

but downhill you get a free ride!

347

By Car

Cars will take you on all kinds of roads. Riding on the highways is fastest!

Driving on back roads is slower but you see more.

You and your family can go wherever or whenever you want. You can bring along lots of your things— if you have room!

You and your family can play word games while you ride. You can take turns reading road signs or looking at different license plates.

It feels good to get out and stretch your legs from time to time.

Switching seats will give you different views.

If you have a cassette player, you can bring your favorite tapes.

Riding the Subway and Bus

In some cities riding underground in a subway is the fastest way to travel.

On a bus you can see what's going on outside. A tour bus driver will point out the sights.

On a subway or bus you must pay a fare to ride.

Subways and buses make many stops. Don't forget to watch for yours!

Taking the Train

You can buy a ticket for the train at the station. Look at the signs for your track and departure time. All aboard! Taking the train is a great way to see new places!

On most trains, you can sit facing forward or backward. The conductor announces each stop the train makes. You can follow along with a timetable.

Trains don't have to stop until they pull into a station. The train stops at many stations so passengers can get on and off.

351

Flying in Planes

At the airport an agent looks at your ticket, checks your luggage, and assigns you a seat on the plane.

Airport security makes sure no one carries anything dangerous or illegal on the plane.

You can bring a small bag on most planes and stow it under or above your seat. Buckle up!

Take off!

As the plane climbs higher, things below look smaller and smaller.

You'll fly up above the clouds!

Coming Home

When it's time to go home, remember to pack all your things. You may want to bring back a gift for someone special. Souvenirs and pictures will remind you of your trip.

At home, things may look different to you.

It's fun to go home again and see friends and relatives.

You can play with all your toys, eat your favorite snacks, and dream about where to travel next!

Think and Respond

1 What are some important things to remember before and as you travel?

2 How can the headings help you understand and summarize "Dinosaurs Travel"?

3 If the Browns asked you to add a travel tip to this book, what would you write?

4 Where would you go for an adventure? Who would your **companions** be?

5 What strategy did you use to figure out the meaning of a word that you didn't know?

355

Meet the Author

Laurie Krasny Brown

Dear Reader,

I've written a lot of books, but *Dinosaurs Travel* is special to me. You see, I wrote the words, and my husband, Marc Brown, drew the pictures.

Whenever I start to write a book, I read all I can on the subject. Next, I make a list of what I need to put in the book. Then, I write and rewrite. When I have finished, I get someone who knows a lot about what's in the book to read it.

Your friend,

Laurie Krasny Brown

Visit *The Learning Site!*
www.harcourtschool.com

356

Meet the Illustrator

Marc Brown

Dear Reader,

Many kids know my artwork from my Arthur books, but I like to do information books, too. I have done several books using these dinosaur characters. I chose to draw dinosaurs because they are powerful animals, and I want my readers to feel powerful. I am proud of these books because I think they help kids feel good about themselves.

When I am not working, I like to spend time gardening. My wife, Laurie, and I grow flowers, fruits, and vegetables.

Your friend,

Marc Brown

KEEPING A ROAD JOURNAL

by Joy Beck • illustrated by Patti H. Goodnow

Road trips are a lot of fun, especially when you keep track of the interesting things you see and do, the neat people you meet, and all the new things you learn. Here's how:

You need:

- A new notebook
  (Spiral-bound notebooks work best.)
- A supply of sharpened pencils
- Adhesive tape
- An inexpensive, disposable camera

Directions:

1. On the first page, print your name, age, date of the trip, and your traveling pals.

2. Turn the page. On the left page, write: "Date," "Time," "Location," and "Weather." On the right page, write: "What Happened Today." These two pages are for the *first* day of the trip.

3. Prepare the next two pages the same way for the *second* day.

4. Prepare enough pages in your journal for the whole trip. (If you do enough in advance, you'll be more likely to actually fill them in later.)

Going on the Record

Gather material for your journal by answering these questions each day:

- Where did we go?
- What did we see?
- What did we do?
- Who did we meet?
- How was all this different from home?

Remember to interview your family. Did they like the same things as you?

Take plenty of pictures, too. Then make a note in your journal so you'll know what they were about and why you took them.

Making Connections

Compare Texts

1 Why do you think "Beginner's World Atlas" comes before "Dinosaurs Travel" in this theme?

2 Think about the pictures in "Dinosaurs Travel" and "Beginner's World Atlas." How do they help you understand the selections?

3 How is the writing in "Dinosaurs Travel" like the writing in "Keeping a Road Journal"?

Invitation to Travel

Think of someone you would like to invite for a visit to your home. Write a short letter to invite that person. Remember to include all the parts of a letter.

Writing
CONNECTION

Dinosaur Details

Find out about actual dinosaurs that lived long ago. Do research to learn about one of these dinosaurs:

- apatosaurus
- stegosaurus
- triceratops
- tyrannosaurus rex

Then make a "Dinosaur Details" poster. Draw pictures of your dinosaur and write facts about it. Tell how your dinosaur was different from other dinosaurs.

Great Escapes

There are many amazing places to visit on Earth. Look on a map to find each of these amazing places:

- Mount Everest
- the Nile River
- the Great Lakes
- the Grand Canyon

Then talk with classmates about what you learned. Name the continent where you would find each.

Words with ou and ough

Read this sentence from "Dinosaurs Travel."

Do _you_ ever wish you could climb a mountain or fly _through_ the air?

Say the underlined words, *you* and *through*. These words have the same vowel sound. The letters **ou** and **ough** stand for that vowel sound.

Look for the letter patterns **ou** and **ough** in the next two words. Say each aloud.

gr<u>ou</u>p   thr<u>ough</u>

Now read the following words. Point to the letters that stand for the vowel sound in **you**.

you'd   grouping   throughout   soup

> **Use these tips to read a longer word.**
> - Look for word parts you know.
> - Break the word into parts.
> - Say each part. Then blend the parts and say the word.

362

Test Prep

Words with *ou* and *ough*

Find the word that has the same sound as the underlined letters in the first word.

Example: th<u>rough</u>

- ○ below
- ● you
- ○ throw

Tip

Look at the underlined letters closely. Be sure you know the sound they make.

1.   g<u>rou</u>p
- ○ grape
- ○ soup
- ○ steep

2.   y<u>ou</u>
- ○ stop
- ○ look
- ○ throughout

Tip

Skip choices that don't make sense.

3.   y<u>ou</u>'ve
- ○ trot
- ○ regroup
- ○ yarn

363

▲ Montigue on the High Seas

Vocabulary Power

cozy

drifted

fleet

launched

looming

realized

It was a cool day, but Juan and his brother felt warm and **cozy** in their jackets. The tall trees were **looming** above them.

Juan and José made paper boats. Soon they had a whole **fleet** of them.

The boys **launched** the boats by pushing them out into the water. The boats **drifted** slowly with the breeze across the pond.

Juan looked at his watch. He **realized** it was time to go. "Come on, José," he said to his brother. "It's almost dinnertime!"

Vocabulary-Writing CONNECTION

Think of something that makes you feel warm and **cozy**. Write a short description of it.

365

Award-Winning
Author

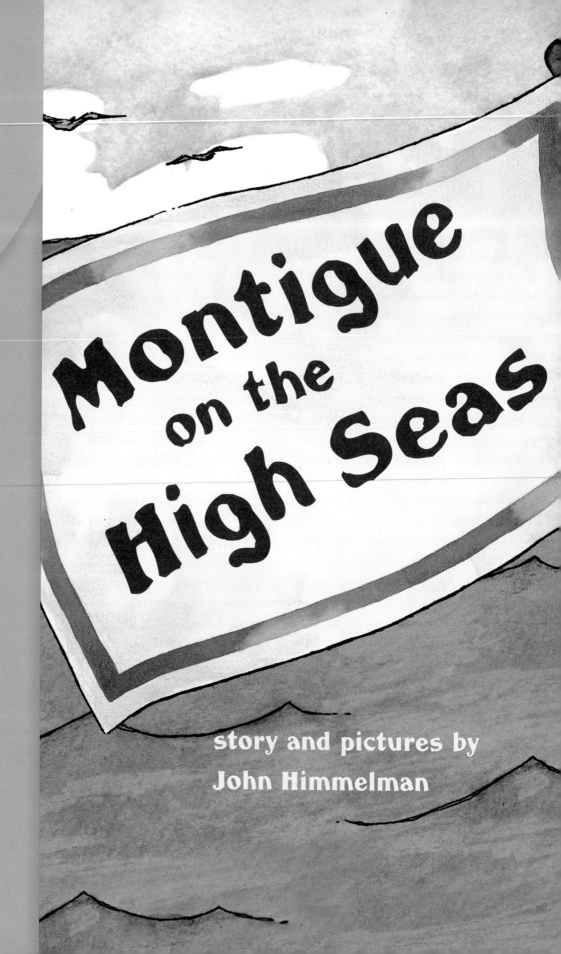

Montigue on the High Seas

story and pictures by
John Himmelman

In a cozy hole by the sea, there lived a young mole. His name was Montigue. Montigue loved his home. It was cool in the afternoons and warm in the evenings.

One day it began to rain. Soon the rain was coming down in buckets. By evening, Montigue's home was flooded. He had to find a safe place to spend the night. Montigue swam and swam until at last he noticed a funny-looking house propped on a rock. He was so tired that he fell into a deep sleep as soon as he crawled inside.

Montigue woke up rested and warm. It was a few moments before he realized that he had been . . .

 . . . swept out to sea!

Poor Montigue drifted for days with nothing to drink except lime soda and nothing to eat but seaweed.

He grew lonely and bored as he stared at the horizon day after day. Then one morning, he noticed a dark shadow beneath him. Suddenly, he was thrown into the air by a giant humpback whale! Montigue clung to the bottle as it slowly filled with water and sank.

371

A passing fish, spotting an interesting
meal, swallowed the bottle, mole
and all! Before Montigue knew what
was happening, the fish was yanked
up by a huge net. Montigue and the bottle fell out
of its mouth and onto the deck of a ship.

Montigue looked up half-dazed and saw a giant
sailor looming over him. He was holding a giant
cat! The cat leapt after him, but Montigue

scuttled into a hole.
"Safe at last," he thought.

"What a funny-looking
mouse," said a voice
beside him.

Montigue was surrounded by mice. "What were you doing out there?" asked one, nervously. "Don't you know that Barnacles the Cat is trying to clear us all off this ship?"

Montigue began to tell them how he came to the ship. He told of battling raging seas, riding giant whales, fighting off mole-eating fish, and he told them of the crash of his bottle ship. Just as he was coming to the end of his story, Montigue fell off his perch and knocked over a box of kitchen supplies.

When things settled down, the mice cheered. Montigue had given them an idea. The mice scurried in every direction, collecting bits of cloth, rags, and other supplies. Even Montigue got caught up in the fun.

376

They all worked together and soon their fleet was launched. The mice elected Montigue their captain. As they glided over the sea, he began to enjoy the thrill of guiding the ships through the waves. In a few days, one of the mice shouted, "LAND HO!"

When they were safely ashore, the mice carried Montigue on their shoulders. They asked him to live with them and he happily accepted. They started building their homes right away.

Montigue loved his new home. It was cool in the afternoons and warm in the evenings. And now he had lots of friendly neighbors.

And if he ever felt the pull of the high seas, he still had his bottle and his sail.

Think and Respond

1 What happened to Montigue after he **drifted** onto the high seas?

2 Why is the setting important to this story?

3 Why do you think the author has Montigue meet the mice on the ship?

4 What part of Montigue's adventure do you like the best?

5 What strategies did you use to help you read this story?

Meet the Author
and Illustrator

John Himmelman

John Himmelman gets the ideas for his stories from the pictures he draws of characters like Montigue. The pictures help him to decide what a character will do in a story. "A story is just a story, but the characters become very real to me," he says. When he's not creating children's books, John Himmelman likes to play the guitar.

Visit *The Learning Site!*
www.harcourtschool.com

379

Making Connections

Compare Texts

1 Why do you think "Montigue on the High Seas" is in the same theme as "Abuela"?

2 Think about the setting at the beginning of the story and at the end. How are the settings alike? How are they different?

3 If Montigue decides to travel on the high seas again, what parts of "Dinosaurs Travel" do you think he should read? Why?

Write a Letter

May 19, 2003

Dear Harold,

You will never believe what happened to me!

Imagine that you are Montigue. Write a short letter to a friend, telling about your adventures. Be sure to include the important details.

Writing CONNECTION

Bottle Music

Fill five bottles with different amounts of water. Tap each bottle gently with a pencil and listen for how high or low the sound is—its *pitch*. Put the bottles in order from highest to lowest pitch. What makes the pitch high or low?

Science CONNECTION

Find the High Seas

Look at a world map, and find the names of all four oceans. Write them down. Now look for the names of the three oceans that touch North America. Circle them on your list.

Social Studies CONNECTION

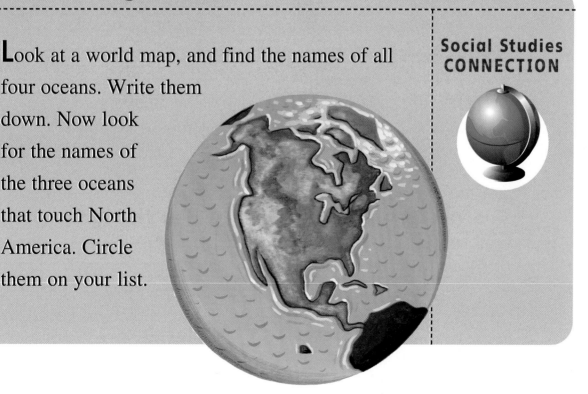

Homophones

Focus
Skill

Homophones are words that sound the same but are spelled differently. They also have different meanings.

I'm eating
a **pear**.

That's a nice
pair of shoes.

The tree is
bare in winter.

The **bear** likes
to eat honey.

He **ate** the
cookie.

I have **eight**
cookies.

Can you complete this sentence with the correct word?

right	write

She will _____ a letter.

Visit *The Learning Site!*
www.harcourtschool.com

See *Skills* and *Activities*

Test Prep

Homophones

Choose the correct word to complete each sentence.

1. It will take an _____ for us to drive home.
    ○ our
    ○ hour

2. At _____, the moon was high in the sky.
    ○ knight
    ○ night

3. I put the book over _____, on the table.
    ○ there
    ○ they're

Tip

Try to picture the right answer in your mind.

4. That dog has a very short _____ .
    ○ tale
    ○ tail

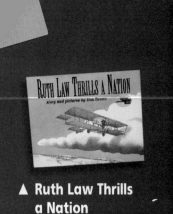

▲ **Ruth Law Thrills a Nation**

feat

heroine

hospitality

refused

spectators

stood

Vocabulary Power

Hi! I'm Dana. I went with my family to see an air show.

With other **spectators**, we watched a pilot fly upside down. That was an amazing **feat**! One pilot held a flying record that **stood** for three years.

I bought a picture of Amelia Earhart. She was a flying **heroine**. She was the first woman to fly across the Atlantic Ocean alone!

384

My brother **refused** to leave at the end of the show. He didn't want to go home.

On the way home, we stopped at my aunt's house. She gave us milk and cookies. We thanked her for her **hospitality**.

Vocabulary-Writing CONNECTION

Think about a time when you did something no one thought you could do. Write a paragraph to tell about your amazing **feat**.

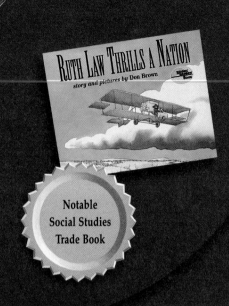

Notable
Social Studies
Trade Book

Genre

Nonfiction: Biography

A biography is the story of a person's life.

Look for

- events in time order.

- information telling why the person's life is important.

RUTH LAW

story and pictures
by Don Brown

THRILLS A NATION

On November 19, 1916, Ruth Law tried to fly from Chicago to New York City in one day.

It had never been done before.

It was a frosty, blustery morning. Ruth woke up before dawn, but she did not feel the cold. To get used to the cold weather, she had slept in a tent on the roof of a Chicago hotel.

She put on two woolen suits, one on top of the other.

Then she put on two leather suits and covered her bulky outfit with a skirt.

In 1916, a polite lady *always* wore a skirt.

It was still dark when Ruth went to Grant Park on the Lake Michigan shore, where her plane was waiting. It was the tiny one she flew in air shows. Ruth called it a baby machine. It was good for stunts like loop-the-loop, but it was small and old. Ruth had tried to buy a newer, bigger plane for her long flight, but Mr. Curtiss, the manufacturer, had refused to sell her one. Hundreds of pilots had already been injured or killed flying, and Mr. Curtiss did not believe a woman could fly a large plane.

Mechanics had worked all night on the plane. They had attached a special windshield to protect Ruth from the cold wind, and had added a second gas tank so she would not have to stop for fuel more than once. Now the plane could carry fifty-three gallons of gasoline. But the additional gasoline made the plane too heavy. To get rid of some extra weight, the mechanics took the lights off the plane. Without them, Ruth would have to reach New York City before nightfall.

The freezing weather made the engine hard to start. More than an hour passed before Ruth could get under way.

At 7:20 A.M., Ruth climbed into the cockpit. She removed her skirt and stuffed it behind her seat—good sense defeated fashion.

She opened the throttle. The plane leaped forward and bounced over bumps and hollows. It raced awkwardly across the ground, then lifted toward the sky.

A fierce wind whipped through Chicago. It shook and tossed the small plane.

A dozen onlookers watched in fear.

A mechanic cried.

Ruth struggled to steady the plane as it dipped and pitched in the wind.

She narrowly topped the buildings and slowly climbed into the sky above Chicago. Ruth Law was on her way to New York City.

A mile above ground, Ruth sliced through the frigid winter air at one hundred miles an hour. She set her course by consulting the crude scroll of maps she had taped together and attached to her leg. She also had a compass, a clock, and a speedometer.

Ruth flew for nearly six hours. She was depending on the wind to help carry her from Chicago to New York City. But the wind died down. Only gasoline propelled the plane.

At approximately 2:00 P.M. eastern standard time, she neared Hornell, New York, where a group of supporters was waiting.

Then the engine quit.

The fuel tank was empty and Hornell was still two miles away.

The plane pitched slightly and sank. Ruth had only one chance to make a safe landing.

She struggled to control the steering gear. The field seemed to come up at her. The crowd of spectators spilled into her path. The plane brushed their heads.

Ruth was on the ground.

She was so cold and hungry that she had to be helped to a nearby car. She was driven to a restaurant for a lunch of scrambled eggs and coffee while her plane was refueled.

She had flown 590 miles nonstop. It was a record. No one in America had ever flown farther.

But Ruth's flight was not over.

397

At 3:24 P.M., Ruth set out again for New York City.

All day, newspapers told the story of Ruth's flight. A crowd in Binghamton, New York, had turned out, hoping to see her fly overhead. They were not disappointed. At first she was just a speck in the sky, but soon she made a striking cameo against the late afternoon sun.

Suddenly the plane slanted toward the ground and disappeared behind some trees.

"She's down! Something's broken!"

Nothing was broken. Ruth had decided to land. New York
City was two hours away, but she would not be able to read her
instruments in the dark. She tied the plane to a tree, wrapped
her skirt around her, and accepted the hospitality of strangers.

The next morning, Ruth flew to New York City.

When she landed, an army general and a military band were there to greet her. Ruth was a heroine. "You beat them all!" the general said as he shook her hand.

Newspapers heralded her feat.

President Woodrow Wilson called her great.

A huge banquet was given in her honor.

On November 19, 1916, Ruth Law tried to fly from Chicago to New York City in one day and failed. Still, she set an American nonstop cross-country flying record—590 miles!—and thrilled a nation.

Her record stood for one year. It was broken by Katherine Stinson, another pilot who dared.

THINK AND RESPOND

1 How did Ruth Law thrill the nation?

2 Why do you think the author chose to tell events in sequence?

3 Why do you think the author wanted to tell about Ruth Law's flying **feat**?

4 What do you think it would have been like to be a member of Ruth Law's plane crew?

5 What strategies did you use to read this story?

Visit *The Learning Site!*
www.harcourtschool.com

Don Brown

Don Brown loves to read and write about history. While
writing a magazine article about flight, he became interested
in the early flyers. He didn't want brave pilots like Ruth Law
to be forgotten. This is his first children's book.

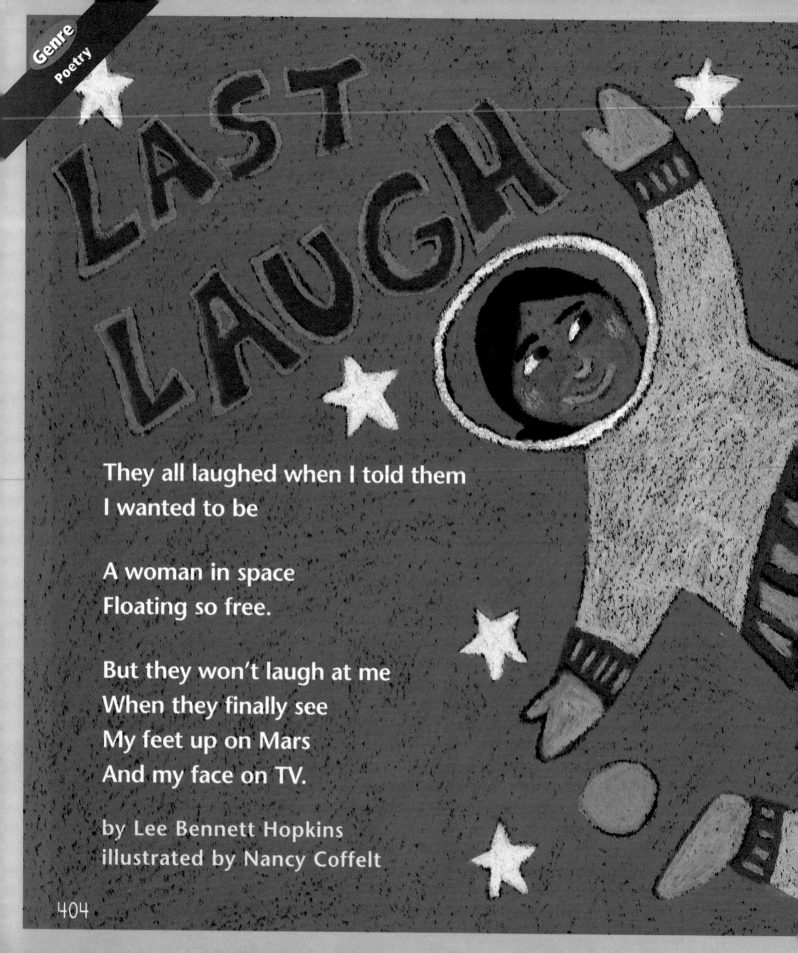

LAST LAUGH

They all laughed when I told them
I wanted to be

A woman in space
Floating so free.

But they won't laugh at me
When they finally see
My feet up on Mars
And my face on TV.

by Lee Bennett Hopkins
illustrated by Nancy Coffelt

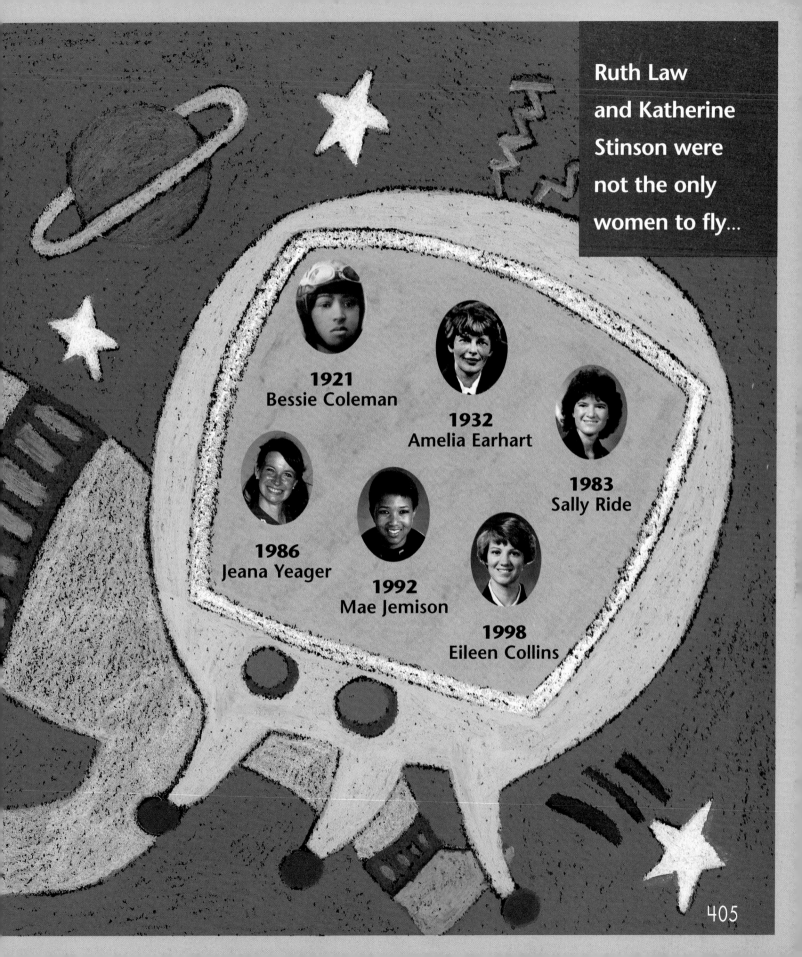

Ruth Law and Katherine Stinson were not the only women to fly...

1921
Bessie Coleman

1932
Amelia Earhart

1983
Sally Ride

1986
Jeana Yeager

1992
Mae Jemison

1998
Eileen Collins

Making Connections

Compare Texts

1 Why do you think "Ruth Law Thrills a Nation" is part of a theme called Travel Time?

2 How might Don Brown use "Beginner's World Atlas" to give more information about Ruth Law's flight?

3 Think about the narrator of the poem "Last Laugh." How is she like Ruth Law? How is she different?

Journal Entry

November 19, 1916

I am so tired! I have had a long, cold day of flying.

Imagine that you are Ruth Law and have landed in Binghamton for the night. Write a short journal entry about your trip so far. Tell how you feel about flying across the country.

Writing
CONNECTION

Airplane Races

Make a paper airplane. Then go outside with your teacher and classmates. Throw your airplane, and use a yardstick or measuring tape to measure how far it goes. With your class, make a chart to compare the distances.

Name	Distance
Emma	37 inches
Duane	42 inches
Ling	55 inches

Science CONNECTION

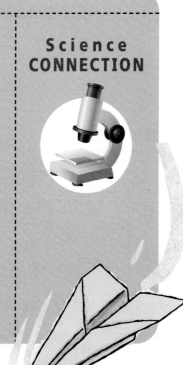

Map Ruth's Route

Look at a map of the United States. Trace Ruth Law's trip from Chicago to New York City. Which states might she have flown over? Think of two possible routes. Then choose the one you think is better. Share your flight plan with classmates.

Social Studies CONNECTION

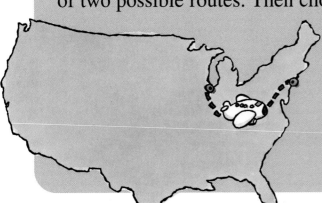

Predict Outcomes

Focus
Skill

Story details are like clues in a mystery. You can use them to figure out what will happen next. When you use clues to figure out what will happen, you make a **prediction**.

Look at the chart. Read each clue. Then predict what will happen next.

Clue #1	Clue #2	Prediction
Rosa's friend tells her about the flight museum.	Rosa looks up the address of the flight museum.	*Rosa will go to the flight museum.*
Max's teacher asks him to write a book report.	Max reads a book about Amelia Earhart.	
Ross packs for a trip to his uncle's house.	Ross gets on an airplane.	

Visit *The Learning Site!*
www.harcourtschool.com

See *Skills* and *Activities*

408

Read the story. Then answer the questions.

Nora's Airplane

Nora brought the model airplane kit home from the store. She took the pieces out of the box. Then she read the directions. She carefully glued the pieces together. When the model was finished, she painted it. The airplane gleamed in the light.

1. **Which sentence would go best at the end of the paragraph?**
   ○ She smiled at her new airplane.
   ○ She felt sad and angry about the color.
   ○ She was proud of her model car.

Tip
Read the paragraph with each possible sentence at the end. Choose the sentence that sounds best.

2. **The next thing Nora will do is _____.**
   ○ throw the airplane away
   ○ hang the airplane in her room
   ○ take the airplane apart

Tip
Read all the choices. Choose the one that makes the best sense.

Writer's Handbook

Contents

Purposes for Writing

There are many different **purposes for writing.**
People may write to give information, to entertain, to
give an opinion, or to express ideas.

Some Purposes for Writing	Examples
to give information	• how-to paragraph • research report
to entertain	• funny story • poem
to give an opinion	• poster that persuades • book review
to express ideas	• journal entry • letter

Try This

What would be the purpose for writing a paragraph about
kinds of cats?

The Writing Process

When you write, use a plan to help you. Think about *what* you want to write, for *whom* you are writing, and *why* you are writing. Then use these stages to help you as you write.

Revise
Read what you have written. Add important ideas and details that you left out. Be sure your information is in an order that makes sense.

Draft
Write your ideas in sentences and paragraphs. Do not worry about making mistakes.

Prewrite
Plan what you will write. Choose your topic, and organize your information.

Proofread

Check for errors. Correct mistakes in capital letters, end marks, and spelling.

Publish

Choose a way to share your writing. You can add pictures, graphs, or charts.

Try This

In your journal, list the five writing stages. Draw a picture with five parts like the one above to help you remember each stage.

How to Get Ideas

Writers find **topics,** or ideas, for writing in many ways. One way is to **brainstorm** ideas. When you brainstorm, you make a list of all the ideas that come to your mind. This is a list of ideas for a story about places to play.

Where I Like to Play

backyard

park

my bedroom

Writers also brainstorm ideas by using a **word web.**

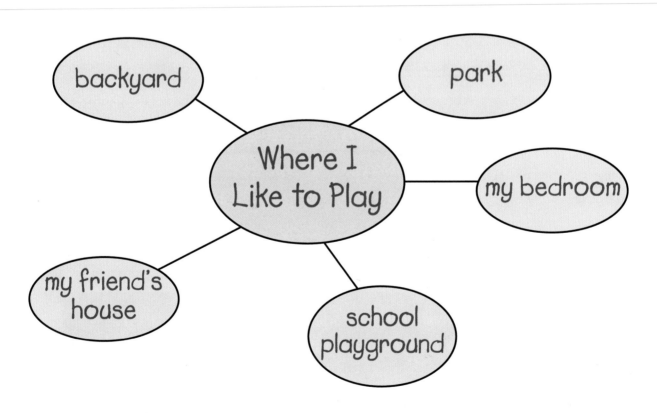

414

Writers ask **questions** to get ideas for their writing. They write a few questions and then find the answers before they begin writing. These questions are for a research report about trucks.

Trucks That Help Us

What kinds of trucks help people do jobs?

What do these trucks do?

Another way to get ideas is to write in your **journal.** You can keep a record of interesting things that happen to write about later.

September 2, 2003

Today was my first piano lesson. I was so nervous, but I loved playing! The half hour flew by. My teacher said I did a great job.

Try This

Choose an animal that you would like to write about. Brainstorm a list of words that tell about it.

...nary

A **dictionary** is a book that gives the meanings of words. It may also give an example sentence that shows how to use the word. A **synonym,** or word that has the same meaning, may come after the example sentence. The **entry words** are in ABC order, or alphabetical order. If a word has more than one meaning, each meaning has a number.

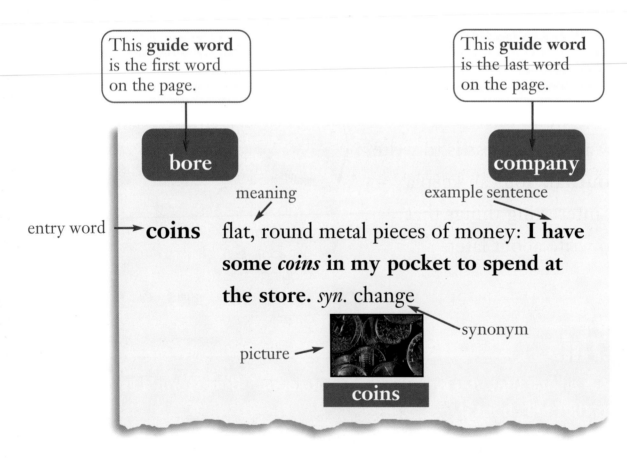

This **guide word** is the first word on the page.

This **guide word** is the last word on the page.

bore

company

entry word → **coins** meaning example sentence

flat, round metal pieces of money: **I have some** *coins* **in my pocket to spend at the store.** *syn.* change

synonym

picture →

coins

Thesaurus

A **thesaurus** is a list of words and their synonyms.
Sometimes a thesaurus lists antonyms, too. An
antonym is a word that has the opposite meaning. A
good time to use a thesaurus is when you are looking
for a more interesting word or a more exact word.

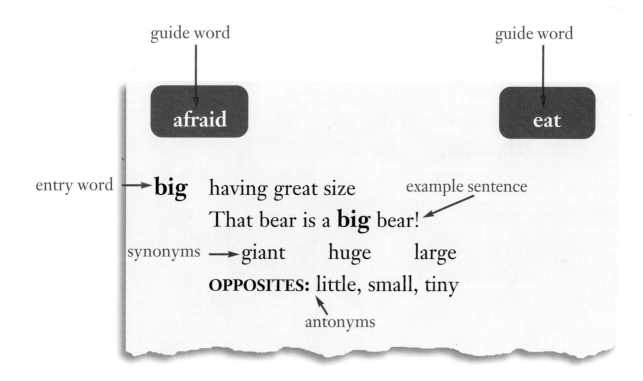

guide word   guide word

afraid   **eat**

entry word → **big**   having great size   example sentence

That bear is a **big** bear!

synonyms → giant   huge   large

OPPOSITES: little, small, tiny

antonyms

Try This

Choose a word. Look it up in the dictionary and in the thesaurus.
What do you find that is the same in both books? What is different?

ok of maps. An atlas of the United
...ps of all the states. The maps show cities,
...aters, and mountains. Sometimes the maps
show where products are made. Look in an atlas's
Table of Contents or Index to find the map you need.

Map of Florida

peanuts

forest
products

corn

Tallahassee

fish

forest
products

fruits and
vegetables

Atlantic Ocean

oranges

Gulf of Mexico

Orlando

grapefruit

fish

Clearwater

fruits and
vegetables

grapefruit

oranges

Lake
Okeechobee

oranges

Miami

dairy and
beef

Newspaper

A **newspaper** gives the news. It can tell what is happening around the world and in your town.

A newspaper tells about many subjects. It can tell about neighborhood events, sports, art, business, and the weather. Newspaper articles tell *who, what, where, when, why,* and *how.*

Magazine

A **magazine** gives information in stories and pictures. Magazines usually come out once a week or once a month.

Magazines can be about one main subject, such as science, skating, baseball, or doll collecting. Some magazines are written for certain groups of people, such as children, parents, or older people.

Try This

Find a newspaper article about a place. Find the place in an atlas. What does the atlas tell about it?

Parts of a Book

Most books have special pages that give information about what is inside. The **table of contents,** in the front, shows the chapters of a book. It also gives the page number for the beginning of each chapter.

A **glossary,** at the back, tells the meanings of important words in the book.

Table of Contents

An **index,** also at the back, lists the subjects in the book. The subjects are in alphabetical order. The index gives the page numbers where you can find those subjects.

Index

Using a Computer

A computer can help you in many ways as you write. You can use **spell-check** to find and correct words that are misspelled.

You can use a computer's **search engine** to find information. A **key word** tells what your topic is. Type a key word and click on *Go*.

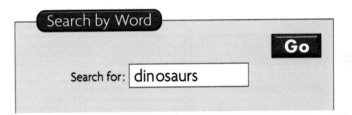

You can also use a computer to get and send e-mail messages. To send e-mail, you need a person's e-mail address.

Try This

Find a book about your favorite sport. Look at the table of contents. Choose a chapter that interests you and read some of it. Then use a word-processing program to write a short paragraph about what you read.

Story

A story has a beginning, a middle, and an end. A good story has strong characters, a setting, and a problem to solve.

A **story map** is a chart that shows the parts of a story. Writers use story maps to plan their stories during the prewriting stage. A writer answers the questions in each part of the story map.

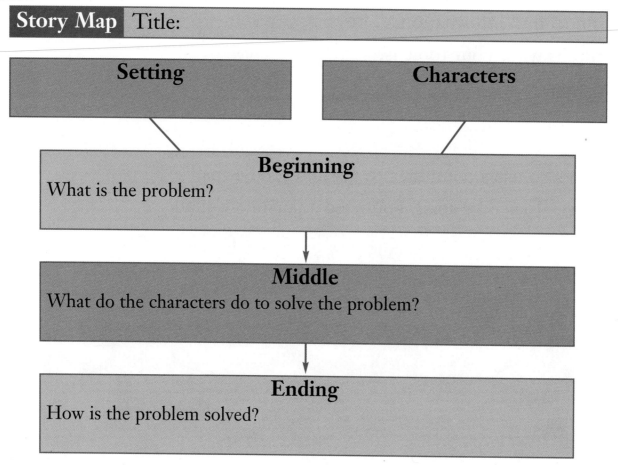

Story Map	Title:

Setting

Characters

Beginning
What is the problem?

Middle
What do the characters do to solve the problem?

Ending
How is the problem solved?

A **sequence chart** is another way to organize a story. Writers often use sequence charts to write personal stories. In a **personal story,** a writer tells about something that happened in his or her life.

In a sequence chart, the writer answers questions about what happens **first, next,** and **last** in a personal story.

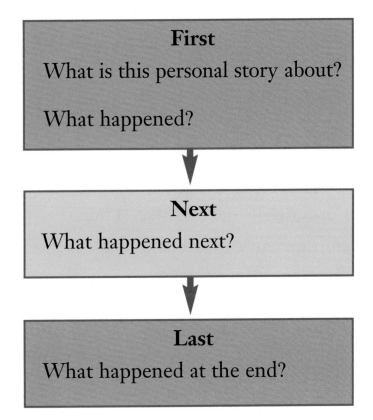

First

What is this personal story about?

What happened?

Next

What happened next?

Last

What happened at the end?

Try This

Think about a story you know. Make a story map to show the parts of the story.

Report: Note Taking

In a **research report**, a writer gives information about a topic. To find information for a report, you can write questions on **note cards.** Then search on a computer and at the library to find the answers. Write the answers on your note cards.

When did dinosaurs live?

- The last dinosaur died about 65 million years ago.
- The first dinosaur lived about 245 million years ago.
- No one knows for sure why they died.

Put your note cards in an order that makes sense. Then use the cards to write an outline. An **outline** shows the order of **main ideas** and **details** in a piece of writing.

Dinosaurs Outline

1. When did Dinosaurs live?
   a. last dinosaur, 65 million years ago
   b. first dinosaur, 245 million years ago
   c. No one knows why they died.
2. What kinds of dinosaurs were there?
   a. Tyrannosaurus rex
   b. Stegosaurus
   c. Troodon

Use your outline to organize your report. The questions become the **main ideas.** Write a paragraph about each main idea. The answers you found are the **details** about the main ideas.

Dinosaurs

Dinosaurs lived millions of years ago. The first dinosaurs lived about 245 million years ago. The last dinosaurs died about 65 million years ago. No one is sure why this happened.

Many different kinds of dinosaurs roamed the Earth. Tyrannosaurus rex was big and fierce and weighed more than 1,400 pounds. Stegosaurus had bony plates on its back. Troodon weighed less than 100 pounds, but some scientists think it was one of the smartest dinosaurs.

Try This

Think about what you do on a weekend morning. Take notes about what you do, and write an outline.

Traits of Good Writing

All good writers ask themselves questions like these
about what they write.

Focus/Ideas

- Is my message clear and interesting?
- Do I have enough information?

Organization

- Do I have a good beginning and a good ending?
- Is my information or my story in the right order?

Development

- Do each of my paragraphs have a main idea?
- Do I include important details in my paragraphs?

Voice

- Do I sound like myself?
- Do I say in an interesting way what I think or feel?

Word Choice

- Do my words make sense?
- Do I use interesting words?

Sentences

- Do I begin my sentences in different ways?
- Does my writing sound smooth when I read it aloud?

Conventions

- Do I indent my paragraphs?
- Are my spelling, punctuation marks, and capital letters correct?

Writers use **editor's marks** like these as they **revise** and **proofread** their writing.

Editor's Marks

⋀	Change.
℘	Take out.
≡	Use a capital letter.
⟨,⟩	Add a comma.
⟨"⟩	Add quotation marks.

Try This

Read a story with a partner. Talk about the traits of good writing that you find in the story.

Using a Rubric

A **rubric** is a checklist you can use to make your writing better. Here is how you can use a rubric.

Before writing   Look at the checklist to find out what your piece of writing should have.

During writing   Check your draft against the list. Use the list to see how to make your writing better.

After writing   Check your finished work against the list. Does your work show all the points?

Your Best Score

✔ Your writing is focused.

✔ You write about your ideas in an order that makes sense.

✔ You give important details about the main idea.

✔ Your writing sounds like you.

✔ You use words that are clear.

✔ Your sentences begin differently and fit together well.

✔ Your writing has few or no mistakes in punctuation, capitalization, or grammar.

Peer Conferences

After you have written your first draft, you are ready to revise your writing. A class partner can help. Follow these steps to have a peer conference. A **peer conference** is a meeting with a partner or small group to help you make your writing better.

Revising Your Writing

1. Read your first draft aloud. Then let your partner read it silently.

2. Talk with your partner about ways to make your draft better.

3. Take notes about changes you need to make.

Revising Your Partner's Writing

1. Listen carefully to your partner's draft read aloud. Then read it slowly yourself.

2. Tell two or three things that you like about it.

3. Give your partner one or two suggestions for making the draft better.

Try This

Meet with a partner to talk about your writing. Together, go over the traits of good writing. Talk about the traits your writing has.

Handwriting Tips

It is important to write neatly and clearly so that others can read your writing. Follow these handwriting tips.

- Hold your pencil and place your paper as shown.

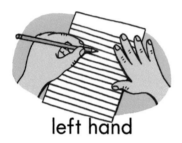
left hand

right hand

- Sit up straight. Face your desk, and place both feet on the floor.

- Make your letters smooth and even.

- Make sure your letters are not too close together or too far apart.

correct	**too close**	**too far apart**
great	great	g r e a t

- Begin writing to the right of the red line on your paper. Leave a space as wide as a pencil.

- The space between words or between sentences should be as wide as a pencil.

- Make sure tall letters touch the top line, short letters touch the midline, and the tails of letters hang below the base line.

Try This

Use your best handwriting to write a letter to a friend.

Using Computer Graphics

You can use your computer to add graphics, or pieces
of art, to your writing.

- **Use different kinds of type.** Using different kinds of
  type and different colors makes writing fun to read.

- **Add pictures to a story.** Use pictures from your word
  processing program, or use a separate drawing program.
  Add art to your story to make a book.

- **Add frames and borders.**

- **Add charts or graphs to a report.** Use your
  computer to make charts and graphs. Show them as
  you share your report with your classmates.

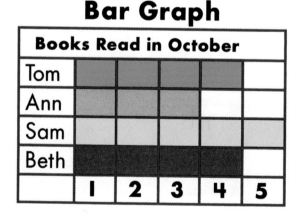

Oral Presentations

You may want to give an **oral presentation** of your writing. Here are some ways to keep your listeners interested.

- Plan your presentation. Decide how you will read or present your writing.

- Hold your paper low so that listeners can see your face.

- Look at your listeners when you speak.

- Use your voice to show funny, sad, or exciting parts of your writing.

- Speak loudly and clearly so that everyone can hear you.

- Use drawings, charts, or time lines to help make your writing interesting and clear.

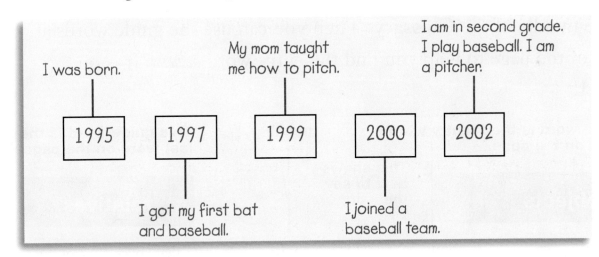

I was born. — 1995

I got my first bat and baseball. — 1997

My mom taught me how to pitch. — 1999

I joined a baseball team. — 2000

I am in second grade. I play baseball. I am a pitcher. — 2002

Try This

Think about something exciting that happened to you. Tell three things you would do to make listeners feel that it is exciting.

Using the Glossary

Get to Know It!

The **Glossary** gives the meaning of a word as it is used in the story. It also gives an example sentence that shows how to use the word. A **synonym**, which is a word that has the same meaning, a **base word**, or **additional word forms** may come after the example sentence. The words in the **Glossary** are in ABC order, also called **alphabetical order**.

Learn to Use It!

If you want to find *oceans* in the **Glossary**, you should first find the *O* words. *O* is near the middle of the alphabet, so the *O* words are near the middle of the **Glossary**. Then you can use the guide words at the top of the page to help you find the entry word *oceans*. It is on page 441.

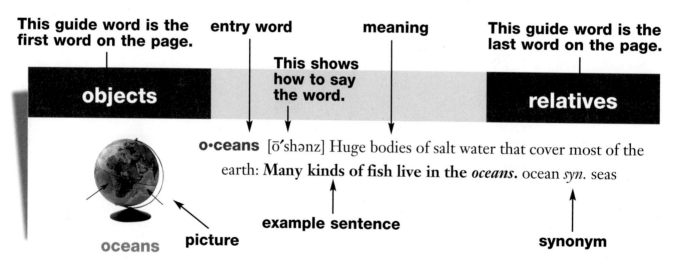

This guide word is the first word on the page.

entry word

meaning

This guide word is the last word on the page.

This shows how to say the word.

objects

relatives

o·ceans [ō′shənz] Huge bodies of salt water that cover most of the earth: **Many kinds of fish live in the *oceans.*** ocean *syn.* seas

oceans

picture

example sentence

synonym

ad·dress·es [ə·dres′əz] The information on pieces of mail telling whom the mail is for and where those people live: **Make sure the *addresses* on the envelopes are correct so the people will get the letters.** address

ad·mired [ad·mīrd′] Liked something or someone: **Sarah's classmates *admired* the nice card she had made.** admire, admiring

ap·peared [ə·pird′] Came into sight: **The rabbit ran into a hole, but it *appeared* again a few minutes later.** appear, appearing

addresses

bor·ing [bôr′ing] Not interesting: **Some stories are exciting, but that story is *boring*.**

cap·tured [kap′chərd] Caught and held by someone: **The horse that ran away was *captured* and brought back to the barn.** capture, capturing

cas·sette [kə·set′] A case holding a spool of tape for putting into a tape recorder or player: **We listened to my favorite *cassette* tape.**

caused [kôzd] Made something happen: **He jumped up so fast that he *caused* the chair to fall over.** cause, causing

cel·e·bra·tions [sel·ə·brā′shənz] Parties or festivals held to mark special days or to honor people: **Our family has many birthday *celebrations* each year.** celebrate, celebration

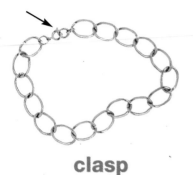

clasp

clerk

conductor

dappled

clasp [klasp] A small piece that holds the ends of something together: **She opened the *clasp* on her necklace and took the necklace off.**

clerk [klûrk] A person who sells things in a store: **The *clerk* at the market took my money and gave me my change.**

com·pan·ions [kəm•pan′yənz] People who spend time together: **My *companions* and I play in the park every day.** companion

con·duc·tor [kən•duk′tər] The person who helps the people riding on a train: **The *conductor* called out each stop so people would know when to get off the train.**

con·fused [kən•fyo͞ozd′] Mixed up; not sure of what is happening: **Jim felt *confused* by all the traffic and noise in the big city.**

connects [kə•nekts′] Joins: **This road *connects* our street to the highway.** connect

cor·nered [kôr′nərd] Trapped, as if in a corner from which one cannot escape: **It looked as if the dog had the cat *cornered*, but it got away.**

co·zy [kō′zē] Warm and comfortable: **We put a blanket in the puppy's basket to make it *cozy* for him.** *syn.* snug

cre·at·ed [krē•āt′əd] Used skill or art to make something new: **The children *created* many pictures and stories.** create, creating

D

dap·pled [dap′əld] Having spots or patches of a different color: **The *dappled* fawns will lose their white spots when they grow up.**

de·tails [di•tālz′ or dē′tālz] Facts about something: **Tell me the *details* of your trip.** detail

436

de·vel·op [di•vel′əp] To come or bring to full growth: **With enough water and sunlight, these tiny plants will *develop* into huge trees.** develops, developing

dis·ap·point [dis•ə•point′] To make someone feel bad by not doing what they want you to do: **I know it will *disappoint* my friend if I don't go to her party.** disappointed, disappointing

dis·tance [dis′təns] The space between two points: **Can you measure the *distance* the football traveled?**

drift·ed [drift′əd] Was carried along by water or air: **When Kim let go of the kite string, her kite *drifted* away.** drift, drifting

ducked [dukt] Got down quickly to keep from being hit by something: **When Jody saw the ball coming, he *ducked* so he wouldn't be hit.** duck, ducking

ducked

E

ex·hi·bi·tion [ek•sə•bish′ən] A display that people come to see: **The museum is having an *exhibition* of paintings by children.**

F

feat [fēt] Something that takes a lot of skill and courage: **Climbing the highest mountain in the world is a great *feat*.**

fea·tures [fē′chərz] The most important parts of something: **One of the nicest *features* of the park is the picnic area.** feature

fleet [flēt] A group of ships or boats that sail together: **We saw a *fleet* of sailboats heading out to sea.**

flip·pers [flip′ərz] Wide, flat legs that help water animals swim: **The seals clapped their *flippers* at the marine park.** flipper

fleet

437

glide

harbor

flock [flok] A group of animals or birds that eat or travel together: **A** *flock* **of about 100 sheep ate grass on the hill.**

for•ci•bly [fôr′sə•blē] Done in a strong way: **The puppy would not come out of the doghouse and had to be** *forcibly* **removed.**

fu•ri•ous [fyōŏr′ē•əs] Very angry: **My father was** *furious* **with me when I disobeyed him.**

fussed [fust] Acted upset about something: **The little children** *fussed* **as they waited in the long line.** fuss, fussing

glide [glīd] To move in a smooth way: **Watch the eagle** *glide* **across the sky.** glided, gliding

grace•ful [grās′fəl] Able to move in a smooth and beautiful way: **Dancers are** *graceful* **both on and off the stage.**

gro•cer•y store [grō′sər•ē stôr] A place where food and household goods are sold: **Besides foods, our new** *grocery store* **sells school supplies, dishes, and even fresh flowers.**

grown [grōn] Finished growing: **That cute little puppy has** *grown* **to become a big dog.** grow, grew, growing

har•bor [här′bər] A place where ships can anchor or be protected in a storm. **The ship sailed into the** *harbor* **after its long trip across the ocean.**

hatch [hach] To come out of an egg: **The baby chicks are beginning to** *hatch.*

haze [hāz] Misty or dusty air, such as you might see on a very hot day: **We could not see the tops of the tall buildings through the** *haze*.

her•o•ine [her′ō•in] A woman or girl who has done something brave or special; a woman or girl who is a hero: **Everyone called Molly a** *heroine* **after she saved the kitten from the pond.**

hon•or [on′ər] A show of pride in someone or something: **We fly the flag in** *honor* **of our country.**

ho•ri•zon [hə•rī′zən] The line where the earth seems to meet the sky: **We were already awake when the sun rose over the** *horizon*.

hos•pi•tal•i•ty [hos•pə•tal′ə•tē] A nice way of treating guests: **We like to eat there because the** *hospitality* **is as good as the food.**

im•ag•i•na•tion [i•maj•ə•nā′shən] The thoughts people use to pretend or to make up stories: **The author must have had a great** *imagination* **to write a story about talking rocks.**

im•i•tat•ed [im′ə•tāt•əd] Copied the way something looked, acted, or sounded: **Jenny** *imitated* **the dance steps she saw on television.** imitate, imitating

in•for•ma•tion [in•fər•mā′shən] Facts: **We went to the library for** *information* **about frogs.**

land•scape busi•ness [land′skāp biz′nis] A kind of business in which workers make outdoor places look better by adding plants and changing the land: **Workers in a** *landscape business* **need to know a lot about flowers, trees, and other plants.**

horizon

imitated

launched [lôncht] Moved, like a boat, from land into the water: **The people on the dock cheered when the ship was** *launched* **into the sea.**

loom·ing [lo͞om′ing] Coming into sight looking large and scary: **We saw the old house** *looming* **before us on the dark hill.** loom, loomed

lug·gage [lug′ij] Suitcases and bags used in traveling: **We put our** *luggage* **in the car.**

man·ners [man′ərz] Ways of acting that show that a person is polite: **Children who have good** *manners* **do not play with their food.**

map·mak·er [map′māk·ər] A person who makes a drawing that shows where things are located: **I would love to watch a** *mapmaker* **draw a map of my town.**

mat·a·dor [mat′ə·dôr] A person who fights bulls for sport: **The** *matador* **waved his red cape as the bull ran around the ring.**

mim·icked [mim′ikt] Copied what someone else said or did: **The boys bent their knees and** *mimicked* **the funny way the circus clown walked.** mimic, mimicking

mis·er·a·ble [miz′ər·ə·bəl] Very unhappy: **Jay was** *miserable* **when he was sick with the flu.**

no·tice [nō′tis] To see or pay attention to: **We didn't** *notice* **the dark clouds in the sky until it began to rain.** noticed, noticing

ob·jects [ob′jikts] Things that can be seen or touched: **The bag was filled with small *objects*, such as coins, buttons, and toys.** object

o·ceans [ō′shənz] Huge bodies of salt water that cover most of the earth: **Many kinds of fish live in the *oceans*.** ocean *syn.* seas

pale [pāl] Light in color: **I mixed white paint and green paint to make a *pale* green color.**

peel [pēl] To strip away or remove: **Bananas are the easiest kind of fruit to *peel*.**

plains [plānz] Flat lands with no trees: **The open *plains* stretched ahead of us as far as we could see.**

pour [pôr] To move in a steady stream: **Children pour out the school's front door when the bell rings.** poured, pouring

ranch [ranch] A kind of large farm where cows, horses, or sheep are raised: **It took the cowhands all day to move the cattle from one part of the *ranch* to another.**

re·al·ized [rē′əl·īzd] Came to understand something: **After a few tries, the boys *realized* that they needed a longer rope.** realize, realizing

re·fused [ri·fyo͞ozd′] Did not do what was asked: **Mother *refused* to give us ice cream before dinner.** refuse, refusing

rel·a·tives [rel′ə·tivz] People in the same family: **My aunts, uncles, cousins, and other *relatives* came to the party.** relative

oceans

plains

ranch

441

relax

spectators

stroke

re·lax [ri·laks´] Take a rest: **After playing ball, we like to sit down and *relax*.** relaxed, relaxing

re·moves [ri·mōōvz´] Takes something off: **He *removes* his shoes and puts on his slippers.** remove, removed, removing

rhythm [rith´əm] A set of sounds repeated again and again: **We clapped our hands to the *rhythm* of the music.**

route [rōōt or rout] The path that a salesperson or delivery person follows: **Our newspaper carrier follows her *route* every day.**

sense [sens] A correct way of thinking: **It makes *sense* to wear a helmet when you ride a bike.**

slip·per·y [slip´ər·ē] Slick and hard to hold onto or stand on: **The sidewalk is very *slippery* when it is covered with ice.**

soared [sôrd] Flew high into the air: **The bird *soared* high above the earth on its strong wings.** soar, soaring

spec·ta·tors [spek´tā·tərz] People who watch something: **The *spectators* cheered when the batter hit a home run.** spectator

star·tled [stär´təld] Surprised and frightened: **The sudden noise *startled* me and made me drop my cup.** startle, startling

stood [stŏŏd] Stayed the same: **The record for the most home runs *stood* for many years.** stand, standing

stroke [strōk] Rub in a gentle way: **My cat likes it when I *stroke* her back.** stroked, stroking

stu·dents [stōōd´ənts] People who learn in a school: **The *students* in Mrs. Santiago's second-grade class are learning Spanish.** *syn.* pupil

stur·dy [stûr´dē] Strong: **The little tree grew to be tall and *sturdy*.**

sup·pose [sə•pōz′] To think something is likely: **Dad's car is in the driveway, so I** *suppose* **he must be home.** supposed, supposing

swoop·ing [swoōp′ing] Coming down in a wide, curving movement: **The hawk was** *swooping* **down from the sky.** swoop, swooped

thou·sands [thou′zəndz] Many, many hundreds: **There are** *thousands* **of leaves on that big oak tree.** thousand

trac·tor [trak′tər] A machine used for pulling a plow: **Kim loves to watch her uncle plow with his** *tractor* **at the farm.**

typ·i·cal [tip′i•kəl] Very much like other things of the same kind: **A** *typical* **school day includes reading and math lessons.**

va·ca·tion [vā•kā′shən] Time off from school or work: **When summer** *vacation* **is over, it's time to go back to school.**

wad·dled [wod′əld] Swayed from side to side when walking: **The duck** *waddled* **to the pond.** waddle, waddling

Page numbers in color tell where you can read about the author.

and Authors

Acknowledgments

For permission to reprint copyrighted material, grateful acknowledgment is made to the following sources:

Curtis Brown, Ltd.: "Last Laugh" from *Blast Off! Poems About Space* by Lee Bennett Hopkins. Text copyright © 1974 by Lee Bennett Hopkins. Published by HarperCollins Publishers.

Candlewick Press Inc., Cambridge, MA, on behalf of Walker Books Ltd., London: *The Emperor's Egg* by Martin Jenkins, illustrated by Jane Chapman. Text © 1999 by Martin Jenkins; illustrations © 1999 by Jane Chapman.

Children's Better Health Institute, Indianapolis, IN: "Keeping a Road Journal" by Joy Beck, illustrated by Patti H. Goodnow from *Jack and Jill* Magazine. Copyright © 1996 by Children's Better Health Institute, Benjamin Franklin Literary & Medical Society, Inc.

Children's Television Workshop, New York, NY: "Cool It!" by Lynn O'Donnell from *3-2-1 Contact* Magazine, July/August 1997. Text copyright 1997 by Children's Television Workshop. From "Birds Do It! Recycle!" in *Kid City* Magazine, April 1995. Text copyright 1995 by Children's Television Workshop.

Clarion Books/Houghton Mifflin Company: *Anthony Reynoso: Born to Rope* by Martha Cooper and Ginger Gordon. Text copyright © 1996 by Ginger Gordon; photographs copyright © 1996 by Martha Cooper.

Crown Publishers, Inc.: *How I Spent My Summer Vacation* by Mark Teague. Copyright © 1995 by Mark Teague.

Dial Books for Young Readers, a division of Penguin Putnam Inc.: From *Snakey Riddles* by Katy Hall and Lisa Eisenberg, illustrated by Simms Taback. Text copyright © 1990 by Katy Hall and Lisa Eisenberg; illustrations copyright © 1990 by Simms Taback. *The Day Jimmy's Boa Ate the Wash* by Trinka Hakes Noble, illustrated by Steven Kellogg. Text copyright © 1980 by Trinka Hakes Noble; illustrations copyright © 1980 by Steven Kellogg.

Dutton Children's Books, a division of Penguin Putnam Inc.: *Abuela* by Arthur Dorros, illustrated by Elisa Kleven. Text copyright © 1991 by Arthur Dorros; illustrations copyright © 1991 by Elisa Kleven.

HarperCollins Publishers: *Good-bye, Curtis* by Kevin Henkes, illustrated by Marisabina Russo. Text copyright © 1995 by Kevin Henkes; illustrations copyright © 1995 by Marisabina Russo.

David Higham Associates: "City Music" by Tony Mitton from *Poems Go Clang!* Text © 1997 by Tony Mitton. Published by Candlewick Press.

Holiday House, Inc.: "June" from *A Child's Calendar* by John Updike, illustrated by Trina Schart Hyman. Text copyright © 1965, 1999 by John Updike; illustrations copyright © 1999 by Trina Schart Hyman.

Henry Holt and Company, LLC: *Chinatown* by William Low. Copyright © 1997 by William Low.

Little, Brown and Company (Inc.): From *Dinosaurs Travel* by Laurie Krasny Brown and Marc Brown. Copyright © 1988 by Laurie Krasny Brown and Marc Brown.

Margaret K. McElderry Books, an imprint of Simon & Schuster Children's Publishing Division: *Dear Mr. Blueberry* by Simon James. Copyright © 1991 by Simon James. Originally published in Great Britain by Walker Books, Ltd. *Cool Ali* by Nancy Poydar. Copyright © 1996 by Nancy Poydar.

National Geographic Society: From *National Geographic Beginner's World Atlas*. Copyright © 1999 by National Geographic Society.

Simon & Schuster Books for Young Readers, an imprint of Simon & Schuster Children's Publishing Division: *Max Found Two Sticks* by Brian Pinkney. Copyright © 1994 by Brian Pinkney.

Ticknor & Fields Books for Young Readers/Houghton Mifflin Company: *Ruth Law Thrills a Nation* by Don Brown. Copyright © 1993 by Don Brown.

Viking Penguin, a division of Penguin Putnam Inc.: *Montigue On the High Seas* by John Himmelman. Copyright © 1988 by John Himmelman.

Franklin Watts, a Division of Grolier Publishing: From "Sports and Exercise" in *Look What Came From China* by Miles Harvey. Text © 1998 by Franklin Watts, a Division of Grolier Publishing.

Photo Credits

Key: (t) = top; (b) = bottom; (c) = center; (l) = left; (r) = right.
Page 32, courtesy, Penguin Putman; 33, Tom Sobolik / Black Star; 40(t), Werner Bertsch / Bruce Coleman, Inc.; 40(b), Dennis Degnan / Corbis; 41(t), Ernest Janes / Bruce Coleman, Inc.; 41(b), Superstock; 59, Black Star; 89, courtesy, Walker Books; 113, Rick Friedman / Black Star; 115(t), G.C. Kelly / Photo Researchers, Inc.; 115(c), Jim Cummins / FPG; 115(b), Jeffrey Sylverster / FPG; 116(t), Rod Planck / Photo Researchers, Inc.; 116(c), Anthony Merceca / Photo Researchers, Inc.; 116(b), John Cancalosi / Tom Stack & Associates; 117(t), John Gerlach / Tom Stack & Associates; 117(c), Renee Lynn / Photo Researchers, Inc.; 122(t), Mark A. Chappell / Animals Animals; 122(b), Keith Kent / SPL / Photo Researchers, Inc.; 123(t), Superstock; 123(b), Richard Kolar / Animals Animals; 145(l), David Levenson / Black Star; 145(r), courtesy, Walker Books; 169(l), Black Star; 169(r), Mark Derse; 170, Roger Wilmshurst / Bruce Coleman, Inc.; 176(t), Michele Burgess / Corbis Stock Market; 176(b), Spencer Grant / Photo Researchers, Inc.; 177(t), Amy Dunleavy; 177(b), Mug Shots / Corbis Stock Market; 194, Black Star; 195, 221, Tom Sobolik / Black Star; 230-245, Martha Cooper; 250(t), Gail Mooney / Corbis; 250(b), Robbie Jack / Corbis; 251(t), Stone; 251(b), Robert Young Pelton / Corbis; 271, Erich Lansner / Black Star; 272, Ann Chwatsky; 273(t), C. Ursillo / H. Armstrong Roberts; 273(b), H. Armstrong Roberts; 280(t), Superstock; 280(b), Rod Planck / Dembinsky Photo Associates; 281(t), Alese & MortPechter / Corbis Stock Market; 281(b), Sam Fried / Photo Researchers, Inc.; 300, Black Star; 301, Dale Higgins; 306, Keith Gunnar / Bruce Coleman, Inc.; 308(tl), Paul Chesley / Stone; 308(tr), Michael Scott / Stone; 308(bl), Ed Simpson / Stone; 308(bc), Connie Coleman / Stone; 308(br), Nicholas DeVore / Stone; 309(t), T. Davis, W. Bilenduke / Stone; 309(b), Frans Lanting / Stone; 314, NASA; 320(2nd), Hugh Sitton / Stone; 320(3rd), Steven Weinberg / Stone; 320(b), Cosmo Condina / Stone; 321(t), Michael Nichols / National Geographic Society; 321(2nd), Andrea Booher / Stone; 321(3rd), Greg Probst / Stone; 321(4th), Stephen & Michele Vaughan; 321(b), Tom Bean; 322, Ed Simpson / Stone; 323, Rosemary Calvert / Stone; 326(tr), Charles Krebs / Stone; 326(cl), Mark Lewis / Stone; 326(b), Bruce Wilson / Stone; 327(t), Dave Bartruff / Artistry International; 327(c), Stephen Krasemann / Stone; 327(b), Stone; 330(tr), Gary Brettnacher / Stone; 330(cl), Mark Lewis / Stone; 330(cr), Ncik Gunderson / Stone; 330(cb), Cosmo Condina / Stone; 330(bl), David Hiser / Stone; 331(tl), George Hunter; 331(cr), Will & Deni McIntyre / Stone; 336(t), Rob Lewine / Corbis Stock Market; 336(b), McCarthy / Corbis Stock Market; 337(t), Myrleen Ferguson / PhotoEdit; 337(b), Superstock; 356, 357, Rick Friedman / Black Star; 379, Black Star; 405(tl), The Granger Collection, New York; 405(tc), Culver Pictures; 405(tr), NASA; 405(bl), Liaison Agency; 405(bc), NASA; 405(br), NASA / Photo Researchers, Inc.; 416, 434, Harcourt Photo Library; 435, Ken Kinzie / Harcourt; 436(t), Victoria Bowen / Harcourt; 436(2nd), Harcourt Photo Library; 436(3rd), Kindra Clineff / Index Stock; 436(b), Stephen J. Krasemann / Photo Researchers, Inc.; 438(t), Daniel J. Cox / Stone; 438(b), Jose Funte Raga / Corbis Stock Market; 439, Herb Schmitz / Stone; 441(t), Harcourt Photo Library; 441(c), Ken Martin / Visuals Unlimited; 441(b), D. R. Stoecklein / Corbis Stock Market; 442(t), Charles Krebs / Corbis Stock Market; 442(b), Claude Charlier / Corbis Stock Market.

Illustration Credits

Steve Johnson/Lou Fancher, Cover Art; Gary Taxali, 4-5, 12-13; Will Terry, 6-7, 150-151; Jennifer Beck-Harris, 8-9, 278-279; Ethan Long 10-11, 36-37, 408; Clare Schaumann, 14-15; Steven Kellogg, 16-33; Simms Taback, 34-35; Mark Teague, 42-59; Nancy Davis, 62-63, 225, 226, 382; Donna Perrone, 66-67; Simon James, 68-89; Jackie Snider, 92-93, 247, 173; Kathi Ember, 96-97; Nancy Poydar, 98-113; Tuko Fujisaki, 119, 303, 406-407; Nancy Coffelt, 120, 147, 275, 333, 404-405; Jane Chapman, 124-145; Cathy Bennett, 148, 197; Ande Cook, 152-153; Mary GrandPré, 154-169; Marisabina Russo, 178-195; Geneviéve Després, 200-201; Brian Pinkney, 202-221; Liz Conrad, 222-223; Craig Spearing, 228-229; William Low, 252-271; Mou-sien Tseng, 272-273; Elisa Kleven, 282-301; Marc Brown, 338-357; Liz Callen, 358-359; Laura Ovresat, 360-361; Amanda Harvey, 364-365; John Himmelman, 366-379; Chris Van Dusen, 380-381; Gail Piazza, 384-385; Don Brown, 386-403; Holly Cooper, 437, 440, 442.